BLEACH
Vol. 37: BEAUTY IS SO SOLITARY
SHONEN JUMP Manga Edition

This volume contains material that was originally published in English in
SHONEN JUMP #105–108. Artwork in the magazine may have been
altered slightly from what is presented in this volume.

STORY AND ART BY
TITE KUBO

English Adaptation/Lance Caselman
Translation/Joe Yamazaki
Touch-up Art & Lettering/Mark McMurray
Design/Yukiko Whitley
Editor/Alexis Kirsch

Printed in the U.S.A.

Published by VIZ Media, LLC
P.O. Box 77010
San Francisco, CA 94107

10 9 8 7 6 5 4 3 2 1
First printing, December 2011

PARENTAL ADVISORY
BLEACH is rated T for Teen and is recommended
for ages 13 and up. This volume contains
fantasy violence.
ratings.viz.com

Mayuri drawn by my assistant Sato. Super cute.

-Tite Kubo

BLEACH is author Tite Kubo's second title. Kubo made his debut with *ZOMBIEPOWDER.*, a four-volume series for *WEEKLY SHONEN JUMP*. To date, *BLEACH* has been translated into numerous languages and has also inspired an animated TV series that began airing in the U.S. in 2006. Beginning its serialization in 2001, *BLEACH* is still a mainstay in the pages of *WEEKLY SHONEN JUMP*. In 2005, *BLEACH* was awarded the prestigious Shogakukan Manga Award in the *shonen* (boys) category.

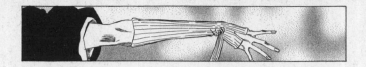

People are not beautiful to me,
But flowers are.

People are only like flowers
When they are cut down.

BLEACH37
BEAUTY IS SO SOLITARY

STARS AND

Sôsuke Aizen

Shinji Hirako

Kisuke Urahara

平子真子

浦原喜助

plot

When high school student Ichigo Kurosaki meets Soul Reaper Rukia Kuchiki his life is changed forever. Soon Ichigo is a soul-cleansing Soul Reaper too, and he finds himself having adventures, as well as problems, that he never would have imagined. Now Ichigo and his friends must stop renegade Soul Reaper Aizen and his army of Arrancars from destroying the Soul Society and wiping out KarakuraTown as well.

The battle finally begins! The Thirteen Court Guard Companies head to Karakura while Ichigo remains in Hueco Mundo to rescue Orihime. Meanwhile, 110 years ago a number of konpaku disappear from the Soul Society soon after Kisuke Urahara is appointed captain of Twelfth Company. Shinji Hirako, captain of Fifth Company, rushes to the place where the investigating task force disappeared and there encounters his own Assistant Captain–Sôsuke Aizen!

BLEACH ALL

ウルキオラ
Ulquiorra

黒崎一護
Ichigo Kurosaki

Orihime Inoue

井上織姫

STORIES

BLEACH 37

BEAUTY IS SO SOLITARY

Contents

-99. Turn Back the Pendulum 10

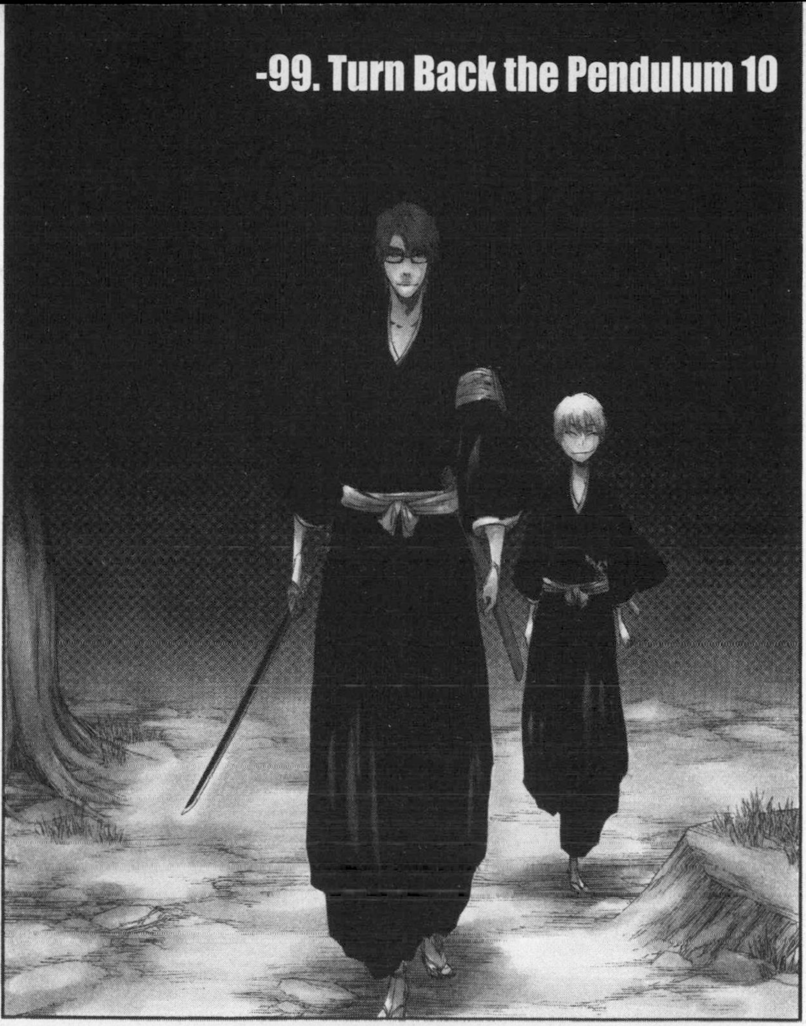

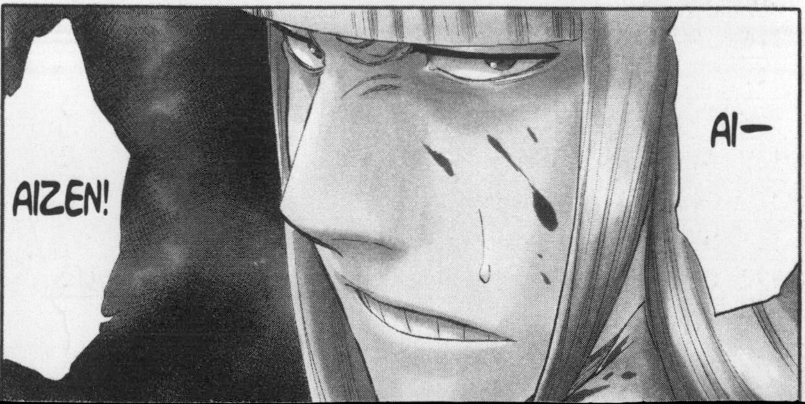
AI—
AIZEN!

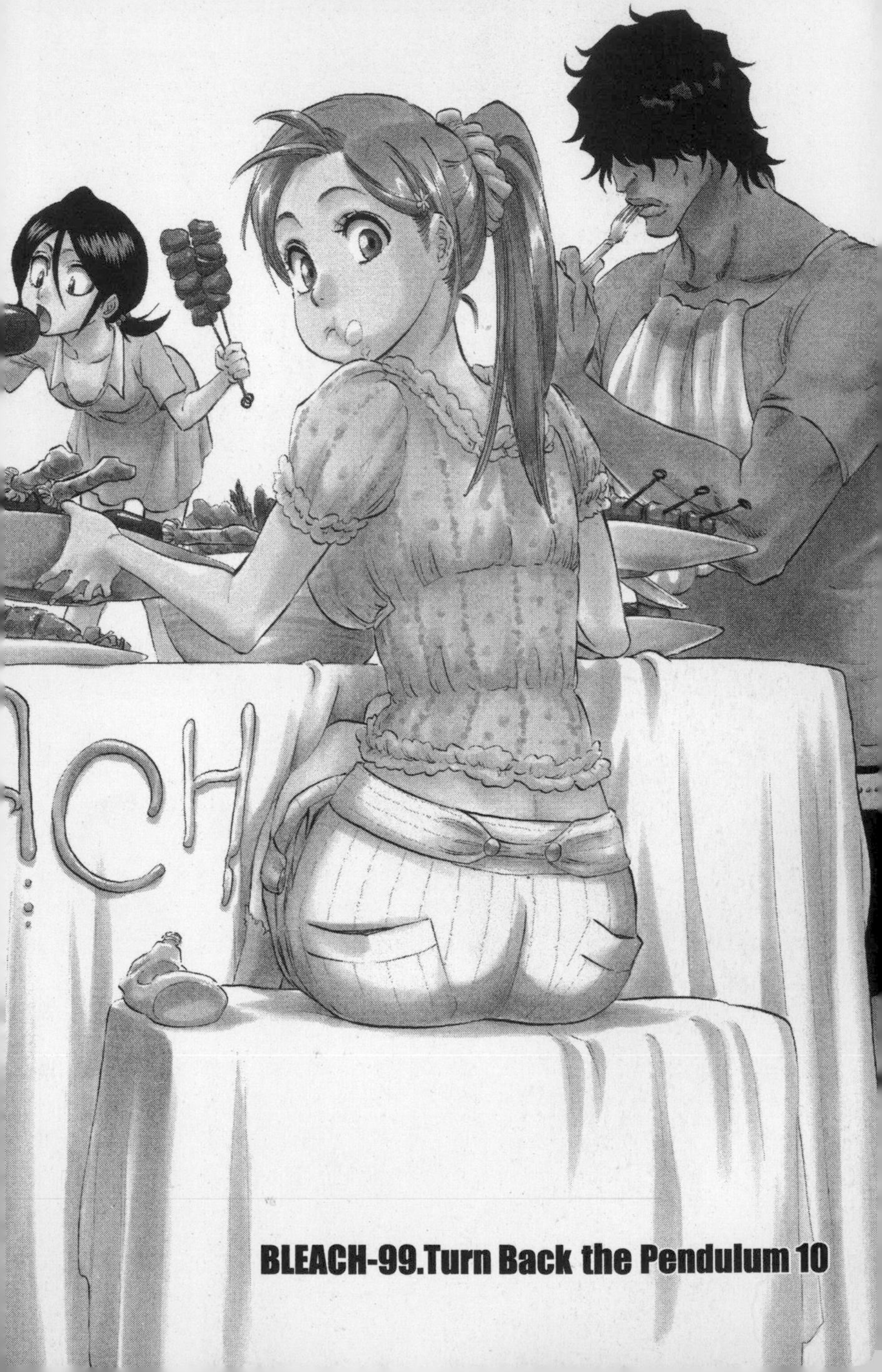
ACH

BLEACH-99.Turn Back the Pendulum 10

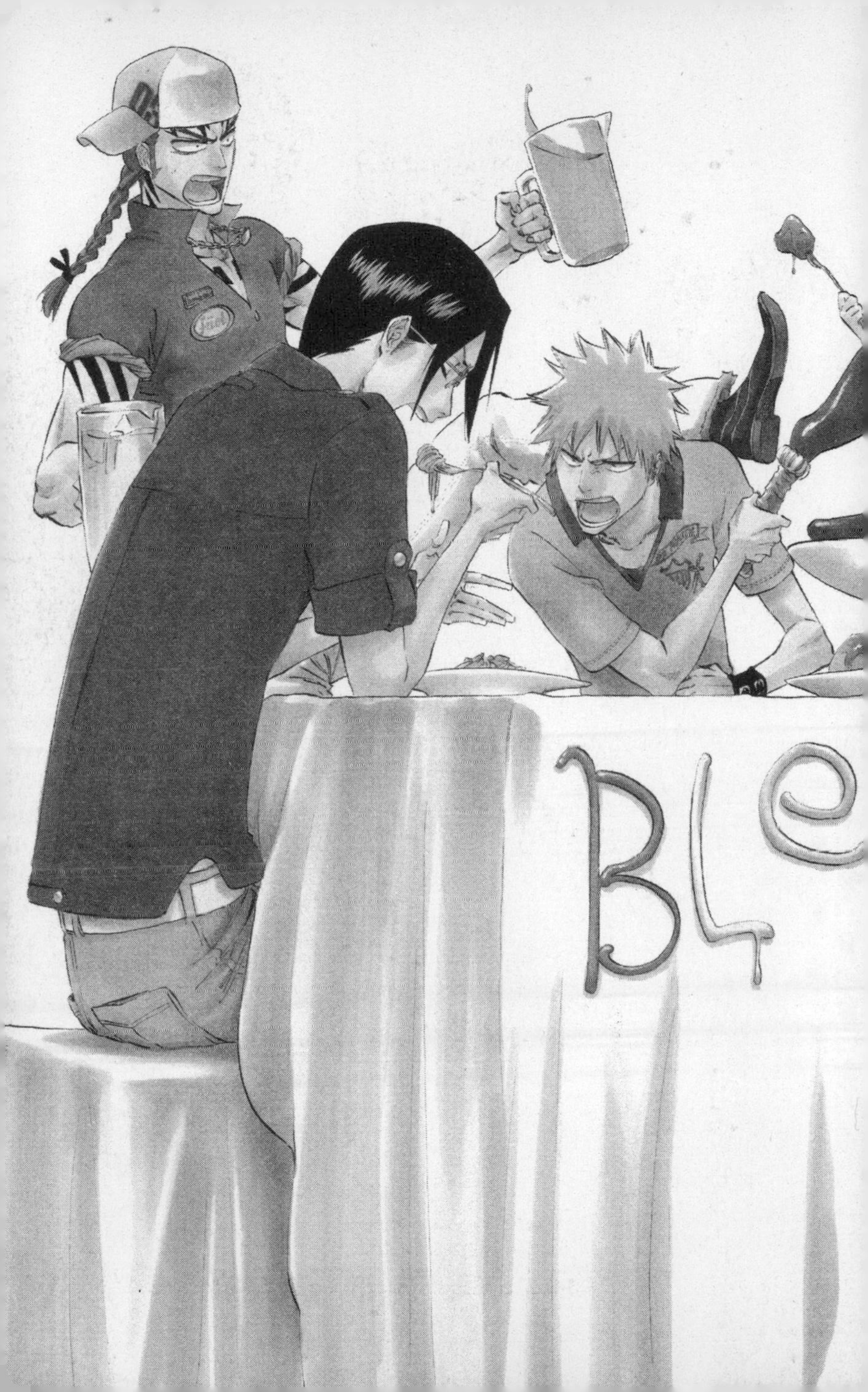
BLe

BLEACH

ブリーチ

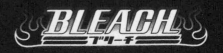

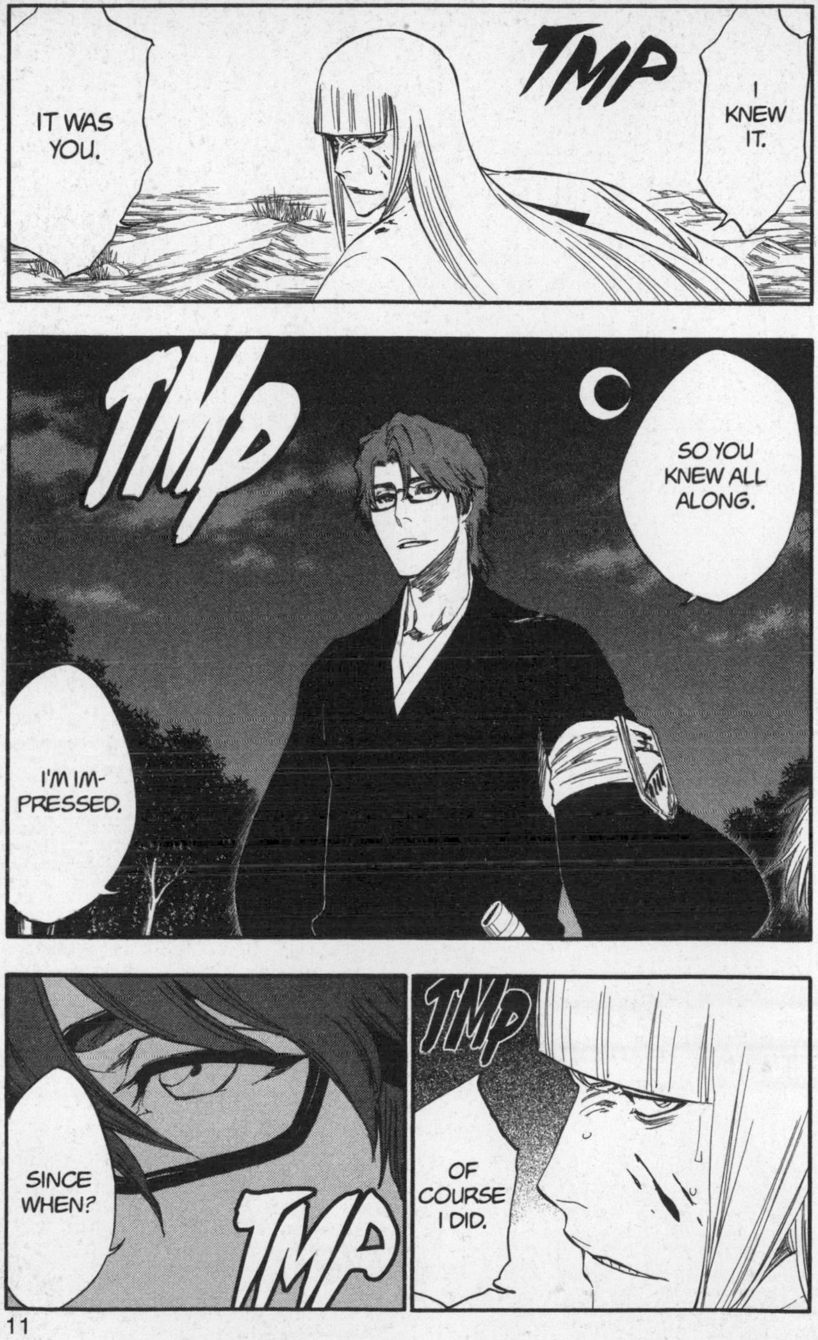
I KNEW IT.
TMP
IT WAS YOU.
SO YOU KNEW ALL ALONG.
TMP
I'M IM-PRESSED.
TMP
OF COURSE I DID.
SINCE WHEN?
TMP

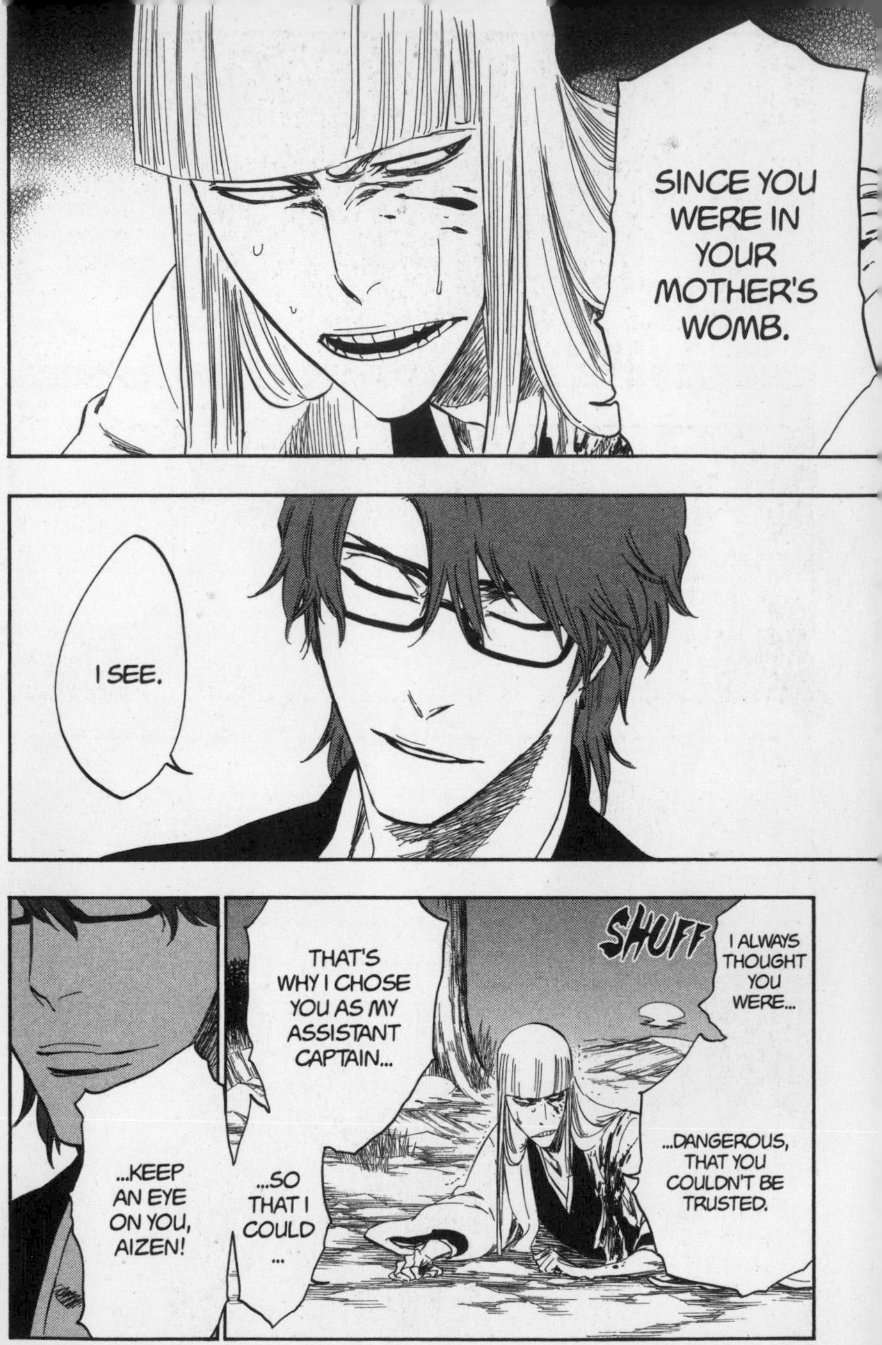
SINCE YOU WERE IN YOUR MOTHER'S WOMB.
I SEE.
SHUFF
I ALWAYS THOUGHT YOU WERE...
...DANGEROUS, THAT YOU COULDN'T BE TRUSTED.
THAT'S WHY I CHOSE YOU AS MY ASSISTANT CAPTAIN...
...SO THAT I COULD ...
...KEEP AN EYE ON YOU, AIZEN!

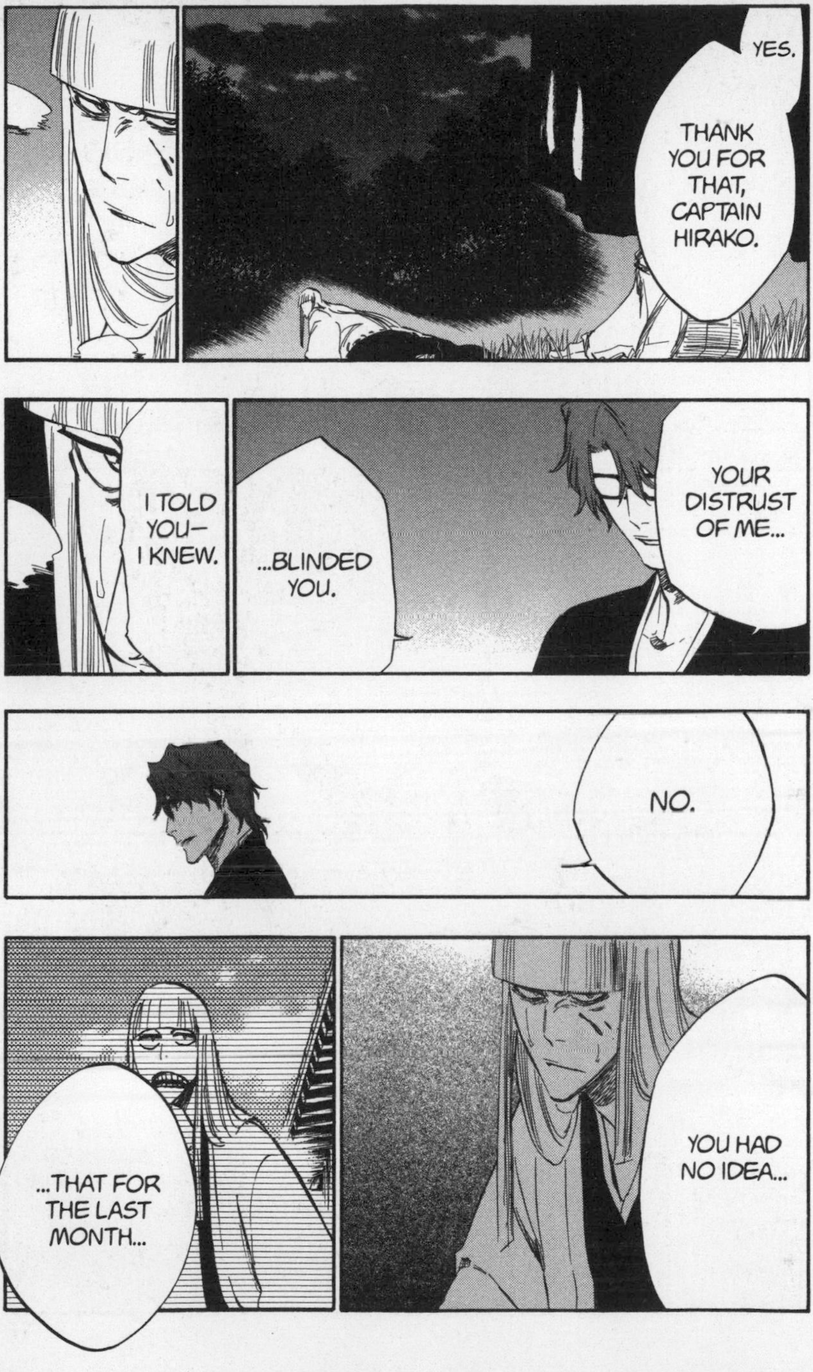
YES.
THANK YOU FOR THAT, CAPTAIN HIRAKO.
YOUR DISTRUST OF ME...
...BLINDED YOU.
I TOLD YOU— I KNEW.
NO.
YOU HAD NO IDEA...
...THAT FOR THE LAST MONTH...

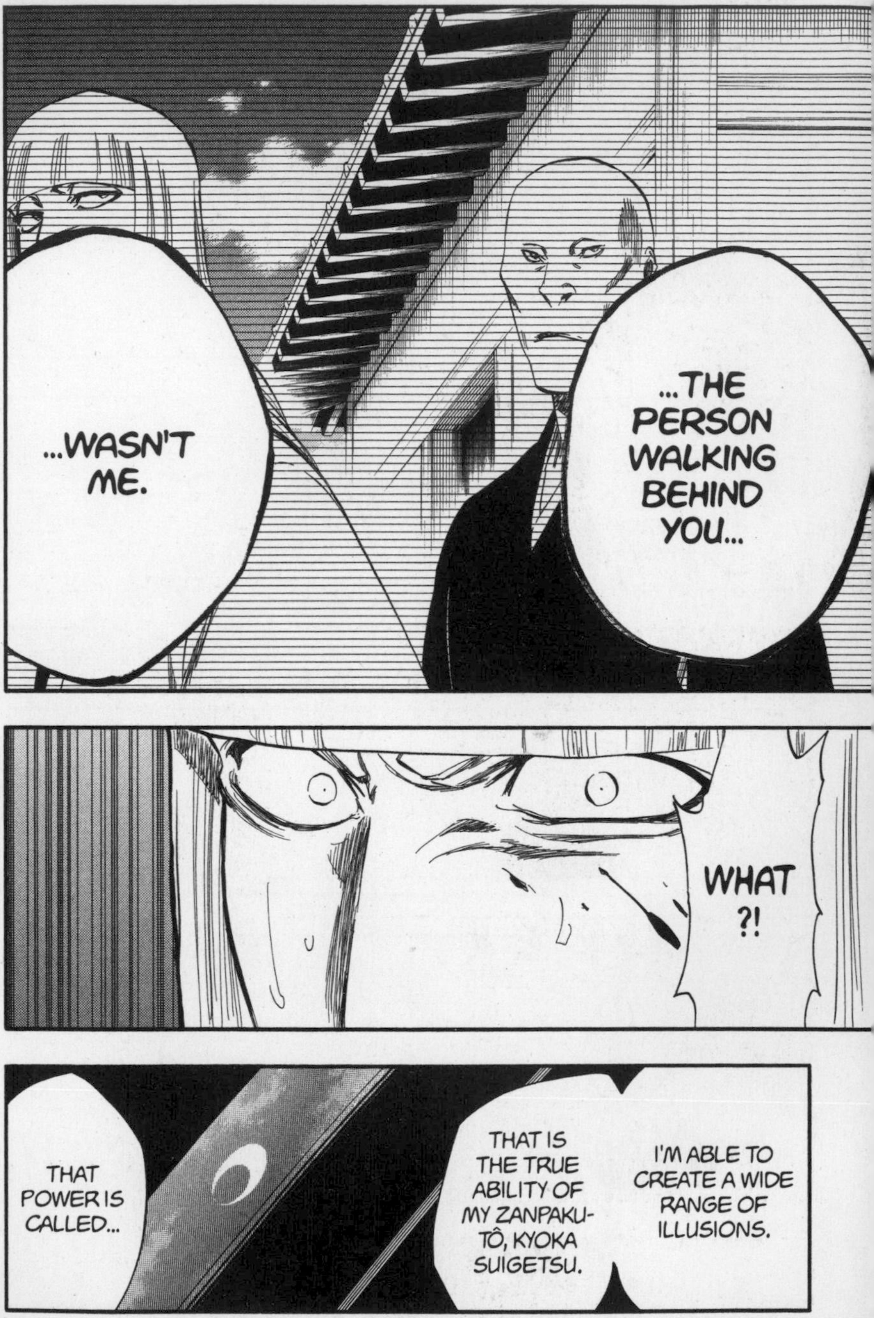
...THE PERSON WALKING BEHIND YOU...
...WASN'T ME.
WHAT?!
I'M ABLE TO CREATE A WIDE RANGE OF ILLUSIONS.
THAT IS THE TRUE ABILITY OF MY ZANPAKU-TÔ, KYOKA SUIGETSU.
THAT POWER IS CALLED...

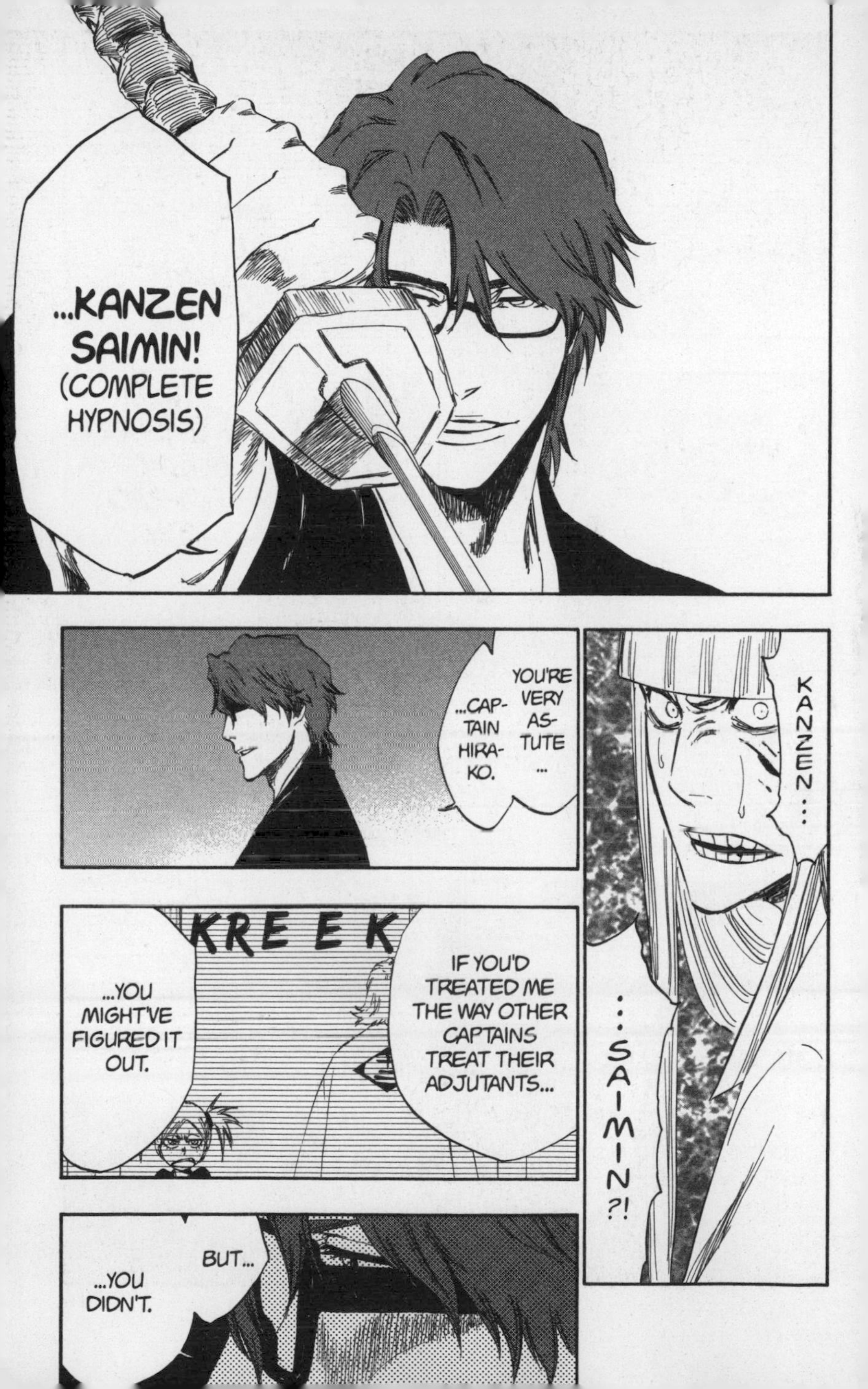
...KANZEN SAIMIN! (COMPLETE HYPNOSIS)
KANZEN...
...SAIMIN?!
YOU'RE VERY AS-TUTE...
...CAP-TAIN HIRA-KO.
KREEK
IF YOU'D TREATED ME THE WAY OTHER CAPTAINS TREAT THEIR ADJUTANTS...
...YOU MIGHT'VE FIGURED IT OUT.
BUT...
...YOU DIDN'T.

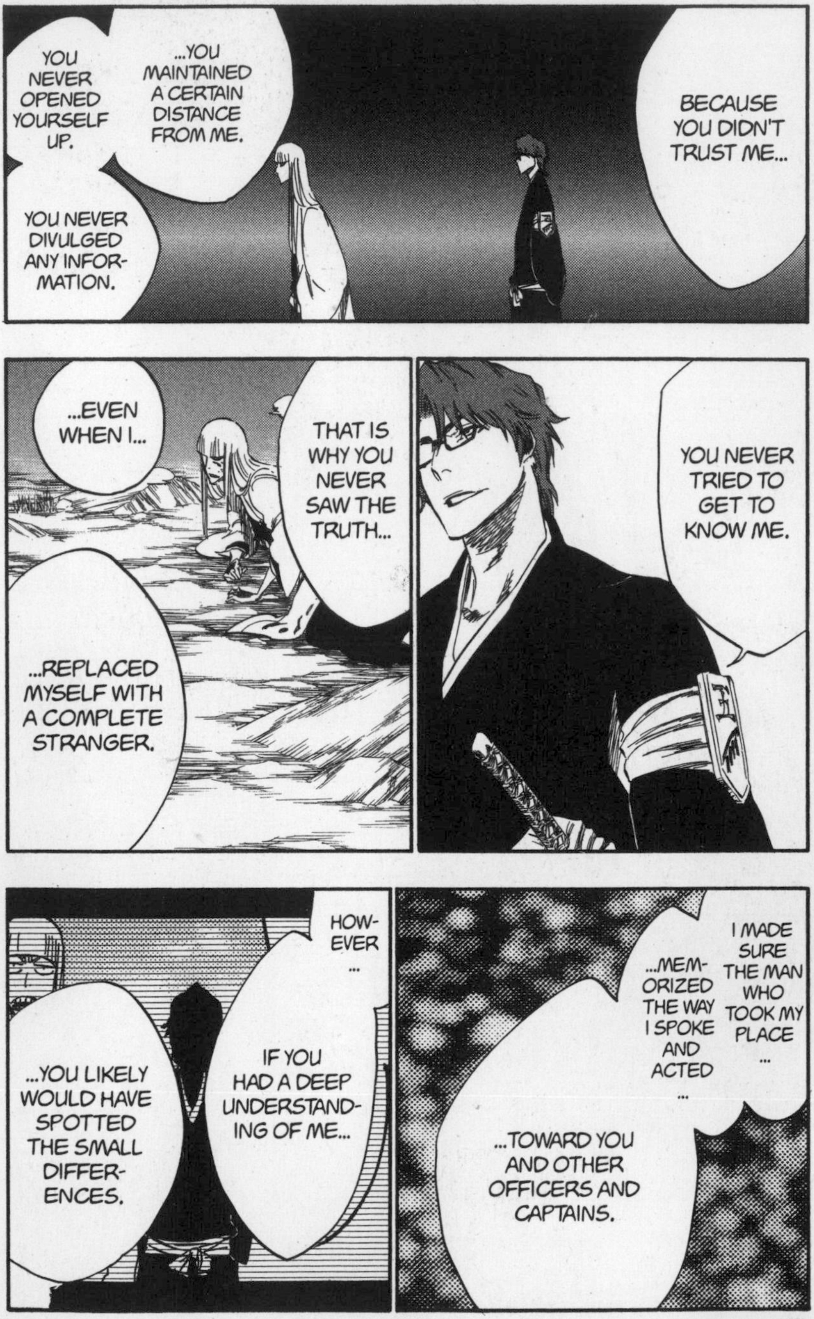
BECAUSE YOU DIDN'T TRUST ME...
...YOU MAINTAINED A CERTAIN DISTANCE FROM ME.
YOU NEVER OPENED YOURSELF UP.
YOU NEVER DIVULGED ANY INFORMATION.
YOU NEVER TRIED TO GET TO KNOW ME.
THAT IS WHY YOU NEVER SAW THE TRUTH...
...EVEN WHEN I...
...REPLACED MYSELF WITH A COMPLETE STRANGER.
I MADE SURE THE MAN WHO TOOK MY PLACE ...
...MEMORIZED THE WAY I SPOKE AND ACTED ...
...TOWARD YOU AND OTHER OFFICERS AND CAPTAINS.
HOWEVER ...
IF YOU HAD A DEEP UNDERSTANDING OF ME...
...YOU LIKELY WOULD HAVE SPOTTED THE SMALL DIFFERENCES.

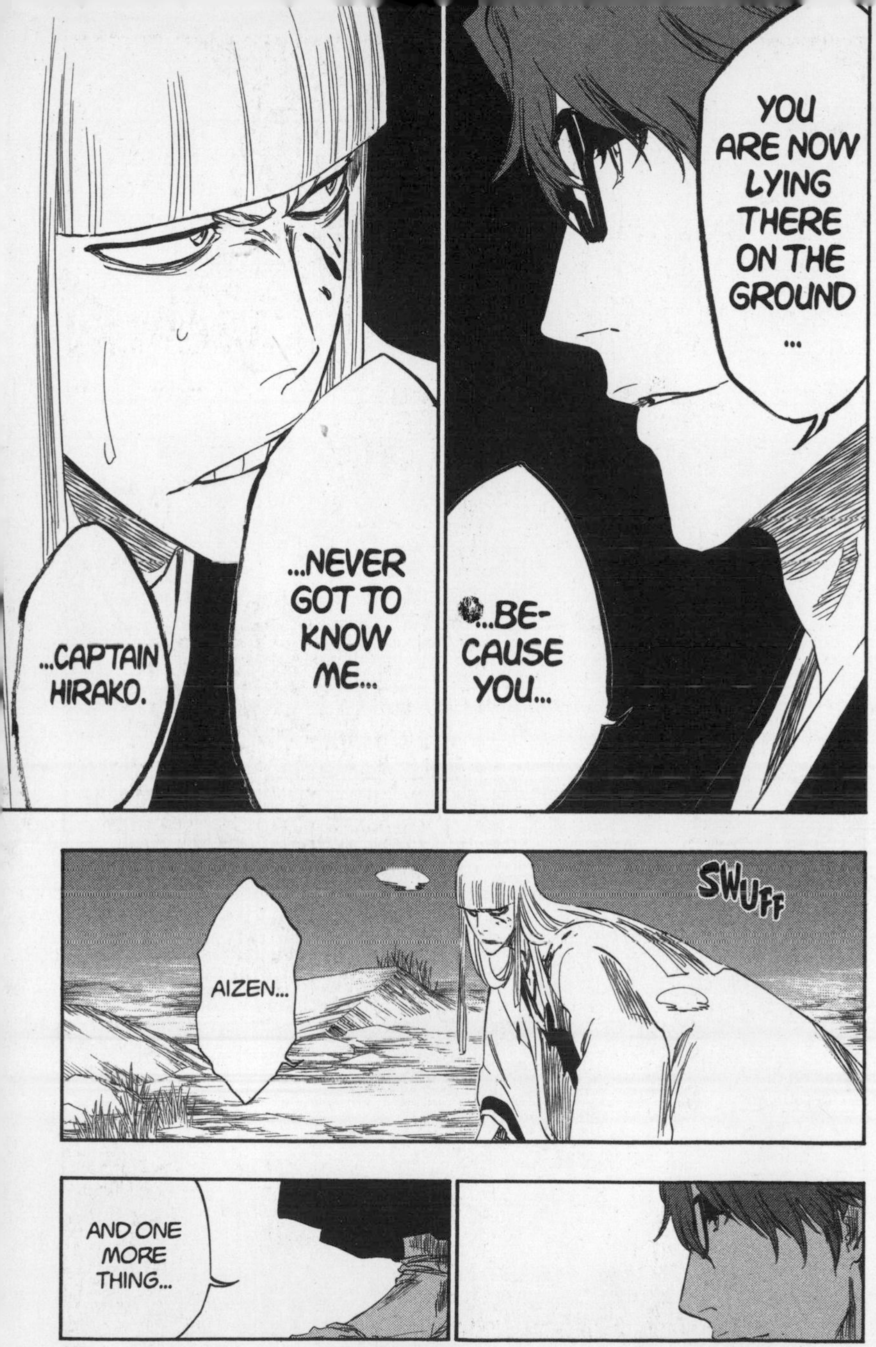

YOU ARE NOW LYING THERE ON THE GROUND ...
...BE-CAUSE YOU...
...NEVER GOT TO KNOW ME...
...CAPTAIN HIRAKO.
SWUFF
AIZEN...
AND ONE MORE THING...

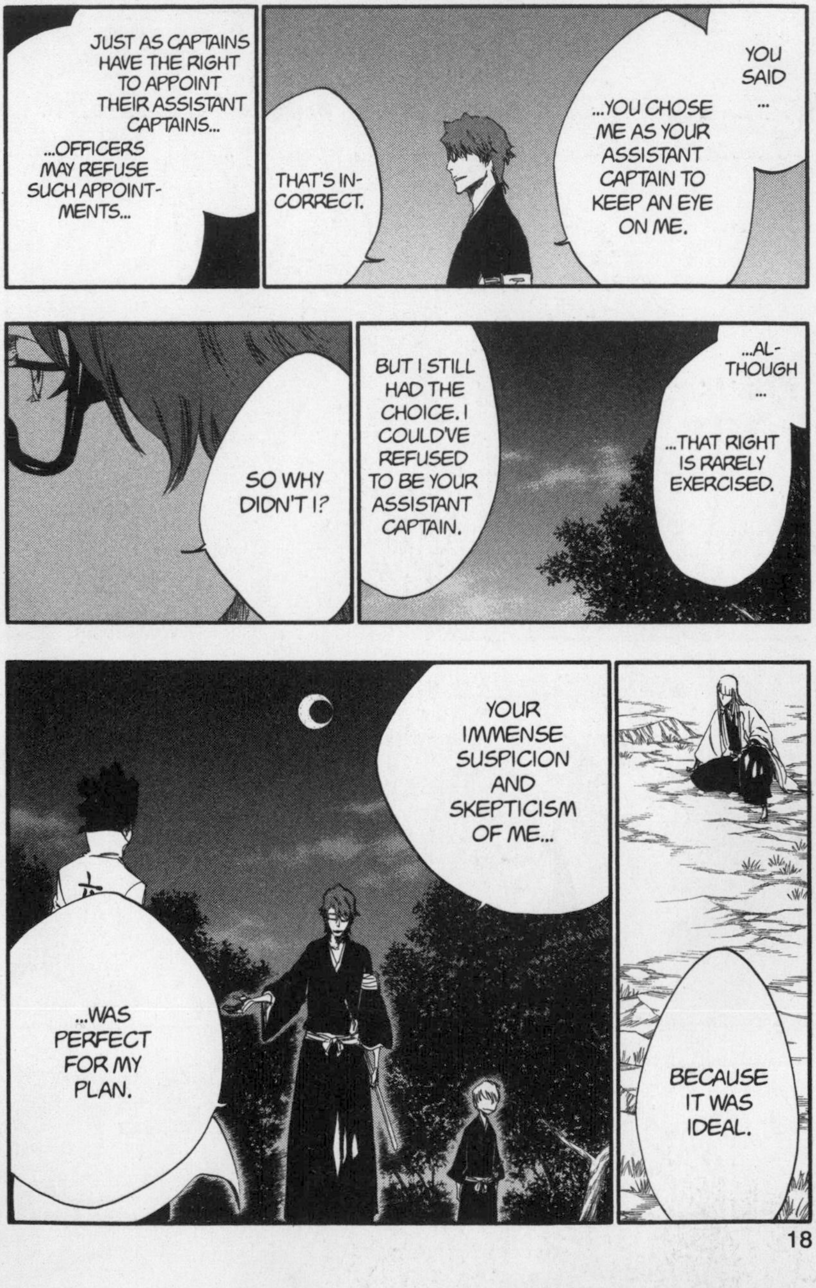
YOU SAID ...
...YOU CHOSE ME AS YOUR ASSISTANT CAPTAIN TO KEEP AN EYE ON ME.
THAT'S IN-CORRECT.
JUST AS CAPTAINS HAVE THE RIGHT TO APPOINT THEIR ASSISTANT CAPTAINS...
...OFFICERS MAY REFUSE SUCH APPOINT-MENTS...
...AL-THOUGH ...
...THAT RIGHT IS RARELY EXERCISED.
BUT I STILL HAD THE CHOICE. I COULD'VE REFUSED TO BE YOUR ASSISTANT CAPTAIN.
SO WHY DIDN'T I?
BECAUSE IT WAS IDEAL.
YOUR IMMENSE SUSPICION AND SKEPTICISM OF ME...
...WAS PERFECT FOR MY PLAN.

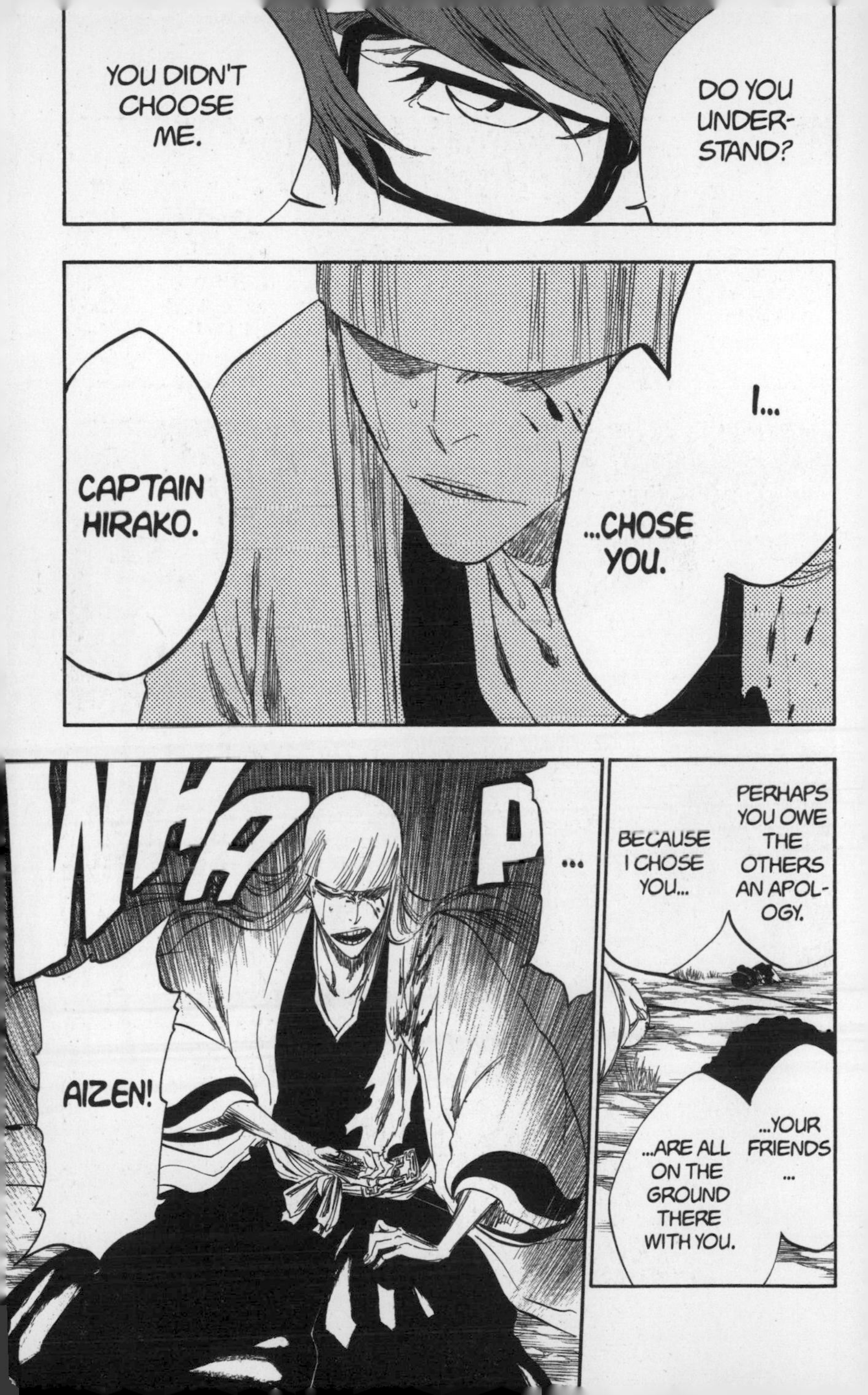
DO YOU UNDER-STAND?
YOU DIDN'T CHOOSE ME.
I...
...CHOSE YOU.
CAPTAIN HIRAKO.
PERHAPS YOU OWE THE OTHERS AN APOL-OGY.
BECAUSE I CHOSE YOU...
...YOUR FRIENDS...
...ARE ALL ON THE GROUND THERE WITH YOU.
WHAP...
AIZEN!

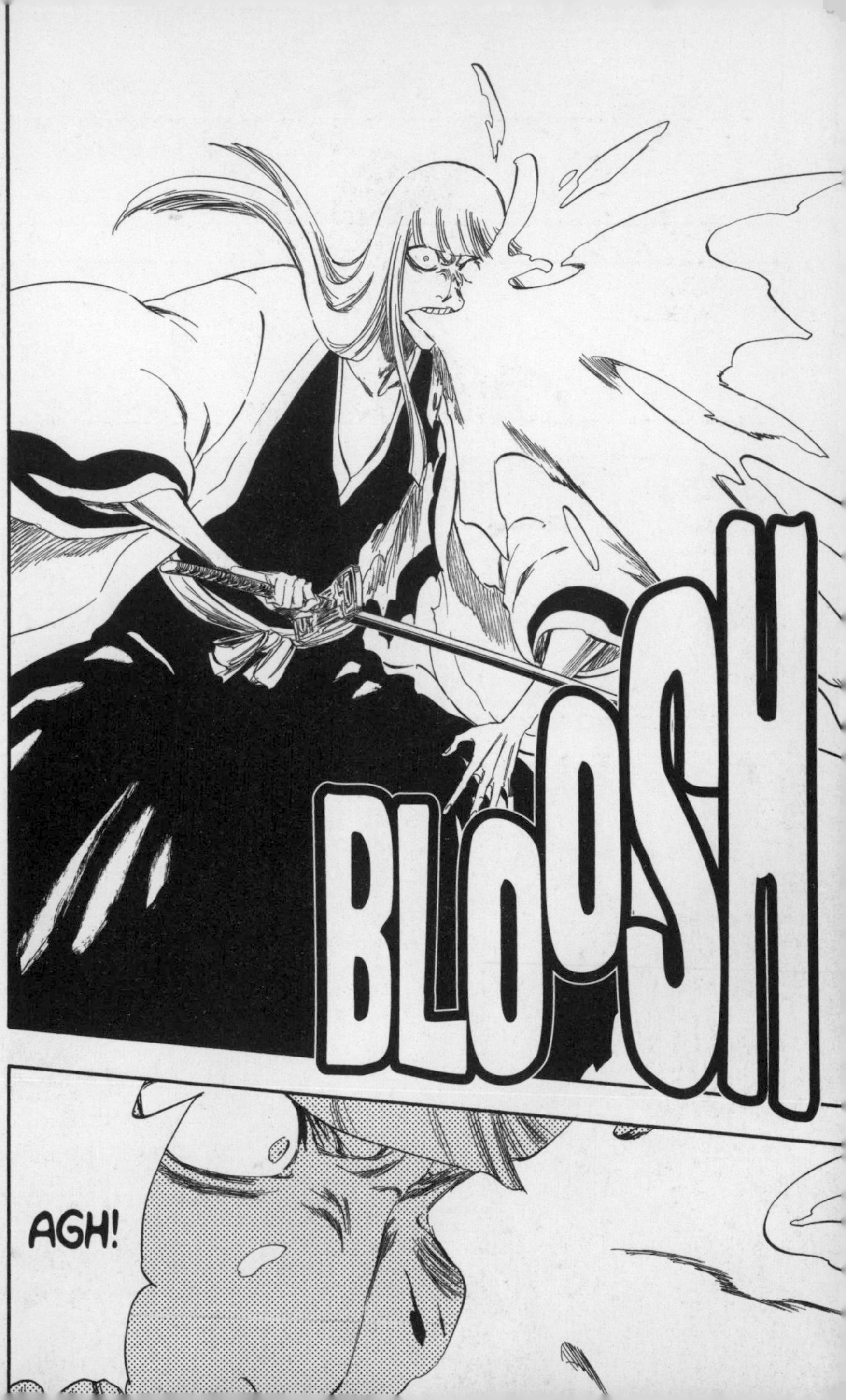
BLOOSH
AGH!

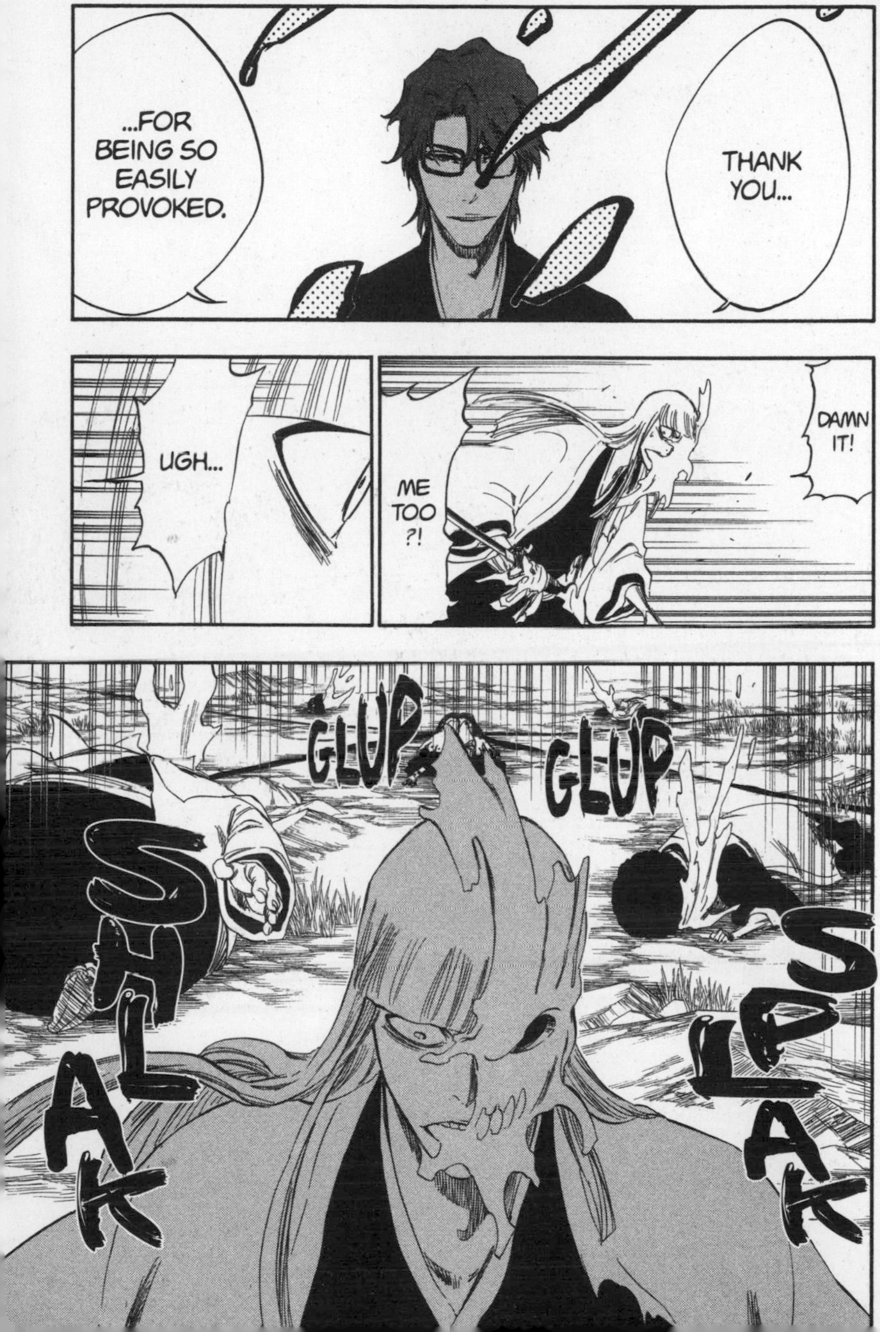
THANK YOU...
...FOR BEING SO EASILY PROVOKED.
DAMN IT!
ME TOO ?!
UGH...
GLUP
GLUP

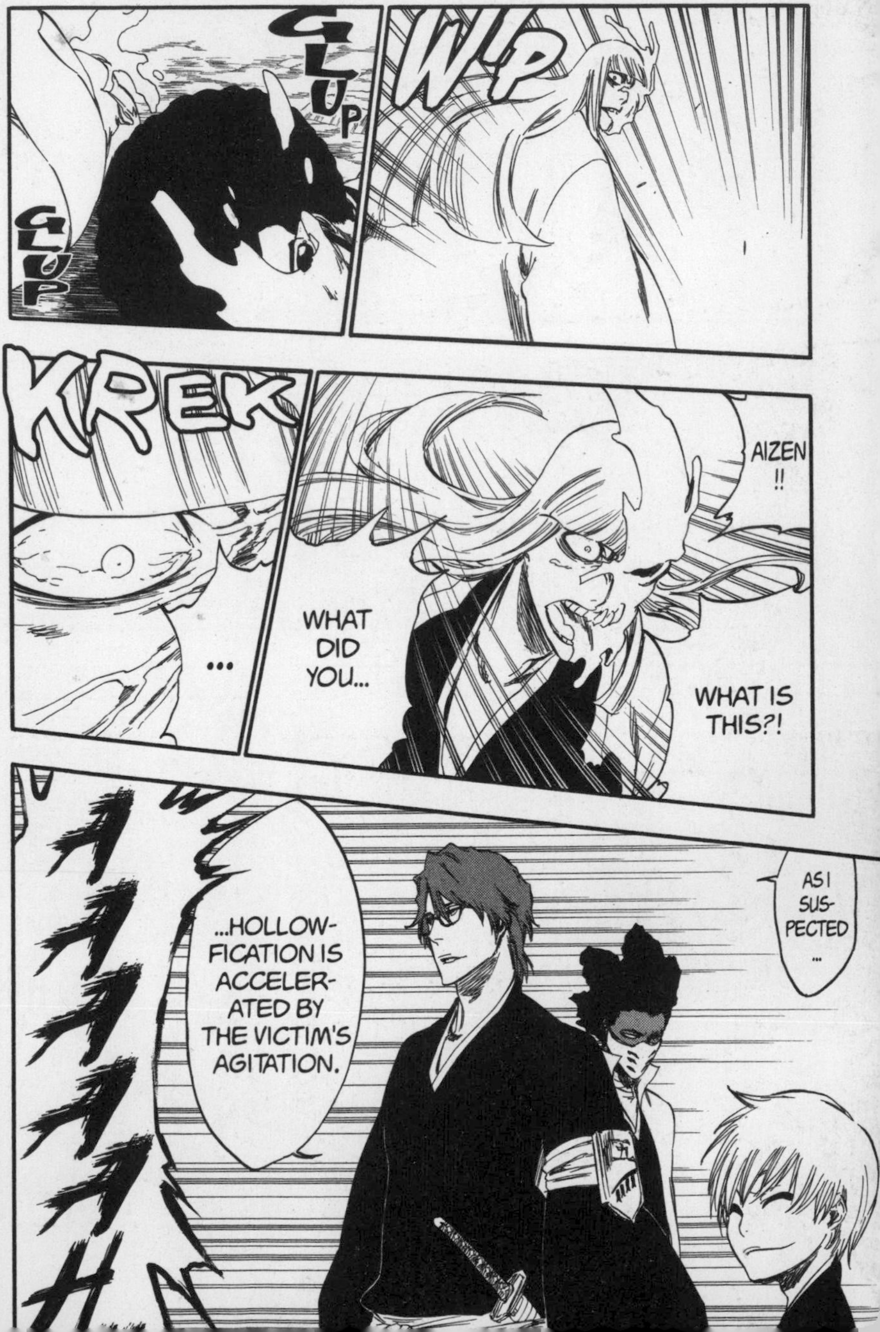
WIP
GLUP
GLUP
AIZEN!!
WHAT IS THIS?!
WHAT DID YOU...
KREK
...
AS I SUSPECTED...
...HOLLOWFICATION IS ACCELERATED BY THE VICTIM'S AGITATION.

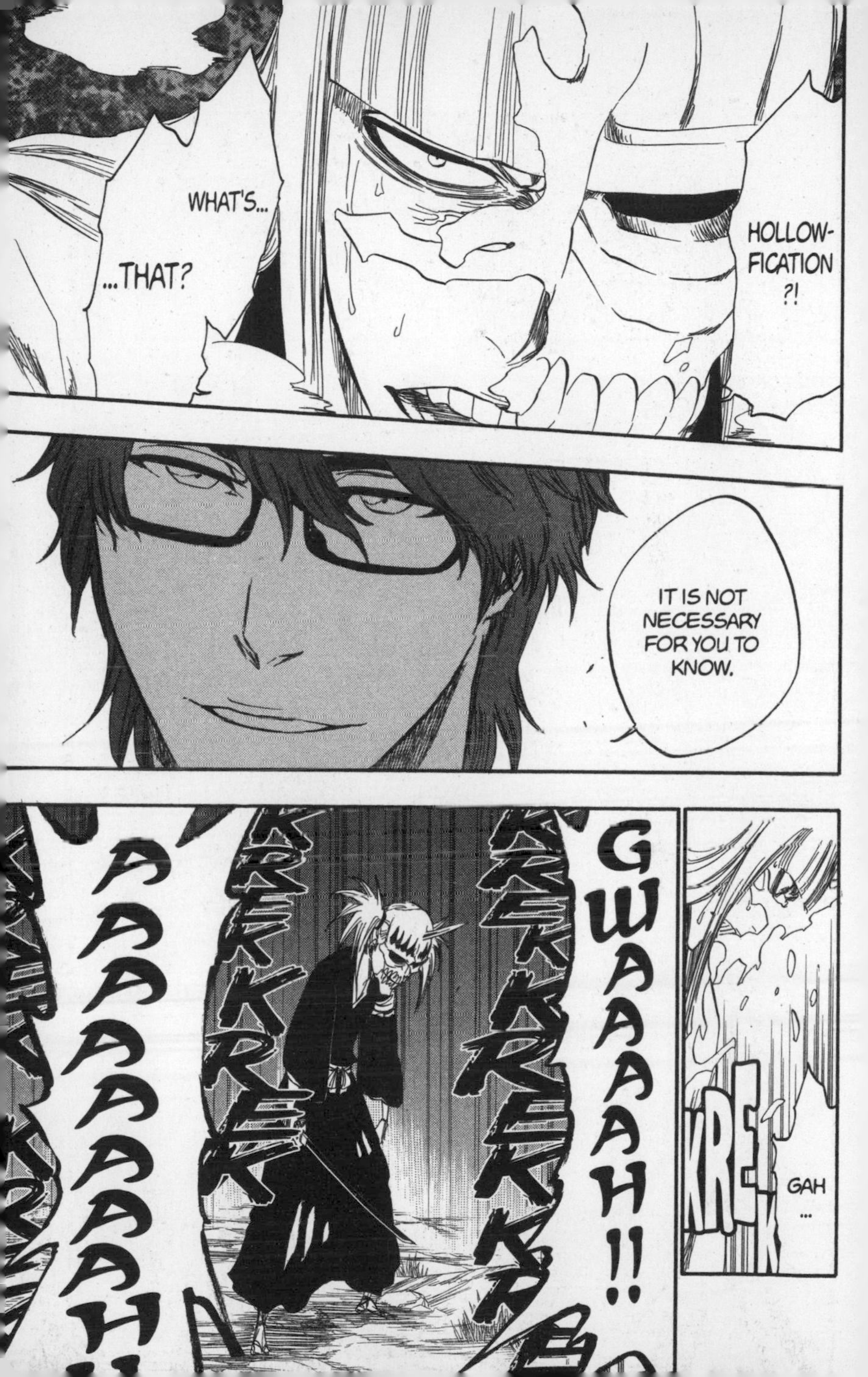
HOLLOW-FICATION ?!
WHAT'S...
...THAT?
IT IS NOT NECESSARY FOR YOU TO KNOW.
KREK
GAH ...

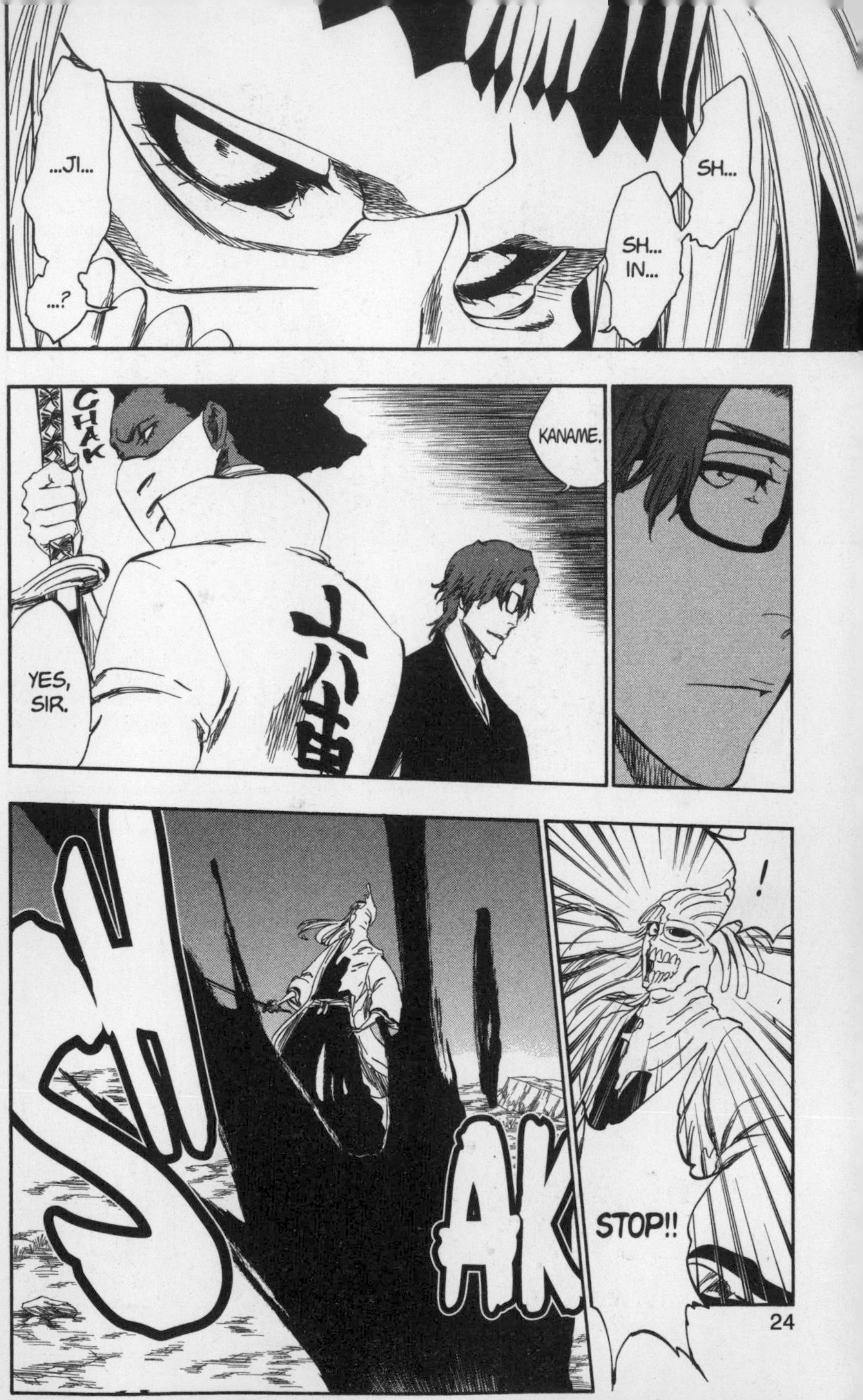
SH...
SH... IN...
...JI...
...?
KANAME.
CHAK
YES, SIR.
!
STOP!!
SH
AK

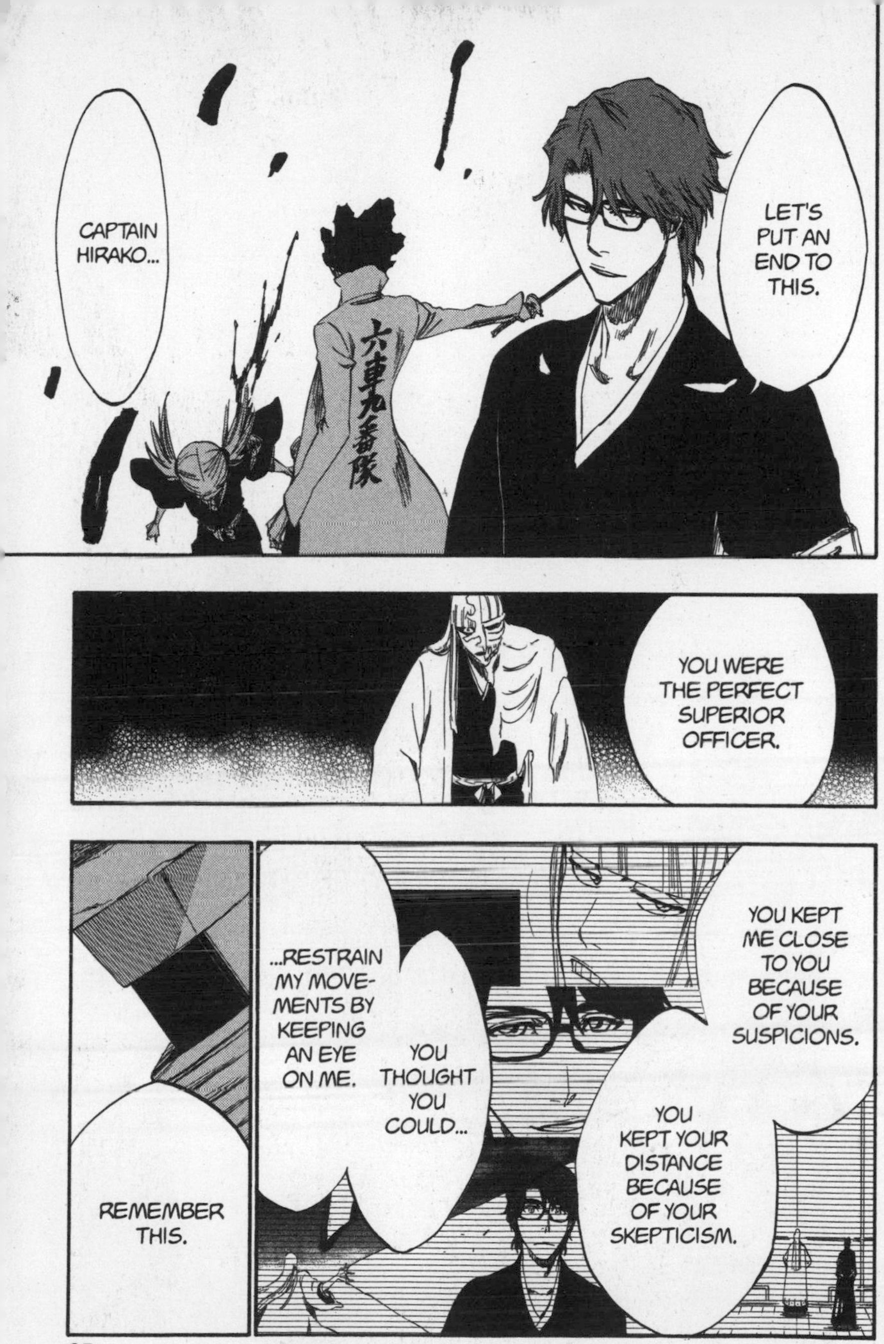
LET'S PUT AN END TO THIS.
六車九番隊
CAPTAIN HIRAKO...
YOU WERE THE PERFECT SUPERIOR OFFICER.
YOU KEPT ME CLOSE TO YOU BECAUSE OF YOUR SUSPICIONS.
YOU KEPT YOUR DISTANCE BECAUSE OF YOUR SKEPTICISM.
YOU THOUGHT YOU COULD...
...RESTRAIN MY MOVEMENTS BY KEEPING AN EYE ON ME.
REMEMBER THIS.

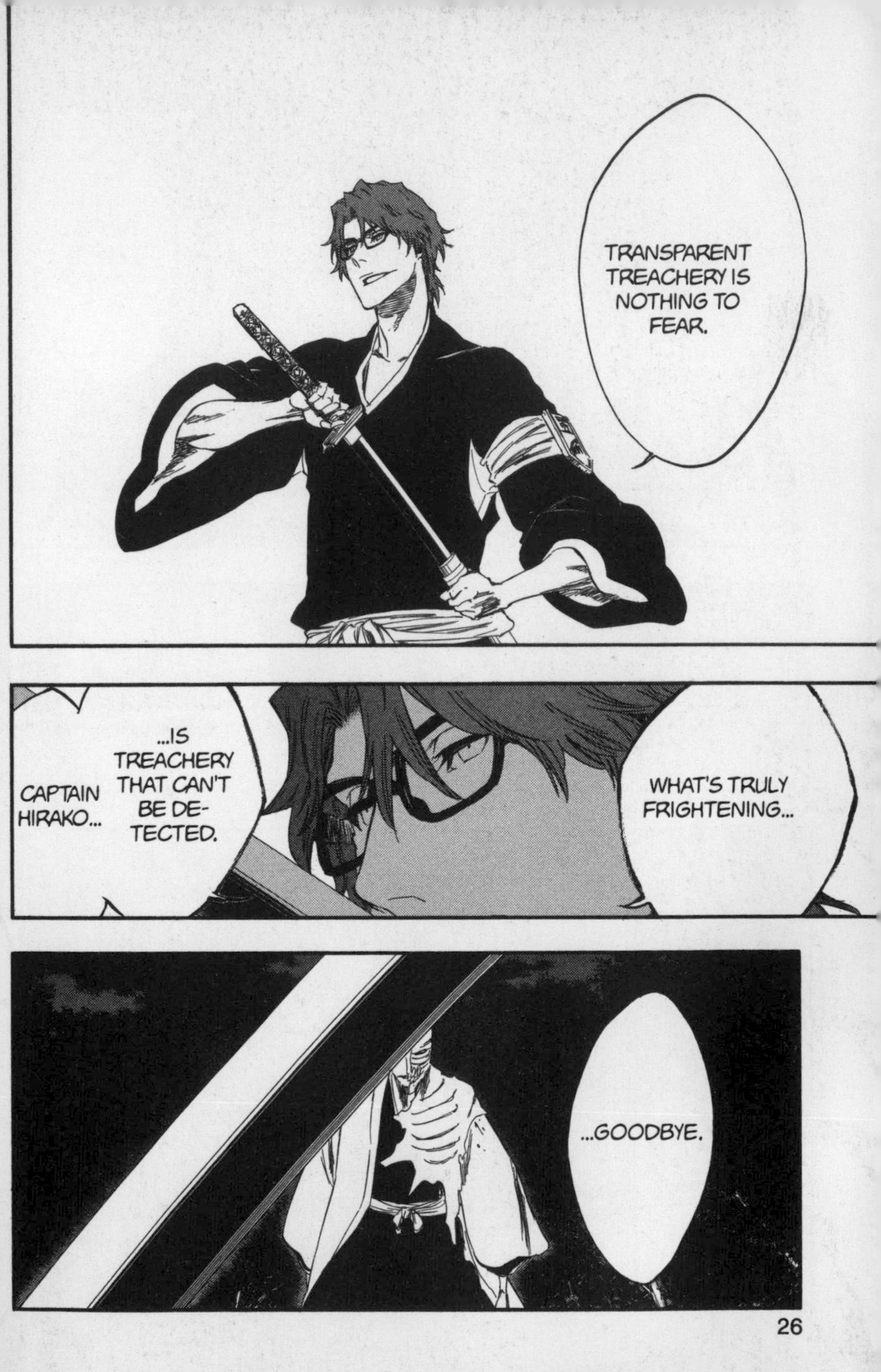
TRANSPARENT TREACHERY IS NOTHING TO FEAR.
WHAT'S TRULY FRIGHTENING...
...IS TREACHERY THAT CAN'T BE DE-TECTED.
CAPTAIN HIRAKO...
...GOODBYE.

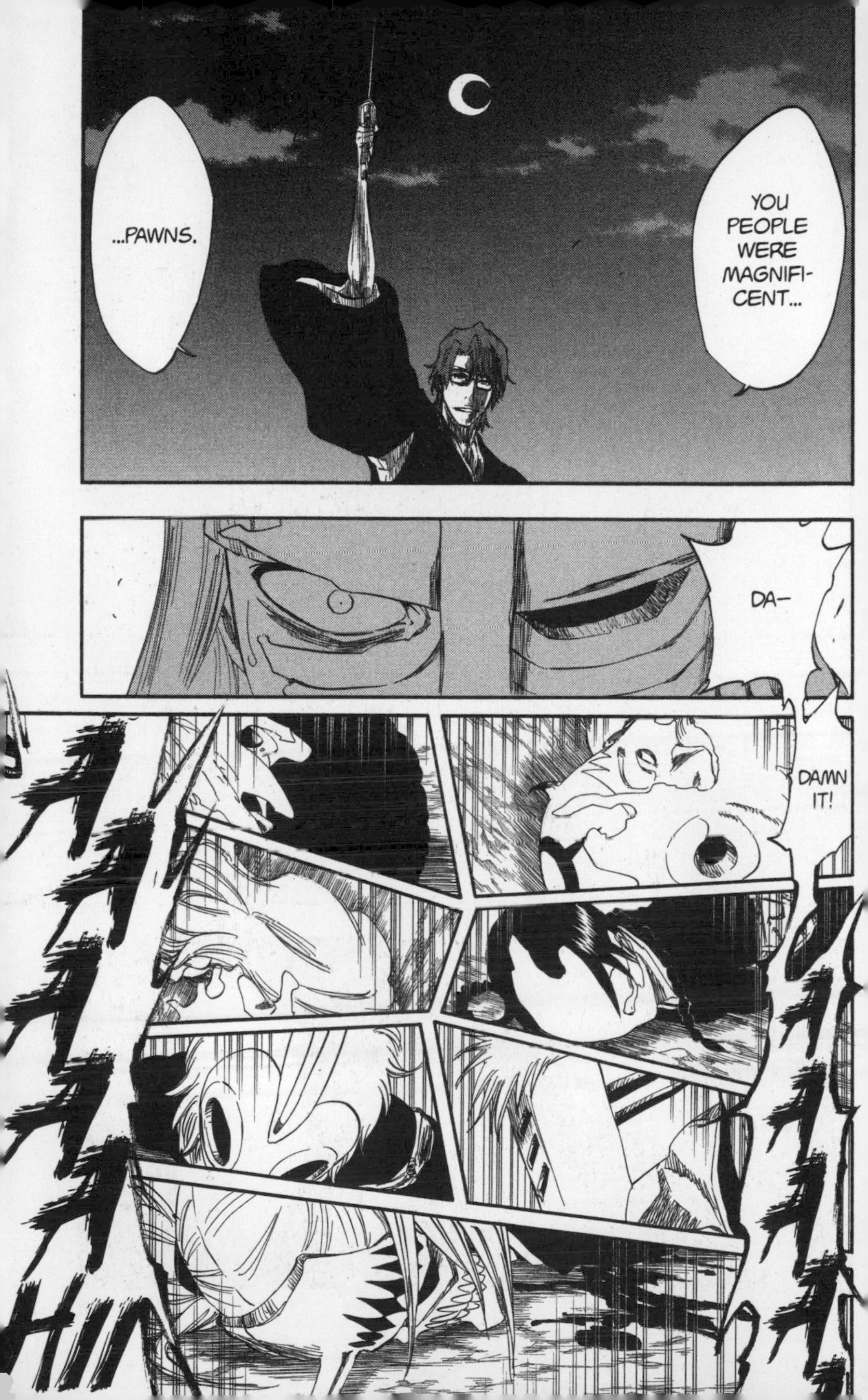
YOU PEOPLE WERE MAGNIFI-CENT...
...PAWNS.
DA—
DAMN IT!

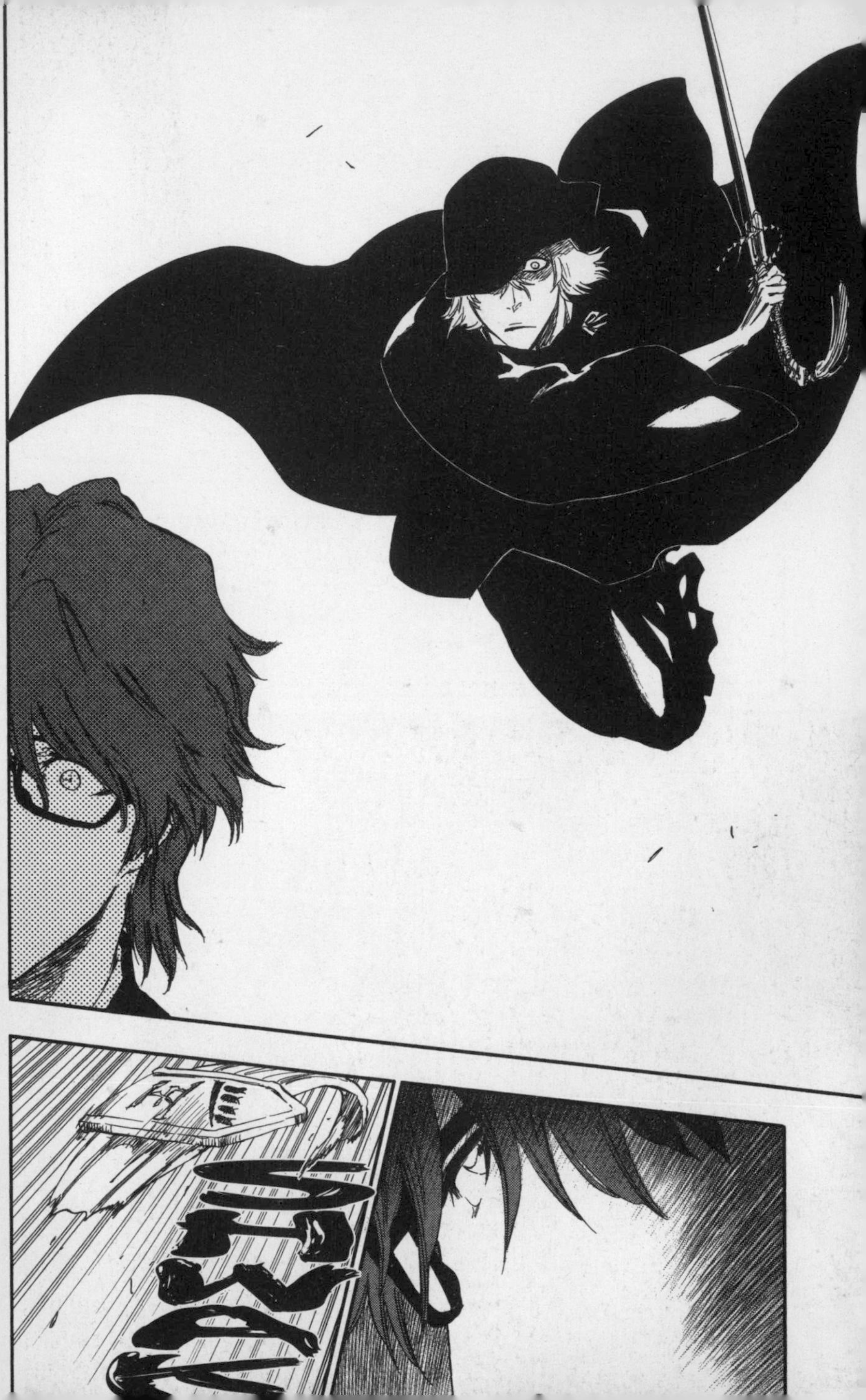

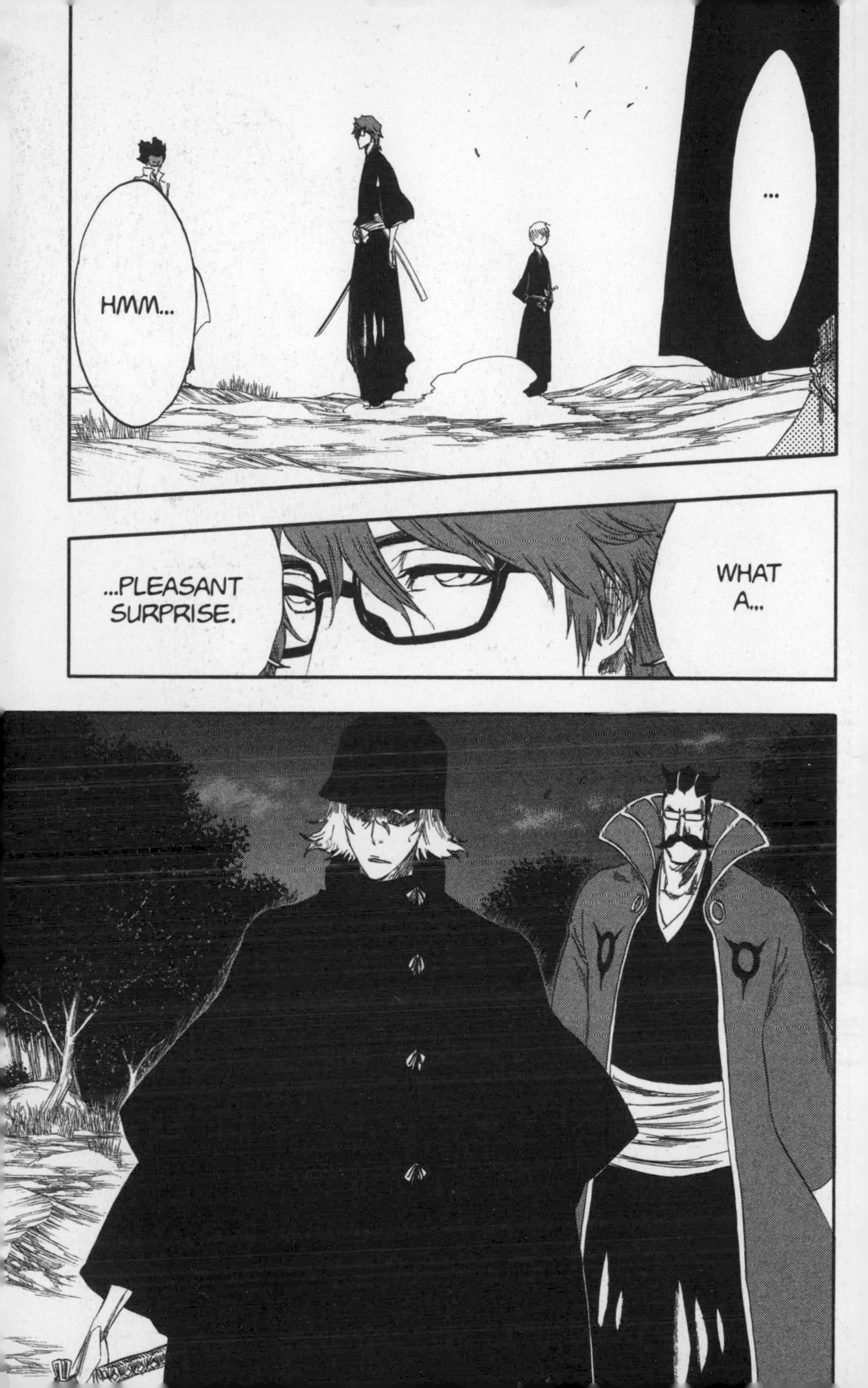
...
HMM...
WHAT A...
...PLEASANT SURPRISE.

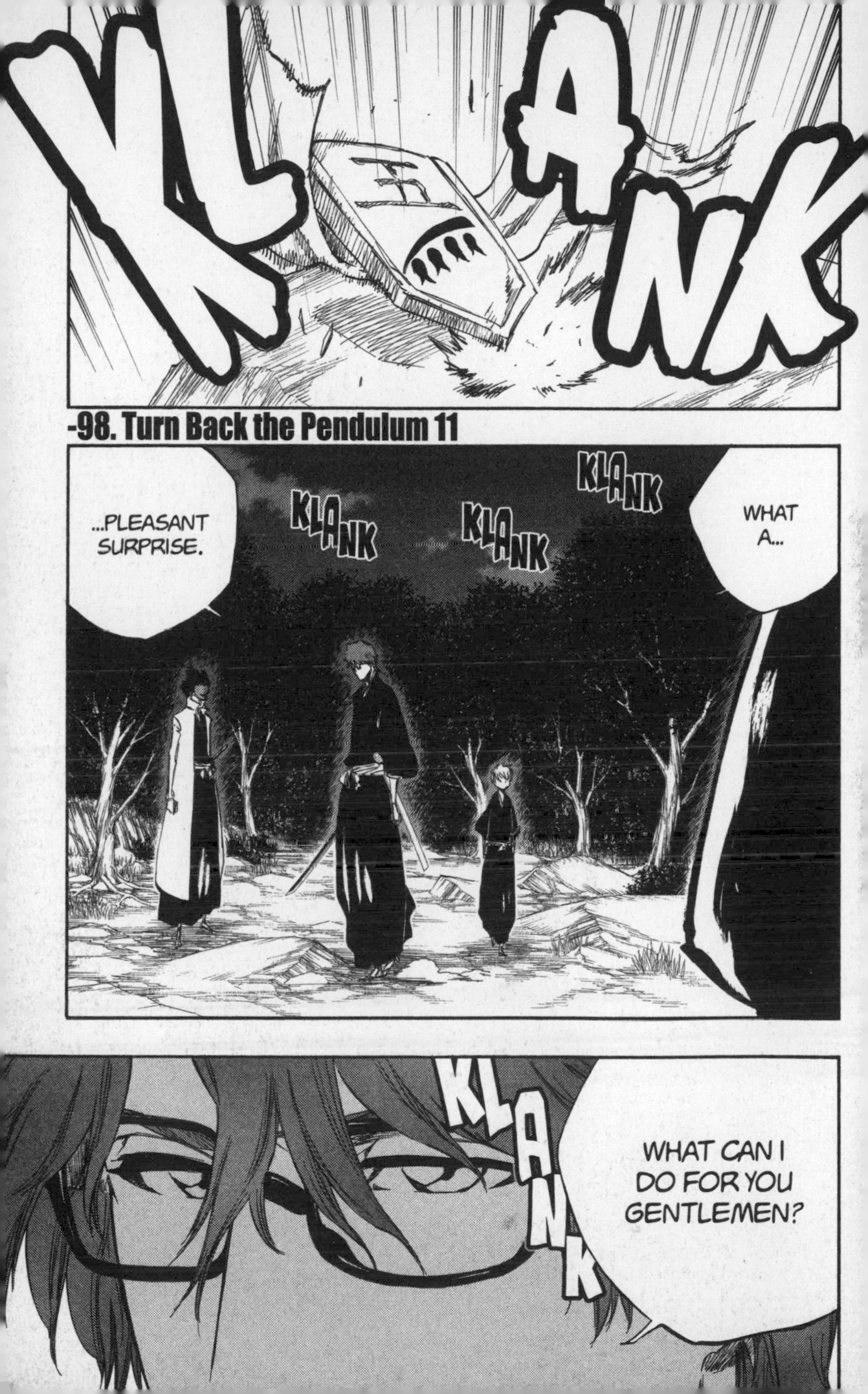
KLANK
-98. Turn Back the Pendulum 11
WHAT A...
KLANK
KLANK
KLANK
...PLEASANT SURPRISE.
KLANK
WHAT CAN I DO FOR YOU GENTLEMEN?

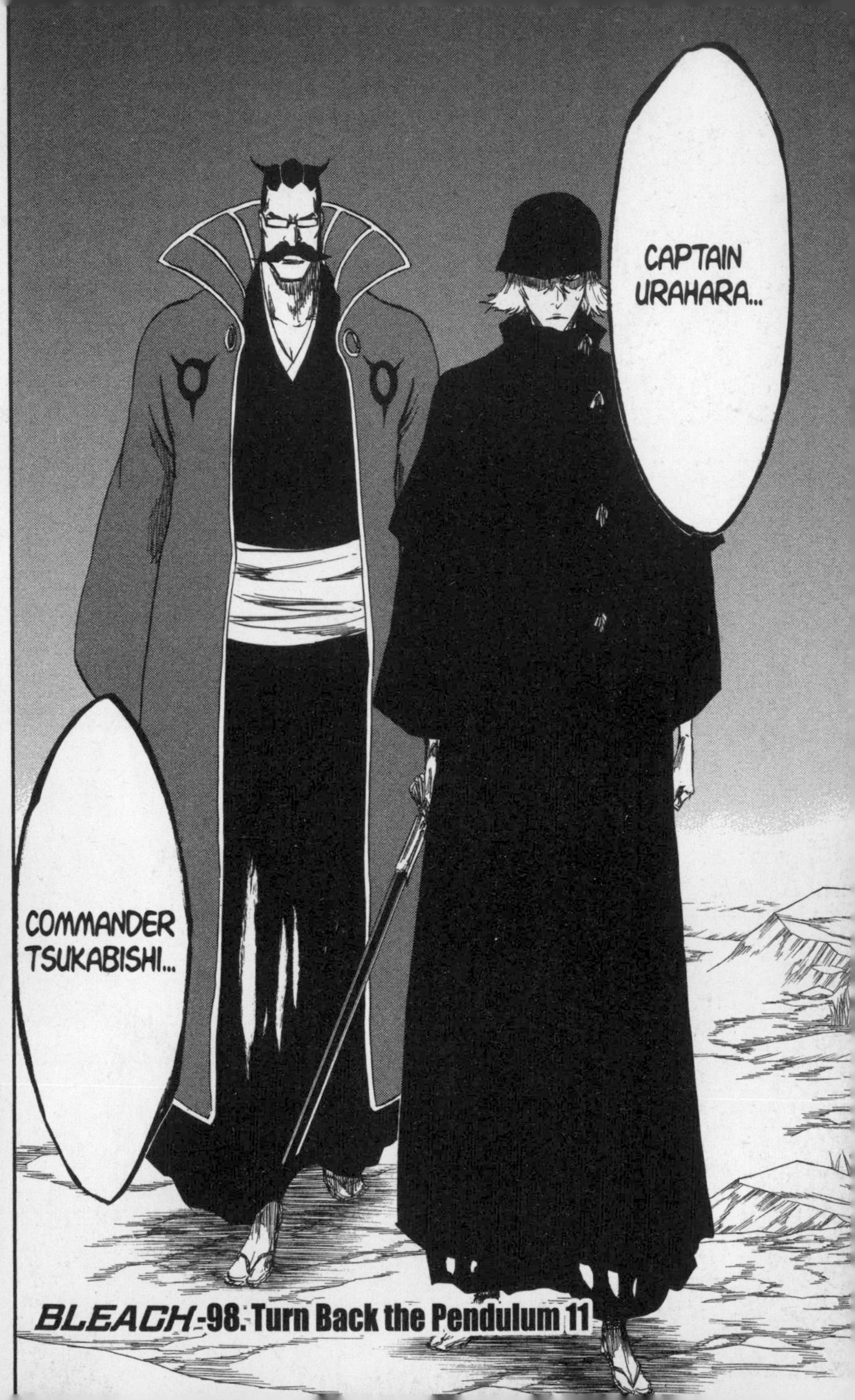
CAPTAIN URAHARA...
COMMANDER TSUKABISHI...
BLEACH -98. Turn Back the Pendulum 11

READ THIS WAY

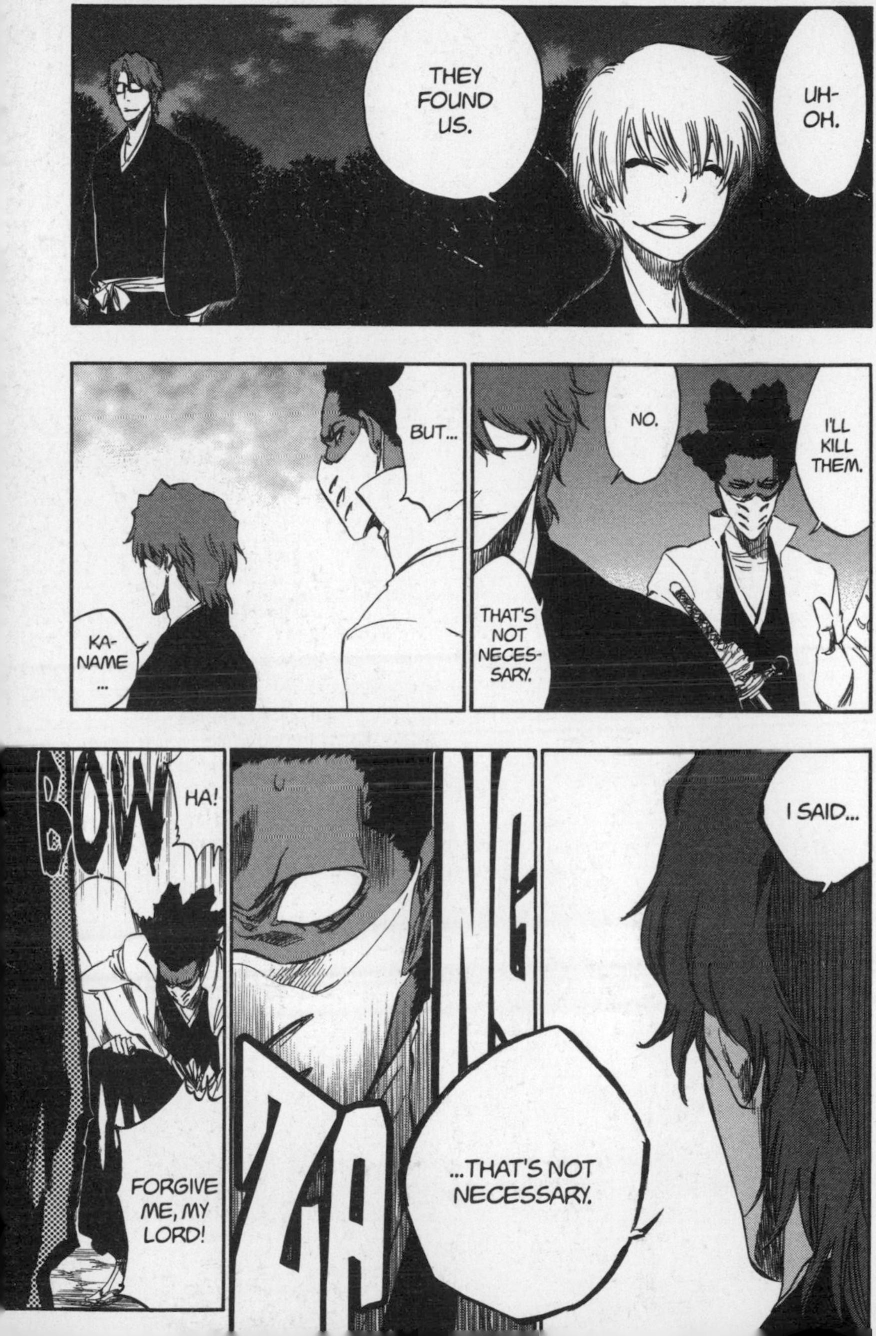
UH-OH.
THEY FOUND US.
I'LL KILL THEM.
NO.
THAT'S NOT NECESSARY.
BUT...
KA-NAME...
I SAID...
...THAT'S NOT NECESSARY.
BOW
HA!
FORGIVE ME, MY LORD!

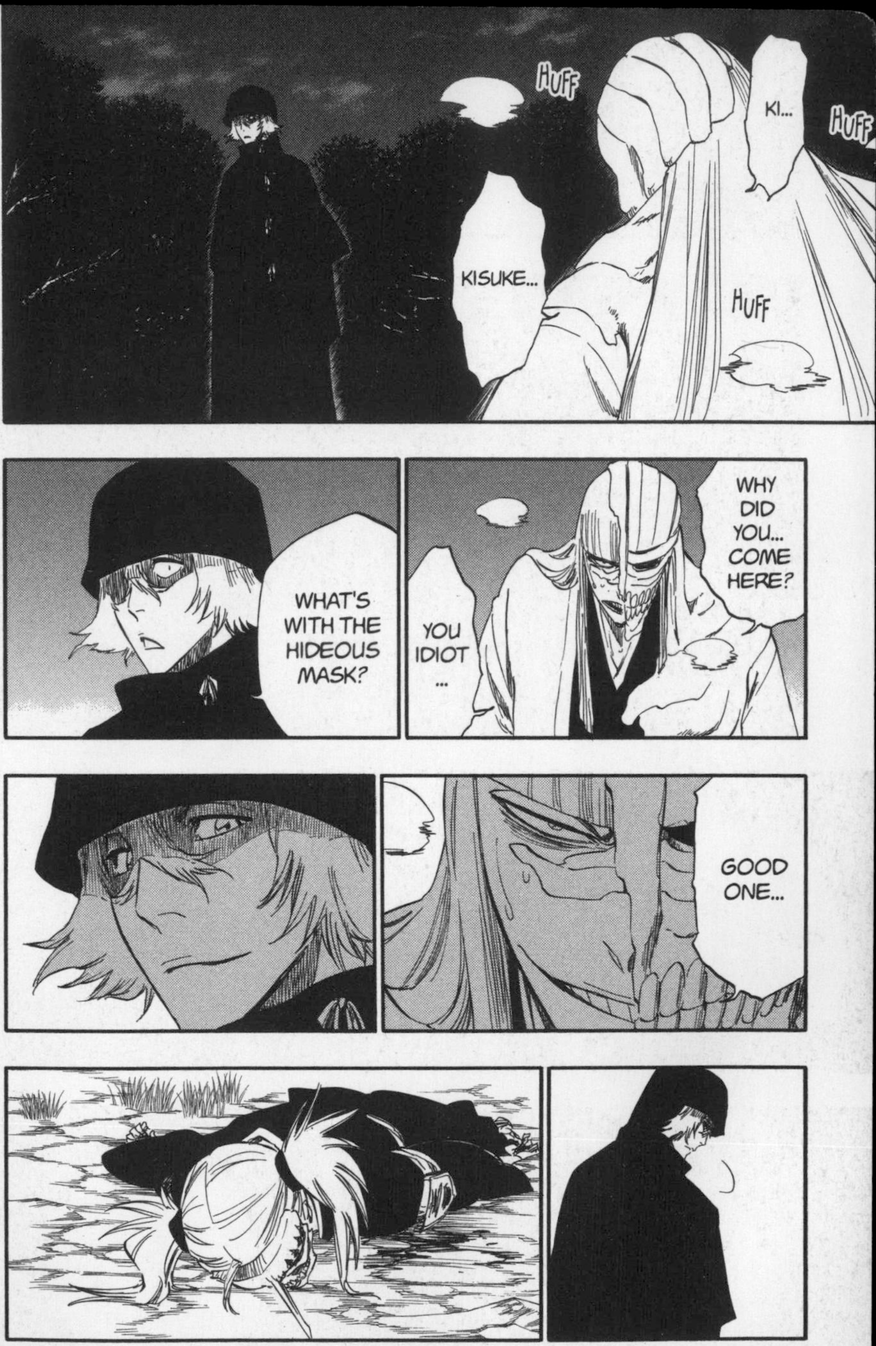
HUFF
KI...
HUFF
HUFF
KISUKE...
WHY DID YOU... COME HERE?
YOU IDIOT ...
WHAT'S WITH THE HIDEOUS MASK?
GOOD ONE...

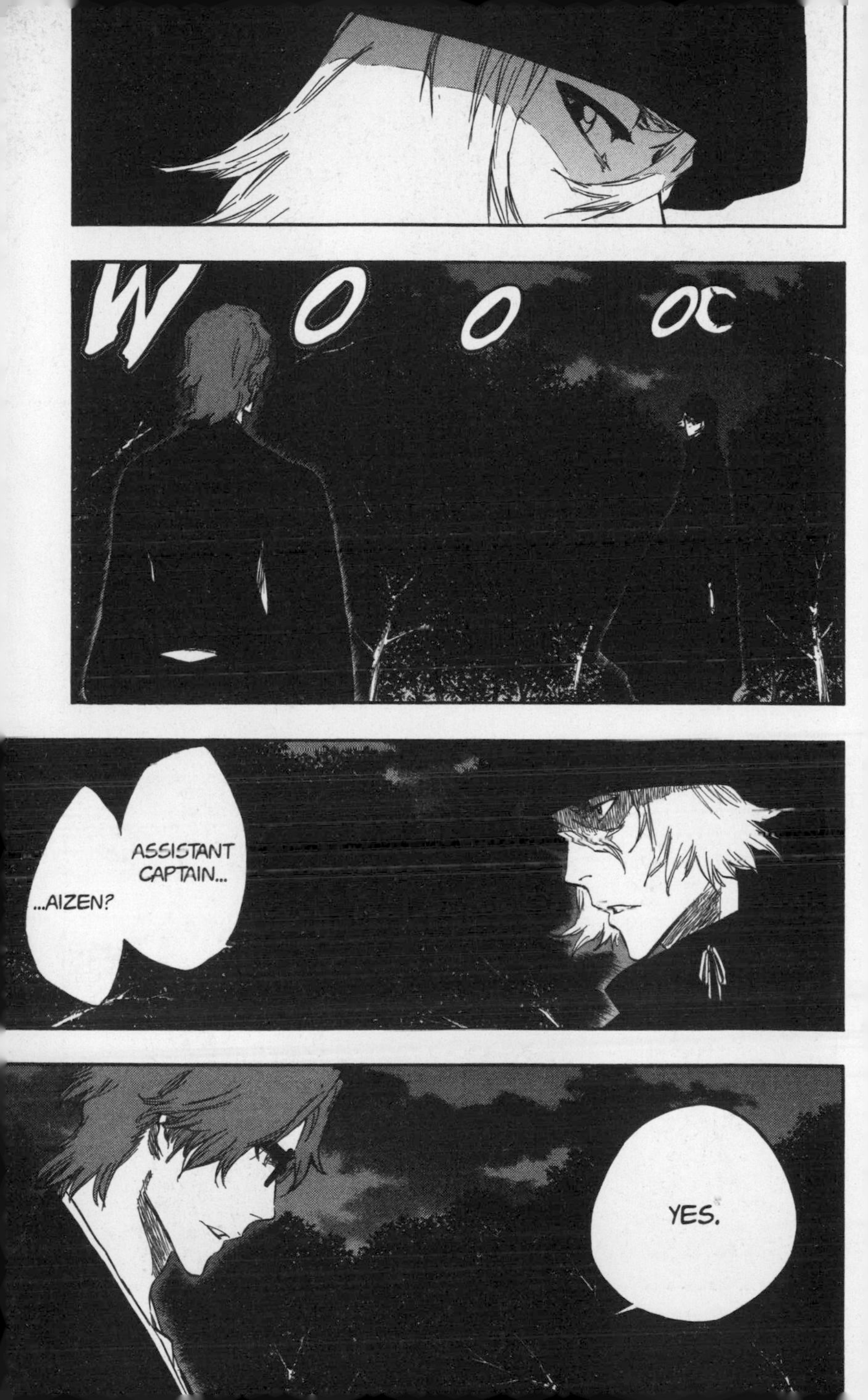
WOOOC
ASSISTANT CAPTAIN...
...AIZEN?
YES.

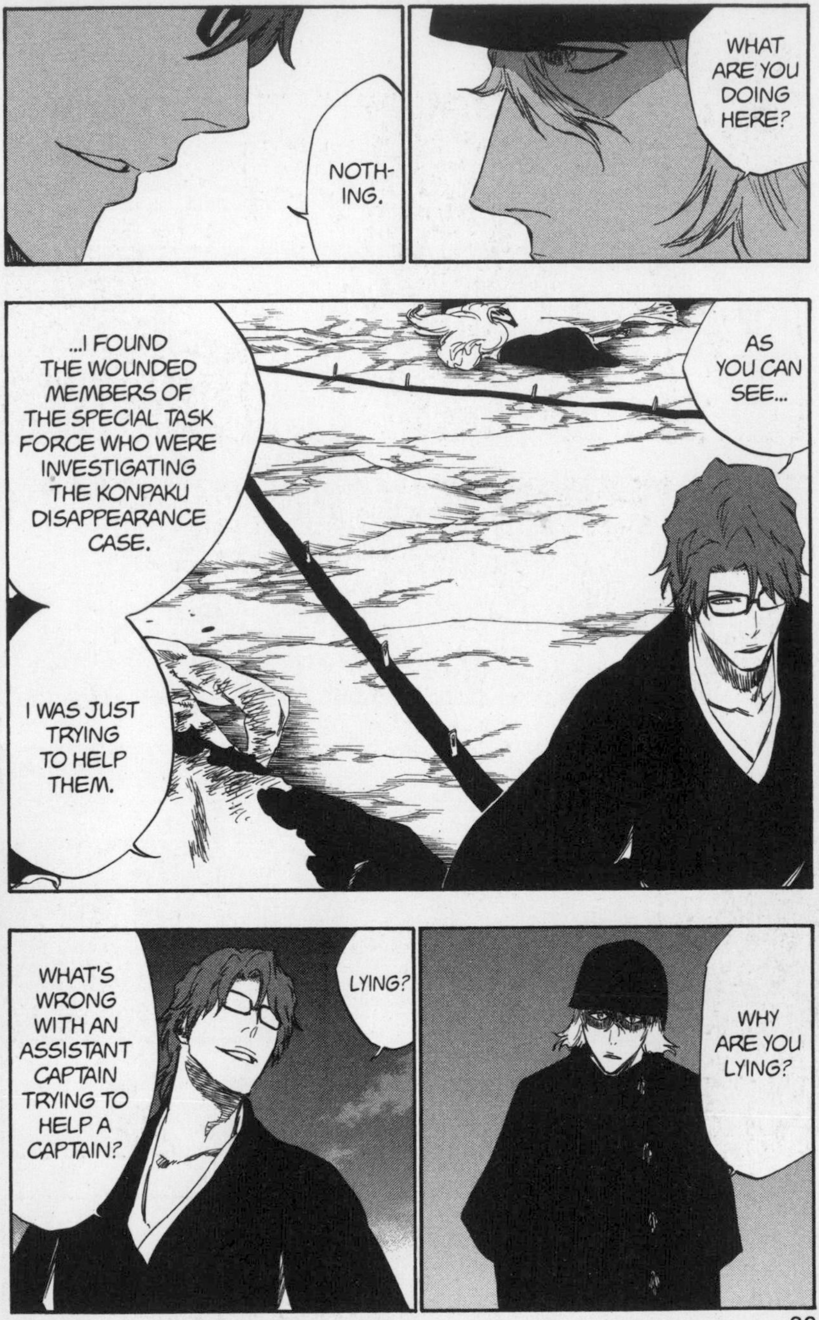
WHAT ARE YOU DOING HERE?
NOTH-ING.
AS YOU CAN SEE...
...I FOUND THE WOUNDED MEMBERS OF THE SPECIAL TASK FORCE WHO WERE INVESTIGATING THE KONPAKU DISAPPEARANCE CASE.
I WAS JUST TRYING TO HELP THEM.
WHY ARE YOU LYING?
LYING?
WHAT'S WRONG WITH AN ASSISTANT CAPTAIN TRYING TO HELP A CAPTAIN?

READ THIS WAY

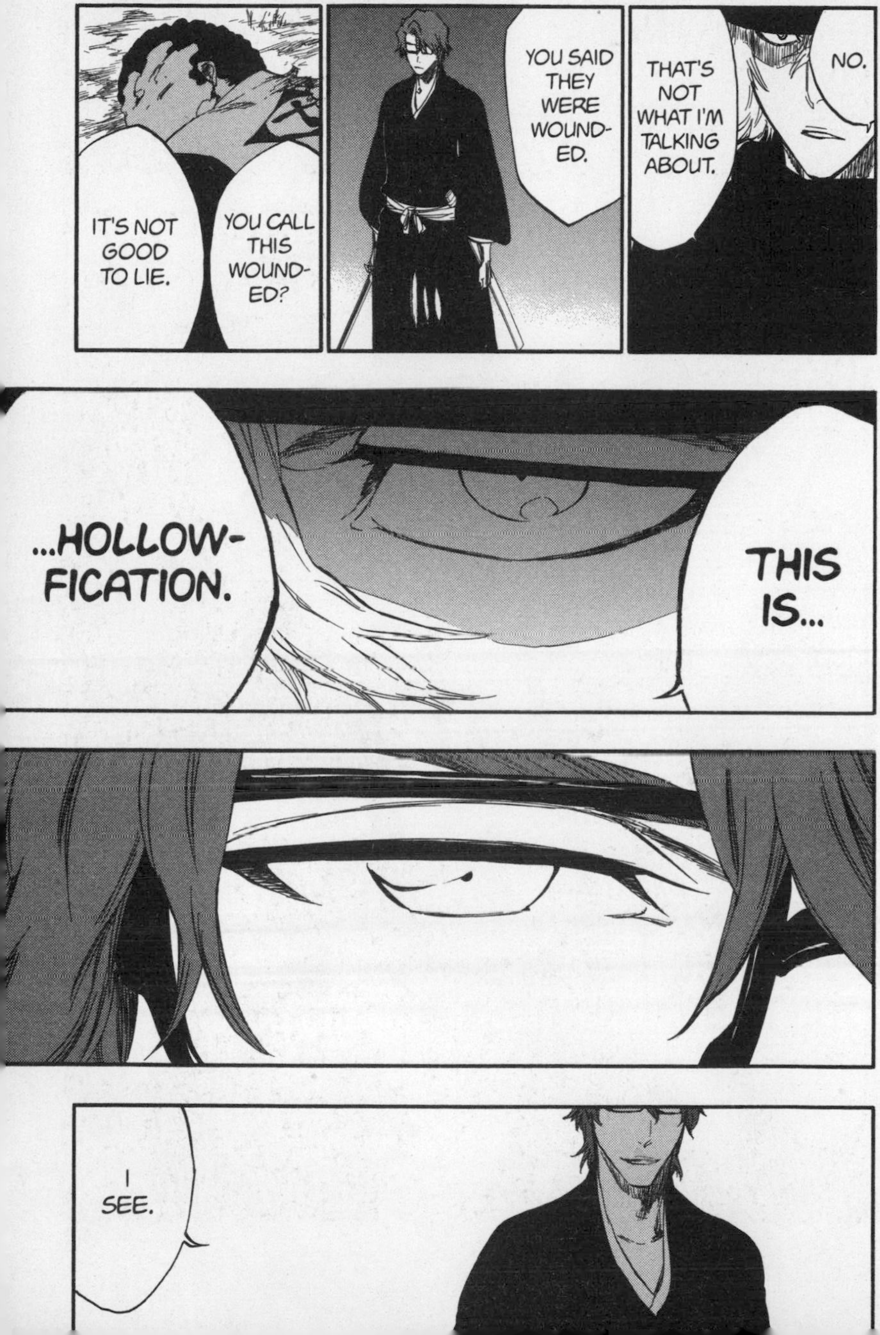
NO.
THAT'S NOT WHAT I'M TALKING ABOUT.
YOU SAID THEY WERE WOUND-ED.
YOU CALL THIS WOUND-ED?
IT'S NOT GOOD TO LIE.
THIS IS...
...HOLLOW-FICATION.
I SEE.

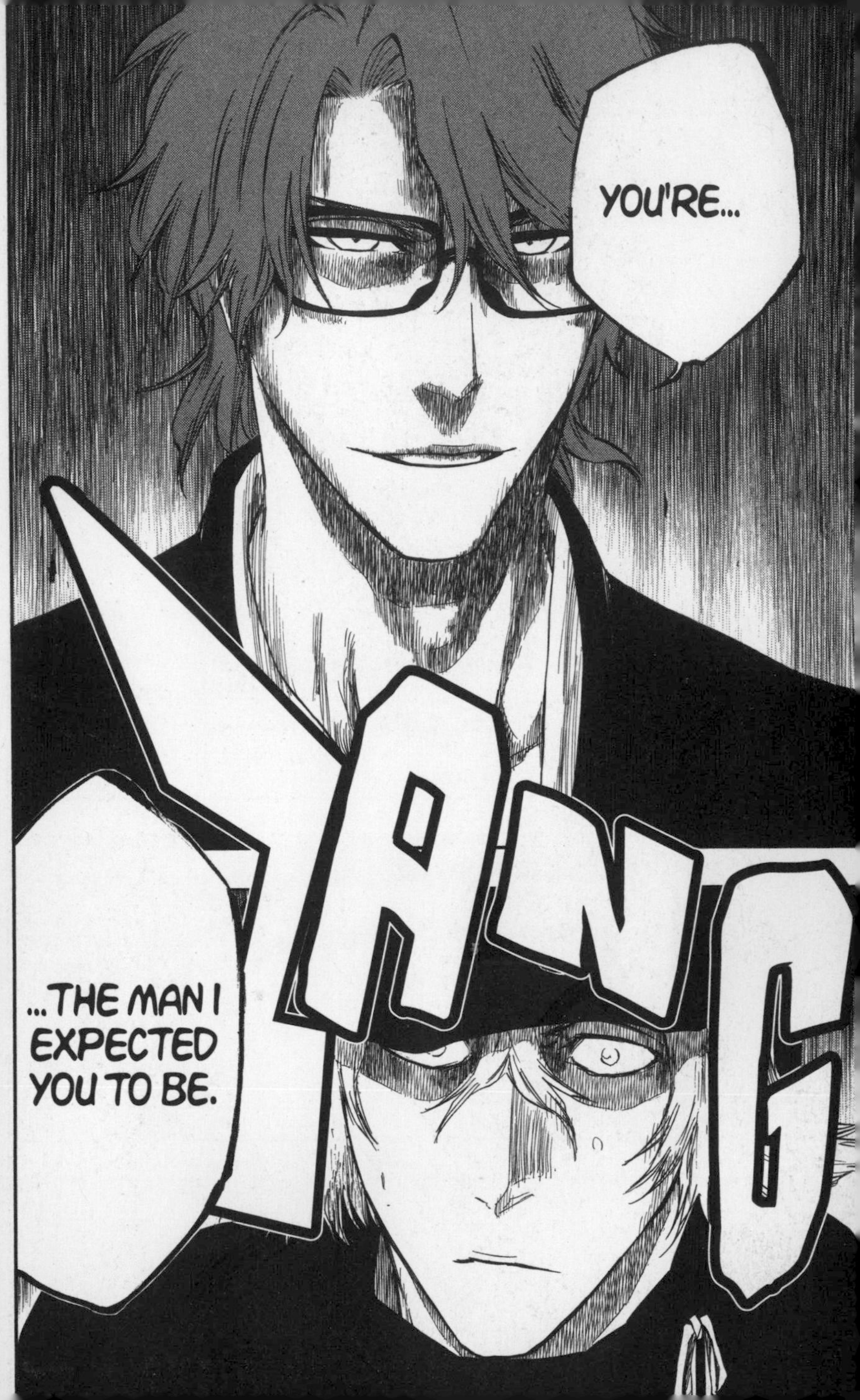
YOU'RE...
ANG
...THE MAN I EXPECTED YOU TO BE.

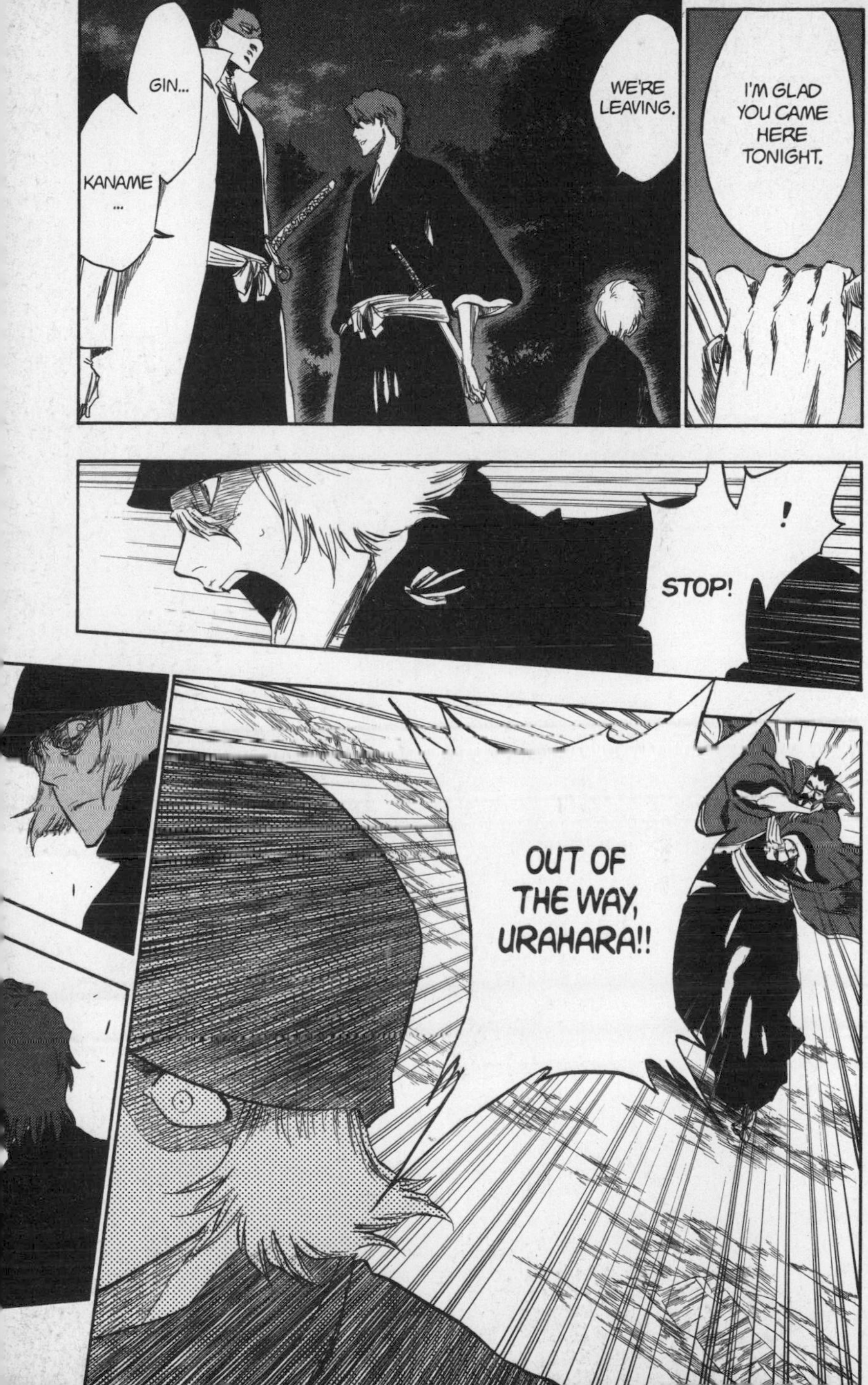
I'M GLAD YOU CAME HERE TONIGHT.
WE'RE LEAVING.
GIN...
KANAME ...
!
STOP!
OUT OF THE WAY, URAHARA!!

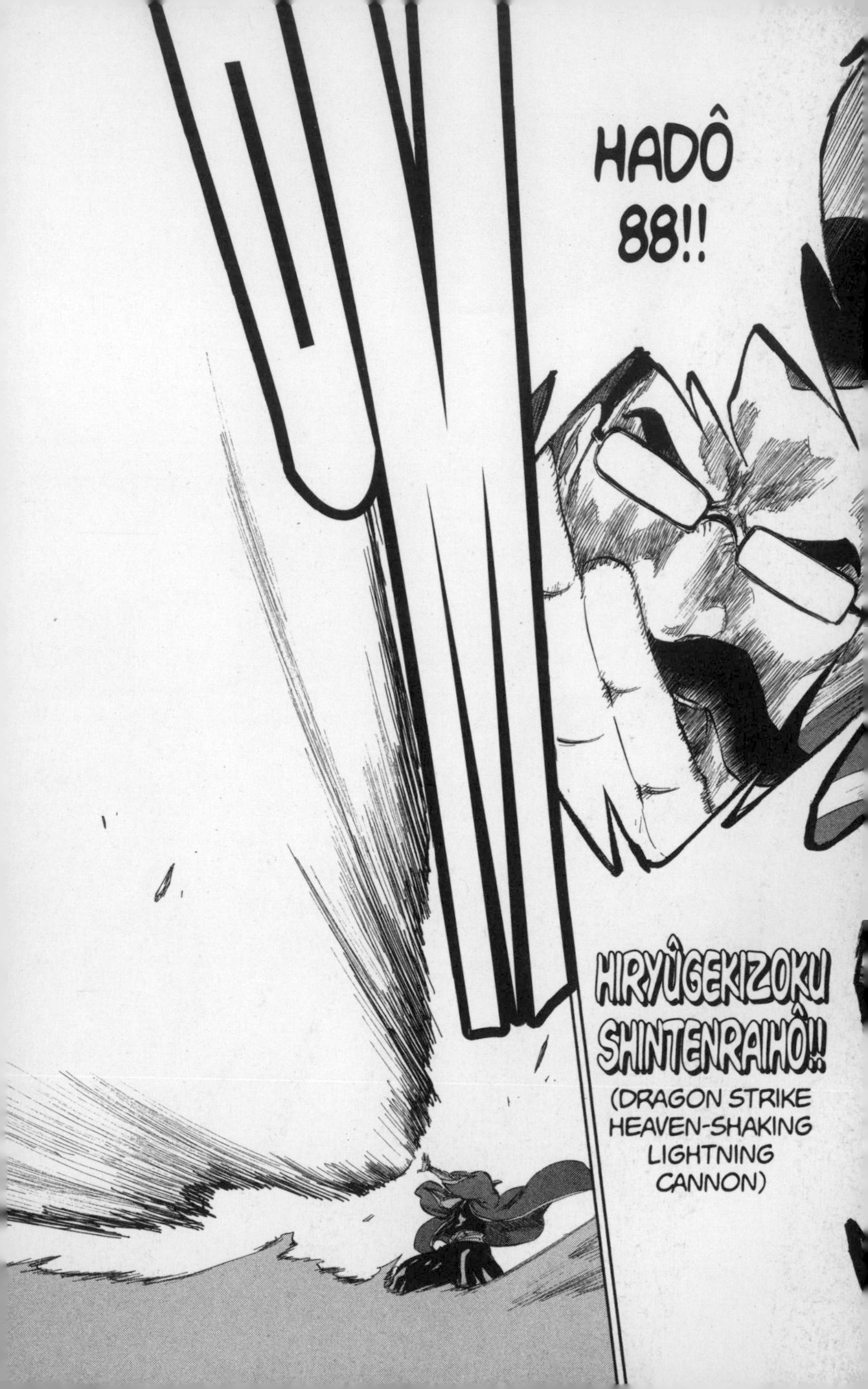
HADÔ 88!!
HIRYÛGEKIZOKU SHINTENRAIHÔ!!
(DRAGON STRIKE HEAVEN-SHAKING LIGHTNING CANNON)

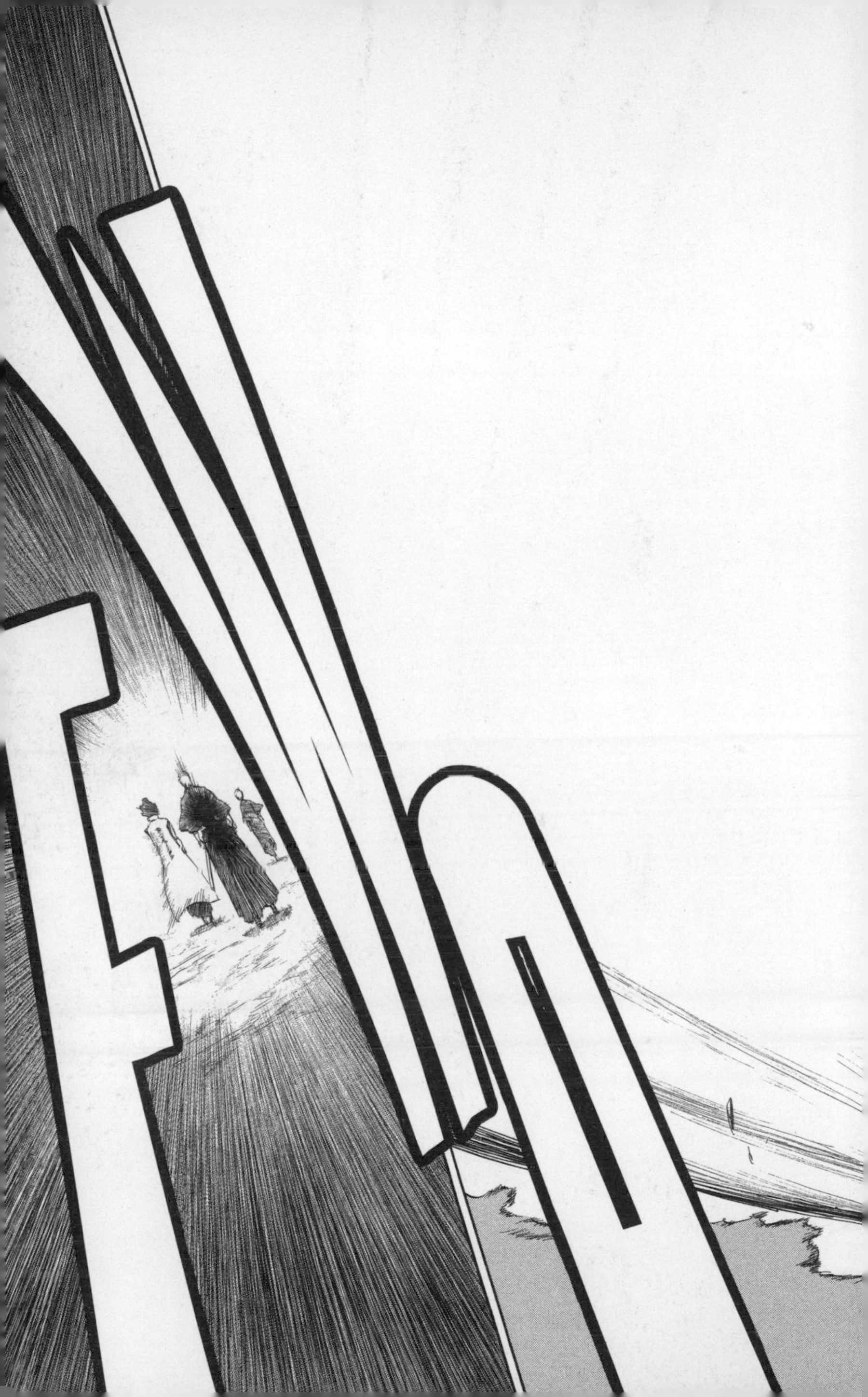

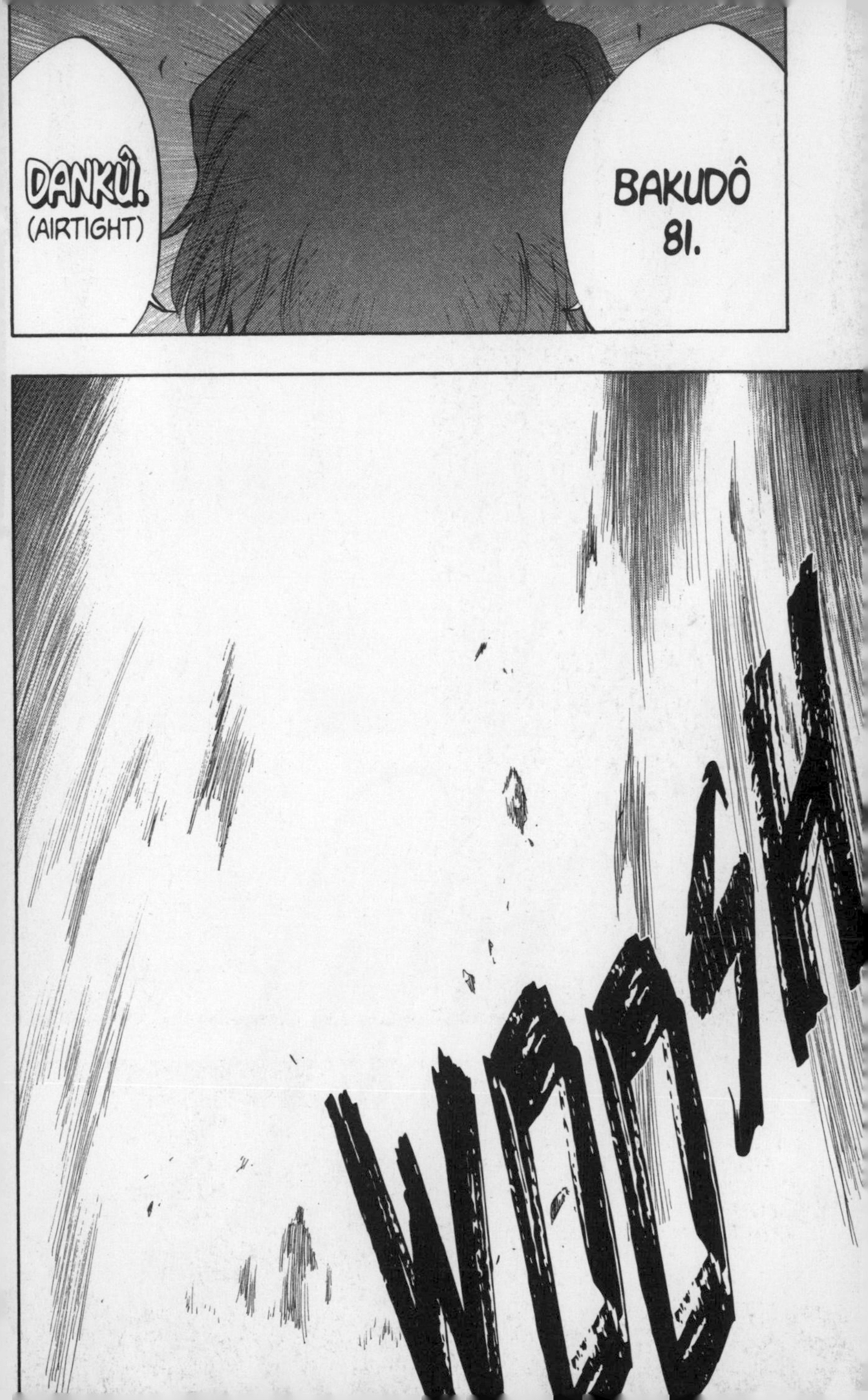
BAKUDÔ 81.
DANKÛ.
(AIRTIGHT)
WOOSH

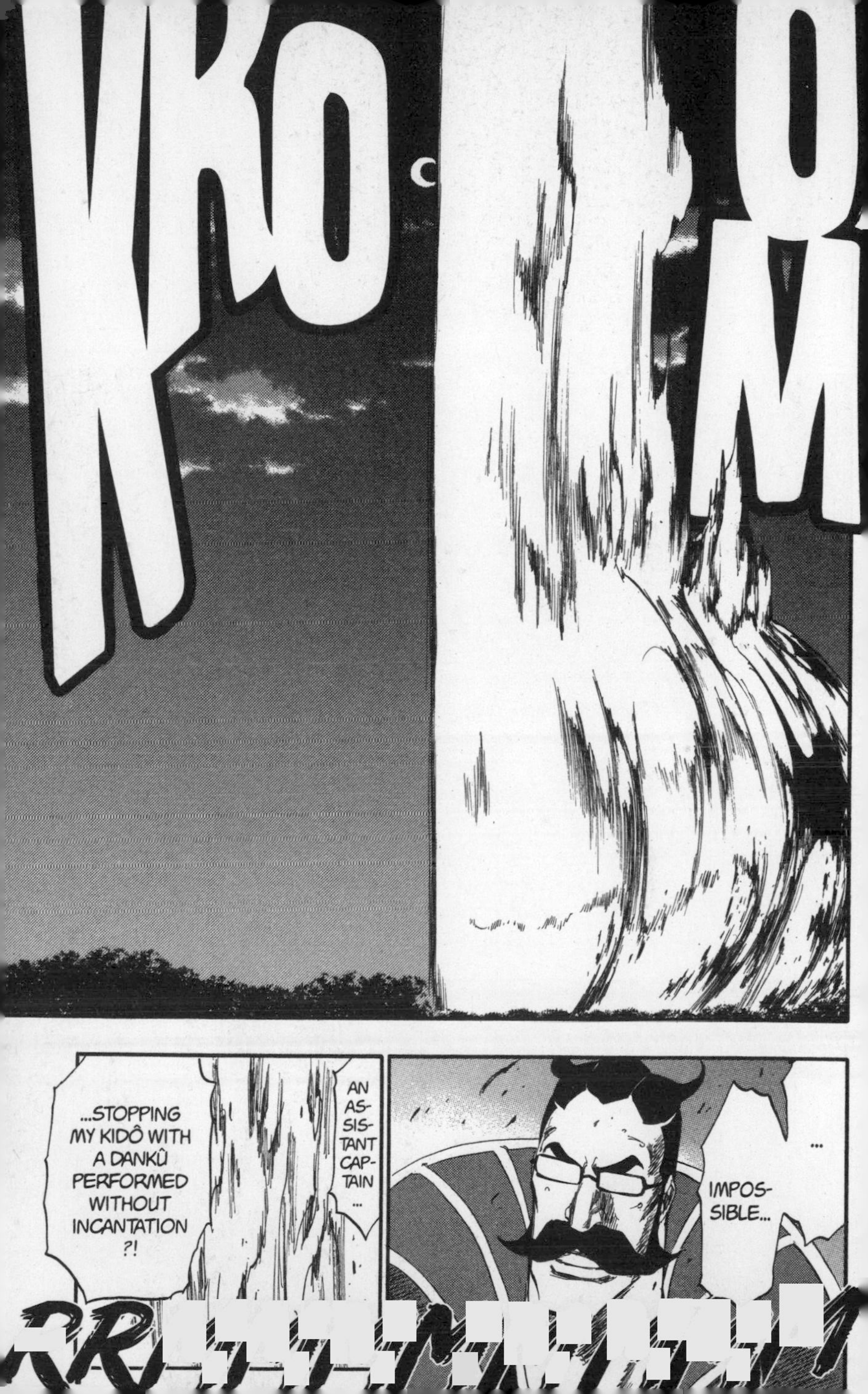
KRO
...
IMPOSSIBLE...
AN ASSISTANT CAPTAIN...
...STOPPING MY KIDÔ WITH A DANKÛ PERFORMED WITHOUT INCANTATION?!

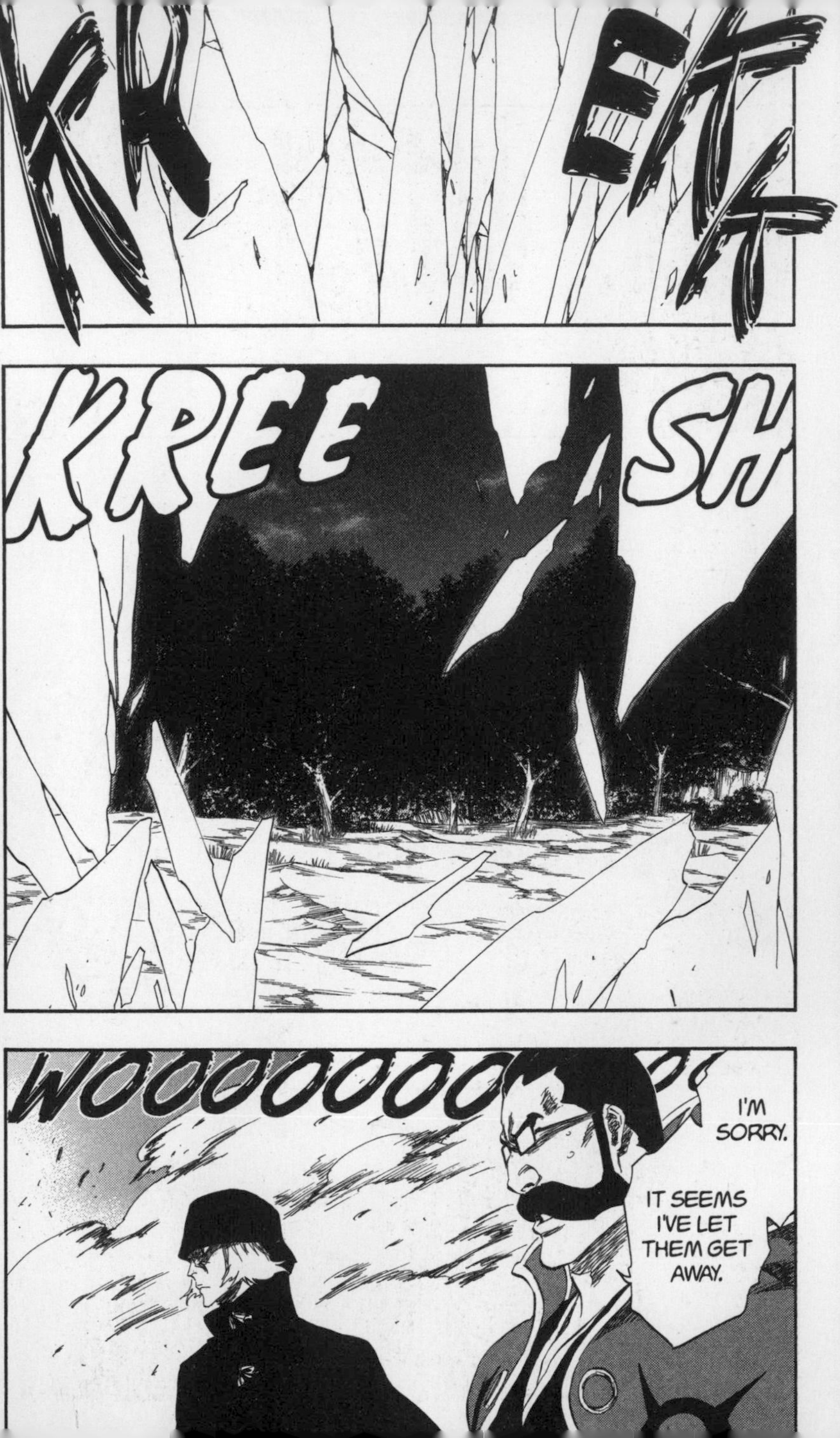
KRRKKT
KREEESH
WOOOOOOOOOOSH
I'M SORRY.
IT SEEMS I'VE LET THEM GET AWAY.

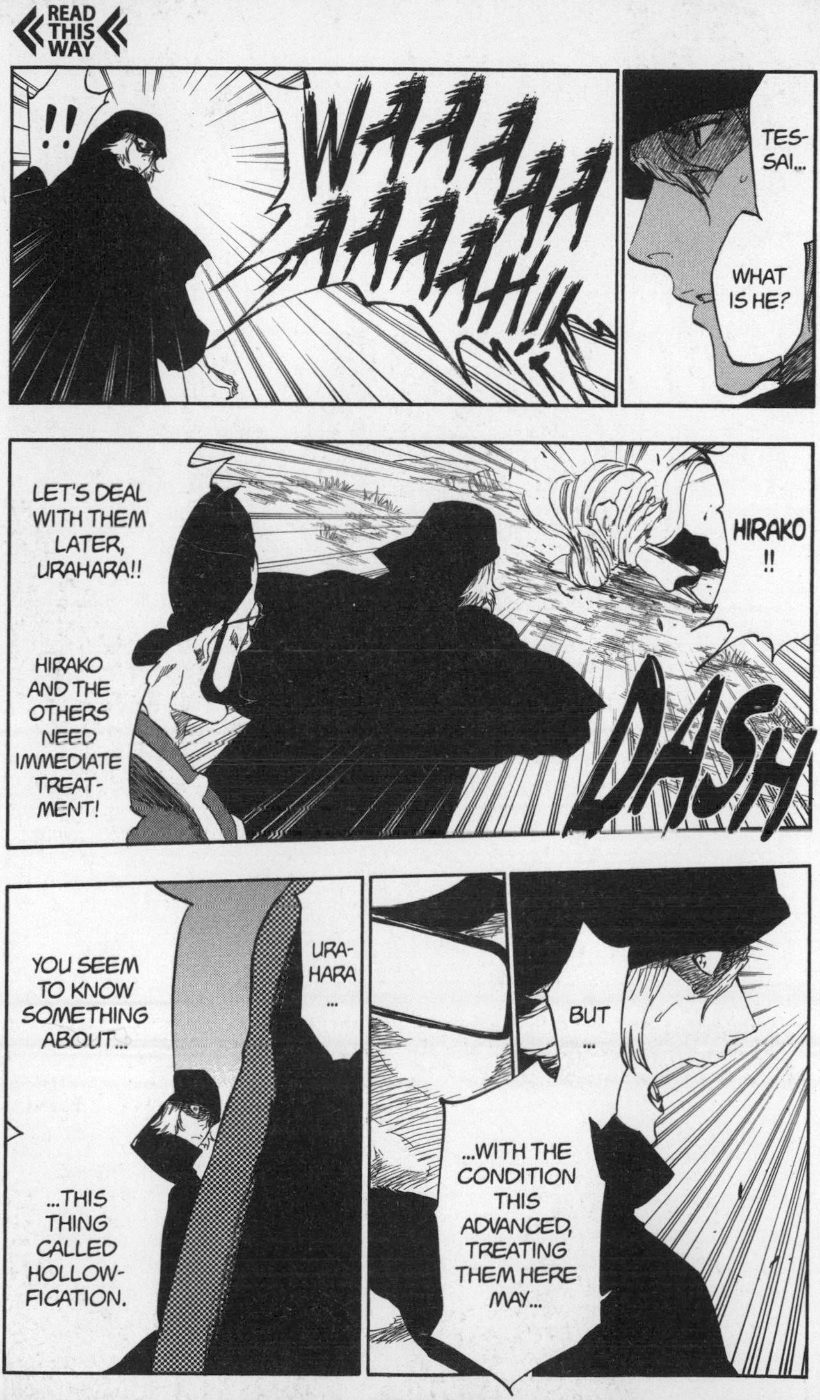
READ THIS WAY
TES-SAI...
WHAT IS HE?
!!
WAAAAAAAAAAAAH!!
HIRAKO !!
DASH
LET'S DEAL WITH THEM LATER, URAHARA!!
HIRAKO AND THE OTHERS NEED IMMEDIATE TREAT-MENT!
BUT ...
...WITH THE CONDITION THIS ADVANCED, TREATING THEM HERE MAY...
URA-HARA ...
YOU SEEM TO KNOW SOMETHING ABOUT...
...THIS THING CALLED HOLLOW-FICATION.

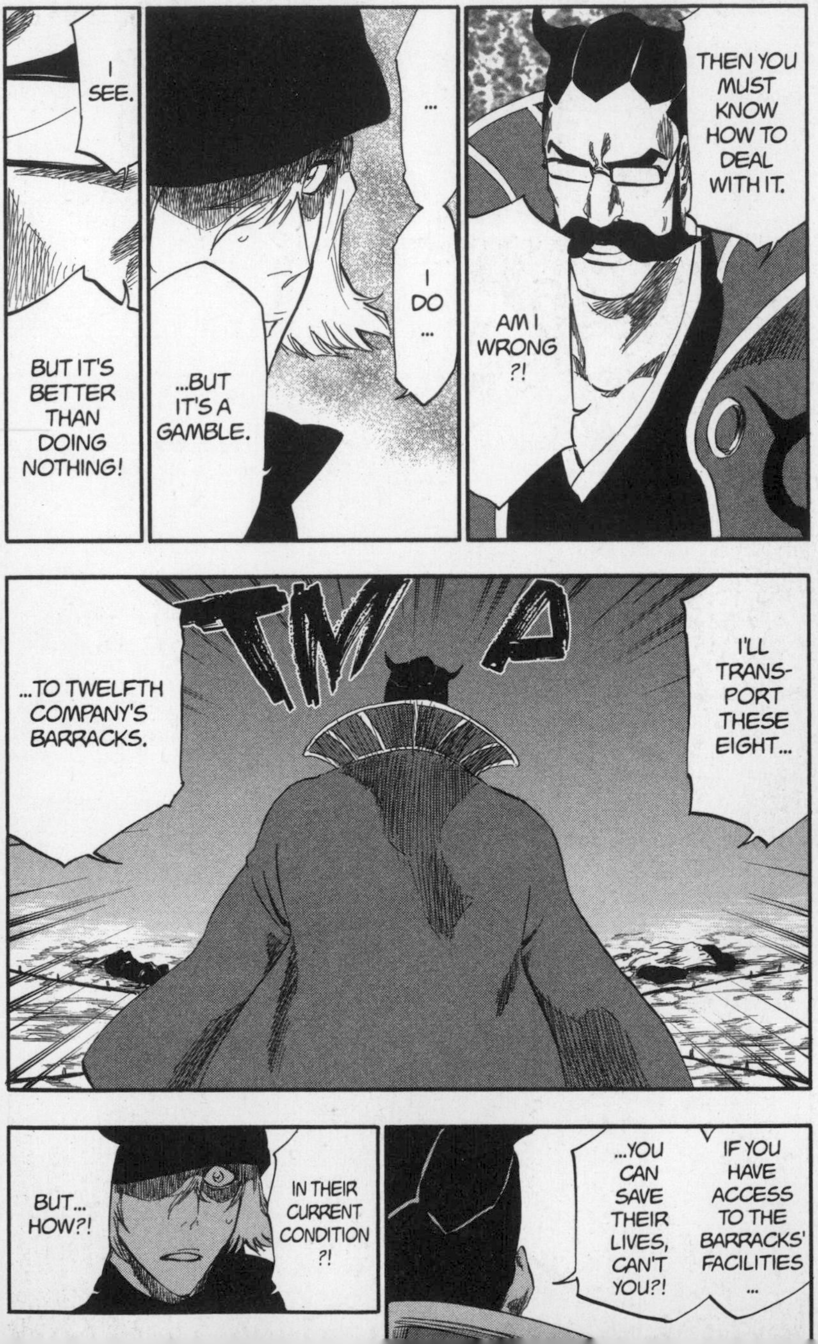
THEN YOU MUST KNOW HOW TO DEAL WITH IT.
AM I WRONG ?!
...
I DO ...
...BUT IT'S A GAMBLE.
I SEE.
BUT IT'S BETTER THAN DOING NOTHING!
TMP
I'LL TRANS-PORT THESE EIGHT...
...TO TWELFTH COMPANY'S BARRACKS.
IF YOU HAVE ACCESS TO THE BARRACKS' FACILITIES ...
...YOU CAN SAVE THEIR LIVES, CAN'T YOU?!
IN THEIR CURRENT CONDITION ?!
BUT... HOW?!

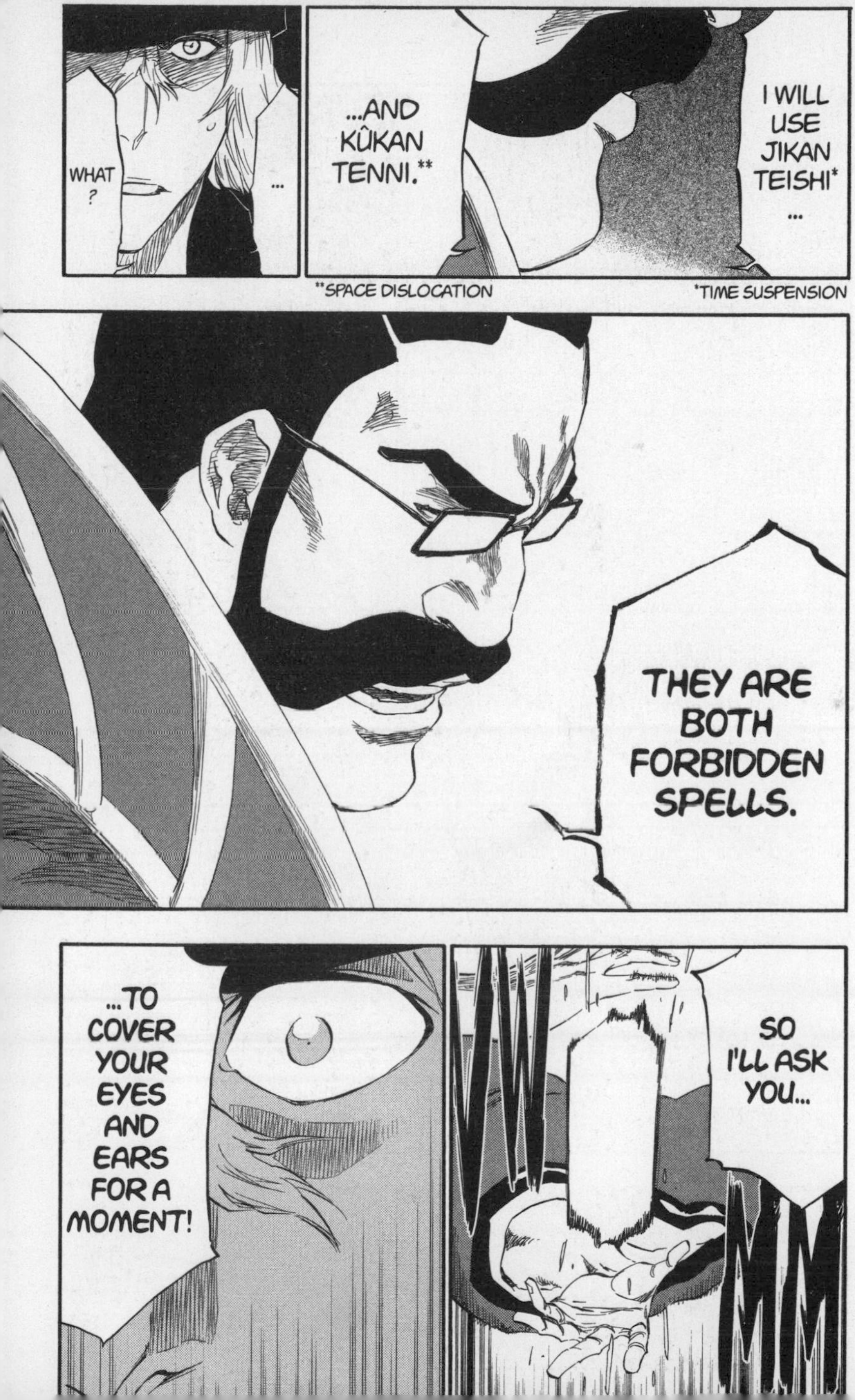
I WILL USE JIKAN TEISHI* ...
...AND KÛKAN TENNI.**
*TIME SUSPENSION
**SPACE DISLOCATION
WHAT?
...
THEY ARE BOTH FORBIDDEN SPELLS.
SO I'LL ASK YOU...
...TO COVER YOUR EYES AND EARS FOR A MOMENT!
SFX: MMM

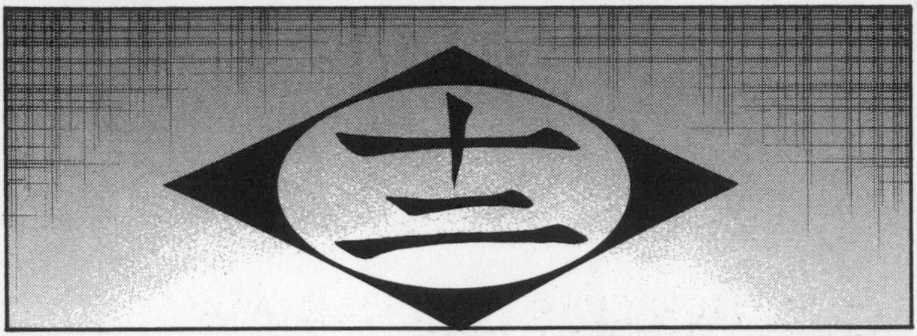

*TWELVE

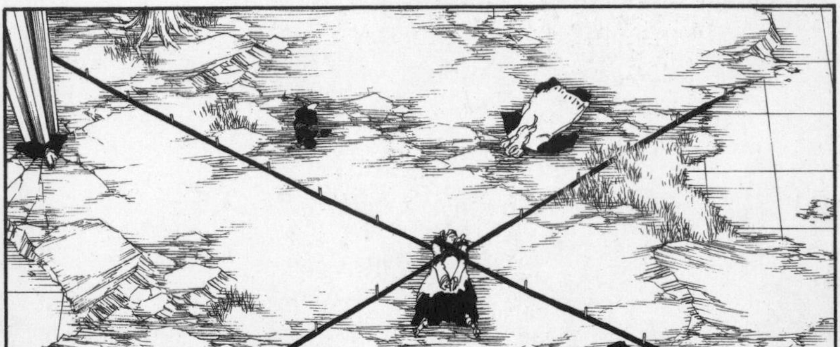

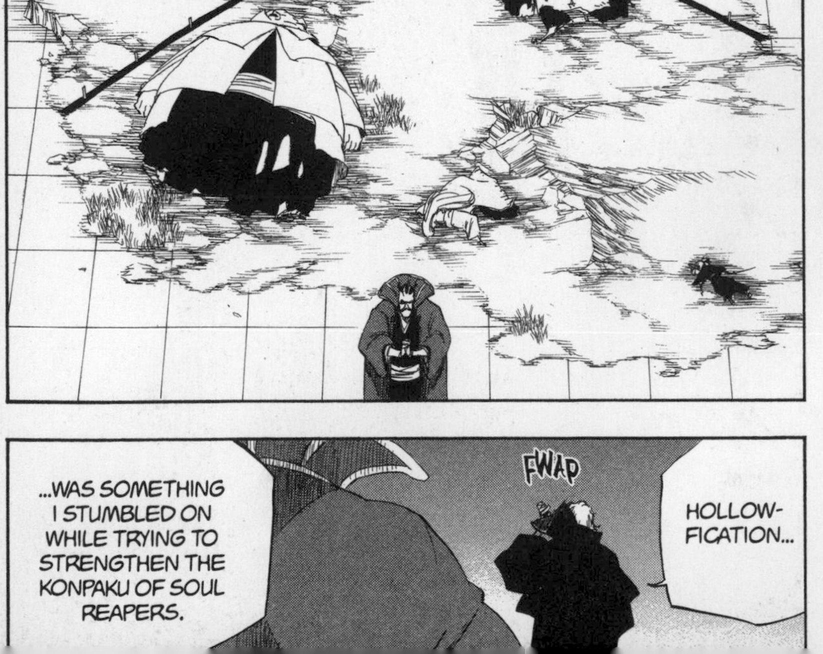
HOLLOW-
FICATION...
FWAP
...WAS SOMETHING I STUMBLED ON WHILE TRYING TO STRENGTHEN THE KONPAKU OF SOUL REAPERS.

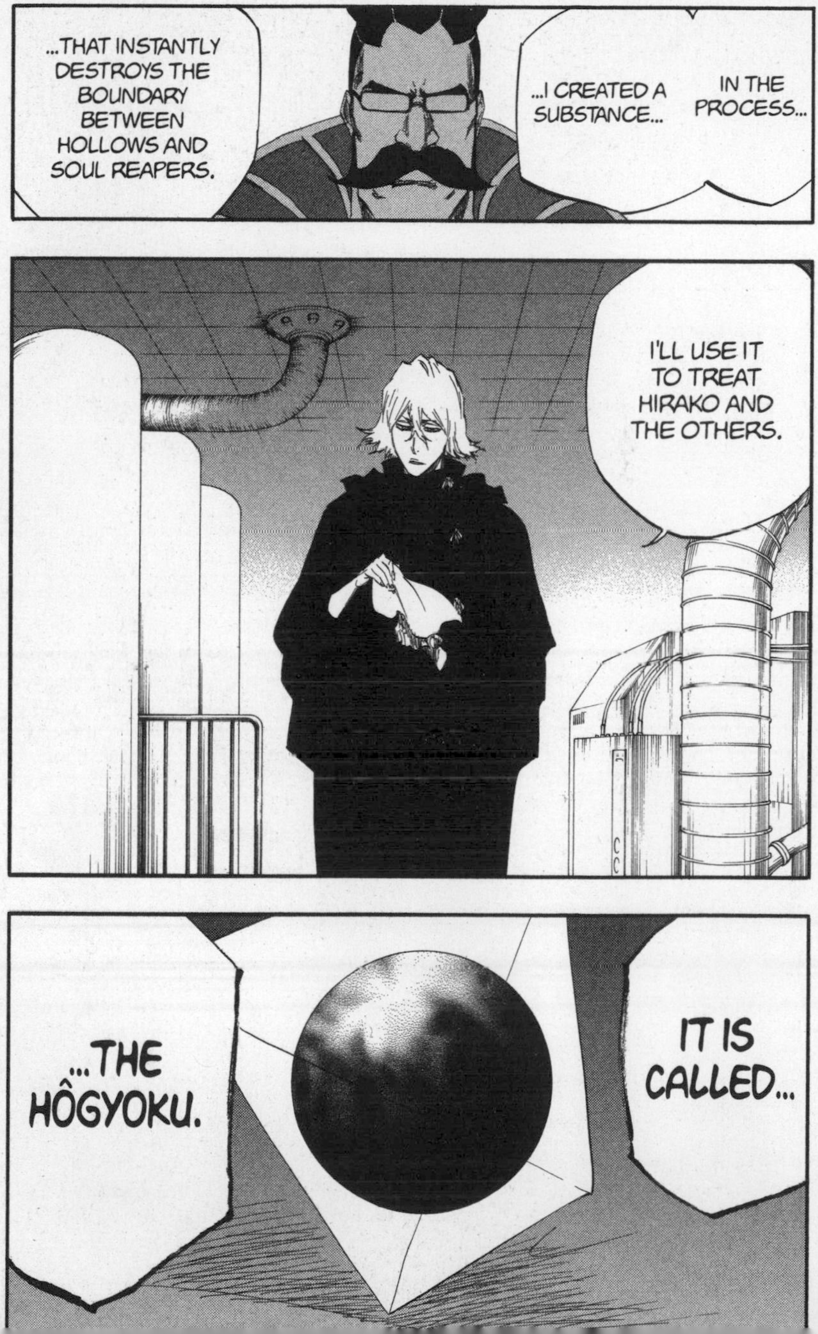
IN THE PROCESS...
...I CREATED A SUBSTANCE...
...THAT INSTANTLY DESTROYS THE BOUNDARY BETWEEN HOLLOWS AND SOUL REAPERS.
I'LL USE IT TO TREAT HIRAKO AND THE OTHERS.
IT IS CALLED...
...THE HÔGYOKU.

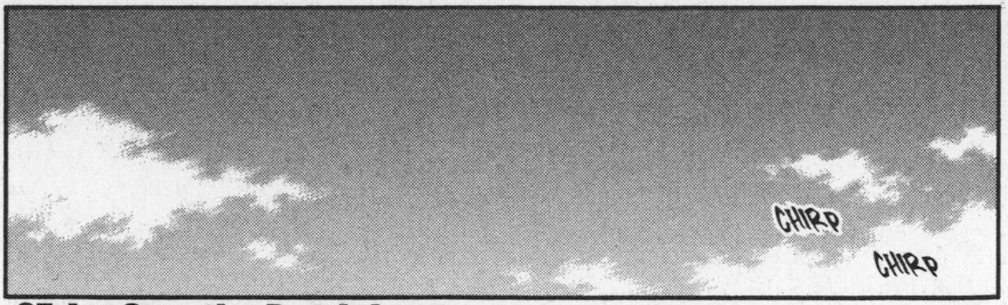
CHIRP
CHIRP

-97. Let Stop the Pendulum

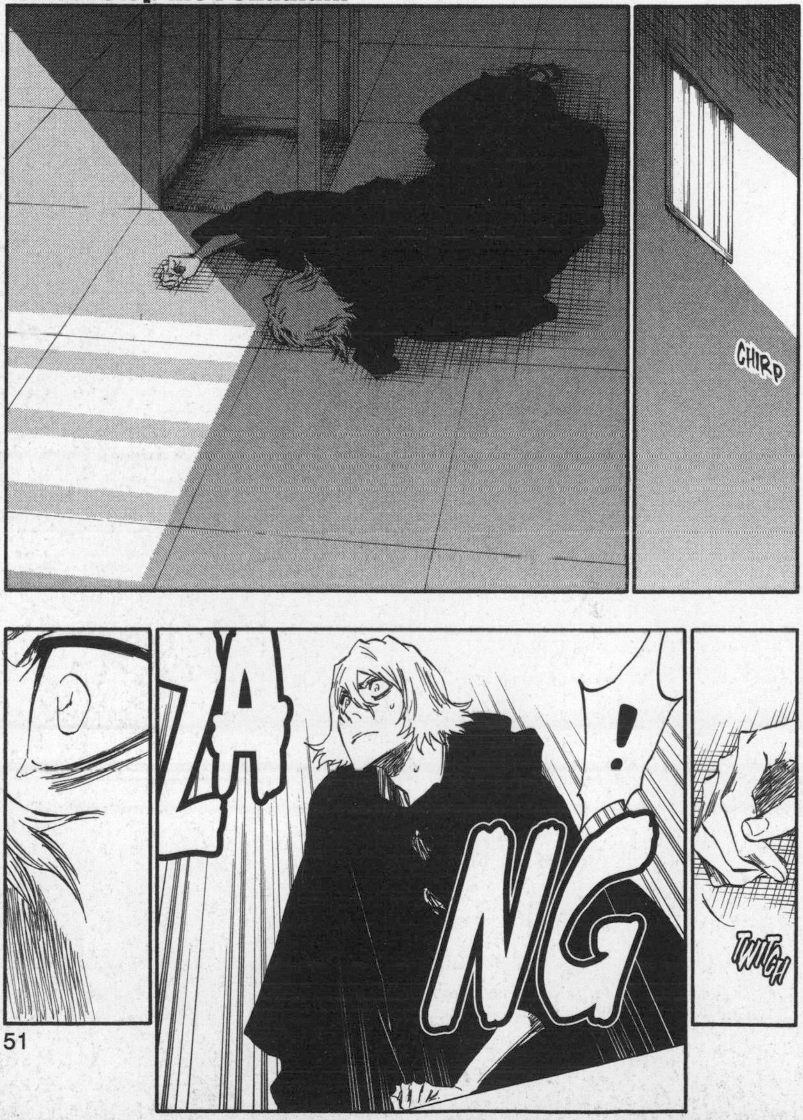
CHIRP
TWITCH
ZANG
!

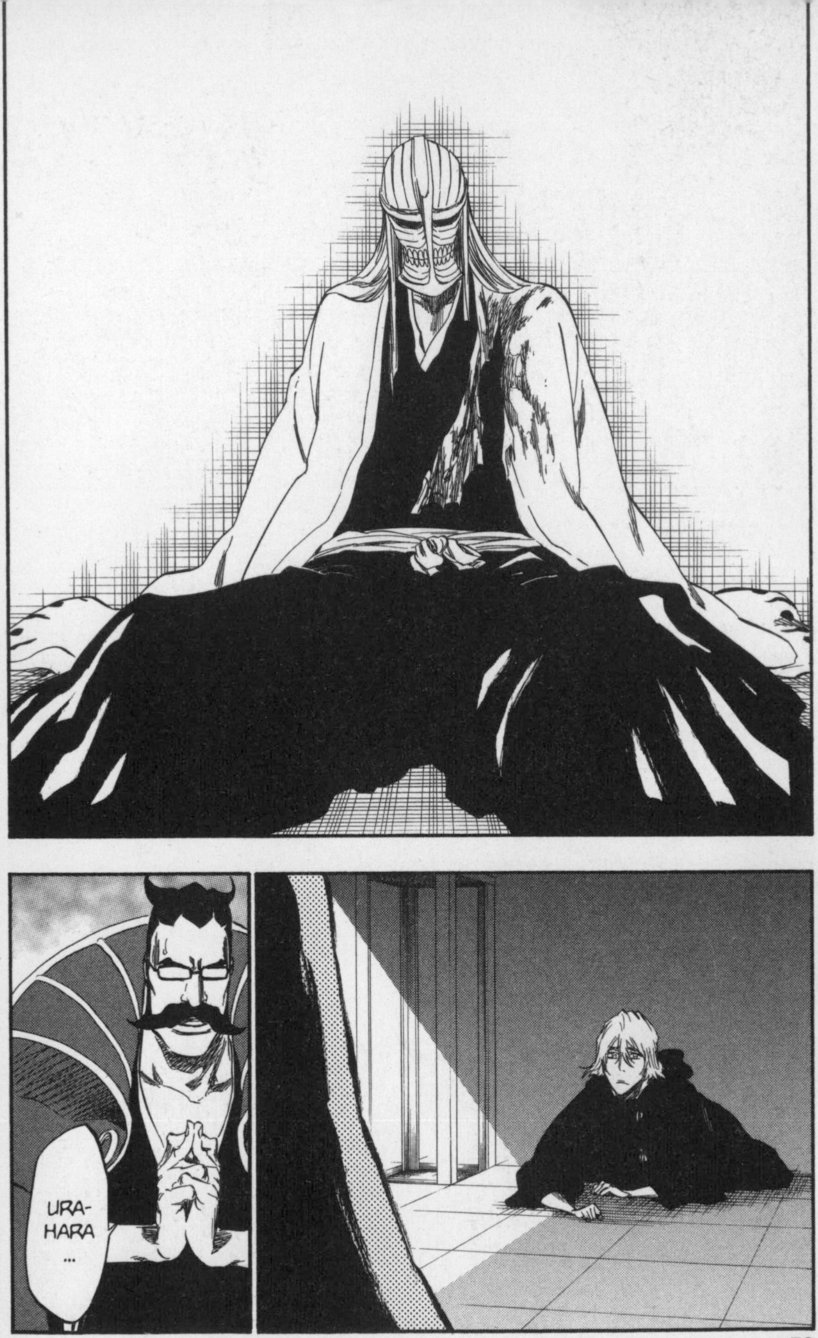
URA-
HARA
...

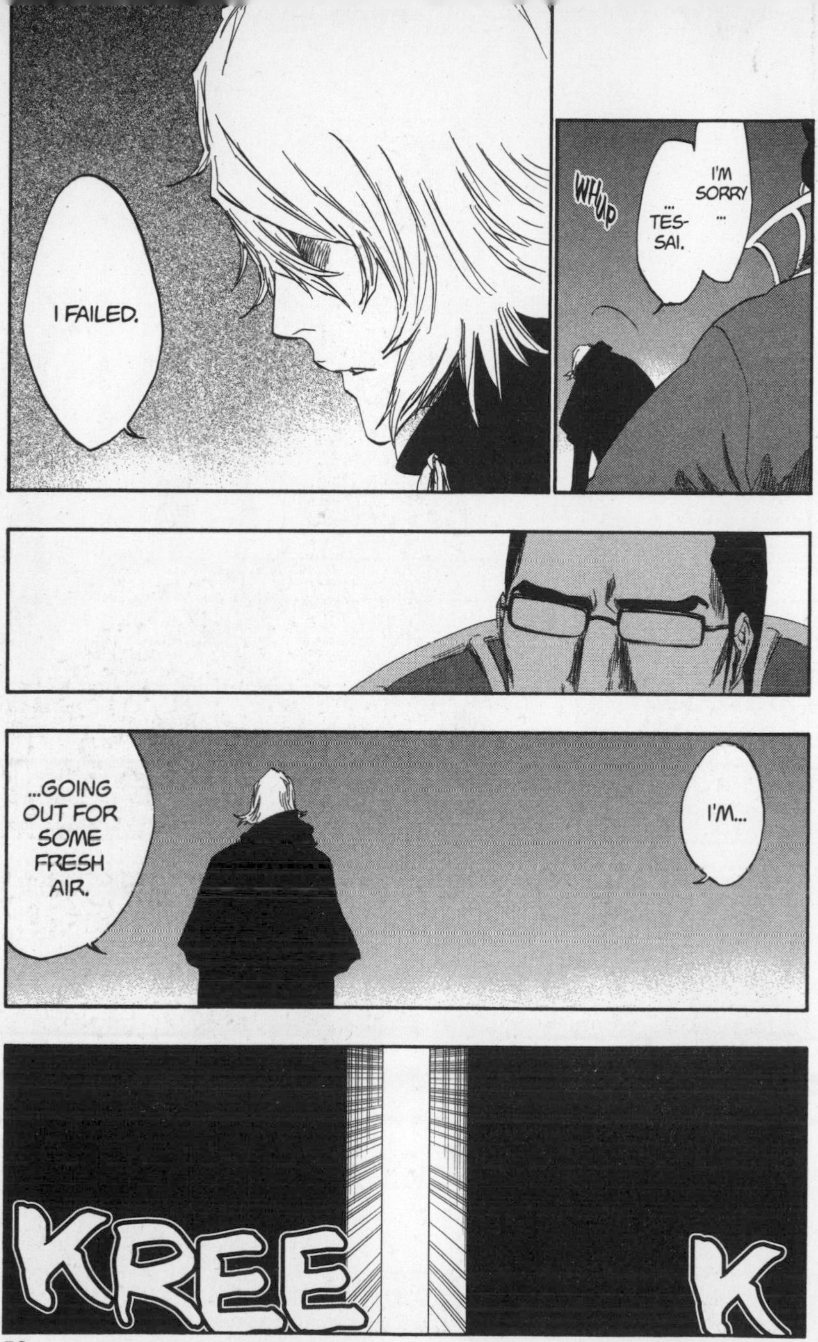
I'M SORRY ...
... TES-SAI.
WHUP
I FAILED.
I'M...
...GOING OUT FOR SOME FRESH AIR.
KREE K

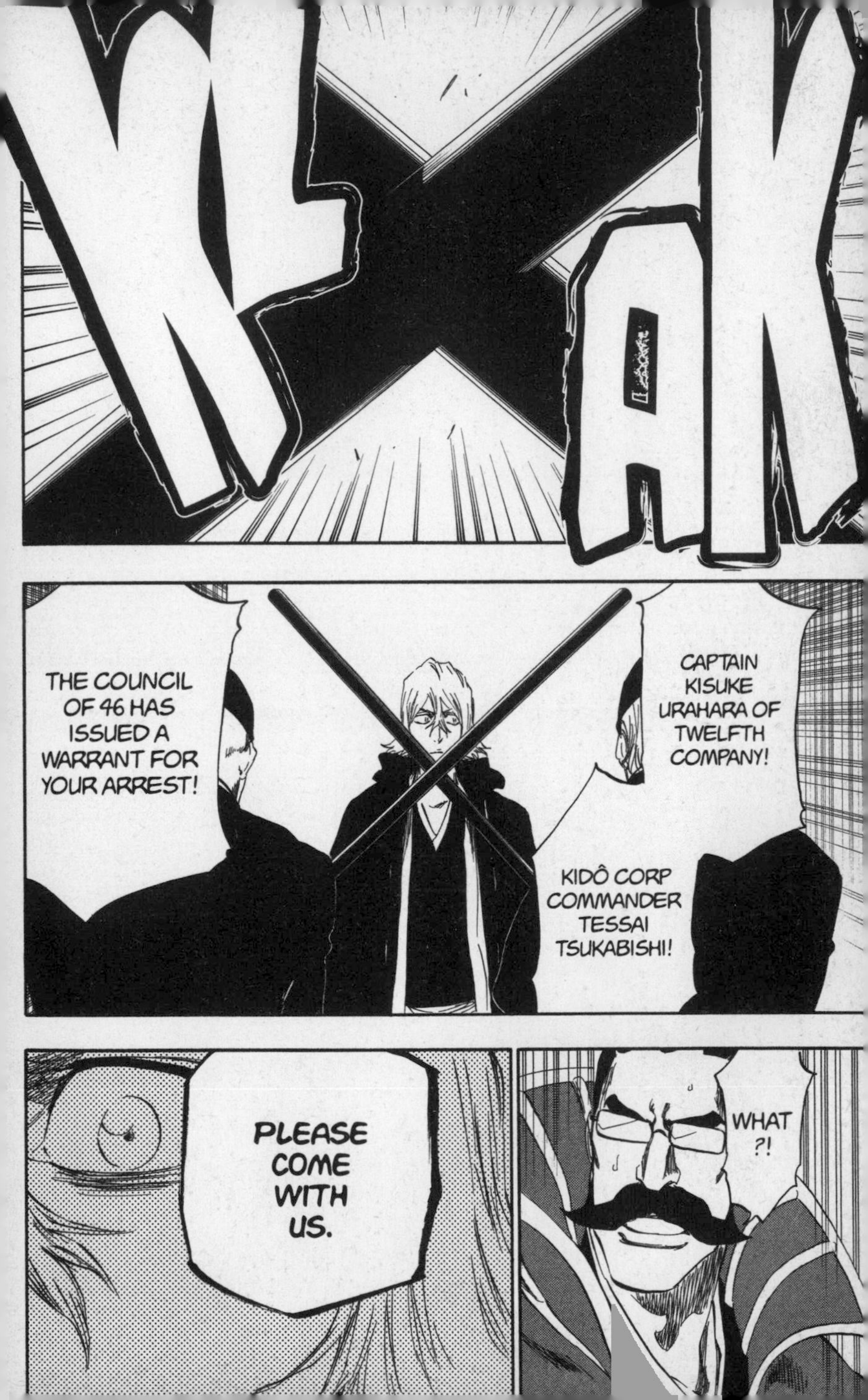
CAPTAIN KISUKE URAHARA OF TWELFTH COMPANY!
KIDÔ CORP COMMANDER TESSAI TSUKABISHI!
THE COUNCIL OF 46 HAS ISSUED A WARRANT FOR YOUR ARREST!
WHAT ?!
PLEASE COME WITH US.

Bleach — 97.

Let Stop The Pendulum.

COUNCIL OF 46

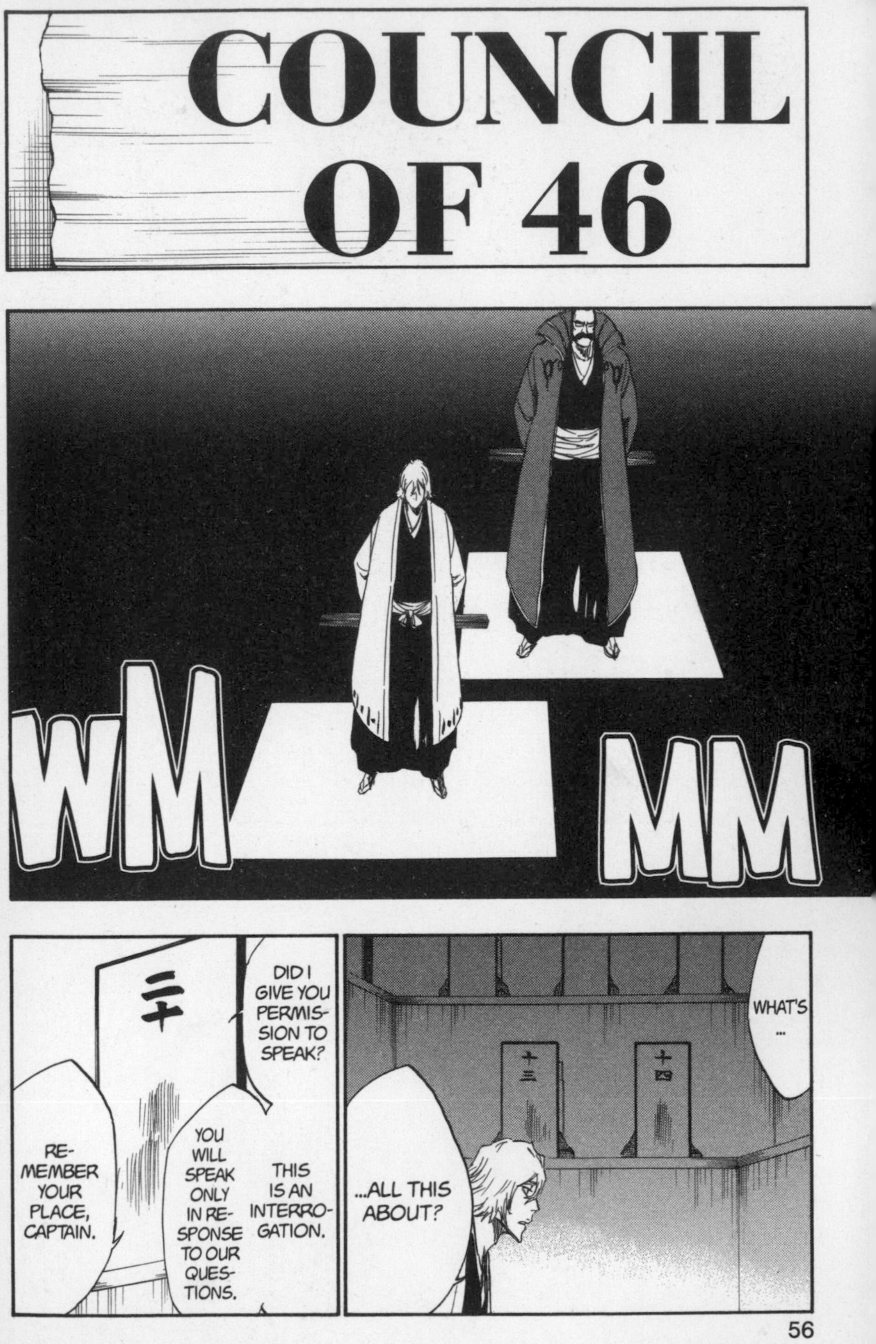
WM
MM
十三
十四
WHAT'S ...
...ALL THIS ABOUT?
二十
DID I GIVE YOU PERMISSION TO SPEAK?
THIS IS AN INTERROGATION.
YOU WILL SPEAK ONLY IN RESPONSE TO OUR QUESTIONS.
REMEMBER YOUR PLACE, CAPTAIN.

READ THIS WAY

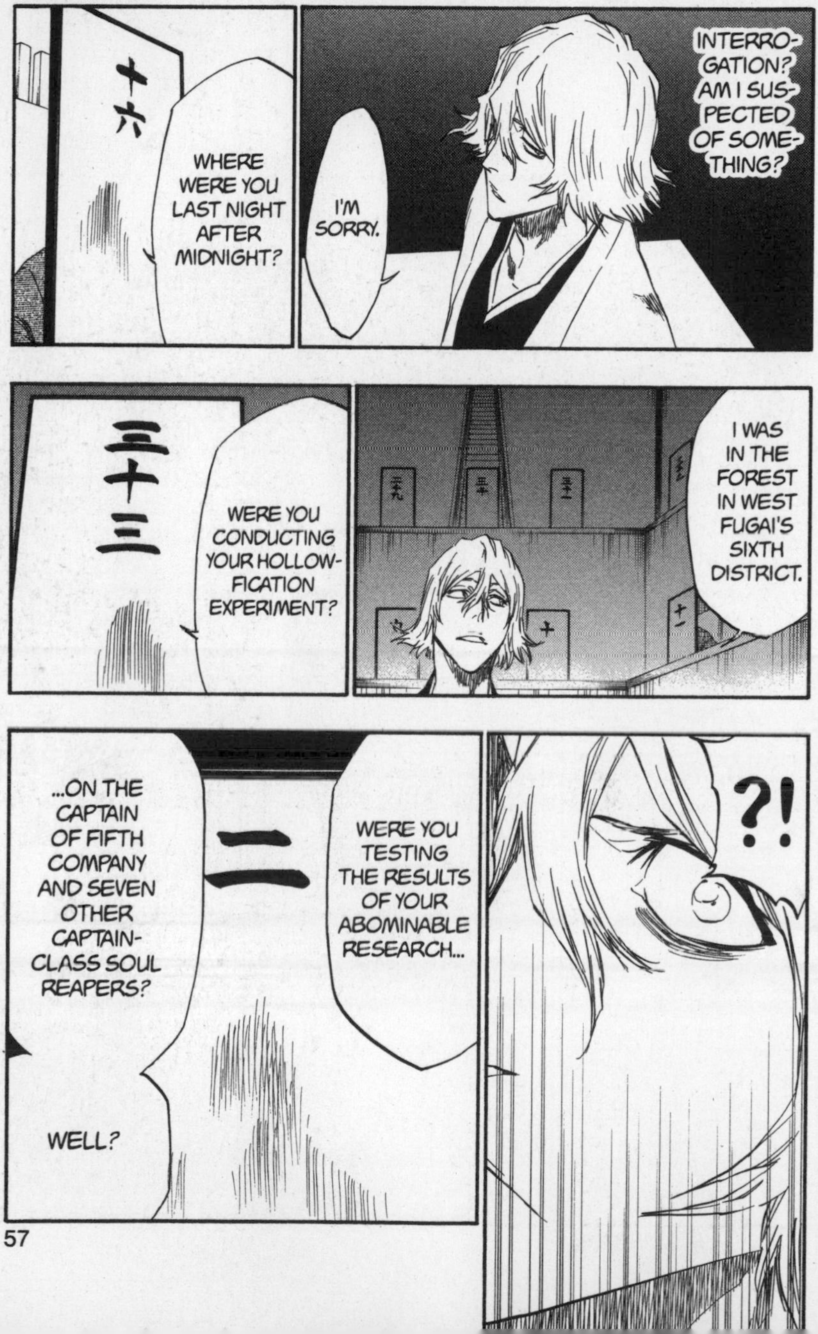

INTERROGATION? AM I SUSPECTED OF SOMETHING?
I'M SORRY.
十六
WHERE WERE YOU LAST NIGHT AFTER MIDNIGHT?
I WAS IN THE FOREST IN WEST FUGAI'S SIXTH DISTRICT.
三十三
WERE YOU CONDUCTING YOUR HOLLOWFICATION EXPERIMENT?
?!
二
WERE YOU TESTING THE RESULTS OF YOUR ABOMINABLE RESEARCH...
...ON THE CAPTAIN OF FIFTH COMPANY AND SEVEN OTHER CAPTAIN-CLASS SOUL REAPERS?
WELL?

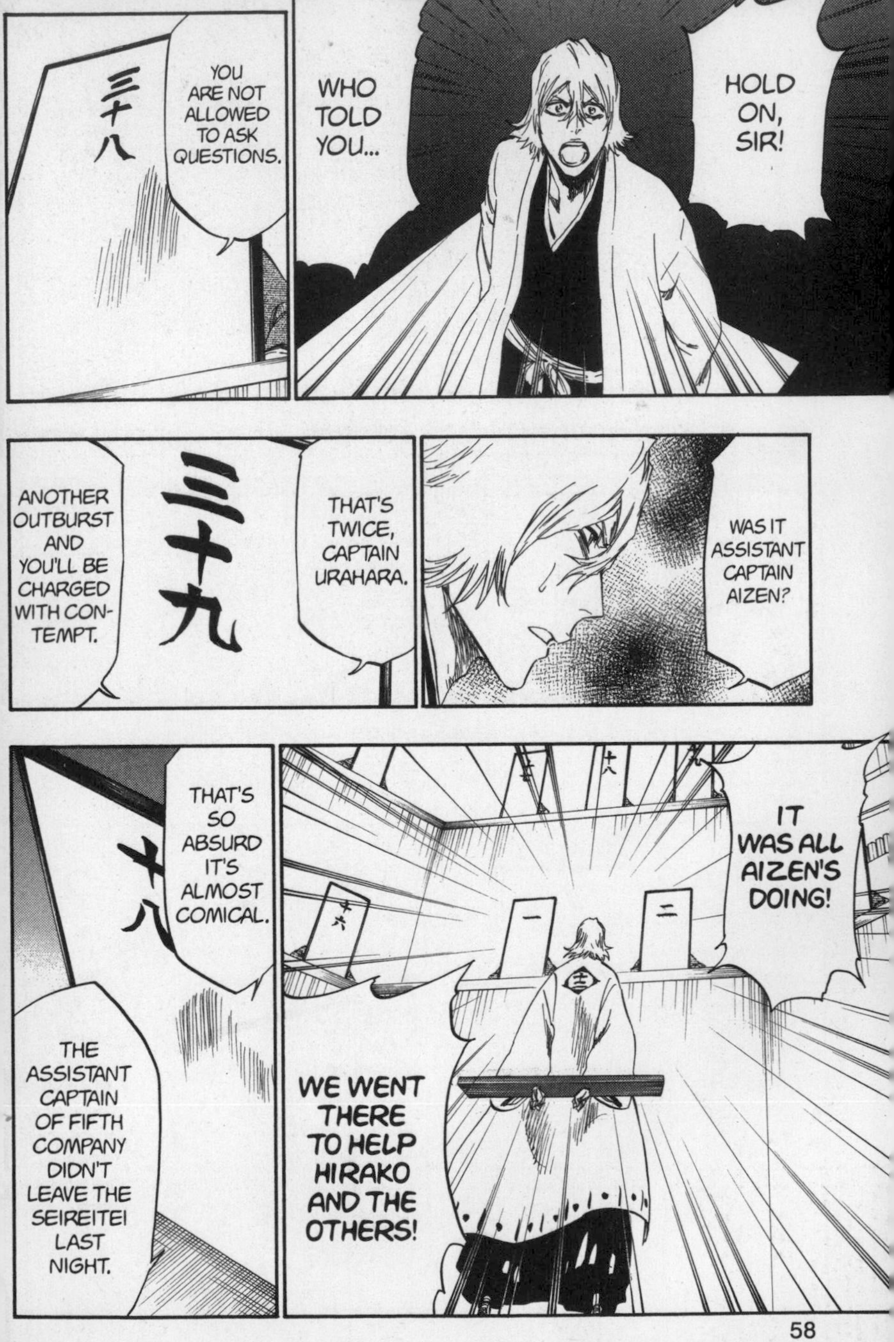
HOLD ON, SIR!
WHO TOLD YOU...
YOU ARE NOT ALLOWED TO ASK QUESTIONS.
三十八
WAS IT ASSISTANT CAPTAIN AIZEN?
THAT'S TWICE, CAPTAIN URAHARA.
三十九
ANOTHER OUTBURST AND YOU'LL BE CHARGED WITH CON-TEMPT.
IT WAS ALL AIZEN'S DOING!
WE WENT THERE TO HELP HIRAKO AND THE OTHERS!
THAT'S SO ABSURD IT'S ALMOST COMICAL.
十八
THE ASSISTANT CAPTAIN OF FIFTH COMPANY DIDN'T LEAVE THE SEIREITEI LAST NIGHT.

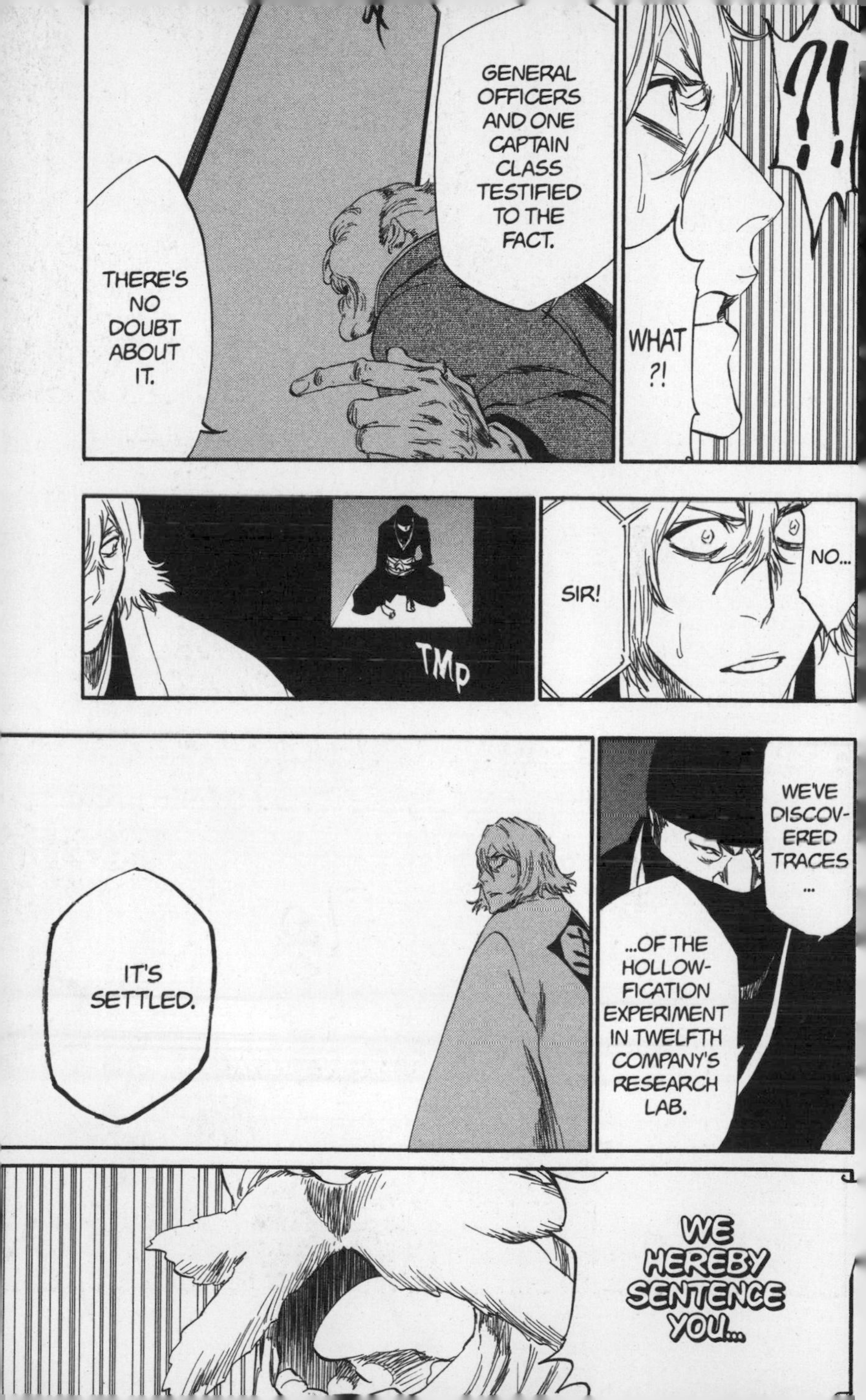
?!
WHAT?!
GENERAL OFFICERS AND ONE CAPTAIN CLASS TESTIFIED TO THE FACT.
THERE'S NO DOUBT ABOUT IT.
NO...
SIR!
TMP
WE'VE DISCOVERED TRACES...
...OF THE HOLLOWFICATION EXPERIMENT IN TWELFTH COMPANY'S RESEARCH LAB.
IT'S SETTLED.
WE HEREBY SENTENCE YOU...

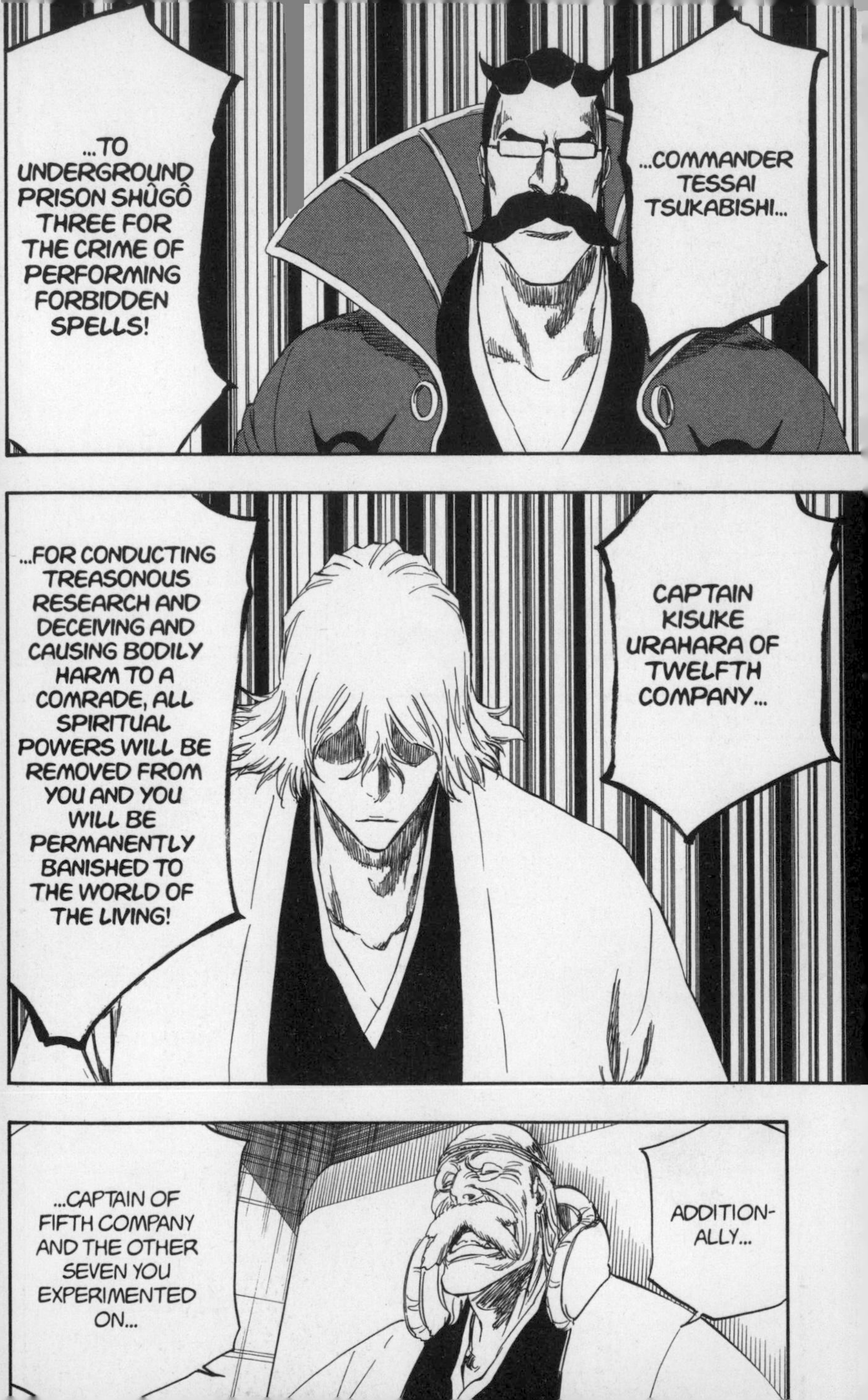
...COMMANDER TESSAI TSUKABISHI...
...TO UNDERGROUND PRISON SHÛGÔ THREE FOR THE CRIME OF PERFORMING FORBIDDEN SPELLS!
CAPTAIN KISUKE URAHARA OF TWELFTH COMPANY...
...FOR CONDUCTING TREASONOUS RESEARCH AND DECEIVING AND CAUSING BODILY HARM TO A COMRADE, ALL SPIRITUAL POWERS WILL BE REMOVED FROM YOU AND YOU WILL BE PERMANENTLY BANISHED TO THE WORLD OF THE LIVING!
ADDITION-ALLY...
...CAPTAIN OF FIFTH COMPANY AND THE OTHER SEVEN YOU EXPERIMENTED ON...

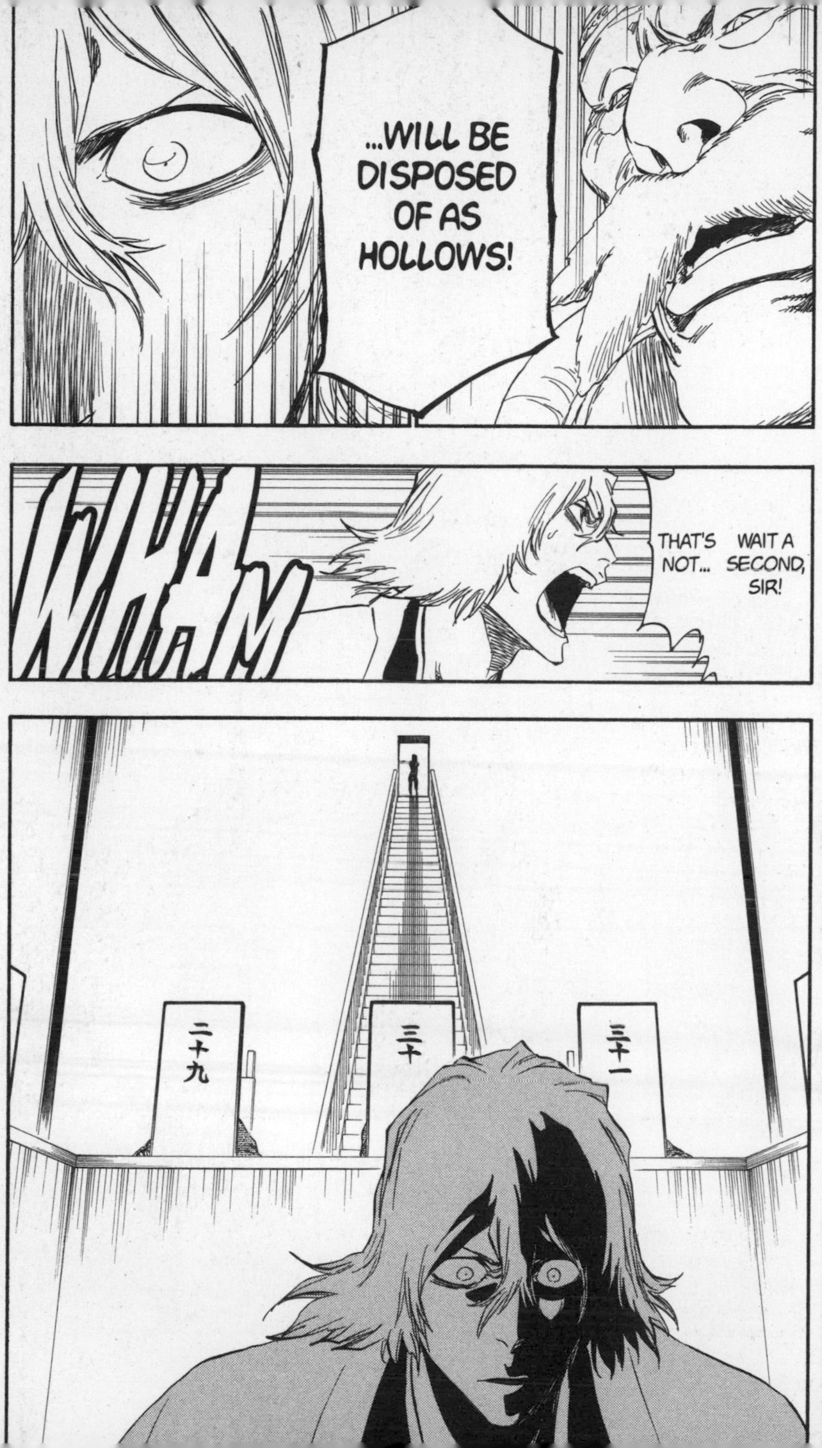
...WILL BE DISPOSED OF AS HOLLOWS!
WAIT A SECOND, SIR!
THAT'S NOT...
WHAM
二十九
三十
三十一

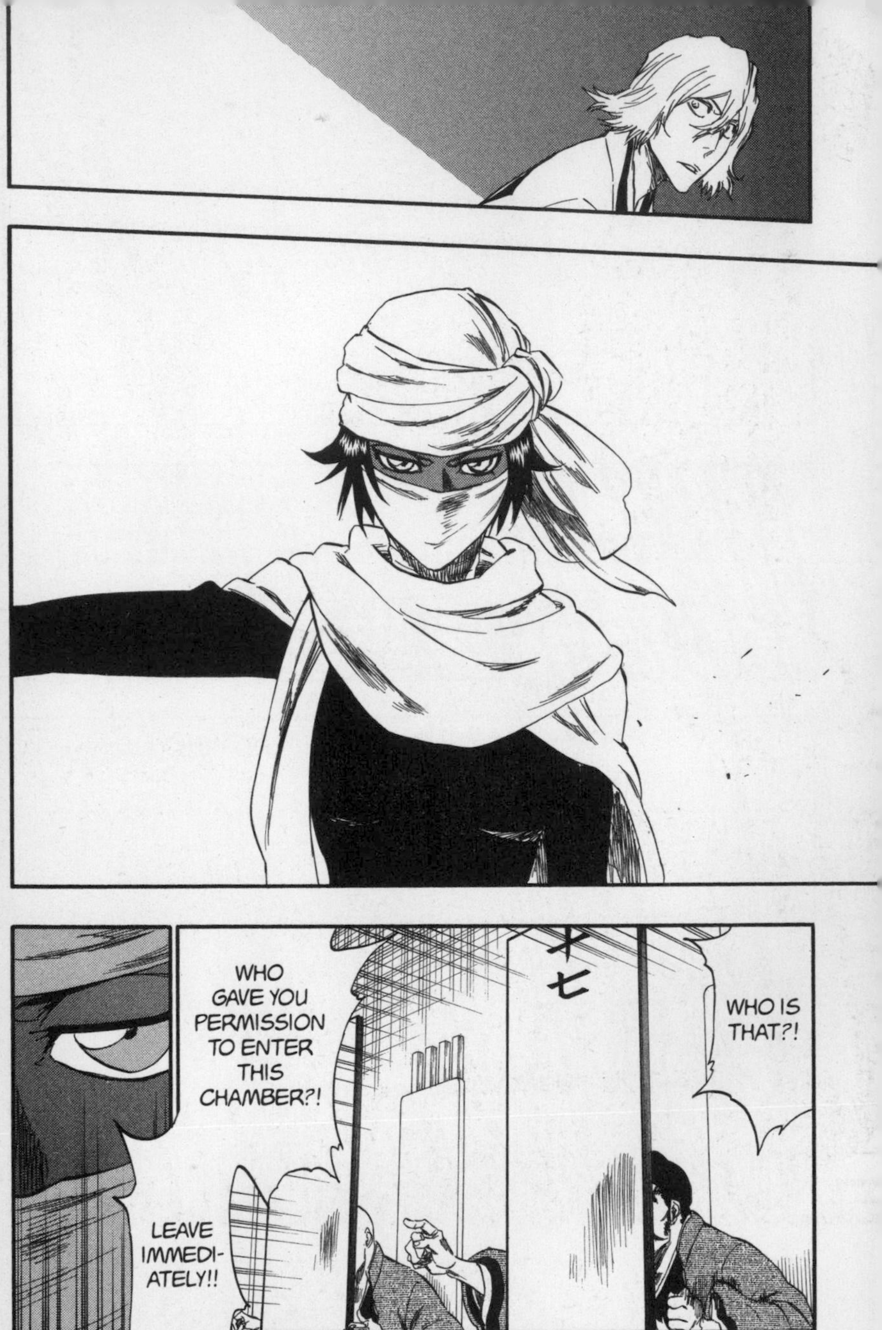
WHO IS THAT?!
WHO GAVE YOU PERMISSION TO ENTER THIS CHAMBER?!
LEAVE IMMEDI-ATELY!!

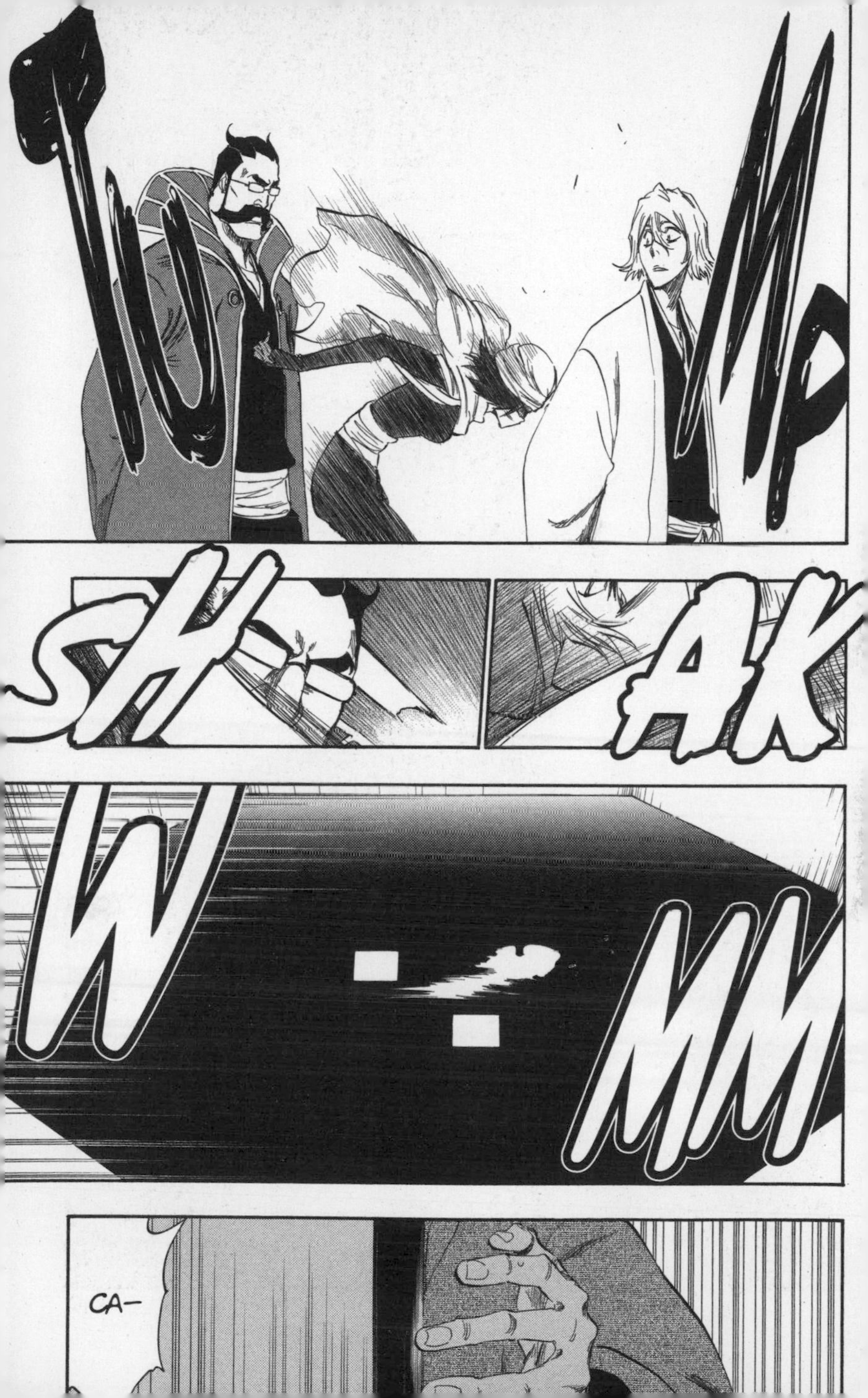
SHAK
WMM
CA—

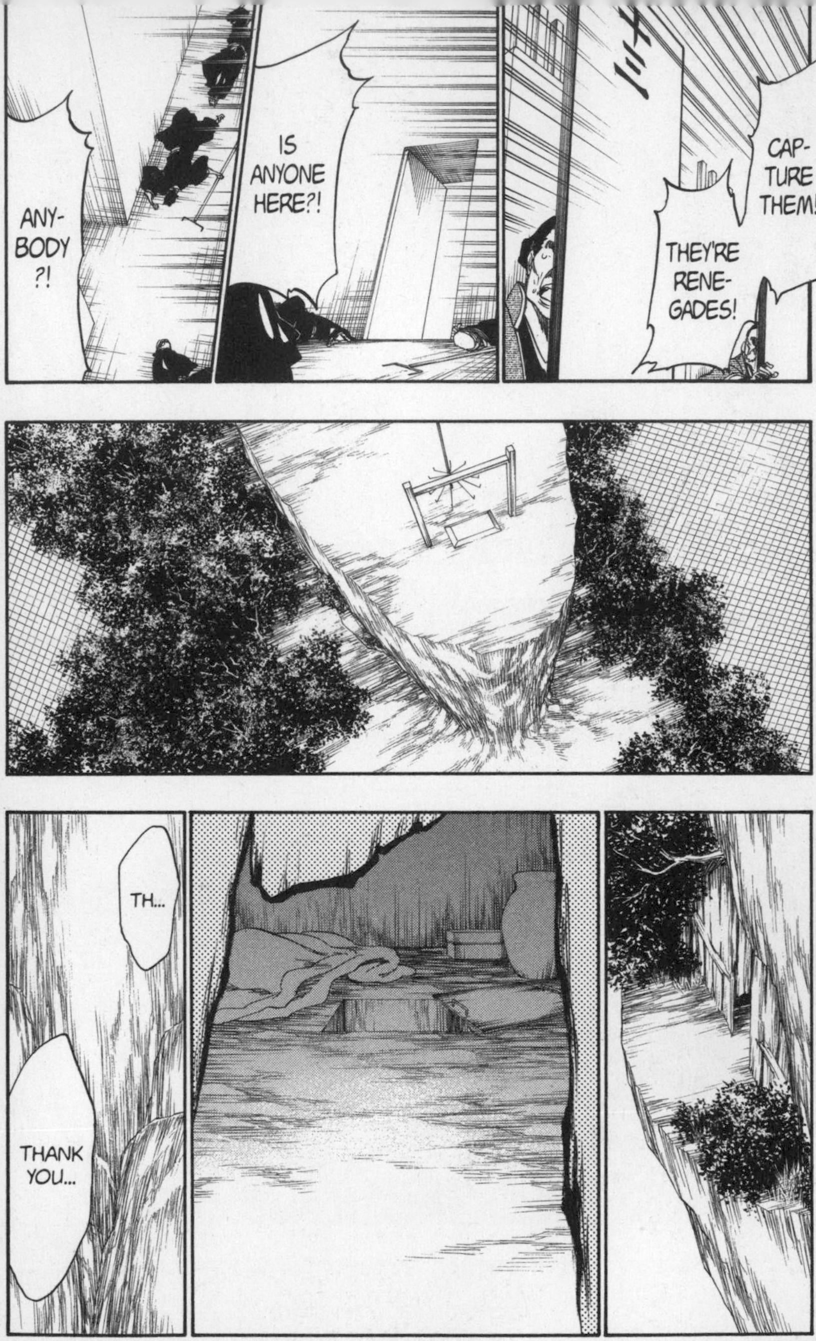
CAP-TURE THEM!
THEY'RE RENE-GADES!
IS ANYONE HERE?!
ANY-BODY?!
TH...
THANK YOU...

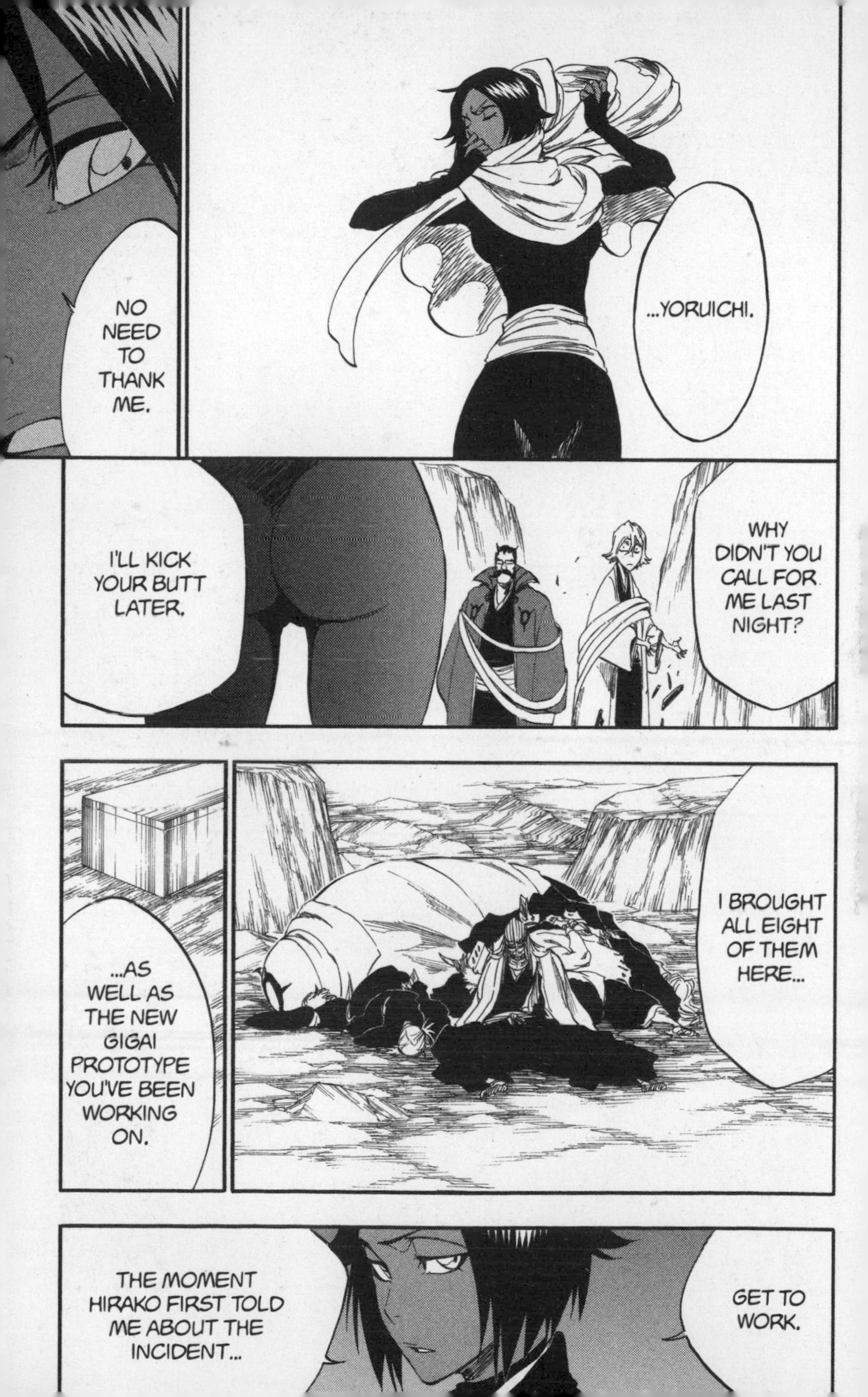
...YORUICHI.
NO NEED TO THANK ME.
WHY DIDN'T YOU CALL FOR ME LAST NIGHT?
I'LL KICK YOUR BUTT LATER.
I BROUGHT ALL EIGHT OF THEM HERE...
...AS WELL AS THE NEW GIGAI PROTOTYPE YOU'VE BEEN WORKING ON.
GET TO WORK.
THE MOMENT HIRAKO FIRST TOLD ME ABOUT THE INCIDENT...

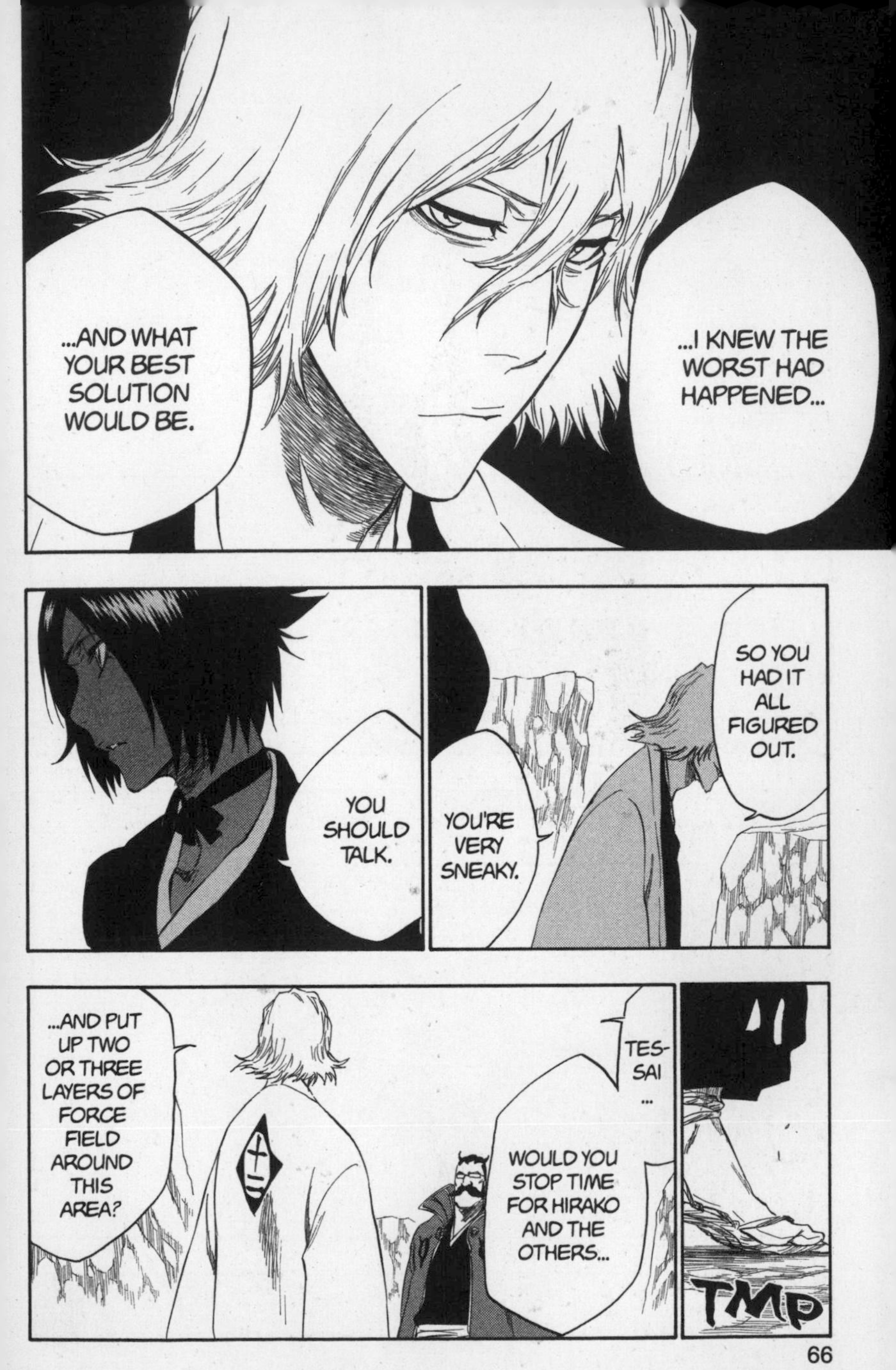
...I KNEW THE WORST HAD HAPPENED...
...AND WHAT YOUR BEST SOLUTION WOULD BE.
SO YOU HAD IT ALL FIGURED OUT.
YOU'RE VERY SNEAKY.
YOU SHOULD TALK.
TMP
TES-SAI...
WOULD YOU STOP TIME FOR HIRAKO AND THE OTHERS...
...AND PUT UP TWO OR THREE LAYERS OF FORCE FIELD AROUND THIS AREA?

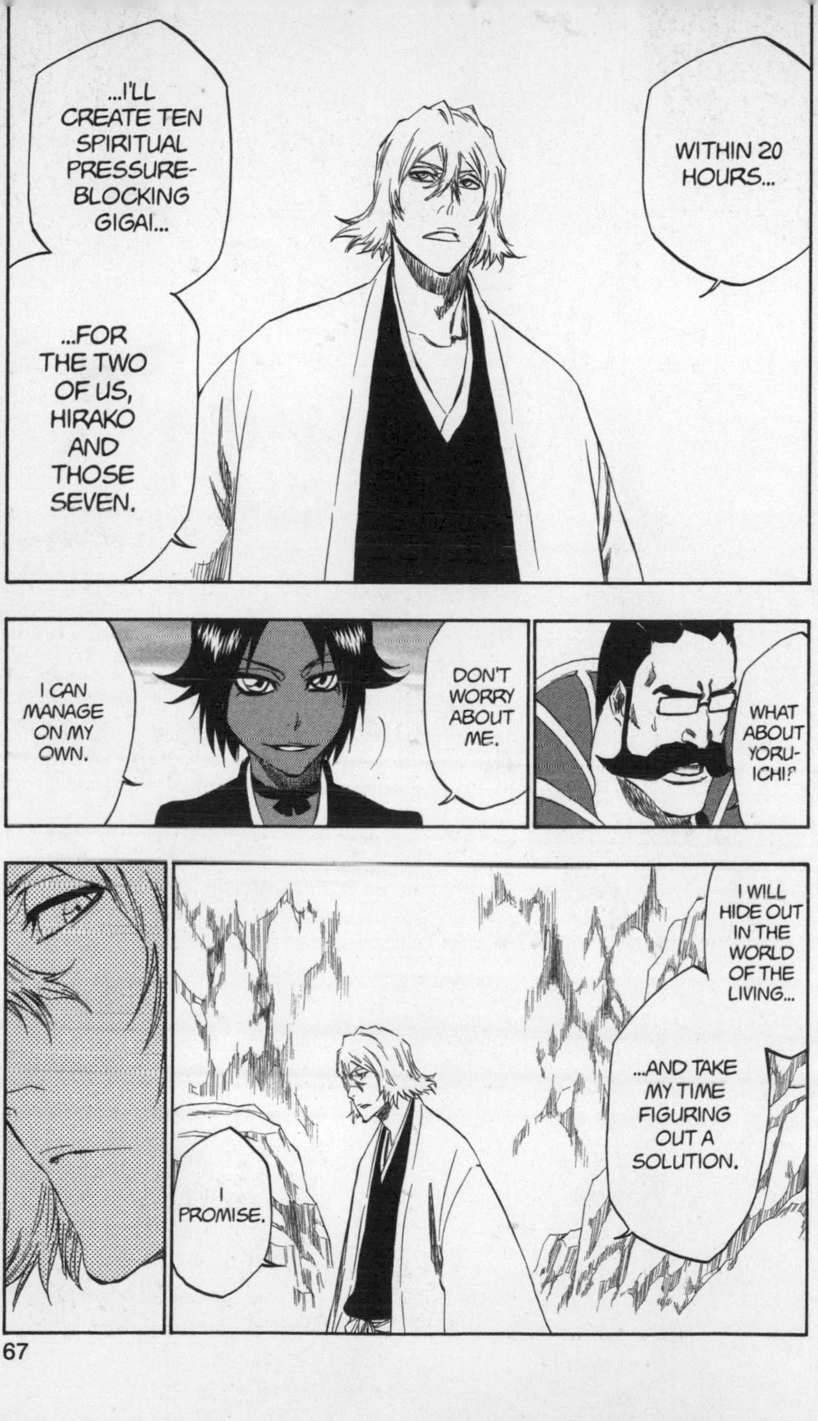
WITHIN 20 HOURS...
...I'LL CREATE TEN SPIRITUAL PRESSURE-BLOCKING GIGAI...
...FOR THE TWO OF US, HIRAKO AND THOSE SEVEN.
WHAT ABOUT YORU-ICHI?
DON'T WORRY ABOUT ME.
I CAN MANAGE ON MY OWN.
I WILL HIDE OUT IN THE WORLD OF THE LIVING...
...AND TAKE MY TIME FIGURING OUT A SOLUTION.
I PROMISE.

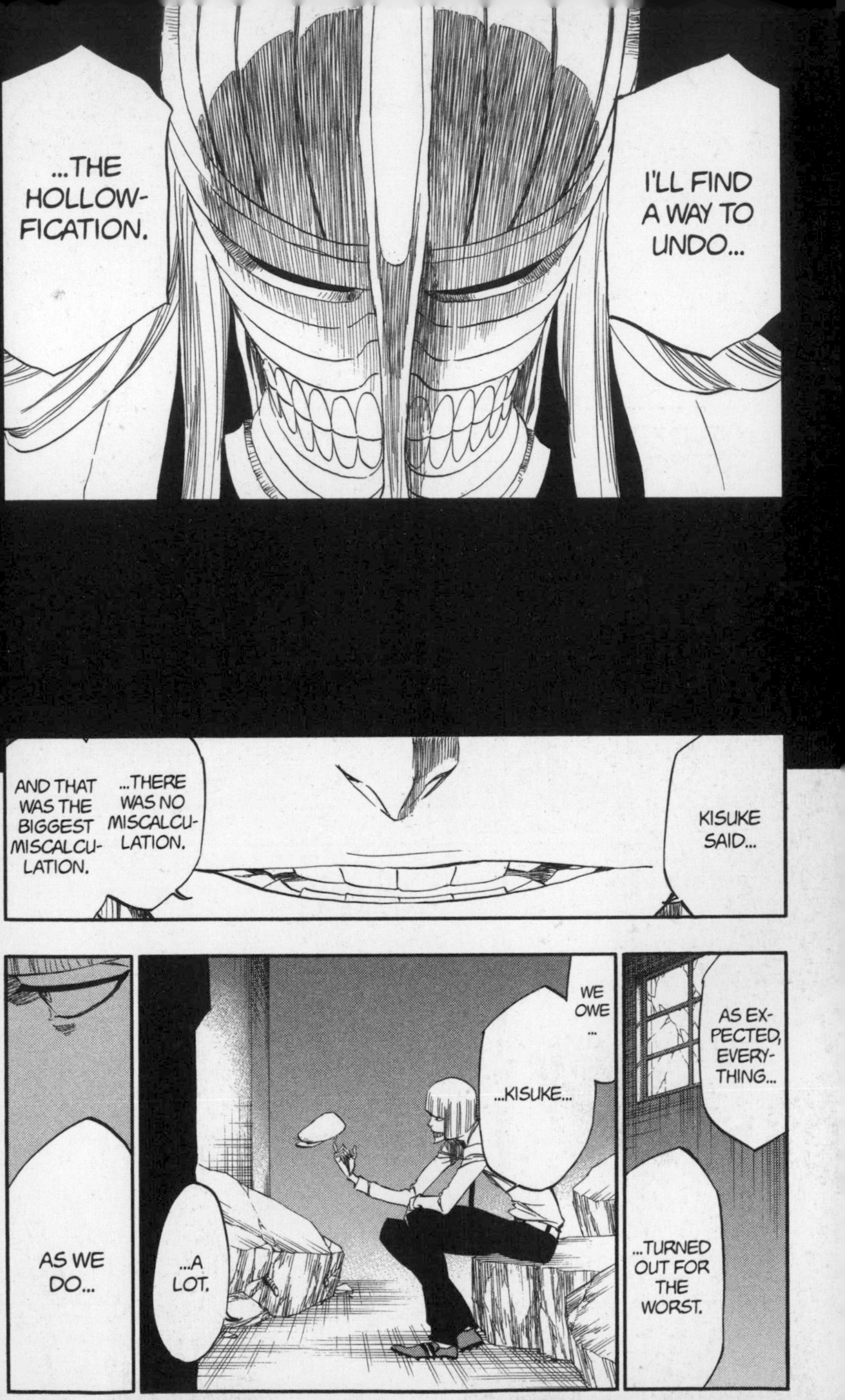
I'LL FIND A WAY TO UNDO...
...THE HOLLOW-FICATION.
KISUKE SAID...
...THERE WAS NO MISCALCU-LATION.
AND THAT WAS THE BIGGEST MISCALCU-LATION.
AS EX-PECTED, EVERY-THING...
...TURNED OUT FOR THE WORST.
WE OWE...
...KISUKE...
...A LOT.
AS WE DO...

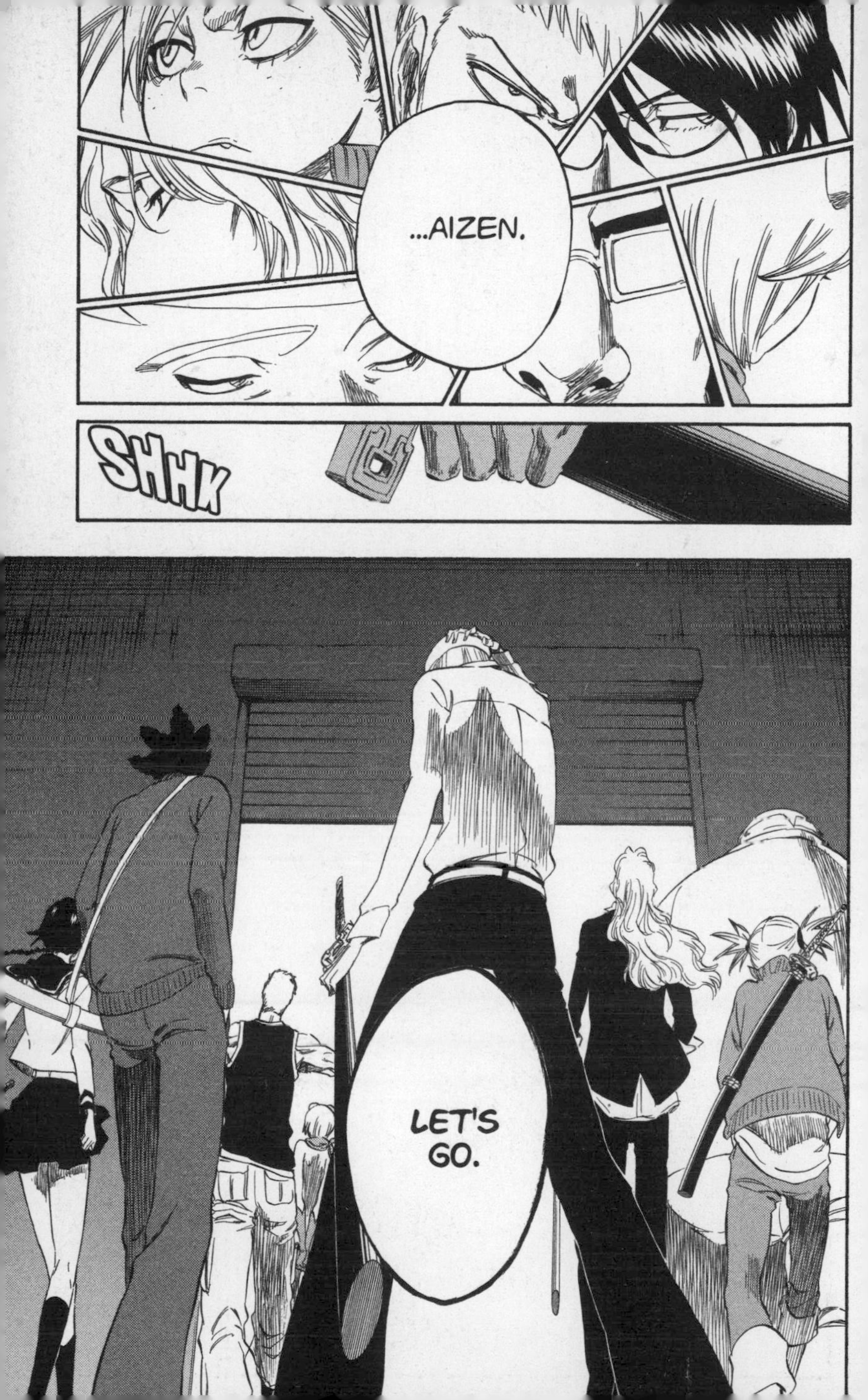
...AIZEN.
SHHK
LET'S GO.

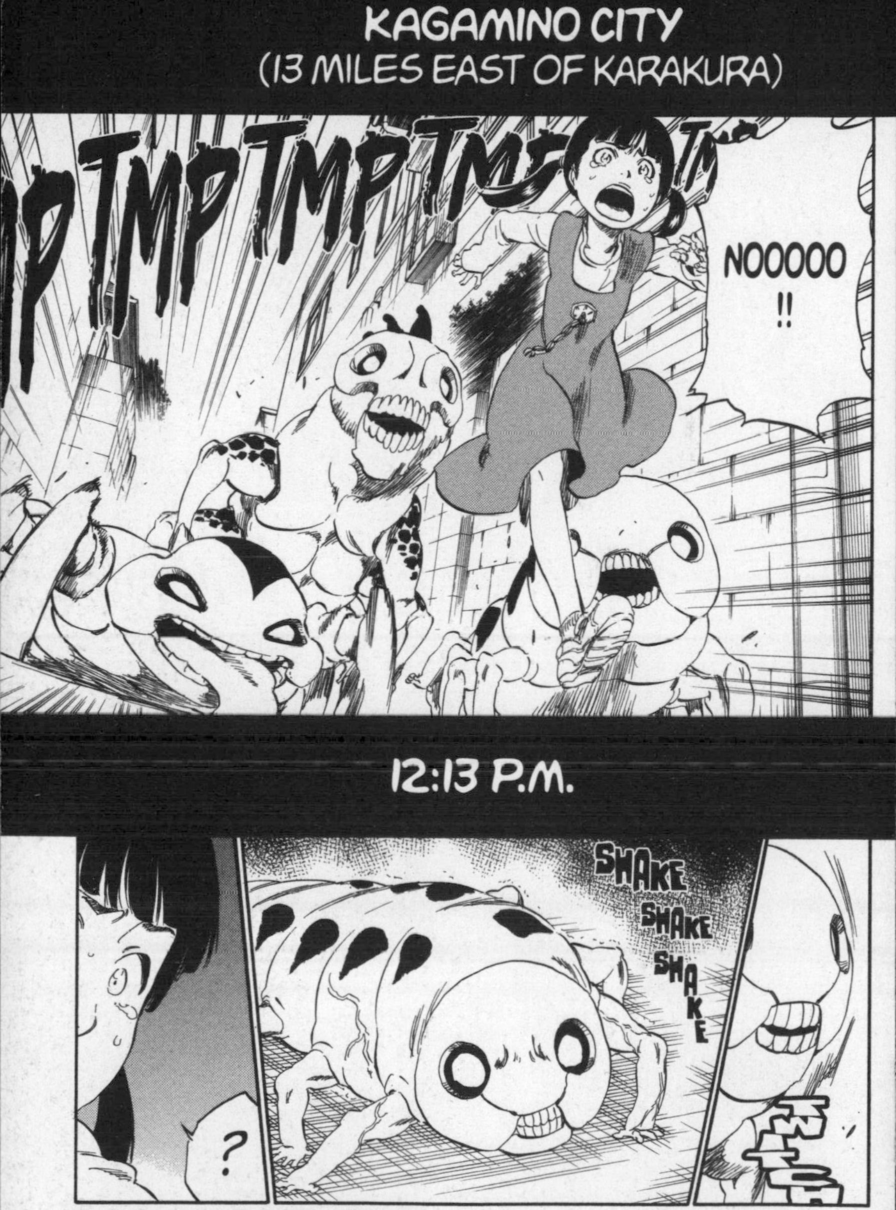
KAGAMINO CITY
(13 MILES EAST OF KARAKURA)
TMP TMP TMP
NOOOOO !!
12:13 P.M.
TWITCH
SHAKE SHAKE SHAKE
?

316. Swang the Edge Down

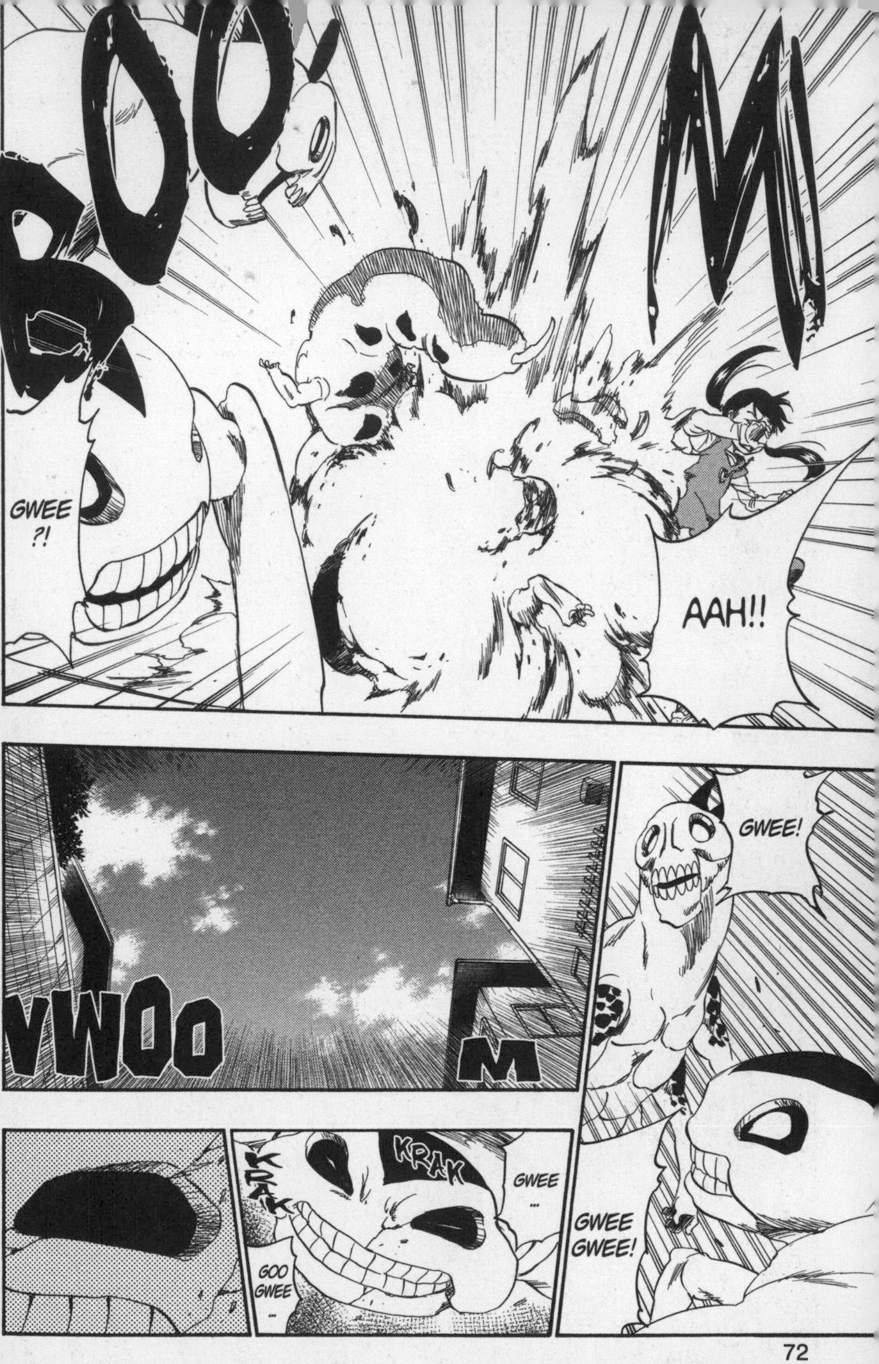
BOOM
AAH!!
GWEE ?!
GWEE!
GWEE GWEE!
VWOOM
KRAK
KRAK
GWEE ...
GOO GWEE ...

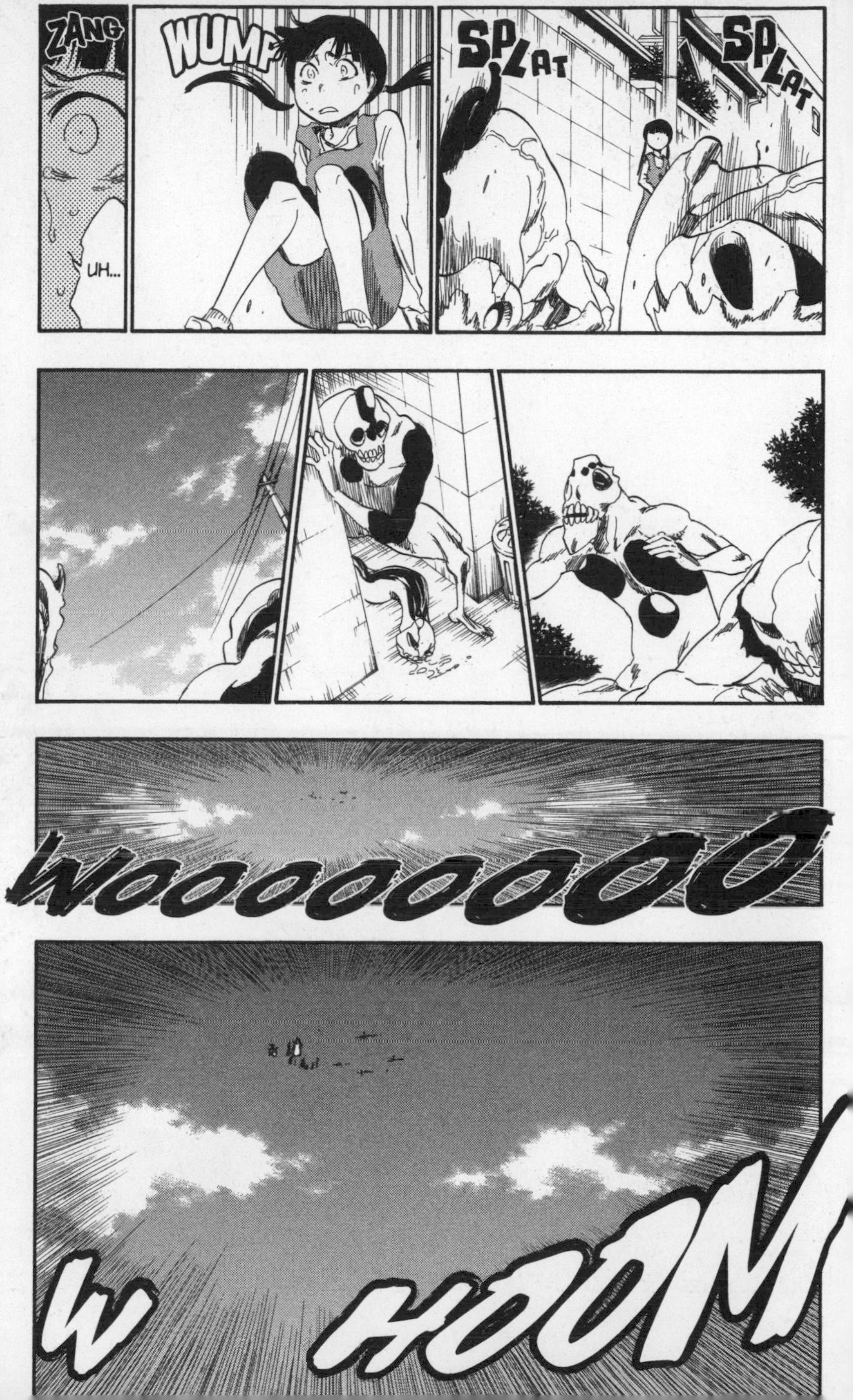
SPLAT
SPLAT
WUMP
ZANG
UH...
WOOOOOOOO
W HOOM

Swang The Edge Down

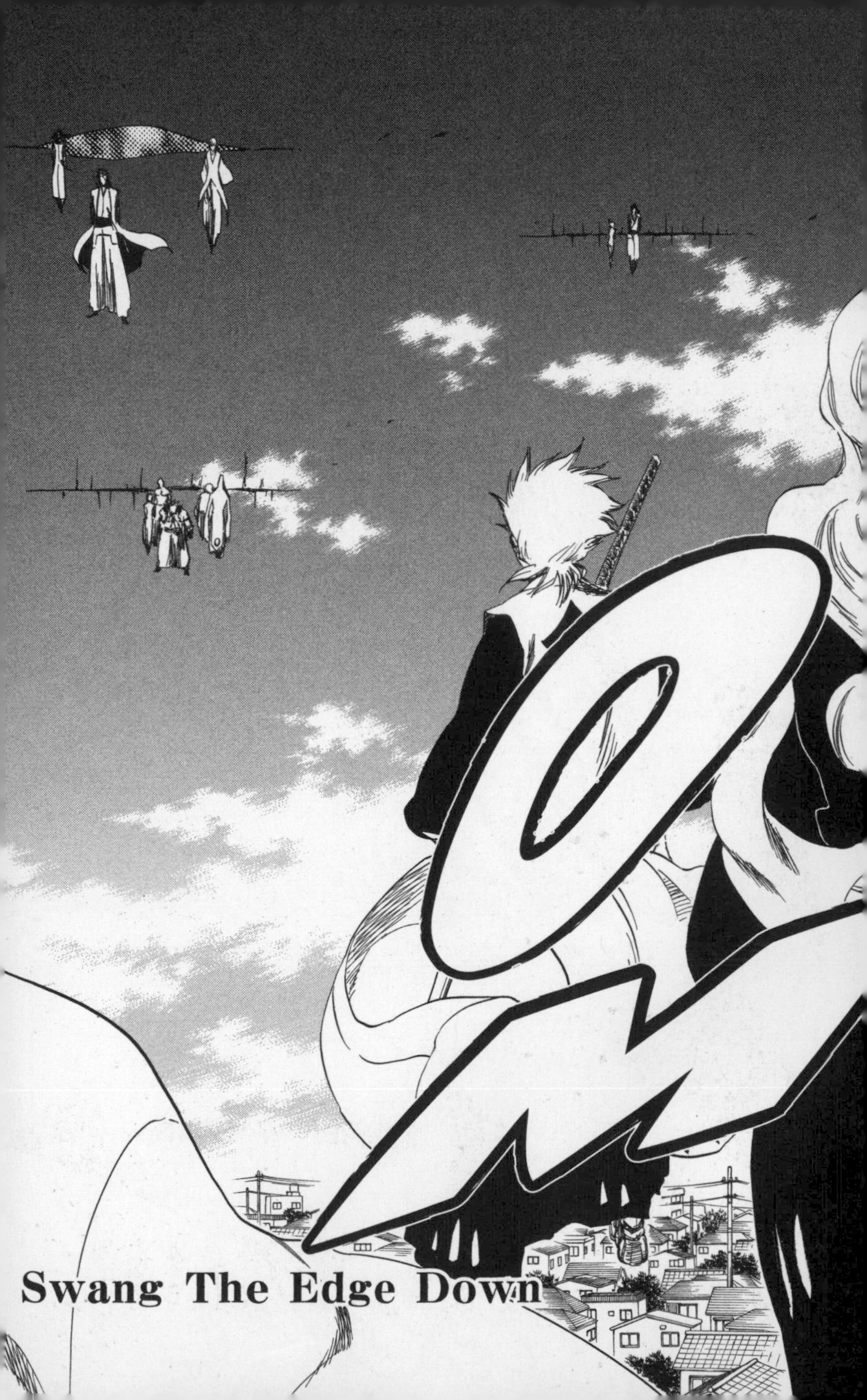

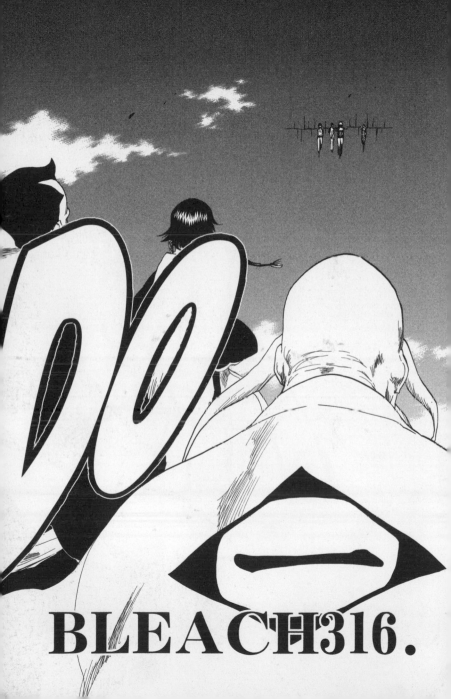

BLEACH316.

WOOOOOOO

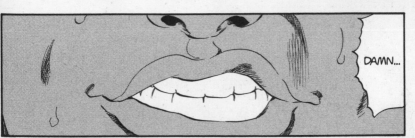

DAMN...

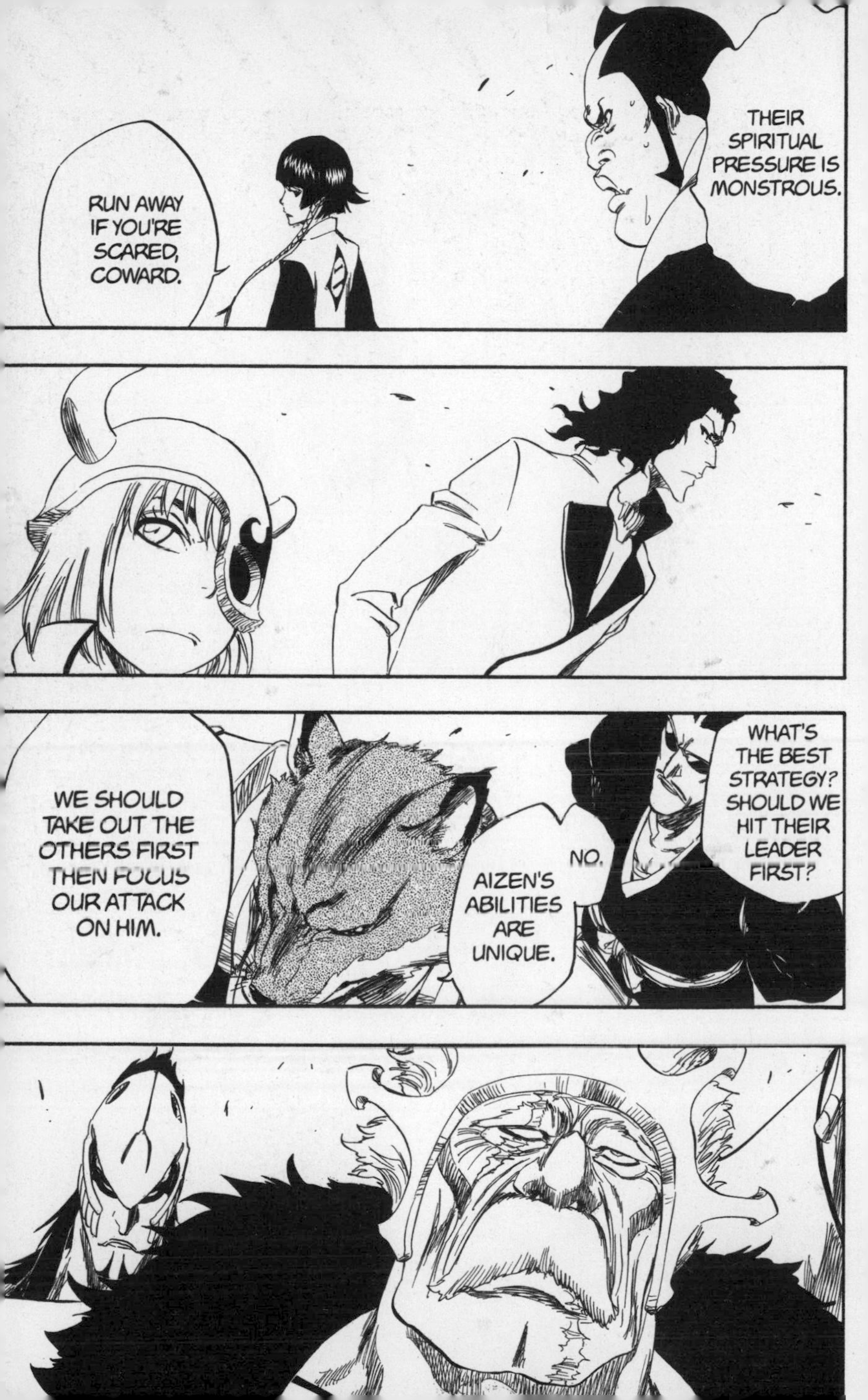
THEIR SPIRITUAL PRESSURE IS MONSTROUS.
RUN AWAY IF YOU'RE SCARED, COWARD.
WHAT'S THE BEST STRATEGY? SHOULD WE HIT THEIR LEADER FIRST?
NO.
AIZEN'S ABILITIES ARE UNIQUE.
WE SHOULD TAKE OUT THE OTHERS FIRST THEN FOCUS OUR ATTACK ON HIM.

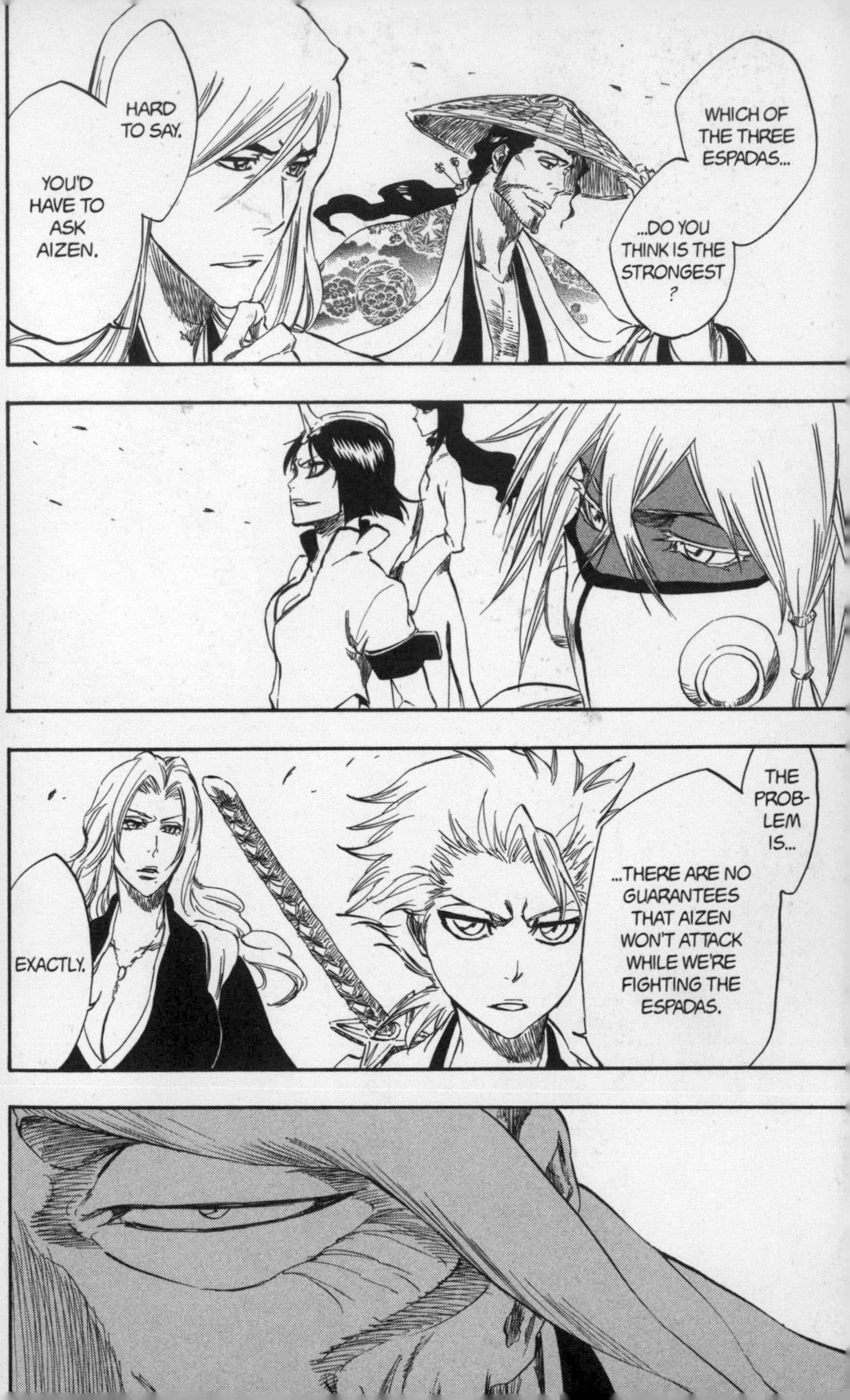
WHICH OF THE THREE ESPADAS...
...DO YOU THINK IS THE STRONGEST?
HARD TO SAY.
YOU'D HAVE TO ASK AIZEN.
THE PROB-LEM IS...
...THERE ARE NO GUARANTEES THAT AIZEN WON'T ATTACK WHILE WE'RE FIGHTING THE ESPADAS.
EXACTLY.

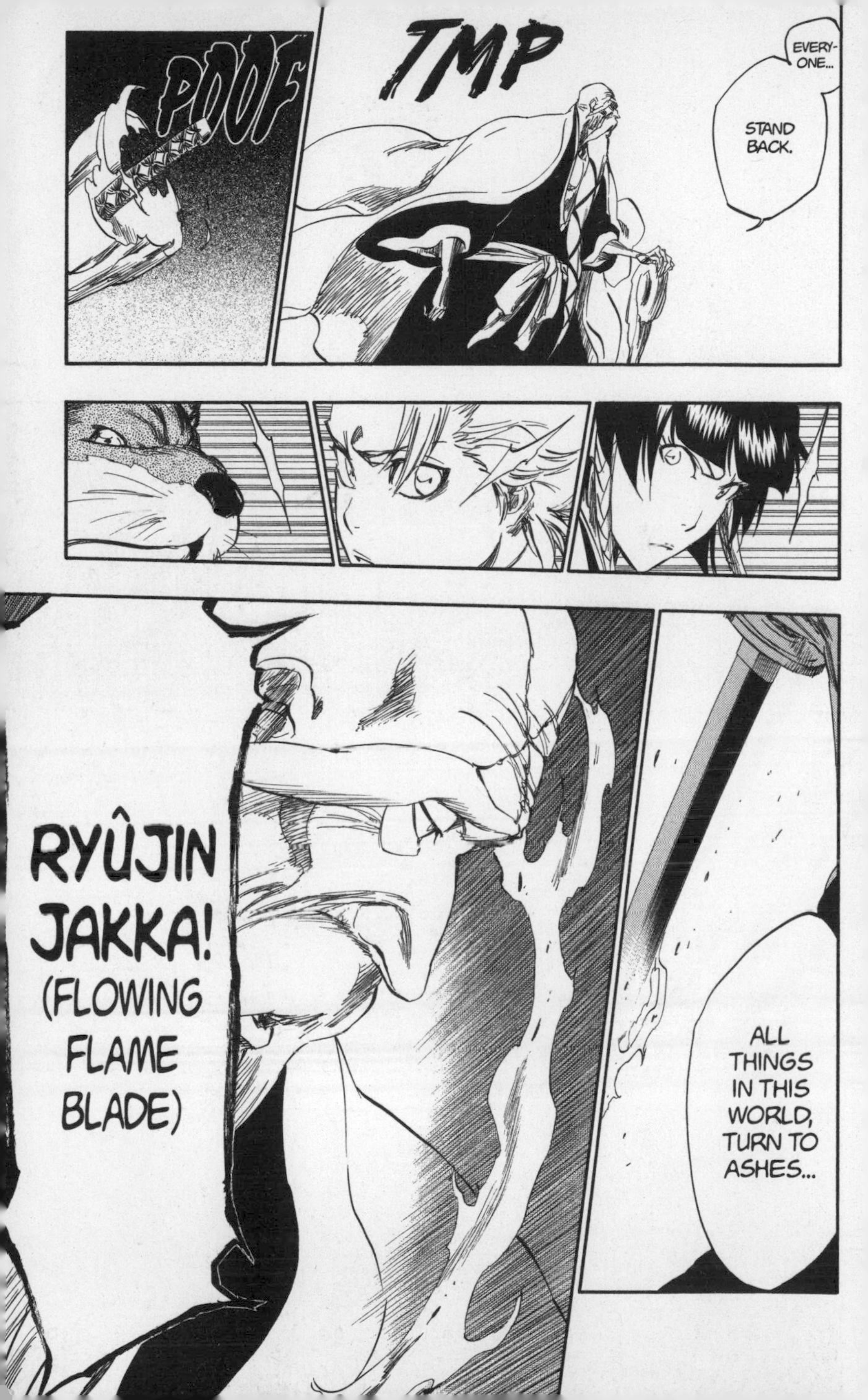
EVERY-ONE...
STAND BACK.
TMP
POOF
ALL THINGS IN THIS WORLD, TURN TO ASHES...
RYÛJIN JAKKA!
(FLOWING FLAME BLADE)

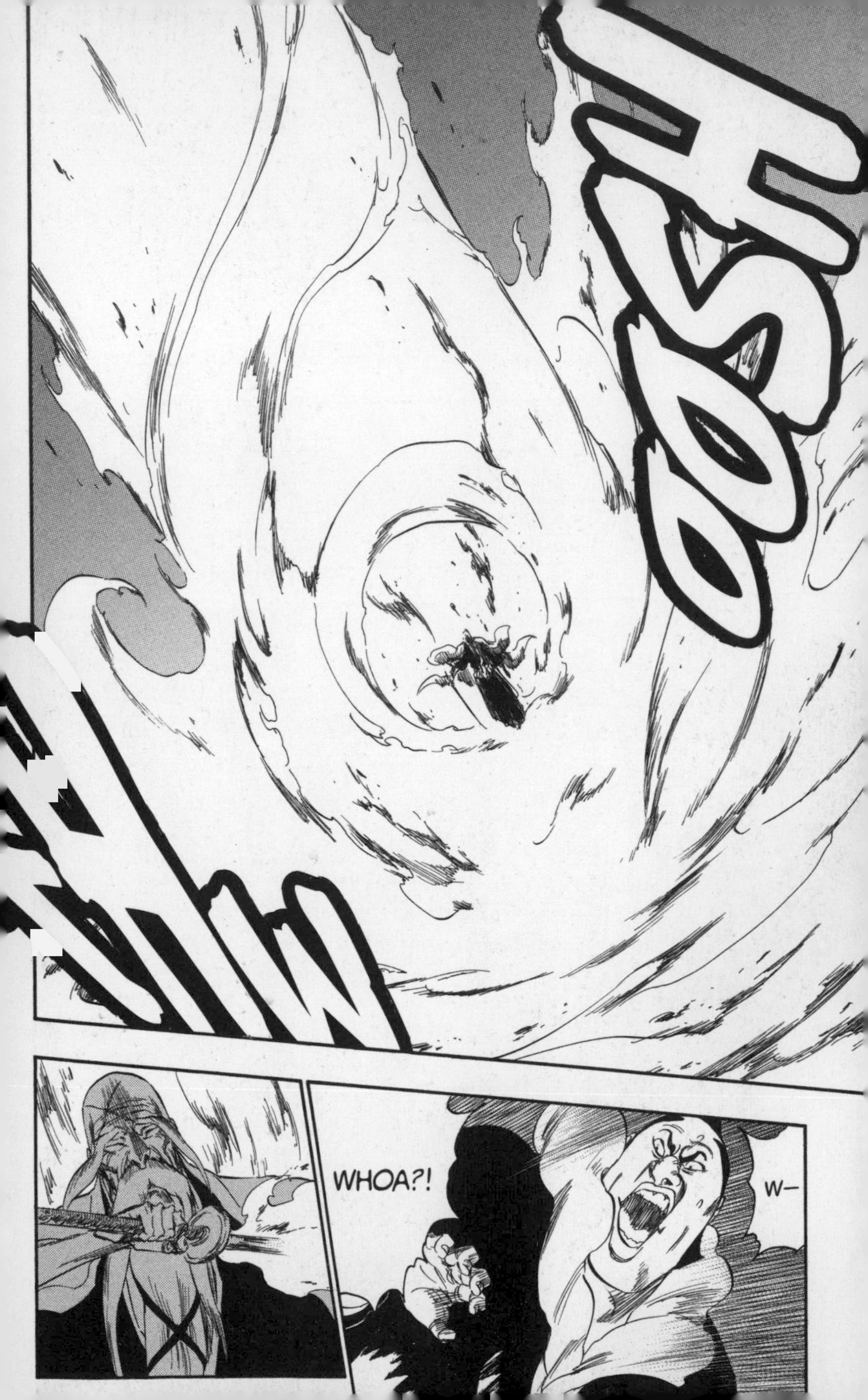
W—
WHOA?!

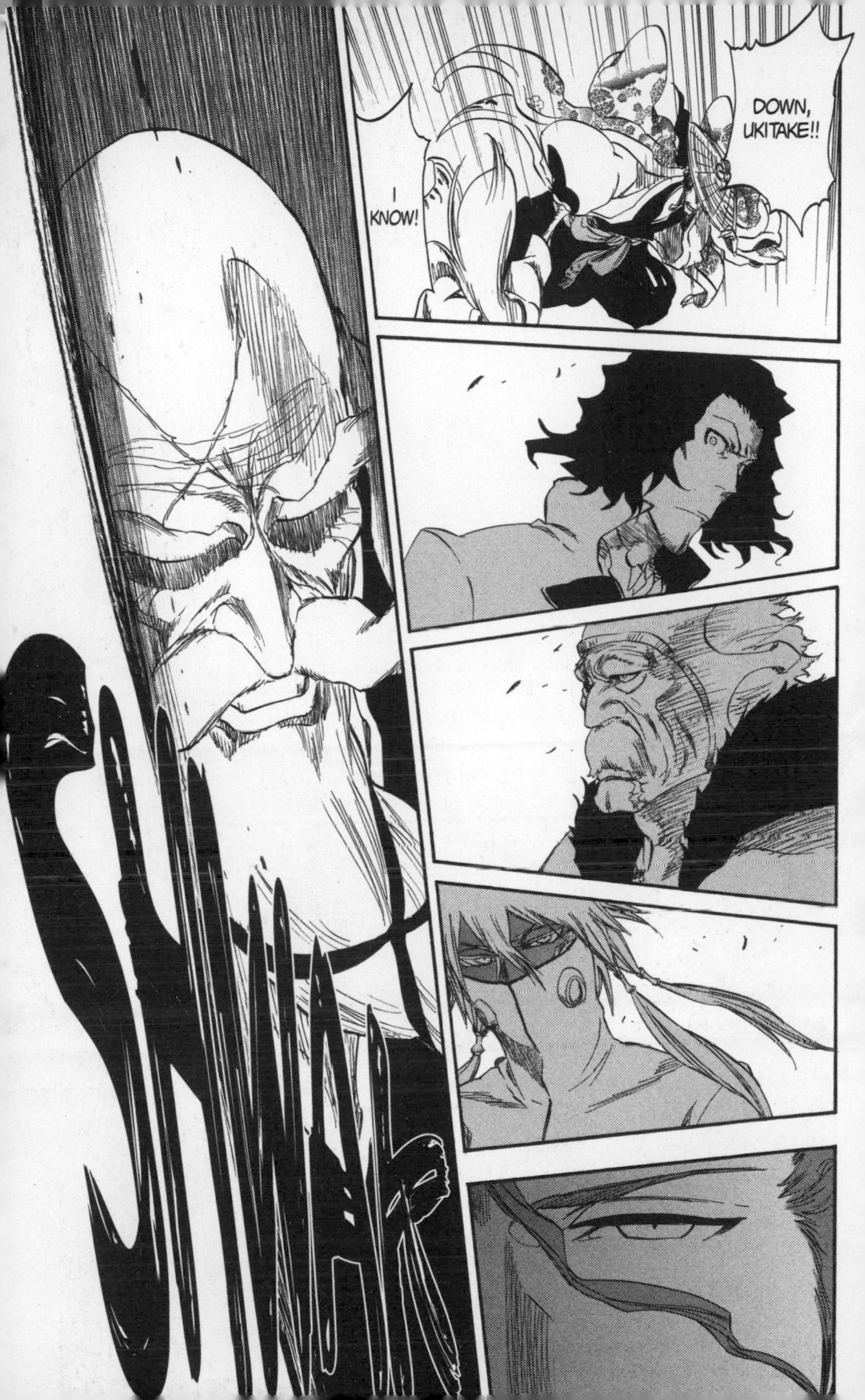
DOWN, UKITAKE!!
I KNOW!

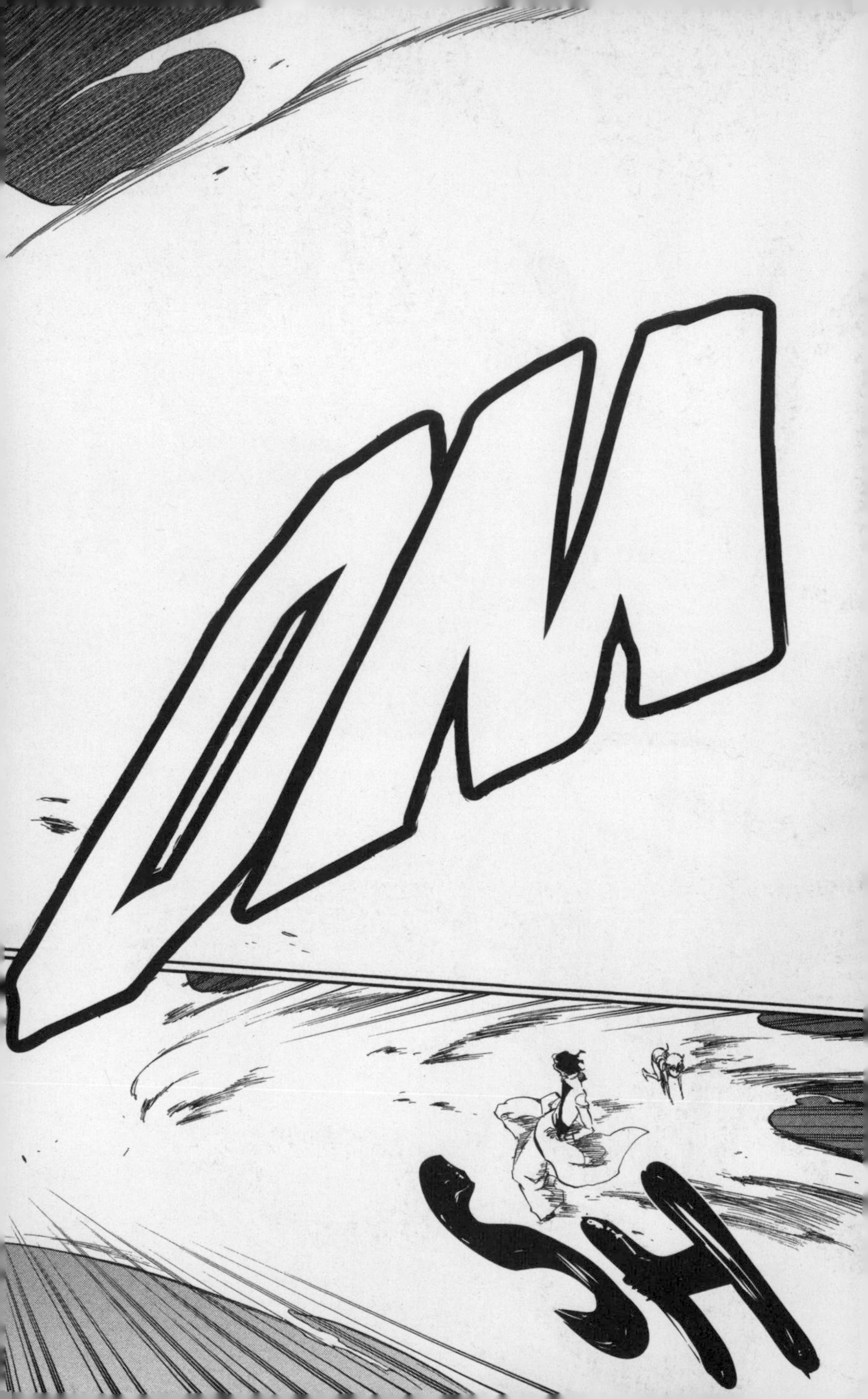
SH

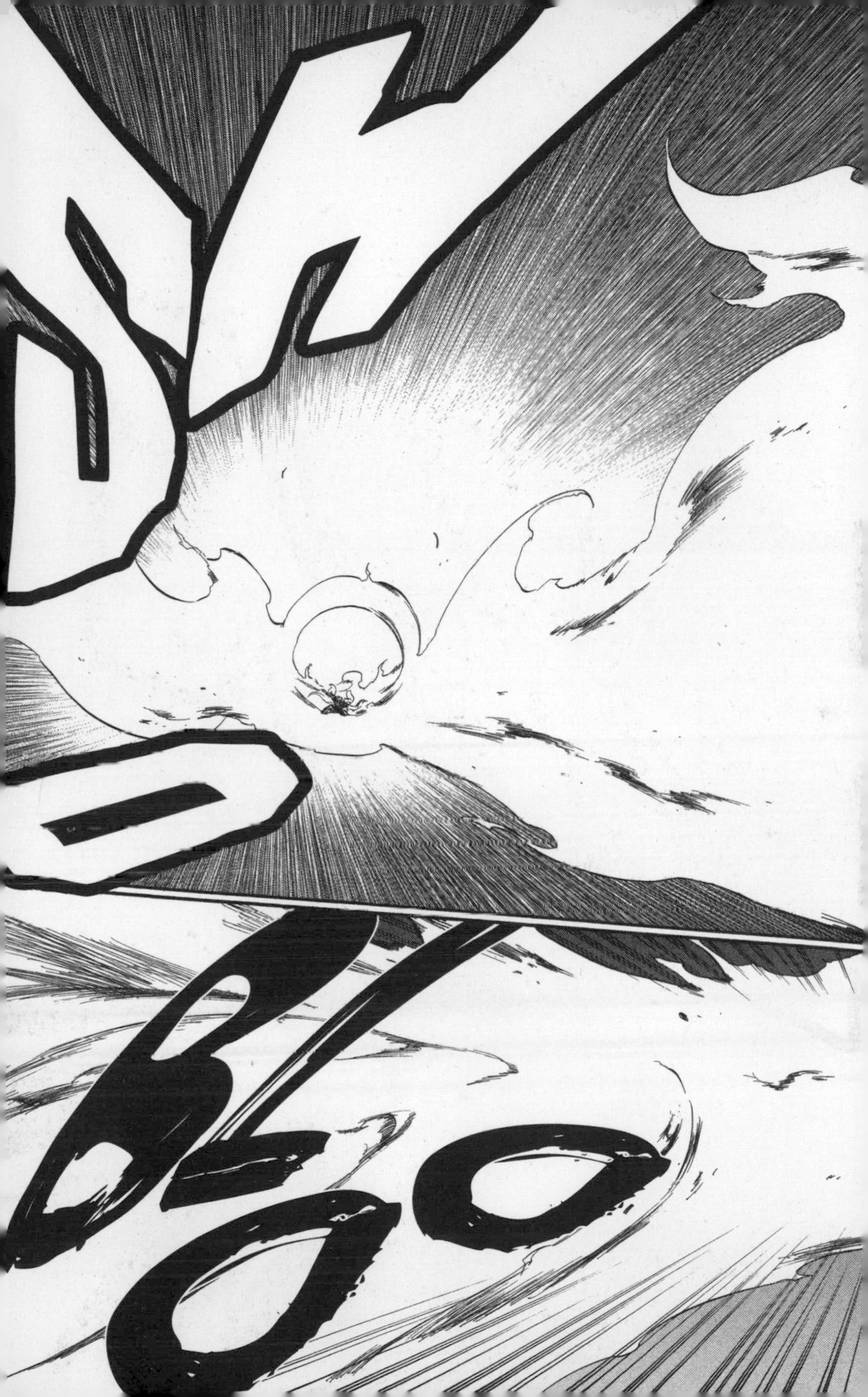

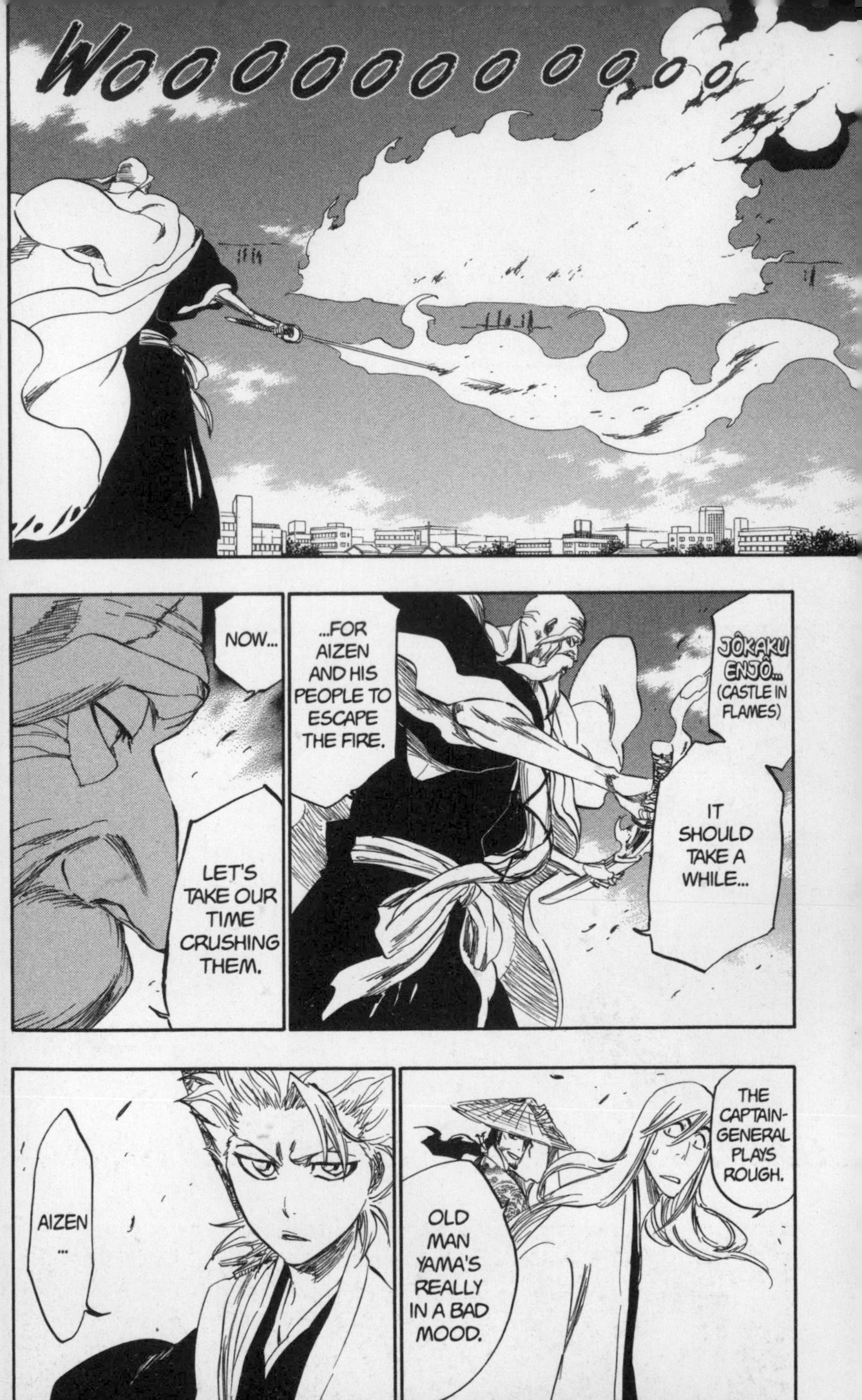
WOOOOOOOOOOOOO
JÔKAKU ENJÔ... (CASTLE IN FLAMES)
IT SHOULD TAKE A WHILE...
...FOR AIZEN AND HIS PEOPLE TO ESCAPE THE FIRE.
NOW...
LET'S TAKE OUR TIME CRUSHING THEM.
THE CAPTAIN-GENERAL PLAYS ROUGH.
OLD MAN YAMA'S REALLY IN A BAD MOOD.
AIZEN ...

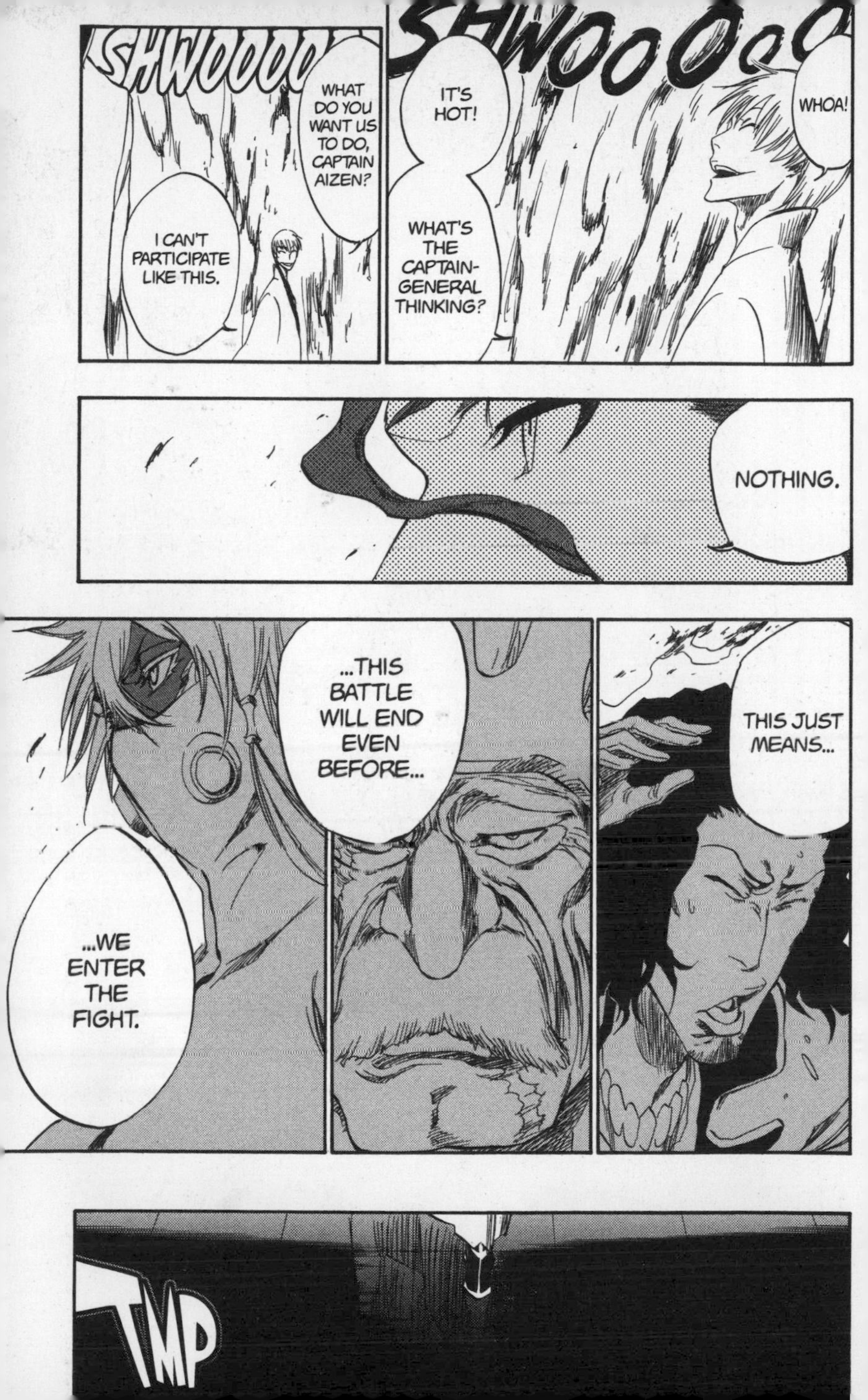
SHWOOOOOO
WHOA!
IT'S HOT!
WHAT'S THE CAPTAIN-GENERAL THINKING?
SHWOOOOO
WHAT DO YOU WANT US TO DO, CAPTAIN AIZEN?
I CAN'T PARTICIPATE LIKE THIS.
NOTHING.
THIS JUST MEANS...
...THIS BATTLE WILL END EVEN BEFORE...
...WE ENTER THE FIGHT.
TMP

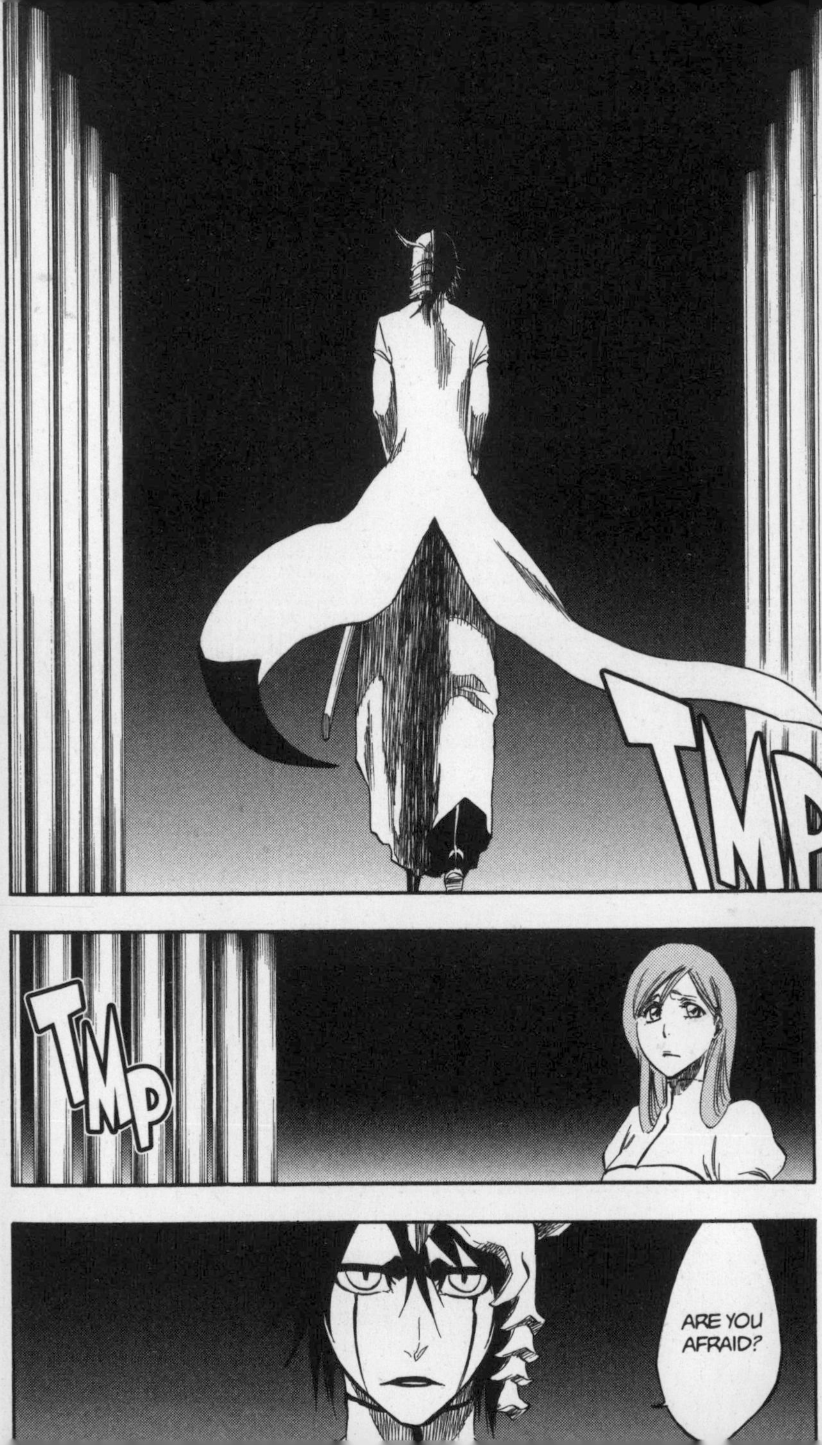
TMP
TMP
ARE YOU AFRAID?

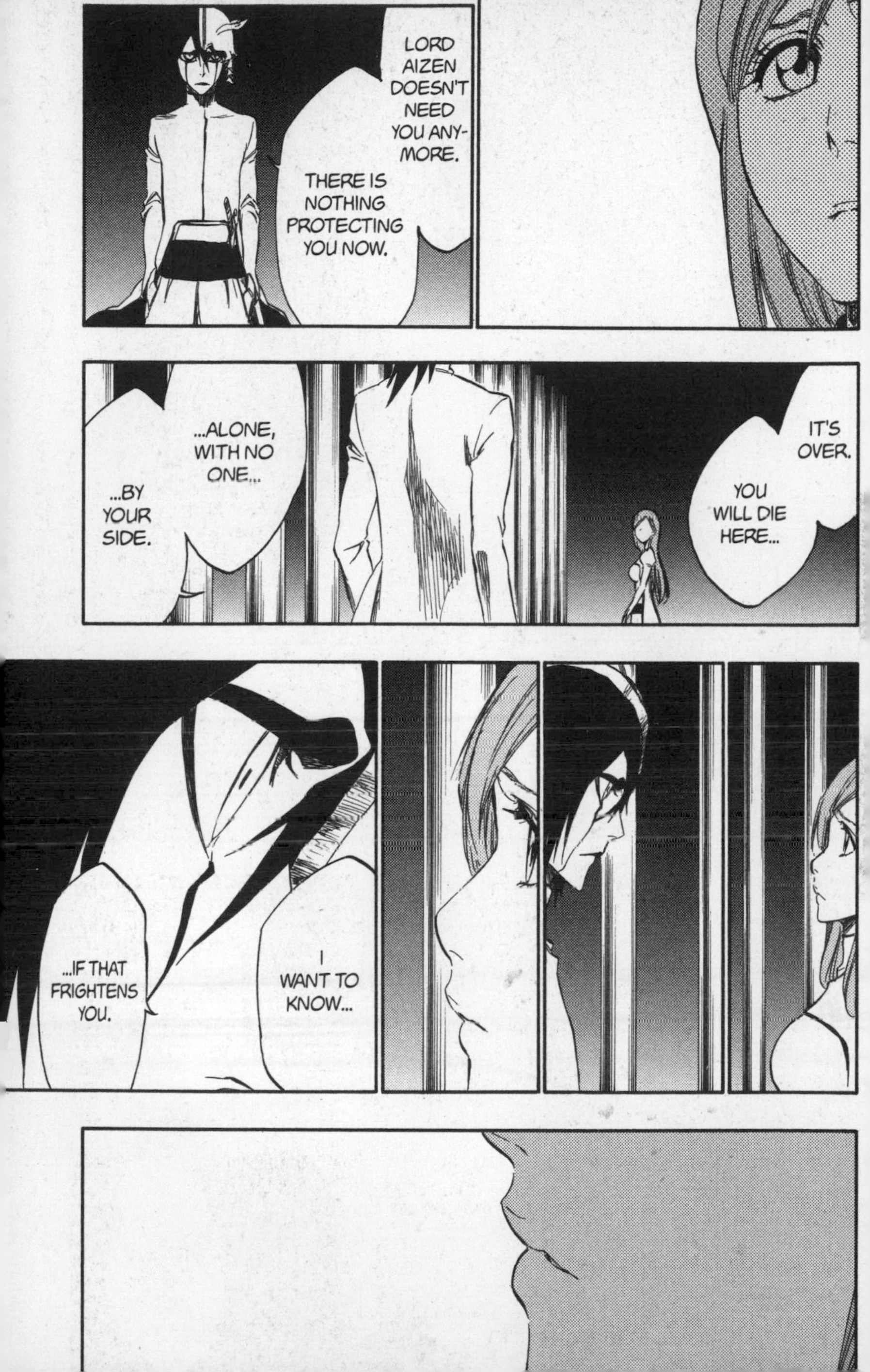
LORD AIZEN DOESN'T NEED YOU ANY-MORE.
THERE IS NOTHING PROTECTING YOU NOW.
IT'S OVER.
YOU WILL DIE HERE...
...ALONE, WITH NO ONE...
...BY YOUR SIDE.
I WANT TO KNOW...
...IF THAT FRIGHTENS YOU.

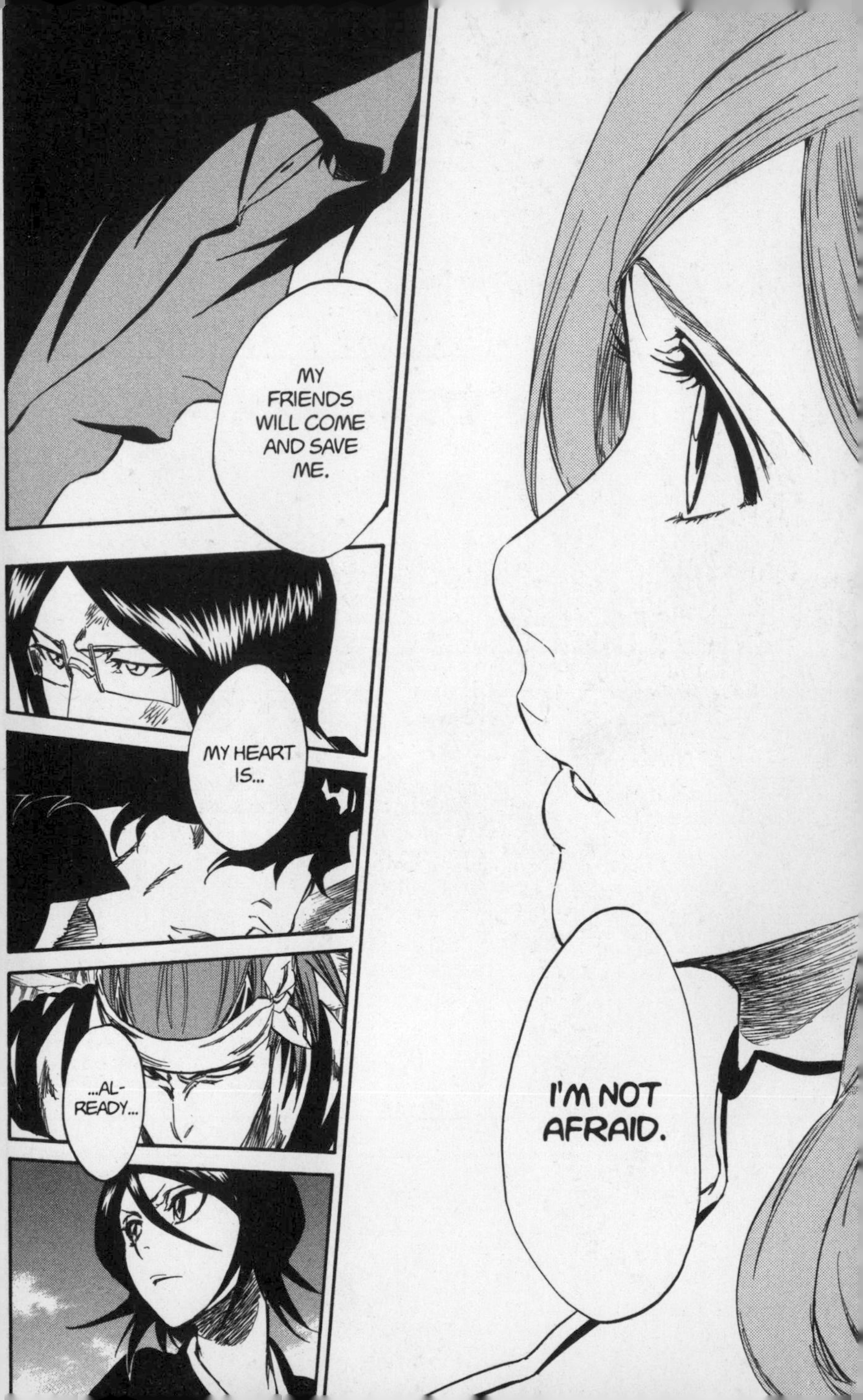
I'M NOT AFRAID.
MY FRIENDS WILL COME AND SAVE ME.
MY HEART IS...
...AL-READY...

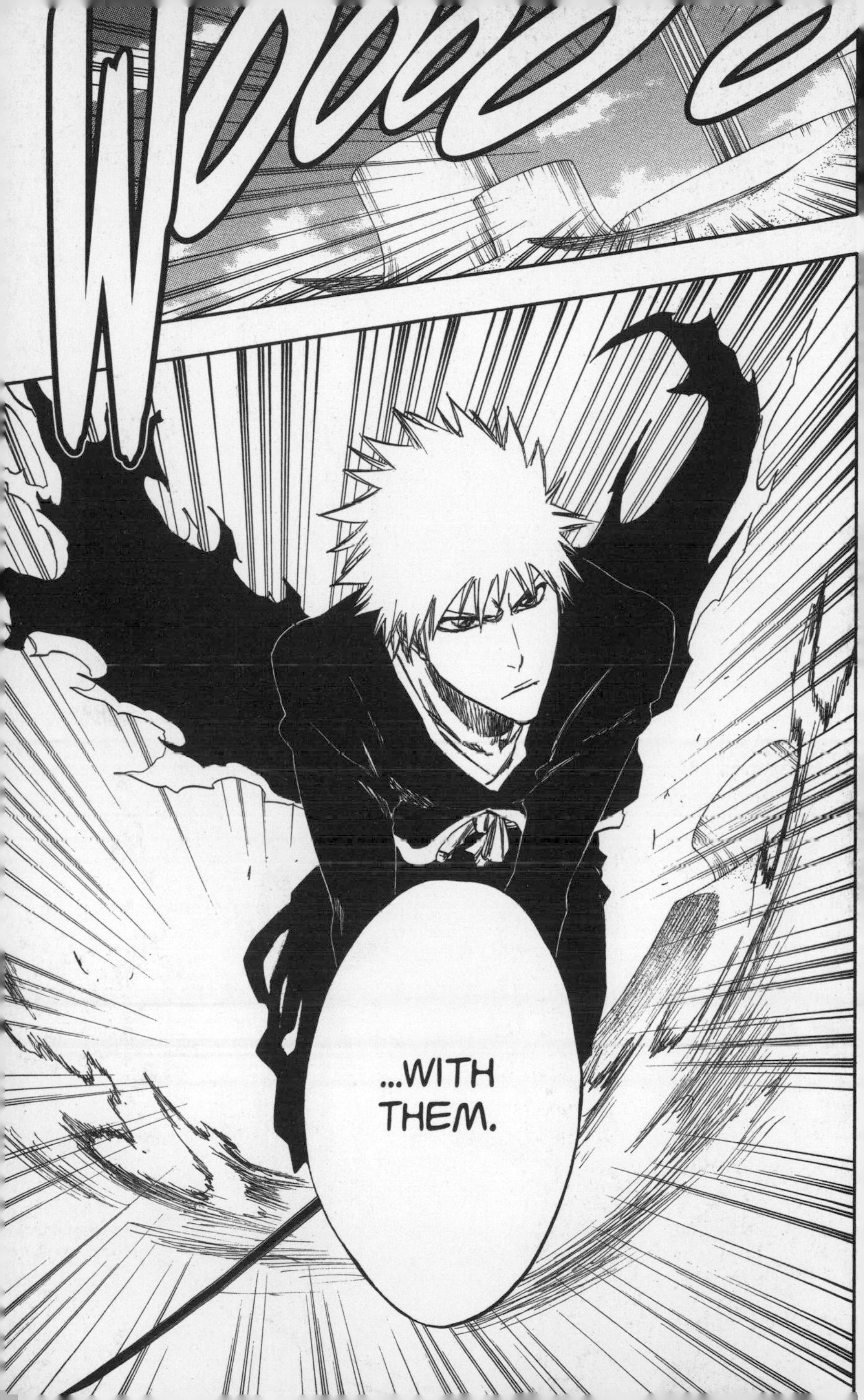
...WITH
THEM.

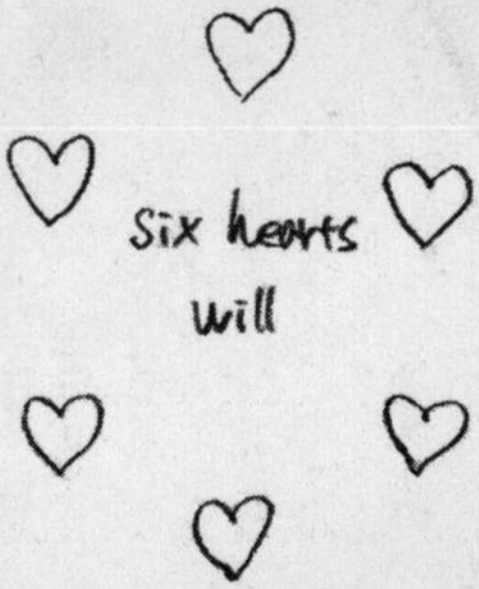
Six hearts
will

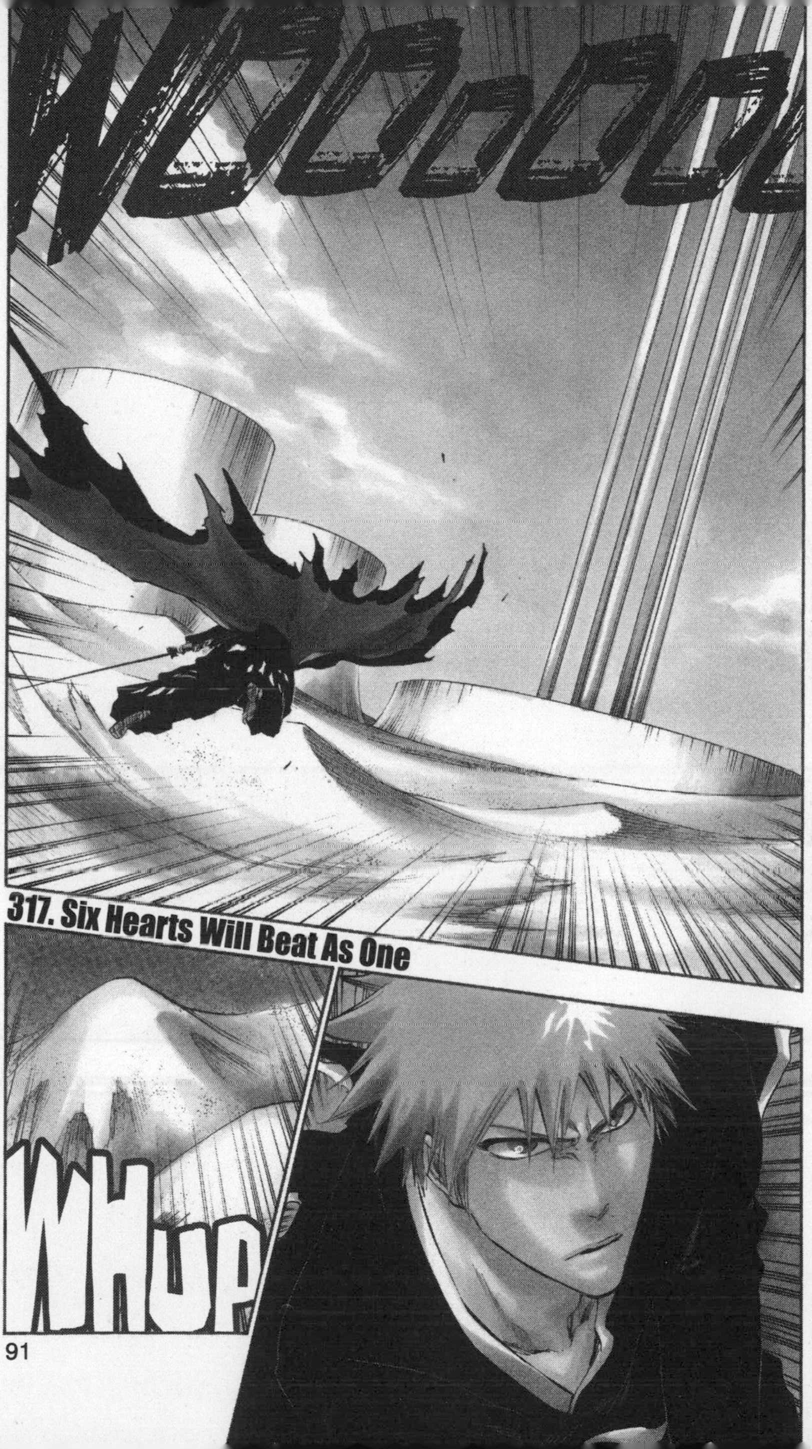
WOOOOOO
WHUP

317. Six Hearts Will Beat As One

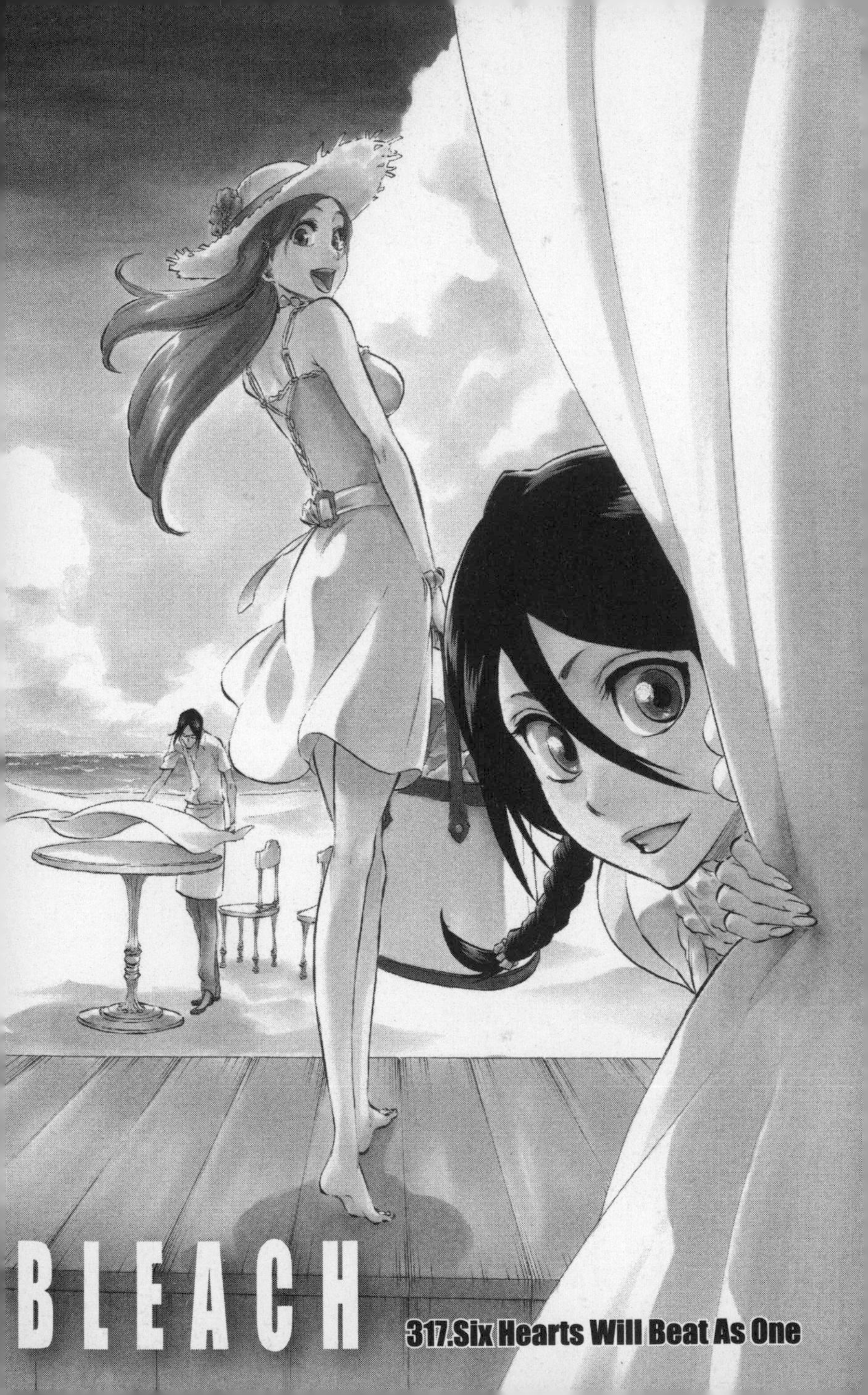
BLEACH
317.Six Hearts Will Beat As One

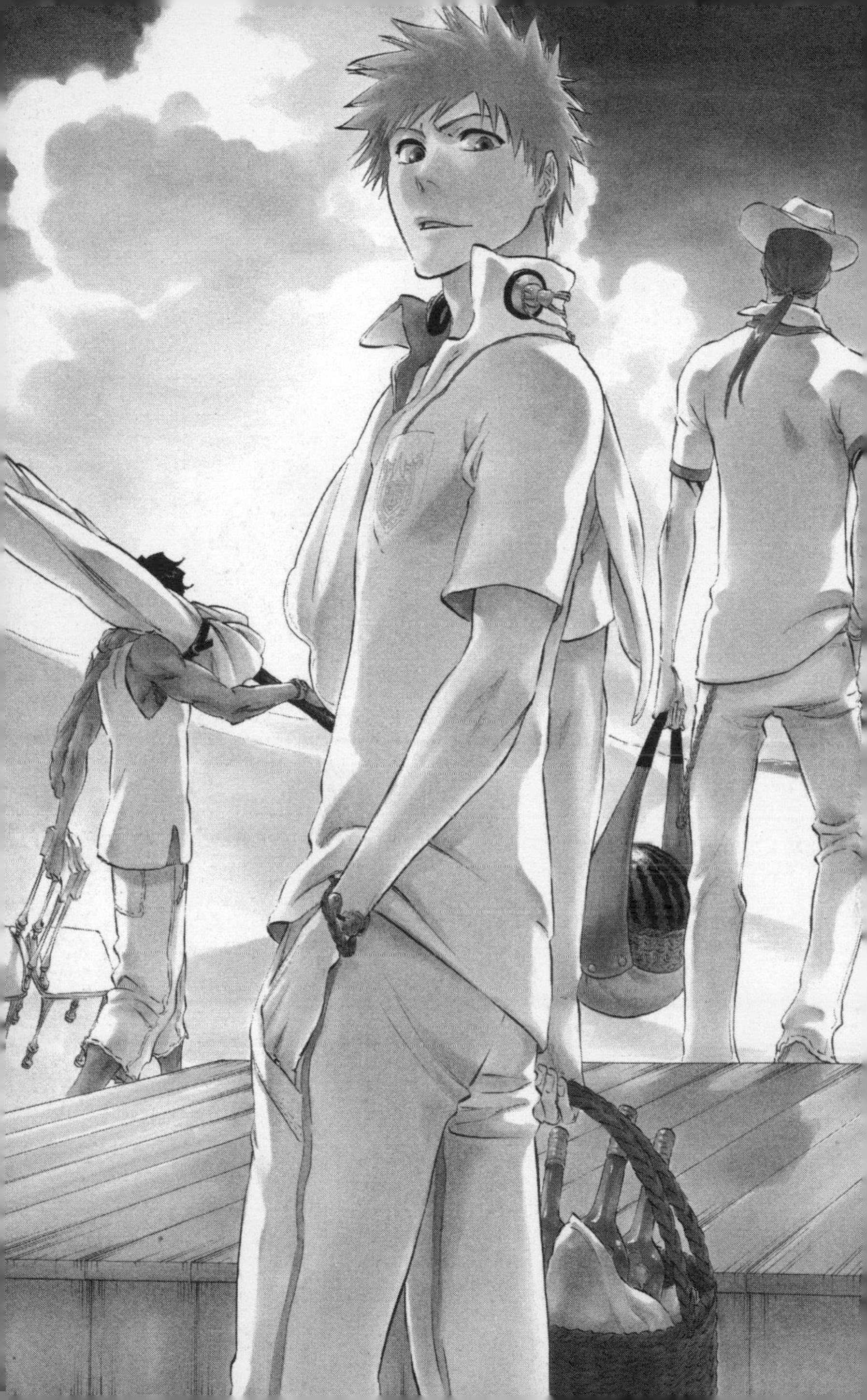

BLEACH

ブリーチ

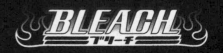

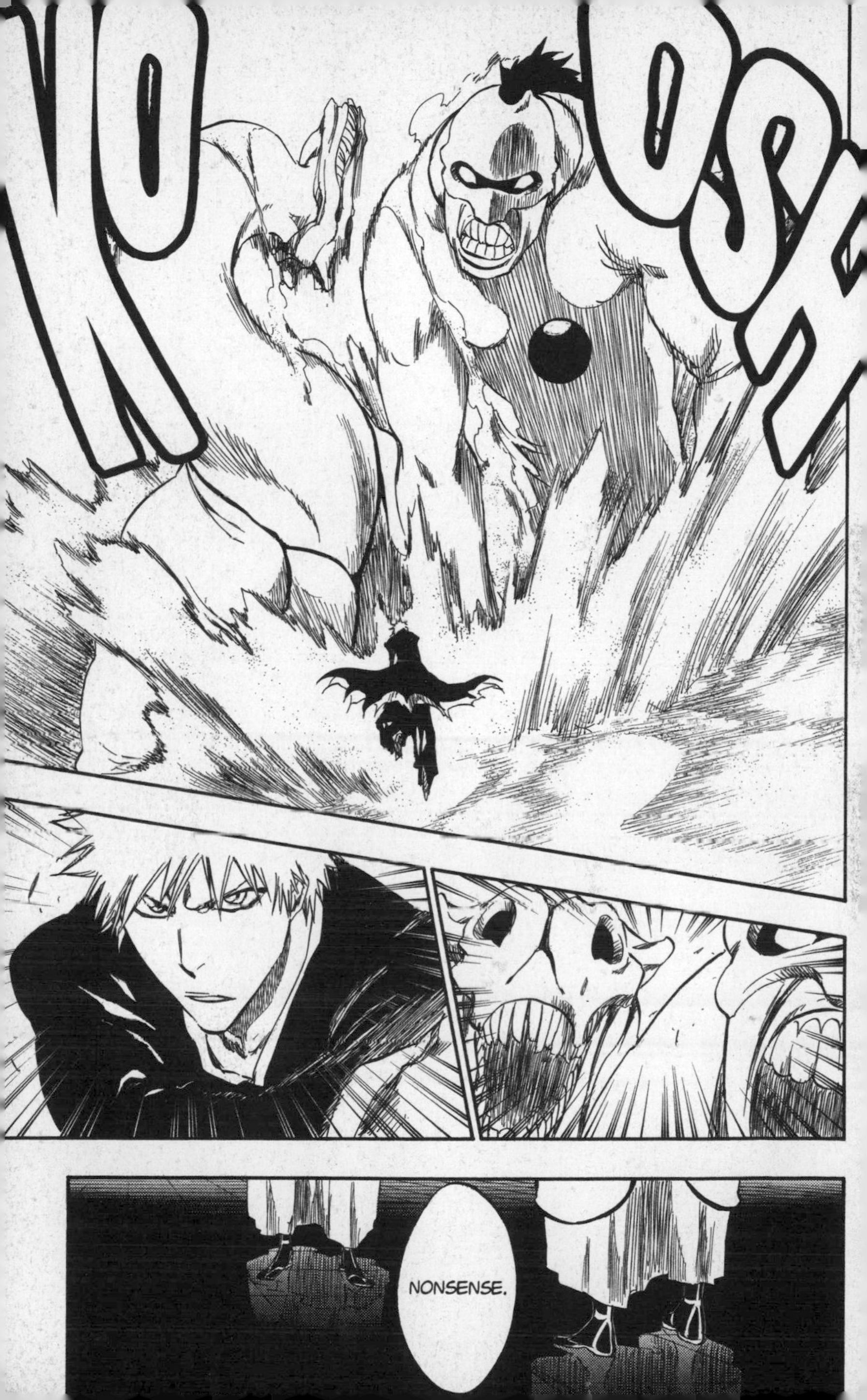
VOOSH
NONSENSE.

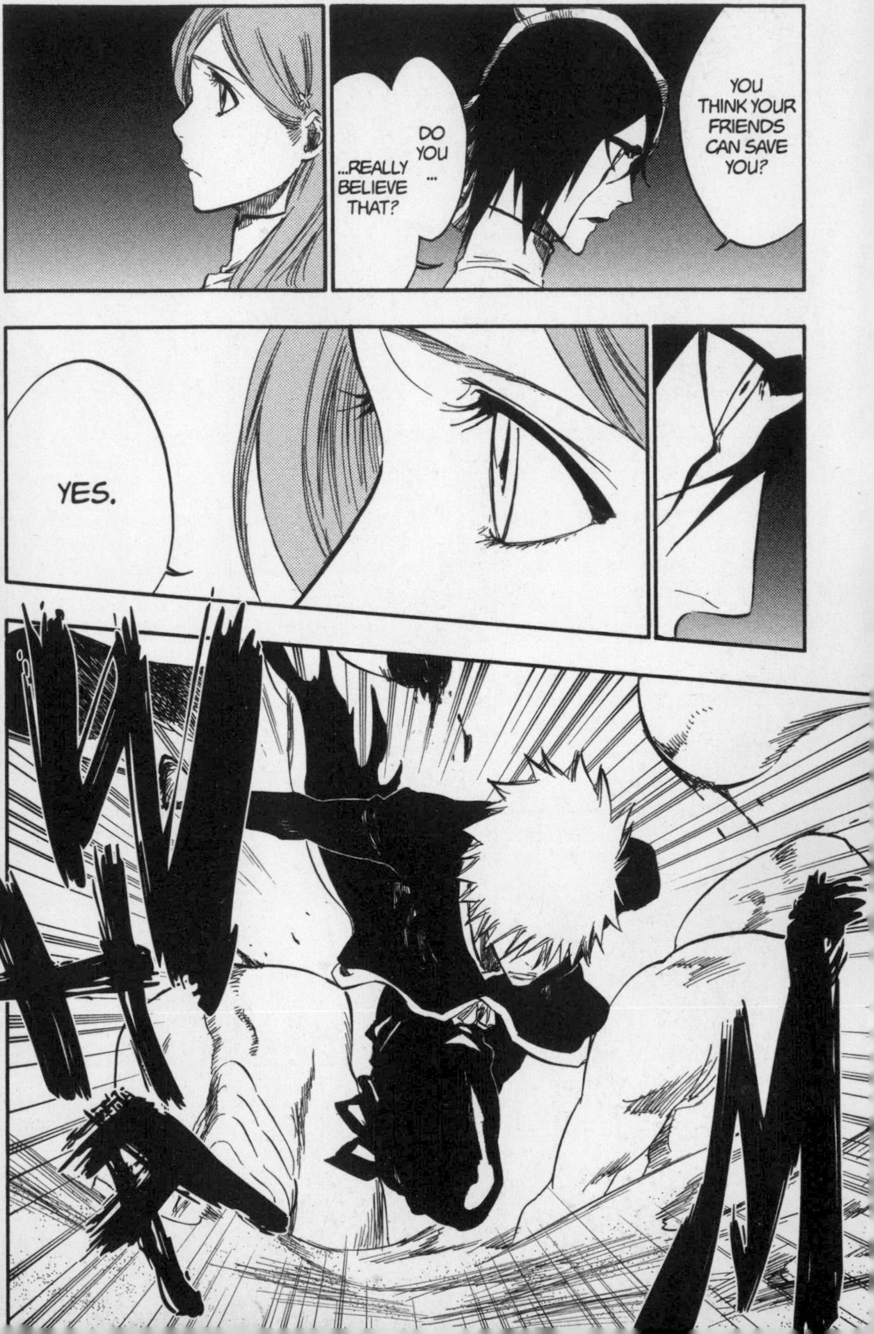
YOU THINK YOUR FRIENDS CAN SAVE YOU?
DO YOU ...
...REALLY BELIEVE THAT?
YES.

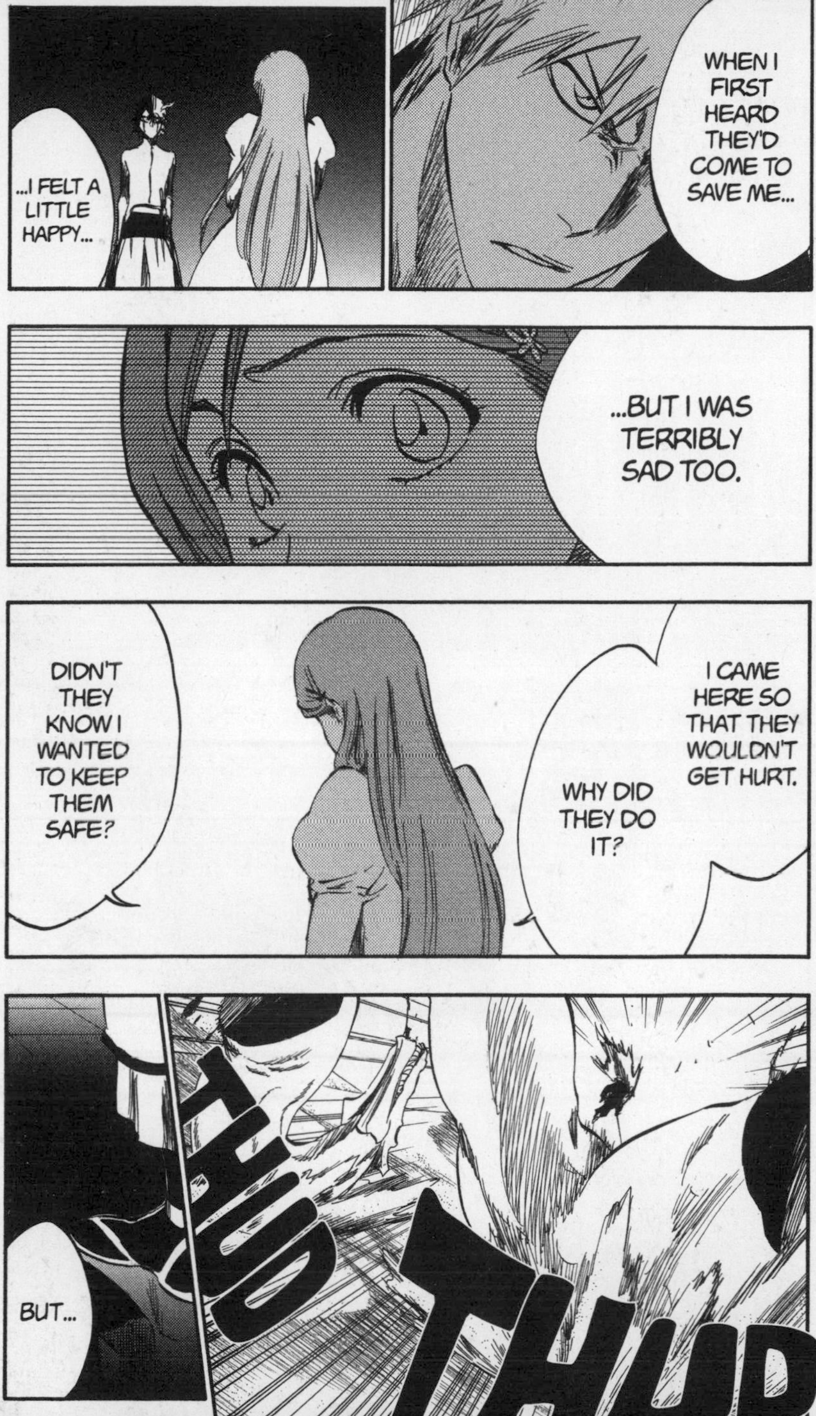
WHEN I FIRST HEARD THEY'D COME TO SAVE ME...
...I FELT A LITTLE HAPPY...
...BUT I WAS TERRIBLY SAD TOO.
I CAME HERE SO THAT THEY WOULDN'T GET HURT.
WHY DID THEY DO IT?
DIDN'T THEY KNOW I WANTED TO KEEP THEM SAFE?
THUD
THUD
BUT...

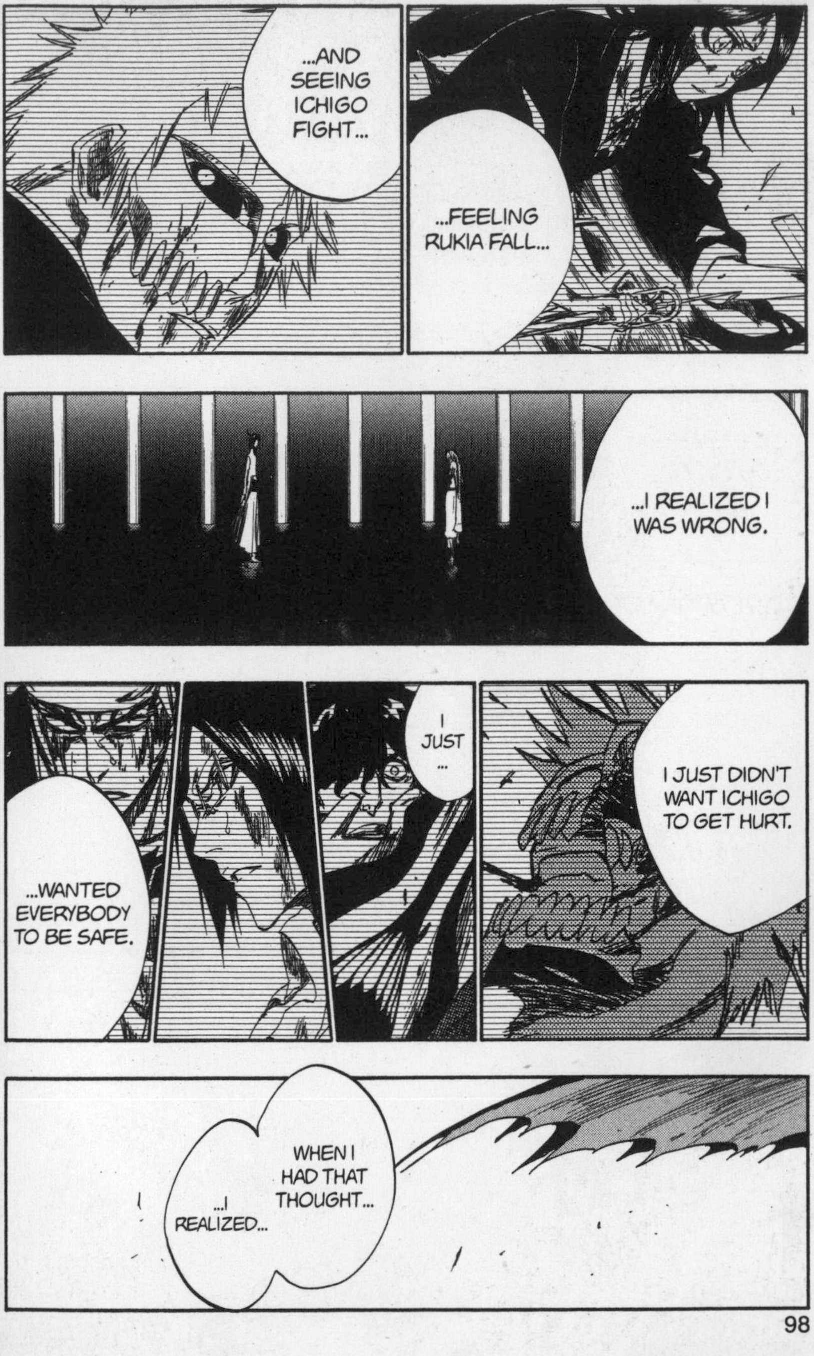

...FEELING RUKIA FALL...
...AND SEEING ICHIGO FIGHT...
...I REALIZED I WAS WRONG.
I JUST DIDN'T WANT ICHIGO TO GET HURT.
I JUST ...
...WANTED EVERYBODY TO BE SAFE.
WHEN I HAD THAT THOUGHT...
...I REALIZED...

THOSE GUYS FEEL THE SAME WAY I DO.

OH...

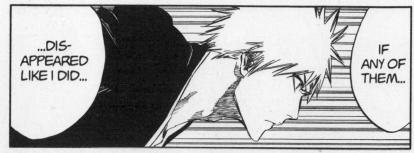

...DIS-APPEARED LIKE I DID...

IF ANY OF THEM...

...COME AFTER THEM.

...I KNOW I'D...

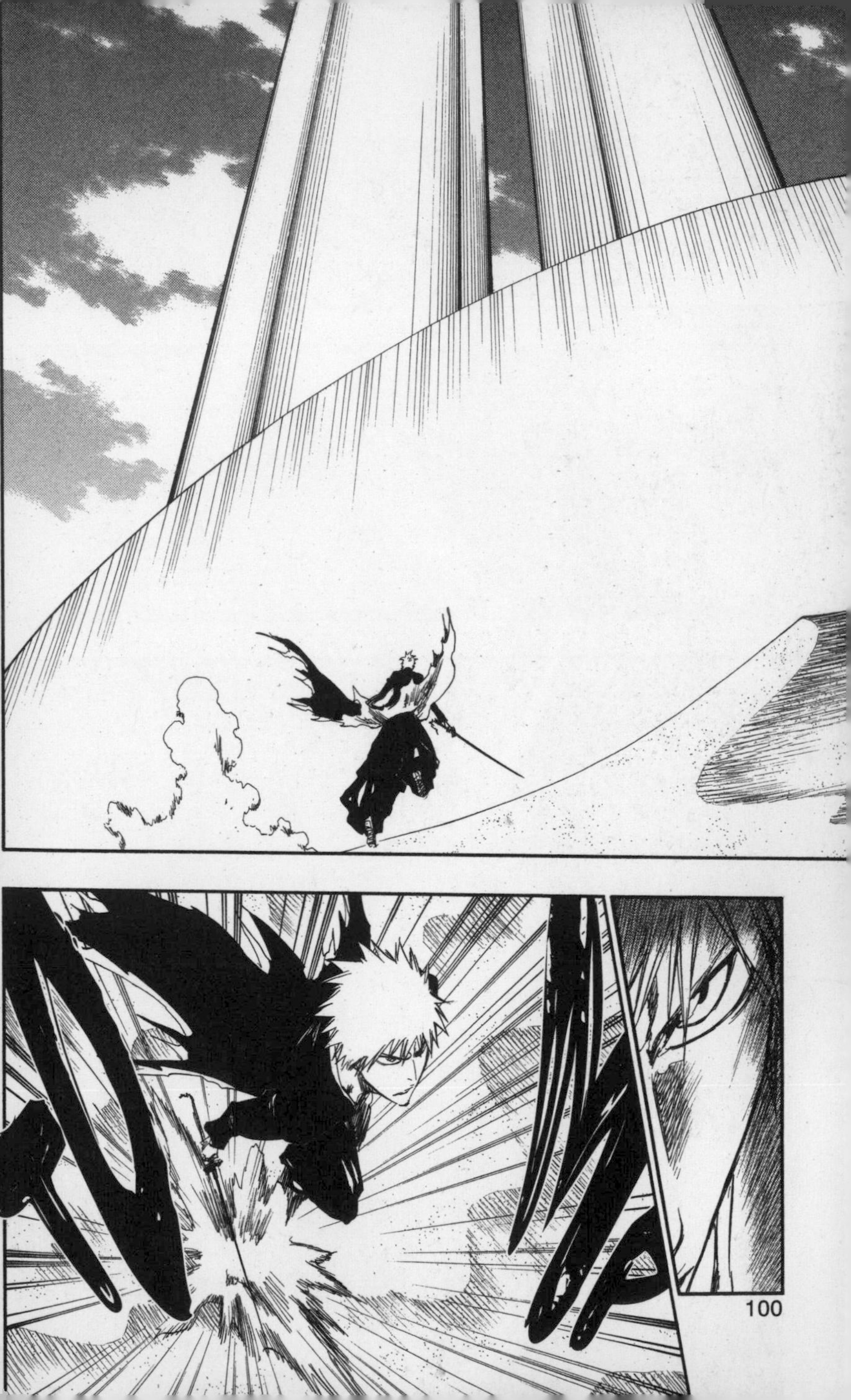

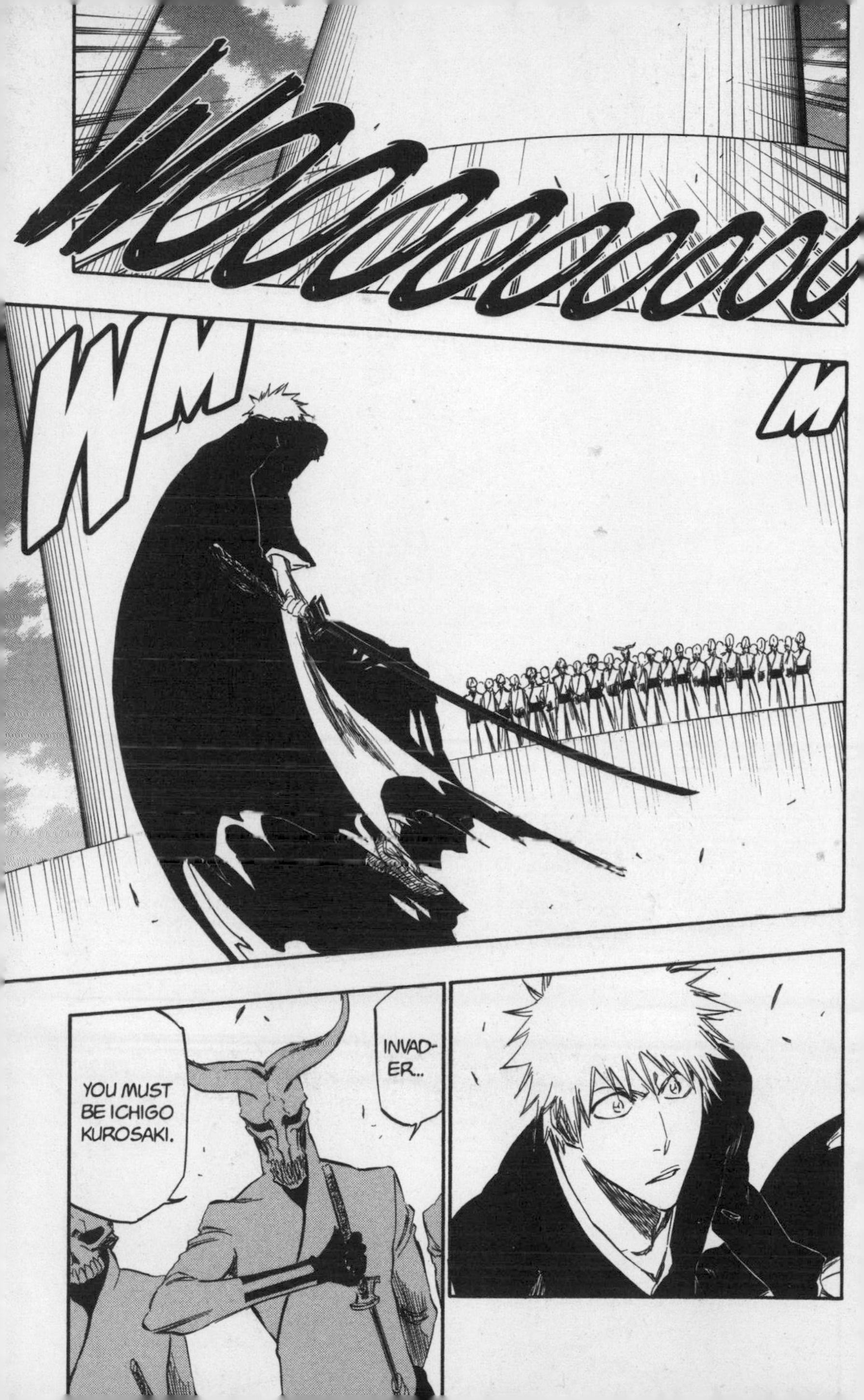
WOOOOOOOOOO
WM
M
INVAD-
ER...
YOU MUST BE ICHIGO KUROSAKI.

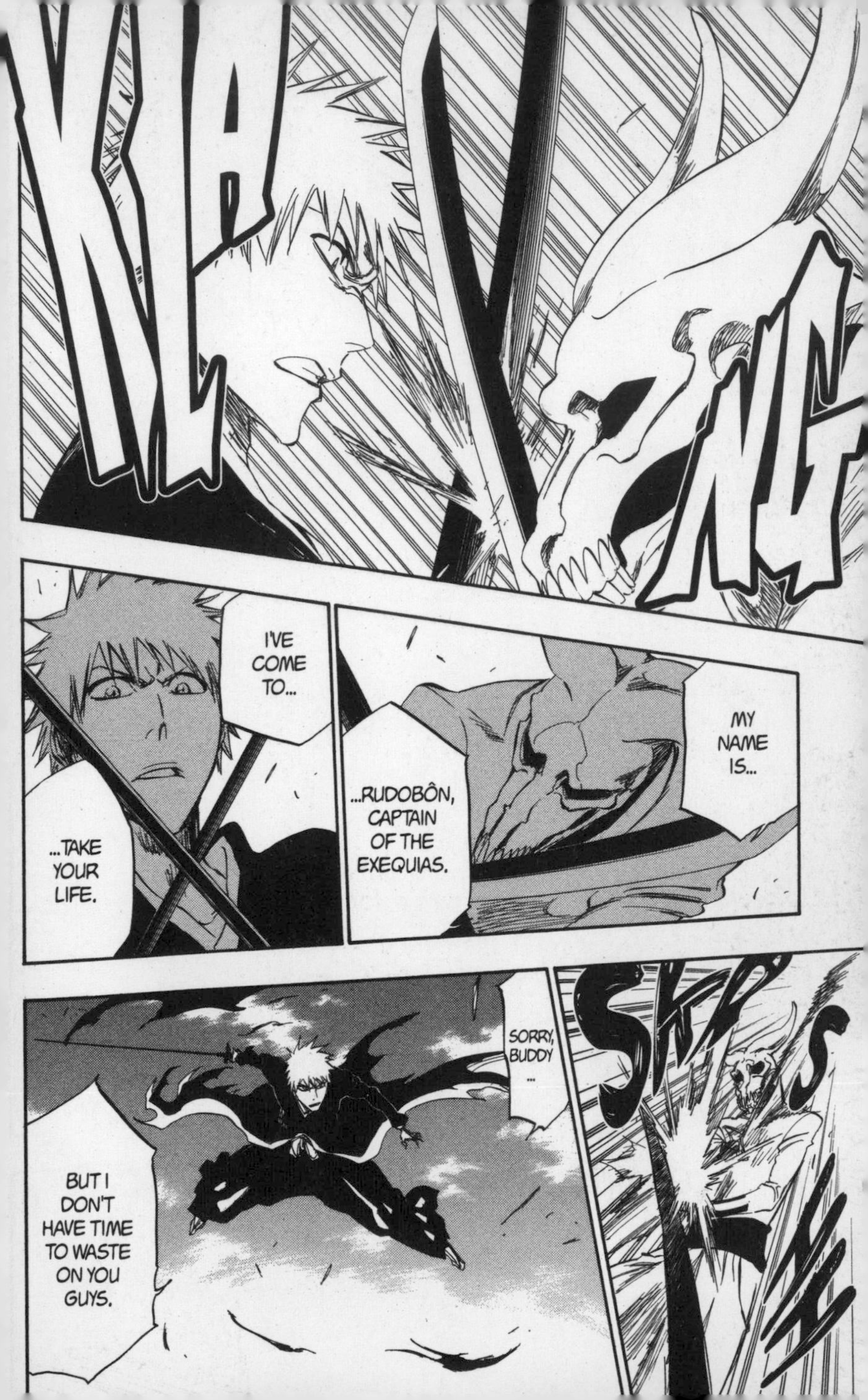
MY NAME IS...
...RUDOBÔN, CAPTAIN OF THE EXEQUIAS.
I'VE COME TO...
...TAKE YOUR LIFE.
SORRY, BUDDY...
BUT I DON'T HAVE TIME TO WASTE ON YOU GUYS.

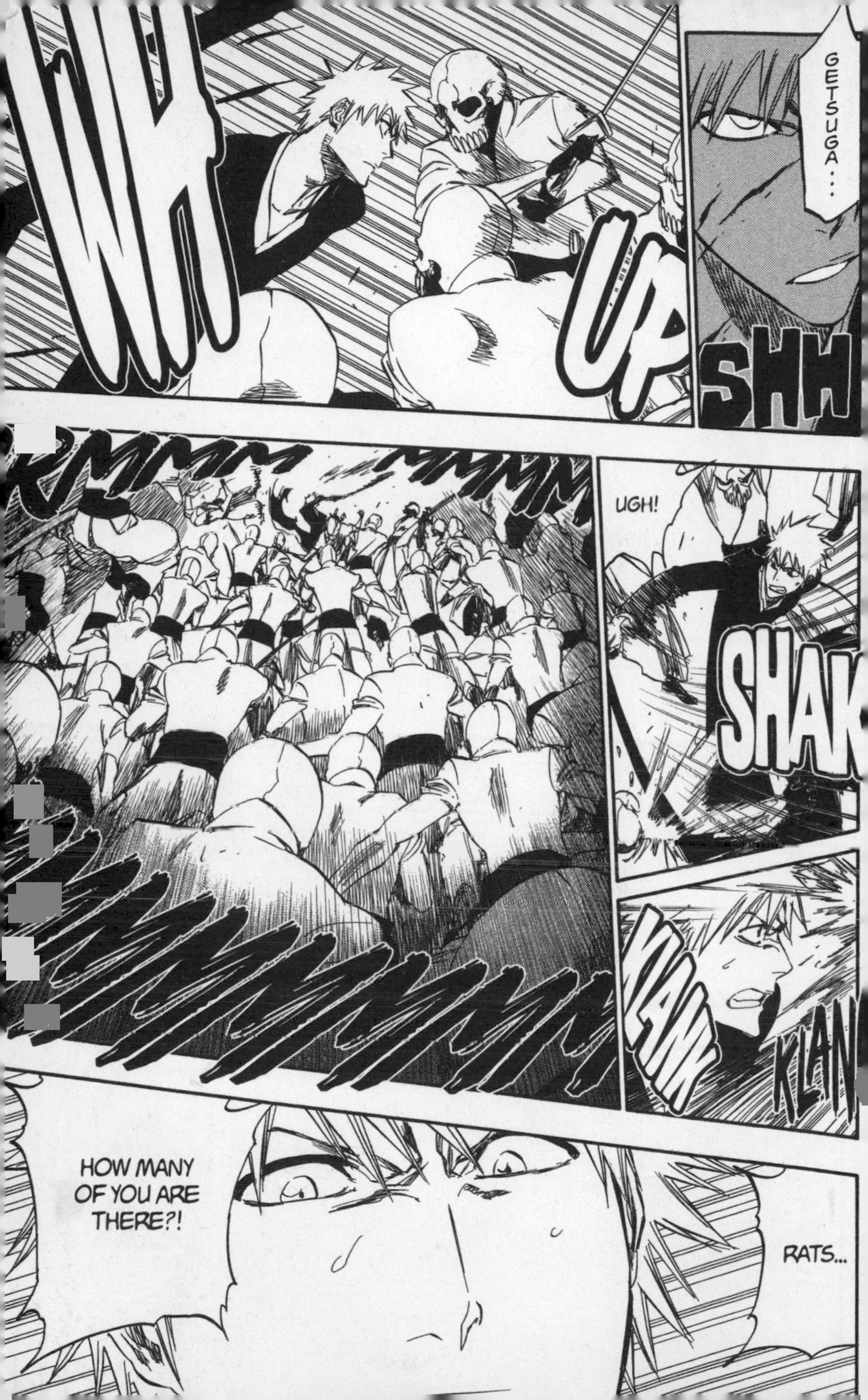
GETSUGA...
SHH
UP
WH
UGH!
SHAK
KLAN
KLANK
RATS...
HOW MANY OF YOU ARE THERE?!

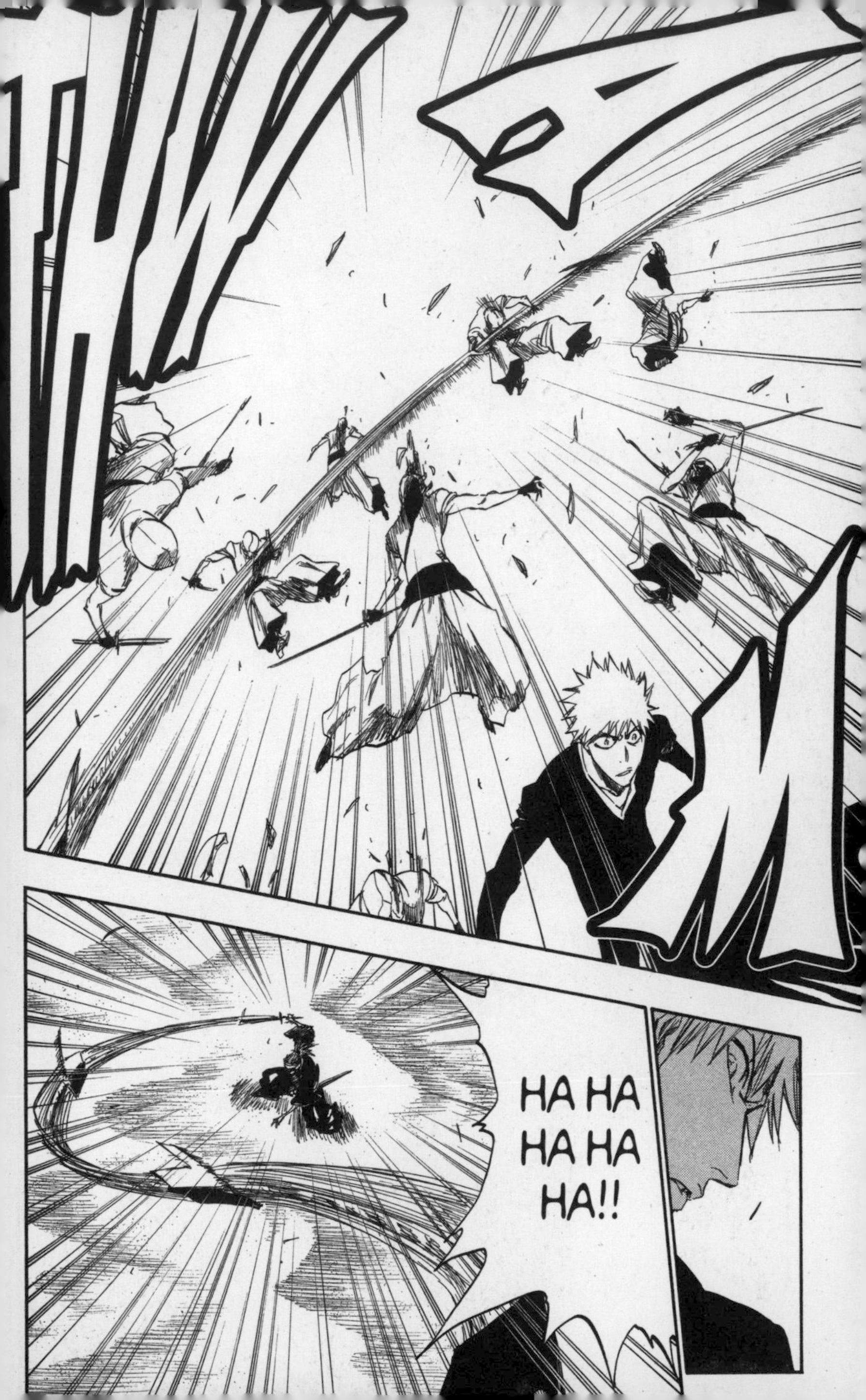
HA HA HA HA HA!!

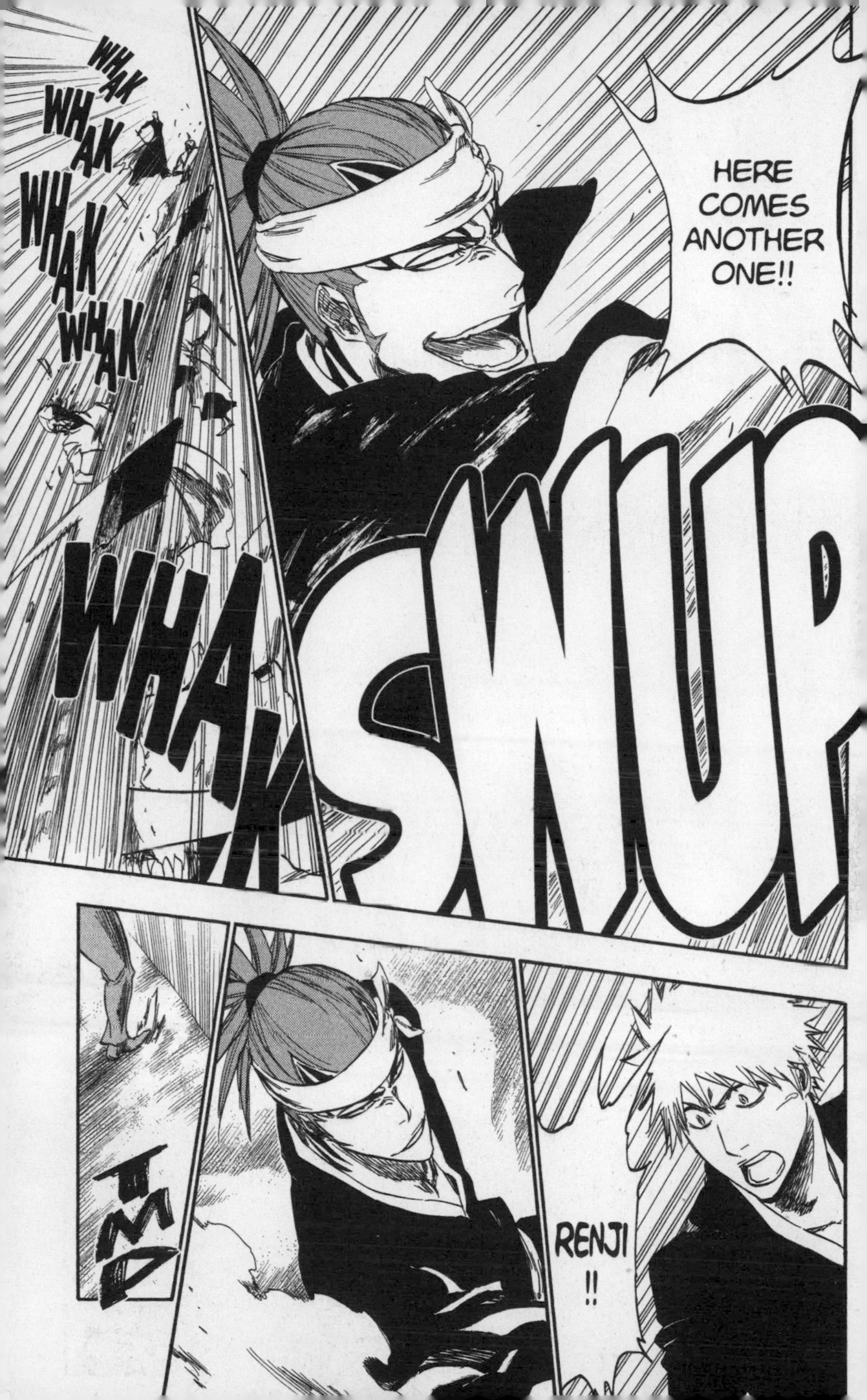
HERE COMES ANOTHER ONE!!
SNUP
WHAK WHAK WHAK WHAK
WHAK
RENJI!!

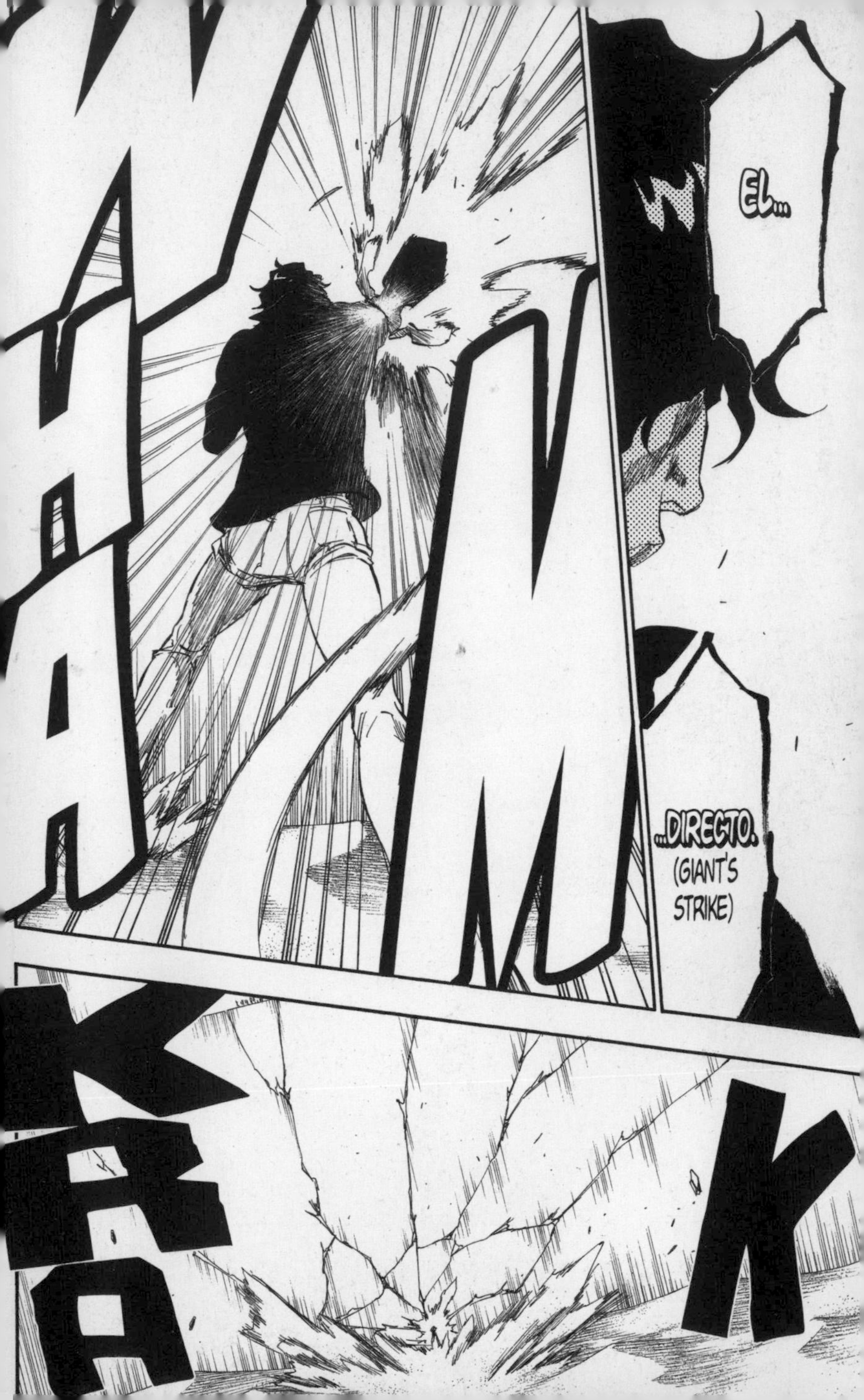
EL...
...DIRECTO.
(GIANT'S STRIKE)
WHAM
KRAK

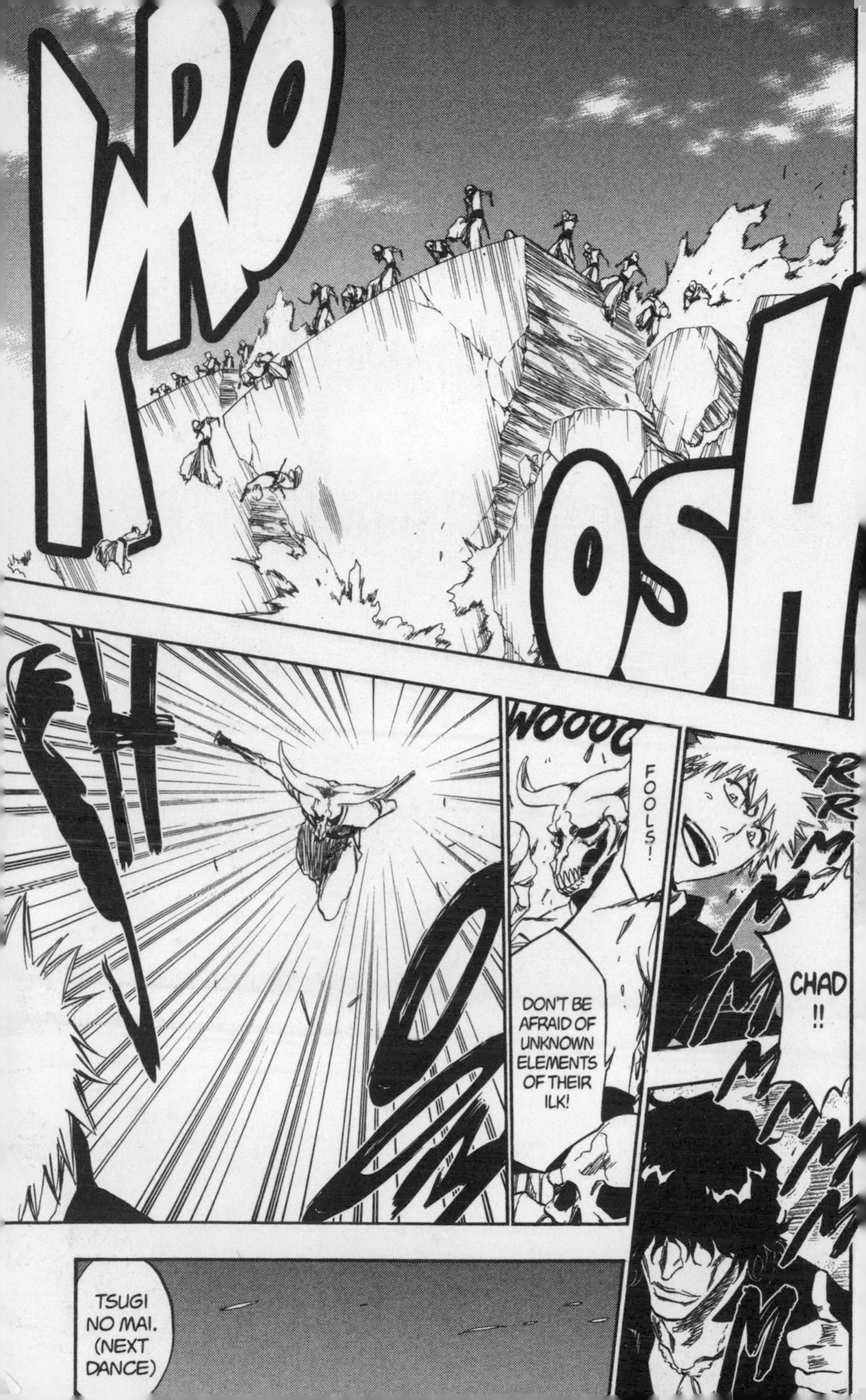
KRO
OSH
CHAD !!
RRMMMMMMMMMM
WOOOO
FOOLS!
DON'T BE AFRAID OF UNKNOWN ELEMENTS OF THEIR ILK!
TSUGI NO MAI. (NEXT DANCE)

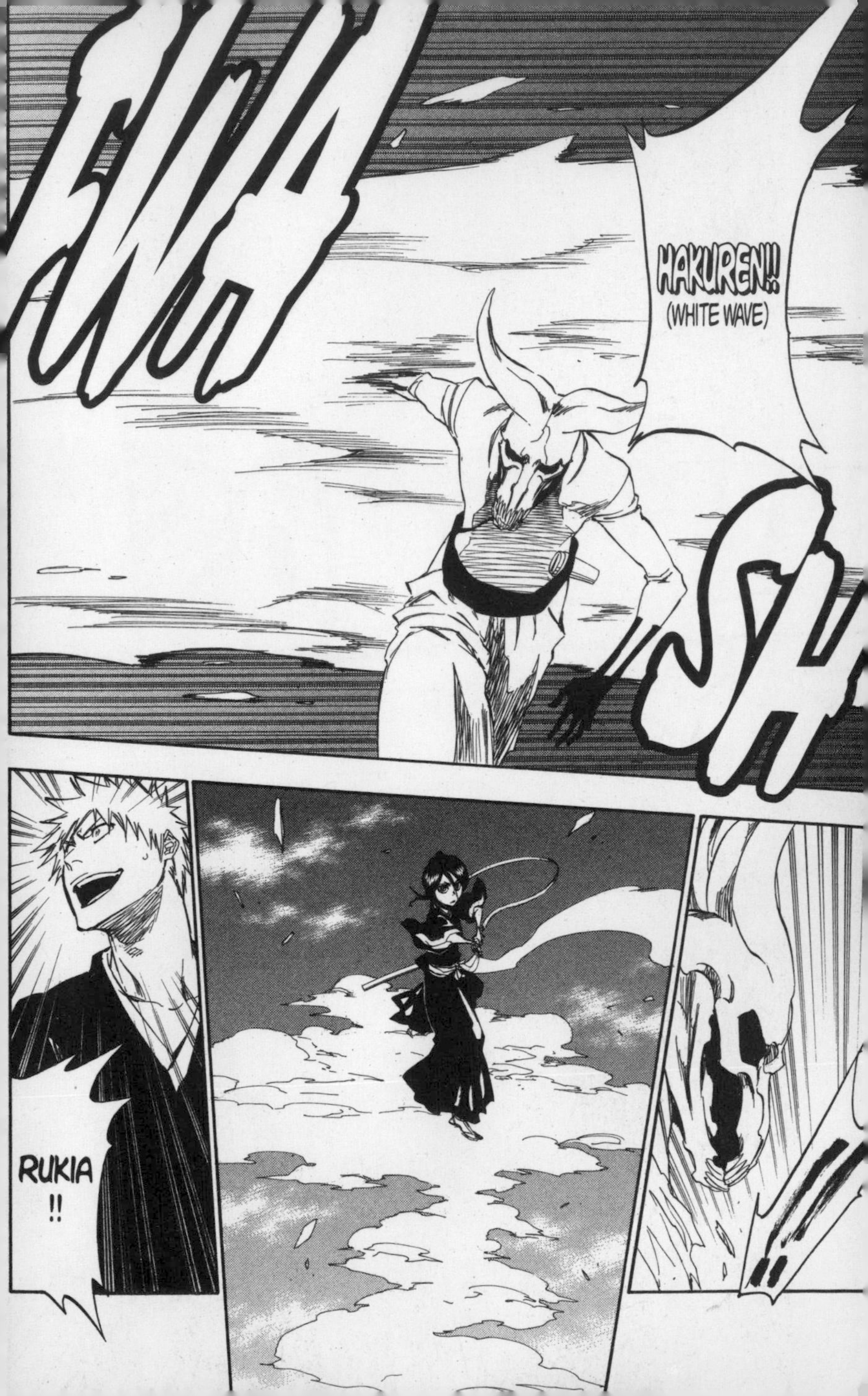

HAKUREN!!
(WHITE WAVE)
!!
RUKIA !!

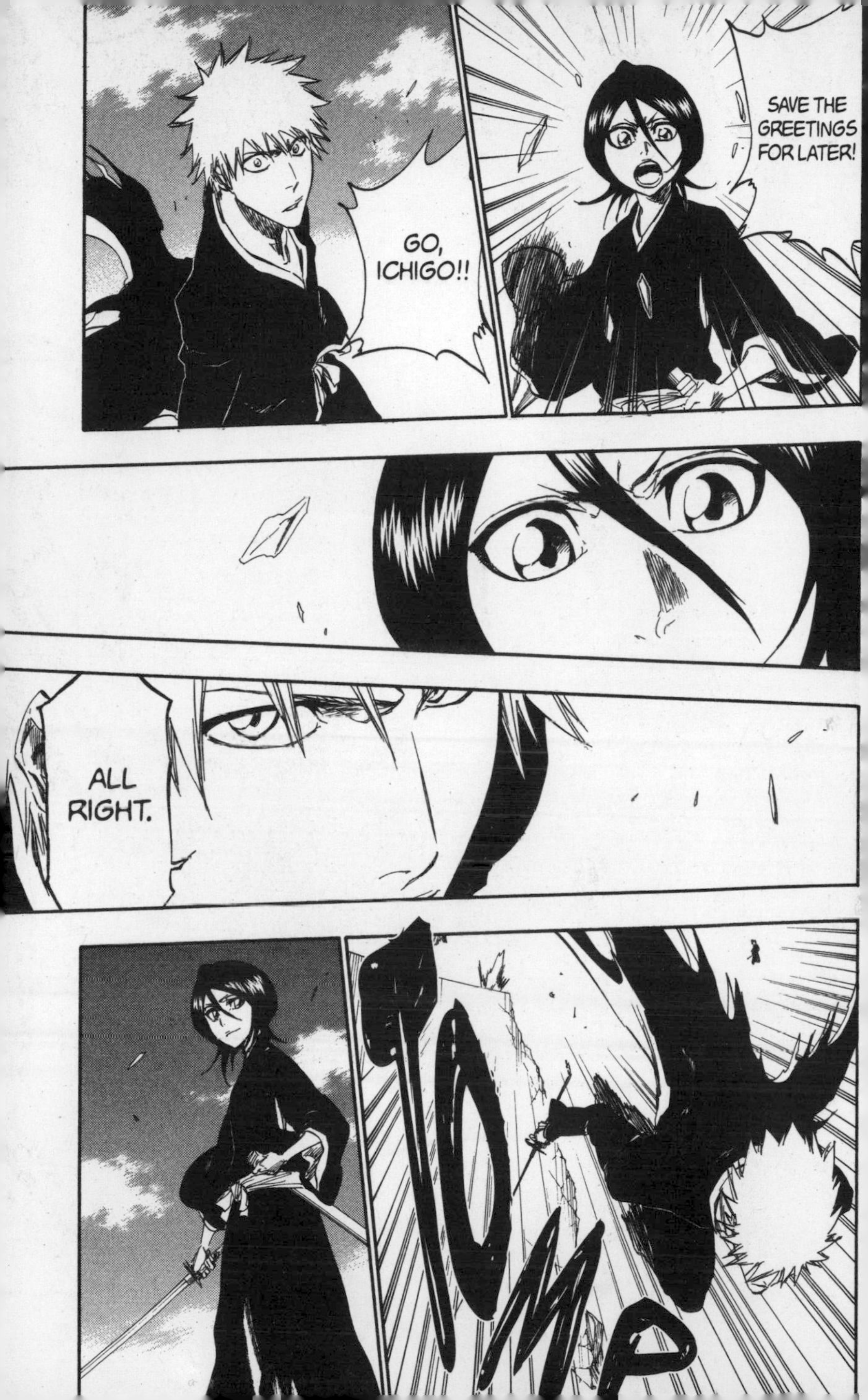

SAVE THE GREETINGS FOR LATER!
GO, ICHIGO!!
ALL RIGHT.
TOMP

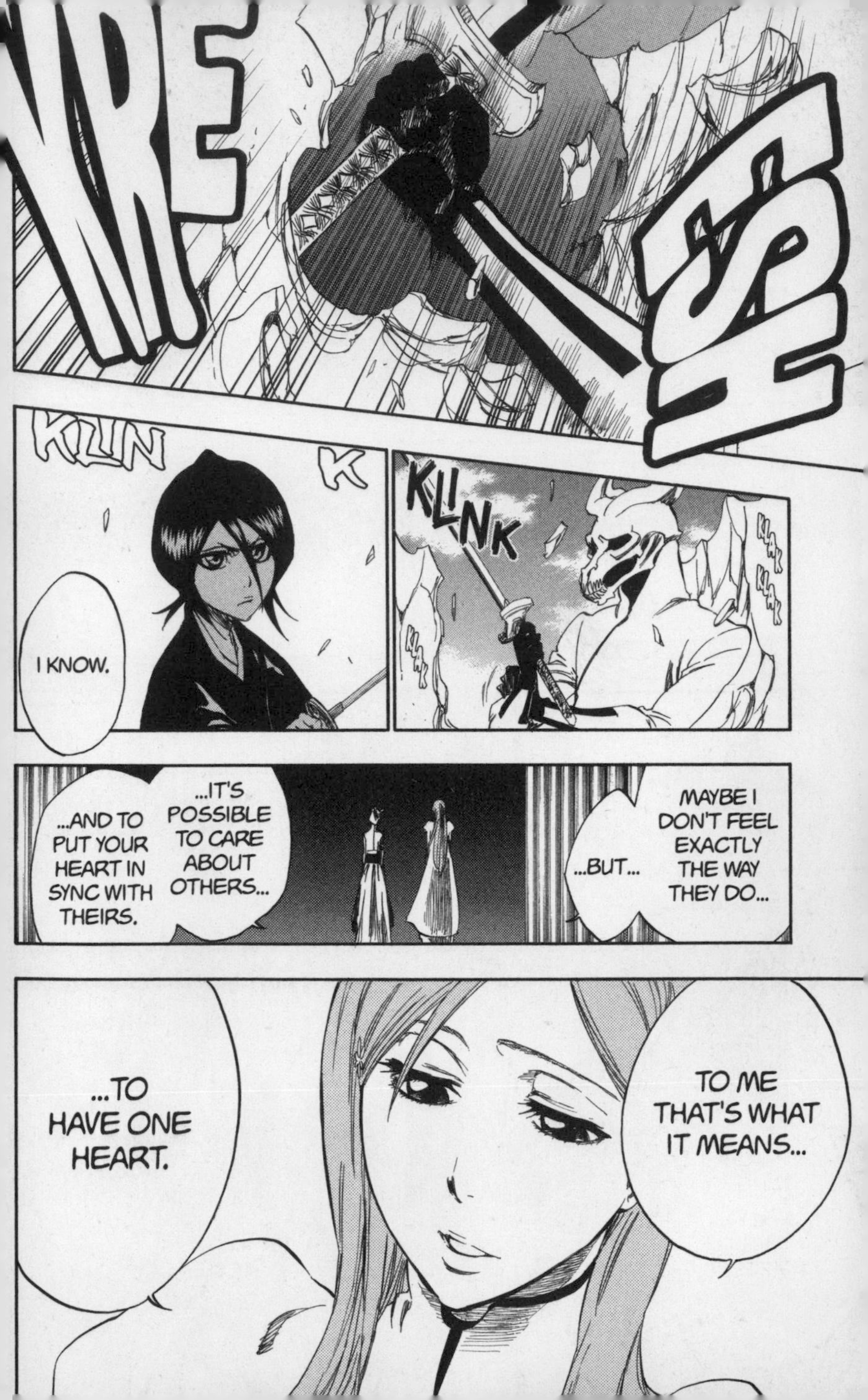
KLINK
KLAK KLAK
KLAK
KLIN K
I KNOW.
MAYBE I DON'T FEEL EXACTLY THE WAY THEY DO...
...BUT...
...IT'S POSSIBLE TO CARE ABOUT OTHERS...
...AND TO PUT YOUR HEART IN SYNC WITH THEIRS.
TO ME THAT'S WHAT IT MEANS...
...TO HAVE ONE HEART.

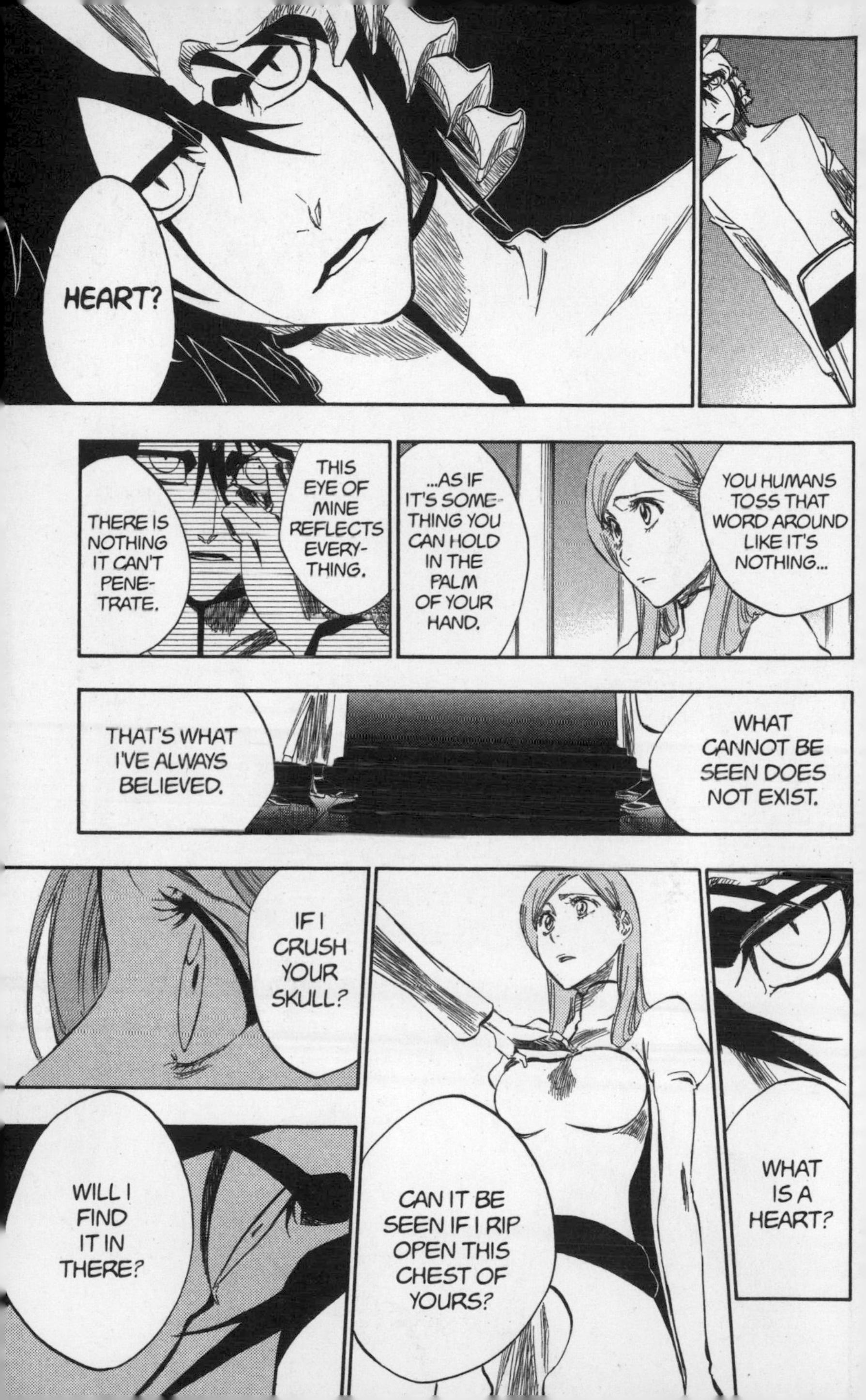
HEART?
YOU HUMANS TOSS THAT WORD AROUND LIKE IT'S NOTHING...
...AS IF IT'S SOMETHING YOU CAN HOLD IN THE PALM OF YOUR HAND.
THIS EYE OF MINE REFLECTS EVERYTHING.
THERE IS NOTHING IT CAN'T PENETRATE.
WHAT CANNOT BE SEEN DOES NOT EXIST.
THAT'S WHAT I'VE ALWAYS BELIEVED.
WHAT IS A HEART?
CAN IT BE SEEN IF I RIP OPEN THIS CHEST OF YOURS?
IF I CRUSH YOUR SKULL?
WILL I FIND IT IN THERE?

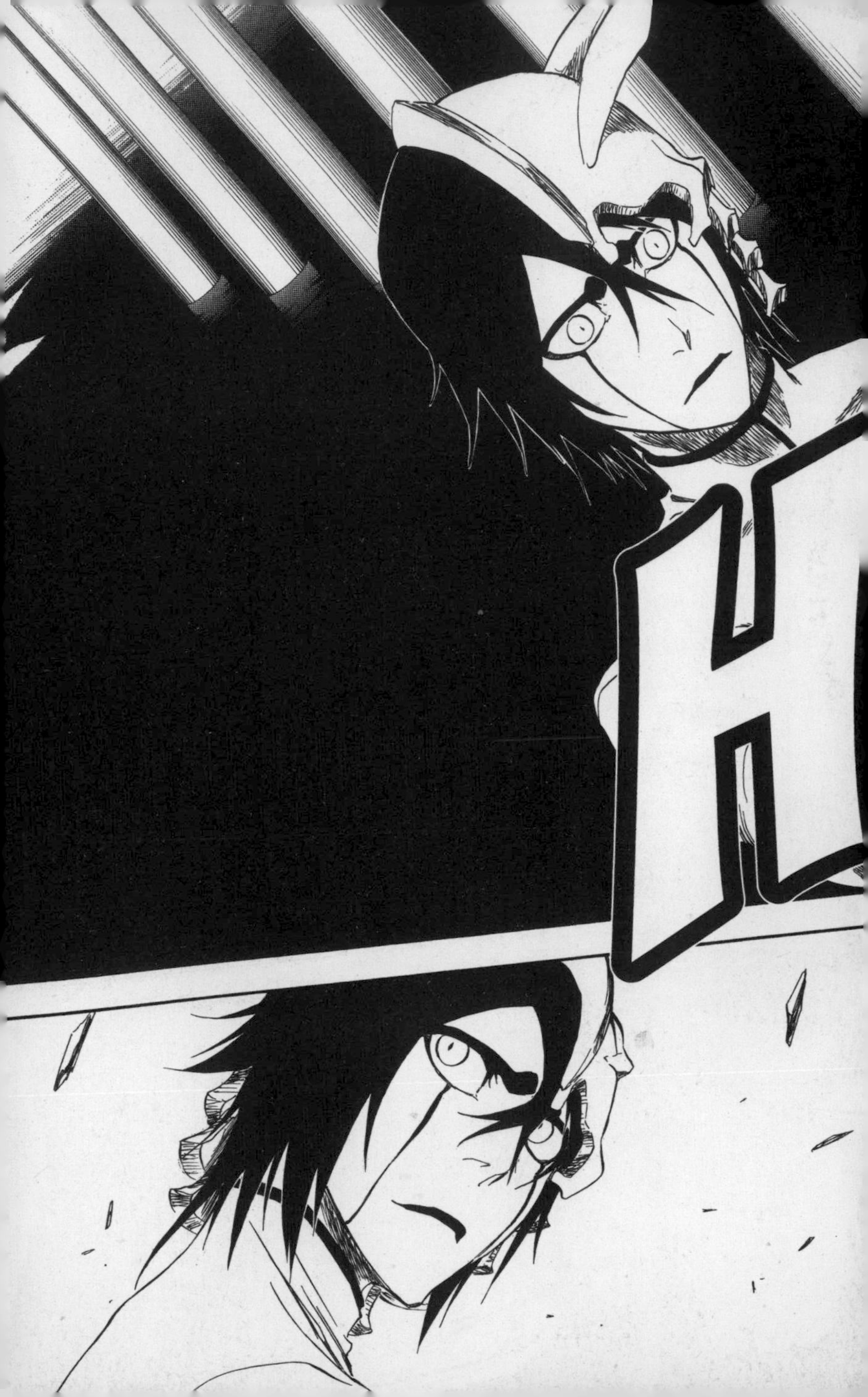
H

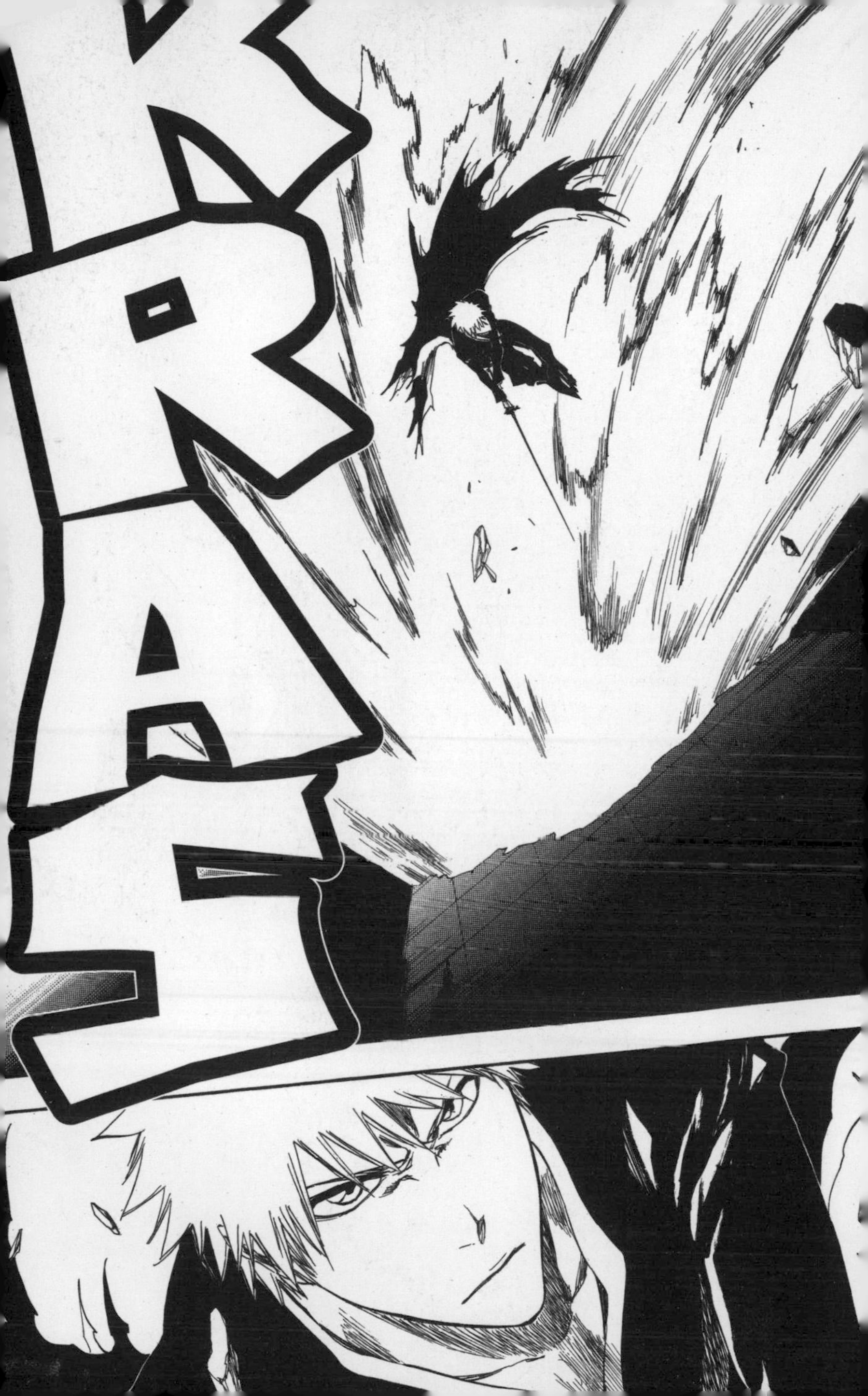

beating as one.

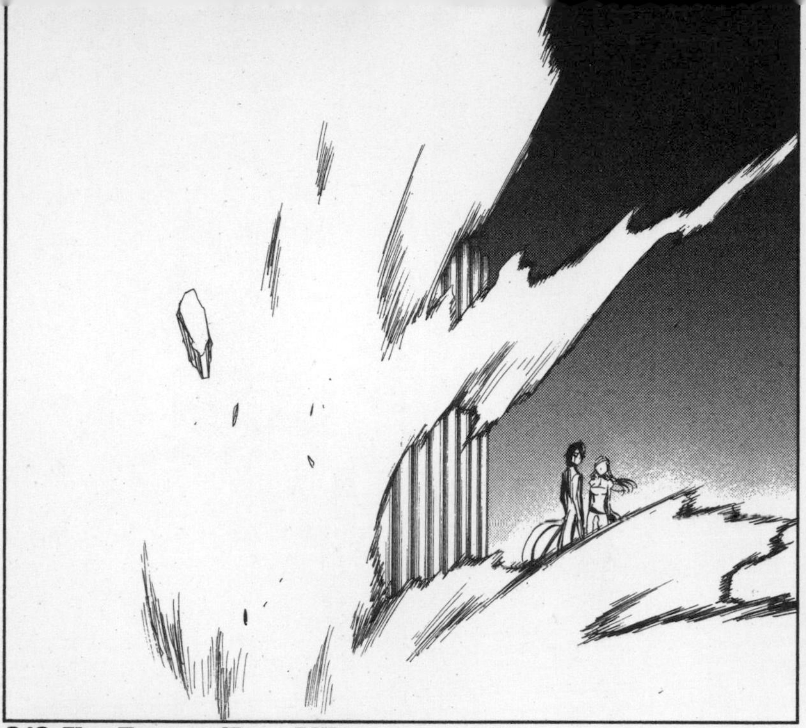

318. Five Towers/Four Pillars

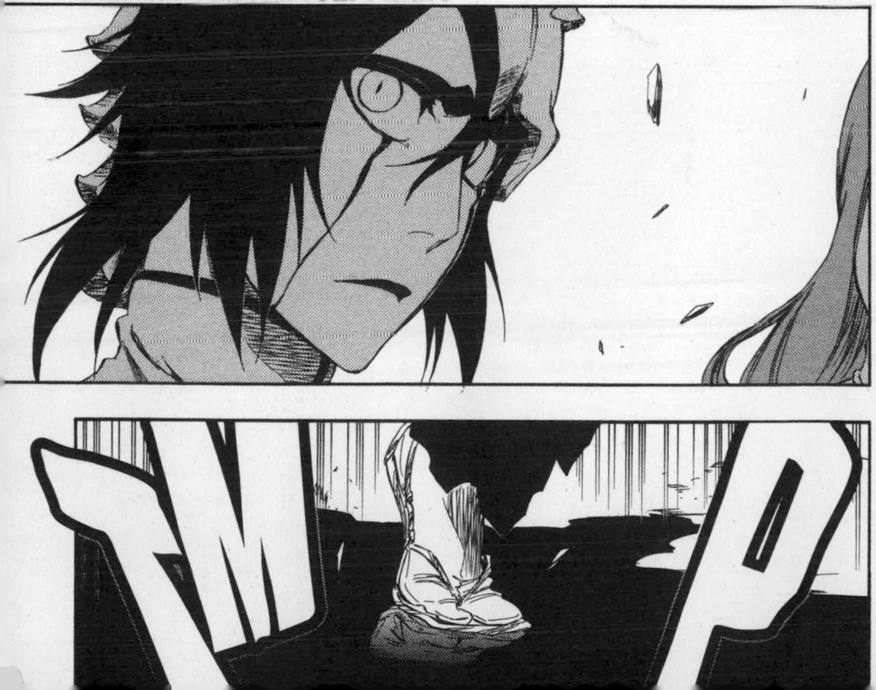

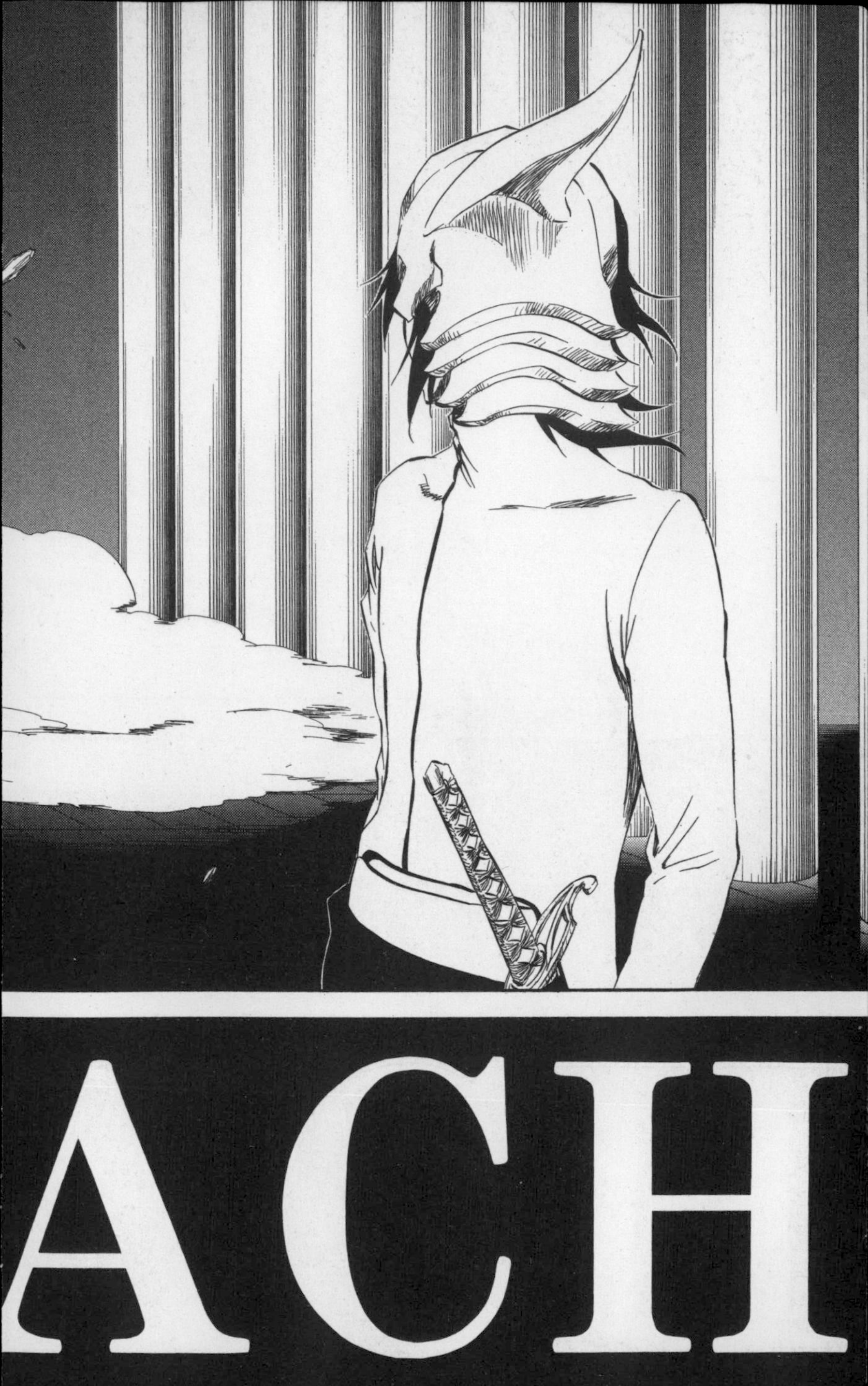
ACH

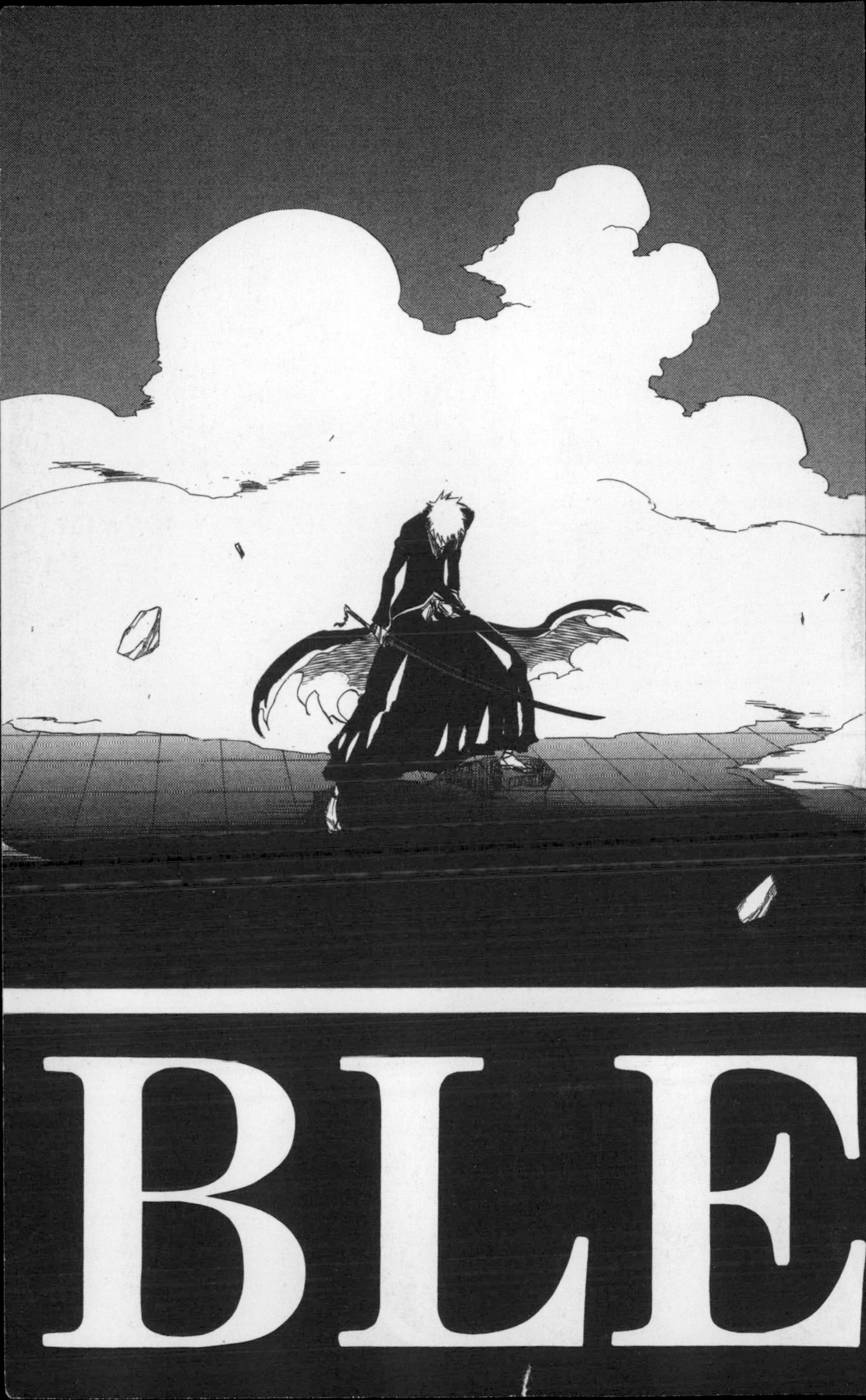
BLE

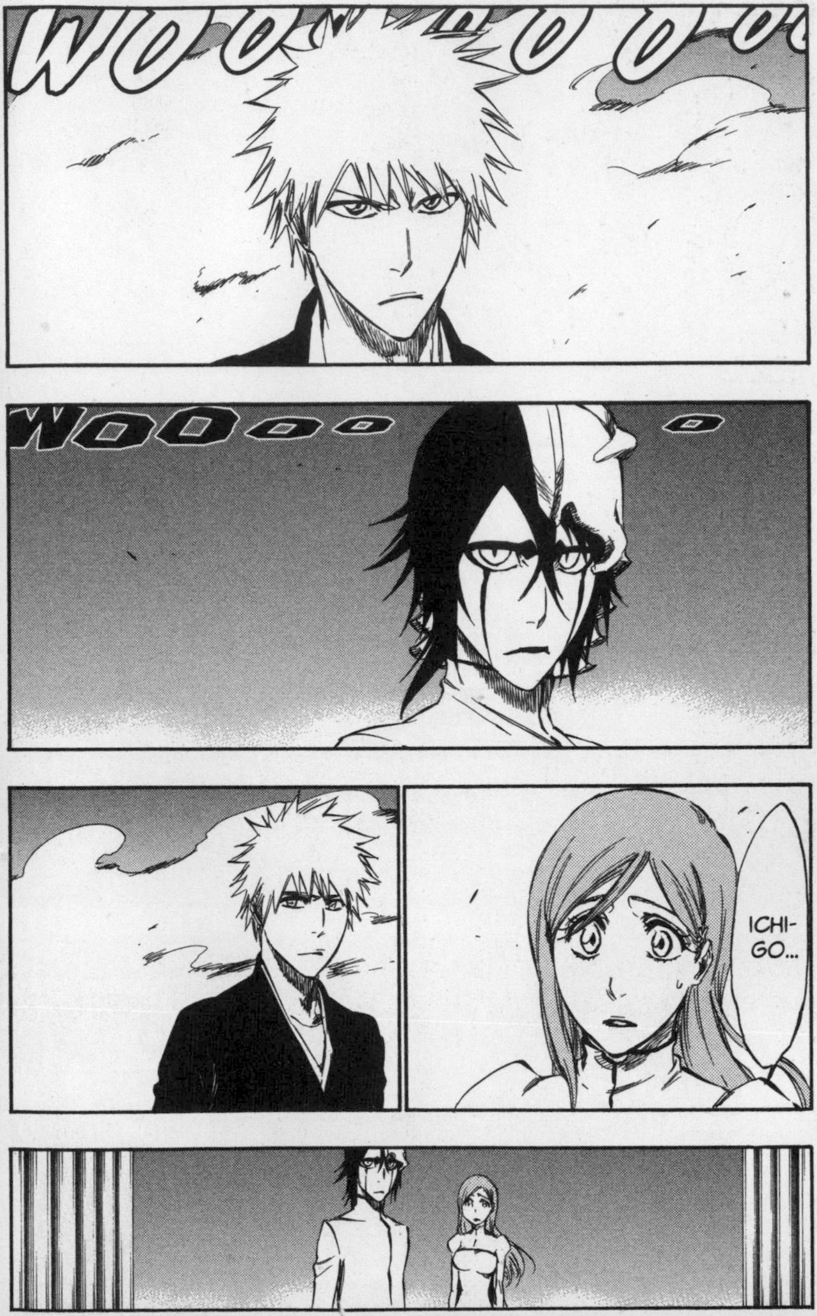
WOOOOOOOO
WOOOOO
ICHI-GO...

READ THIS WAY

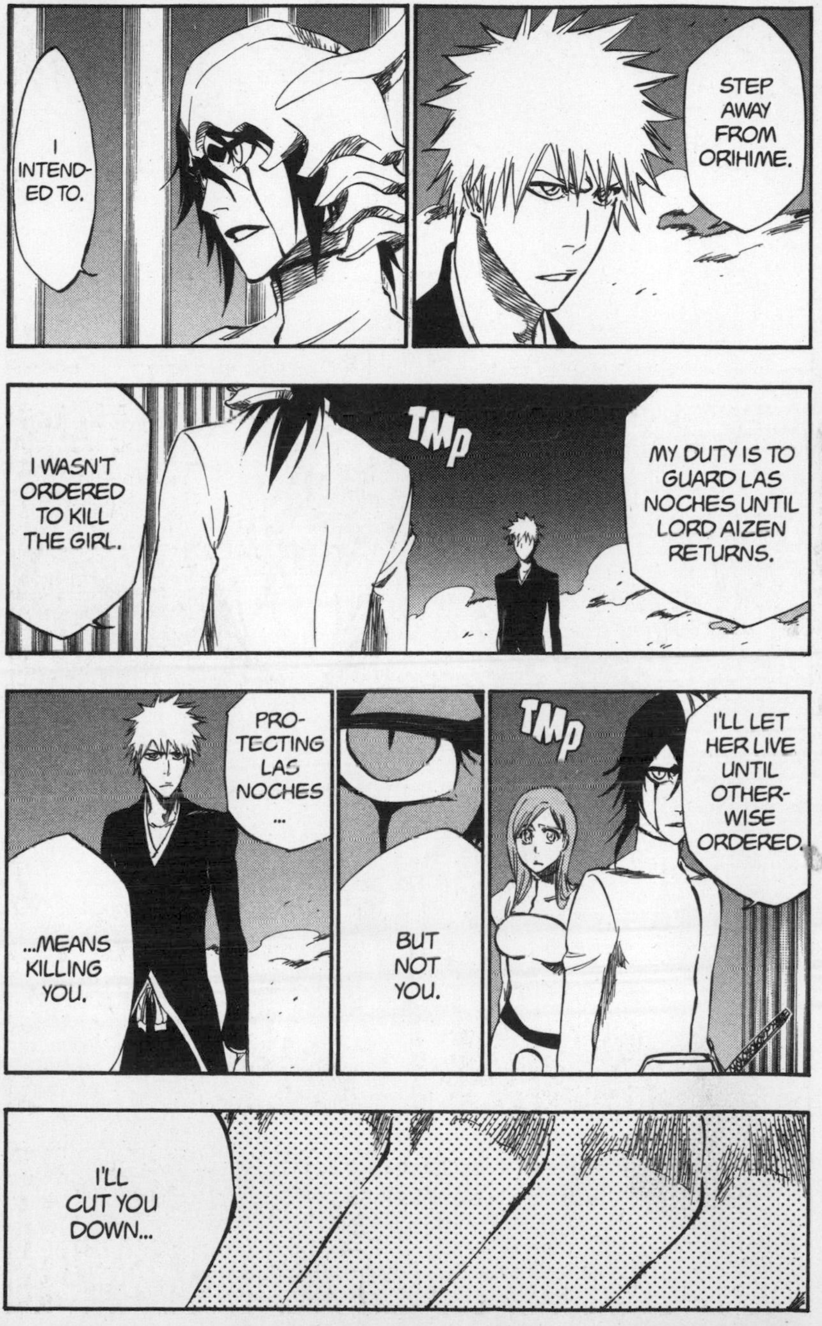
STEP AWAY FROM ORIHIME.
I INTEND-ED TO.
MY DUTY IS TO GUARD LAS NOCHES UNTIL LORD AIZEN RETURNS.
TMP
I WASN'T ORDERED TO KILL THE GIRL.
TMP
I'LL LET HER LIVE UNTIL OTHER-WISE ORDERED.
BUT NOT YOU.
PRO-TECTING LAS NOCHES ...
...MEANS KILLING YOU.
I'LL CUT YOU DOWN...

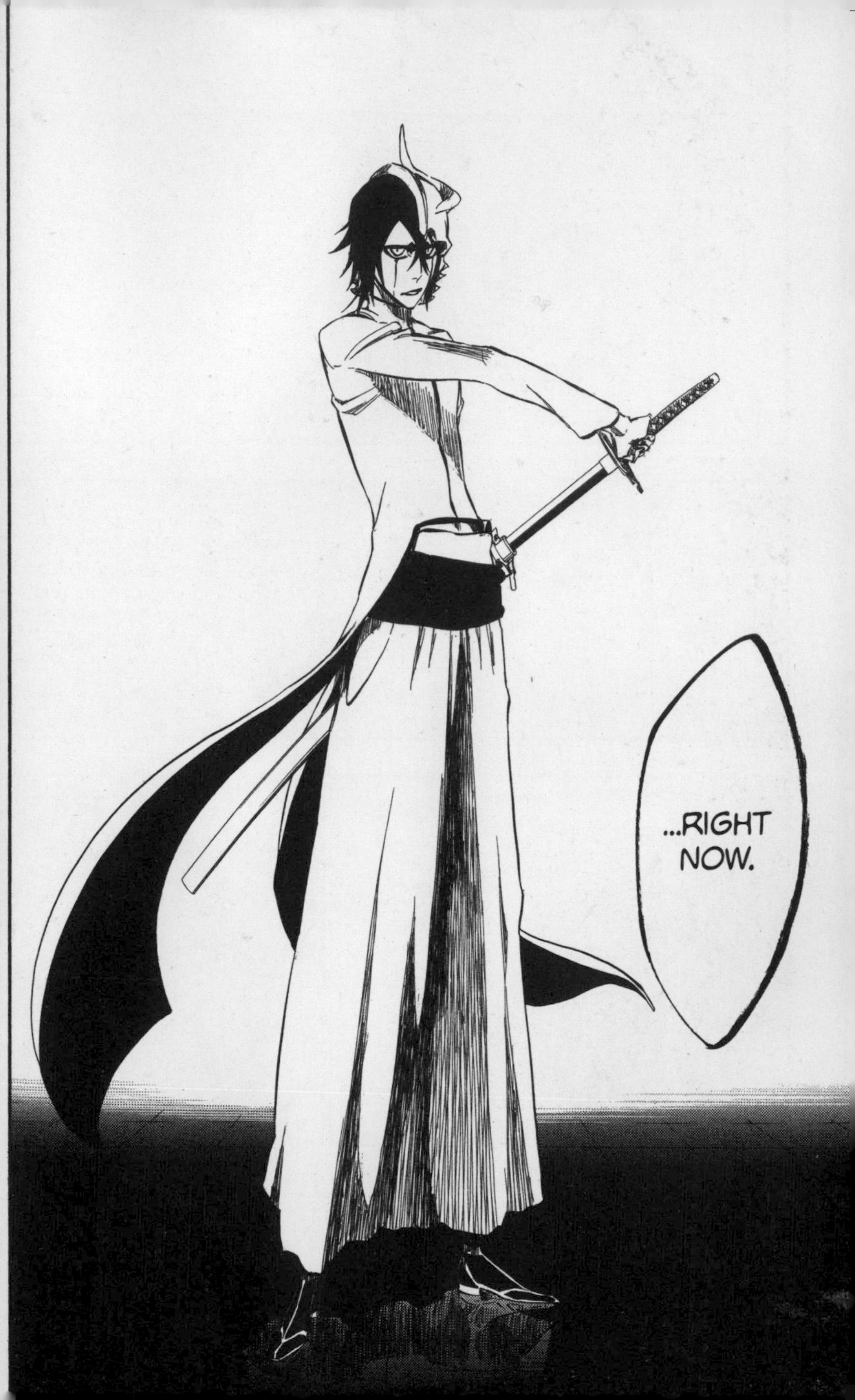
...RIGHT NOW.

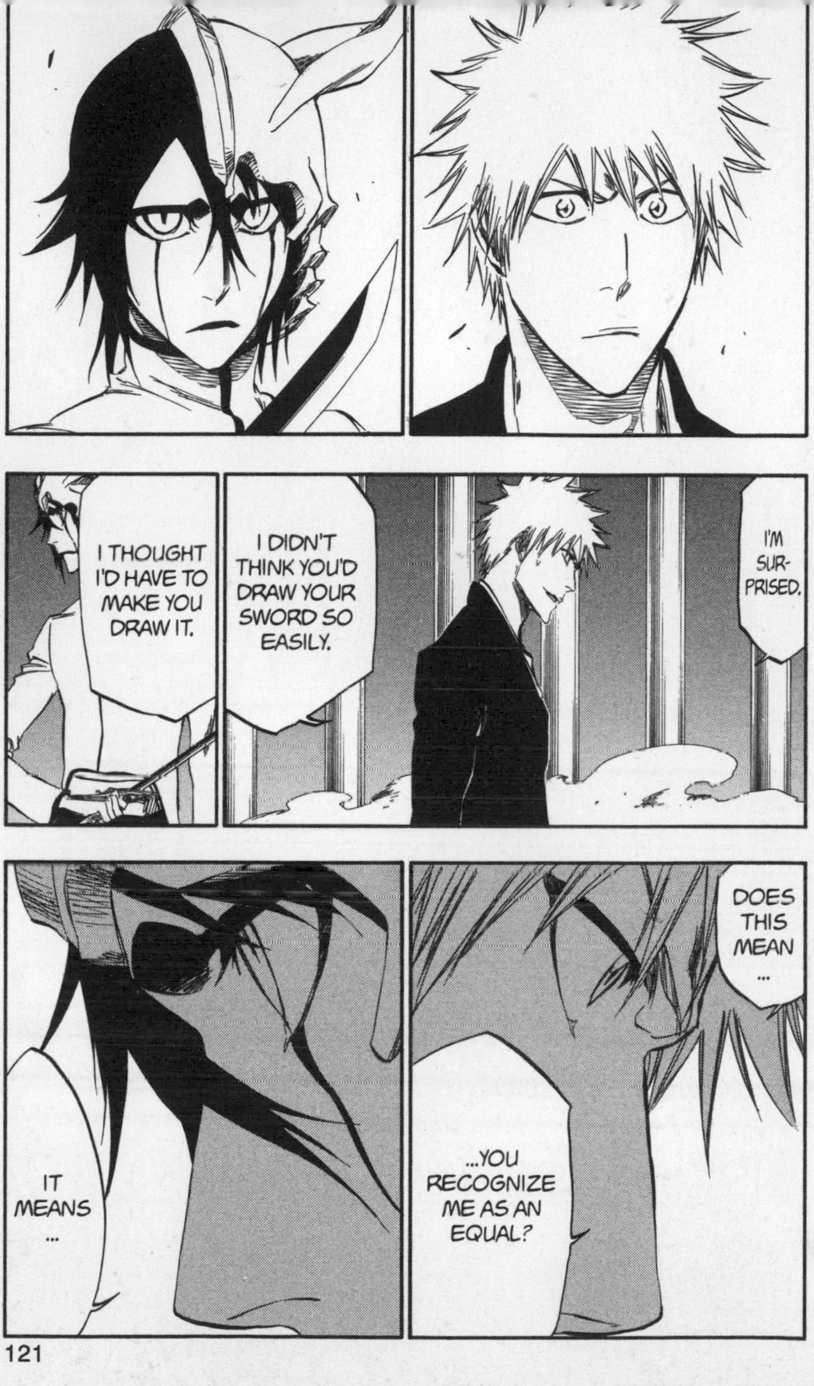
I'M SURPRISED.
I DIDN'T THINK YOU'D DRAW YOUR SWORD SO EASILY.
I THOUGHT I'D HAVE TO MAKE YOU DRAW IT.
DOES THIS MEAN ...
...YOU RECOGNIZE ME AS AN EQUAL?
IT MEANS ...

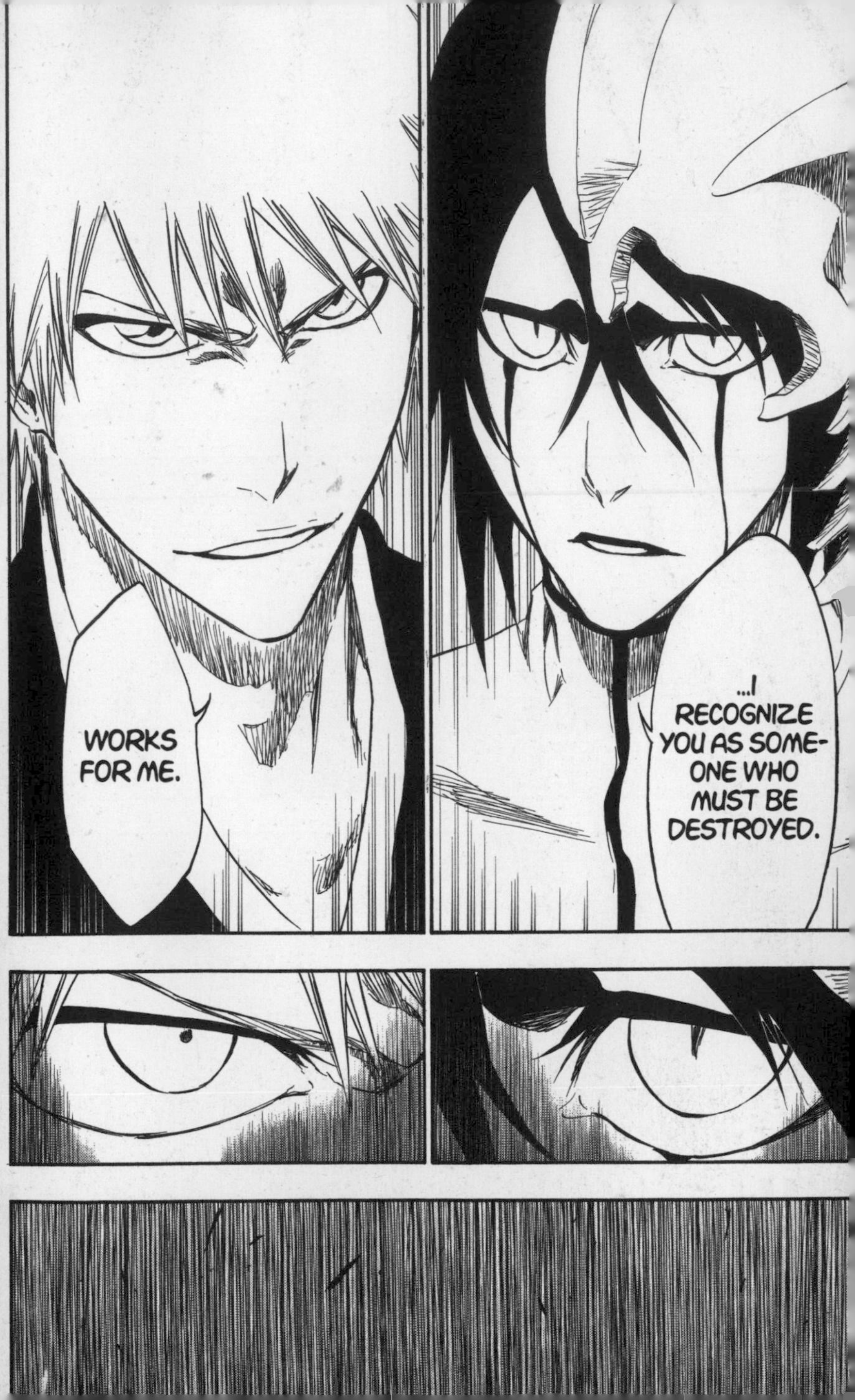
...I RECOGNIZE YOU AS SOME-ONE WHO MUST BE DESTROYED.
WORKS FOR ME.

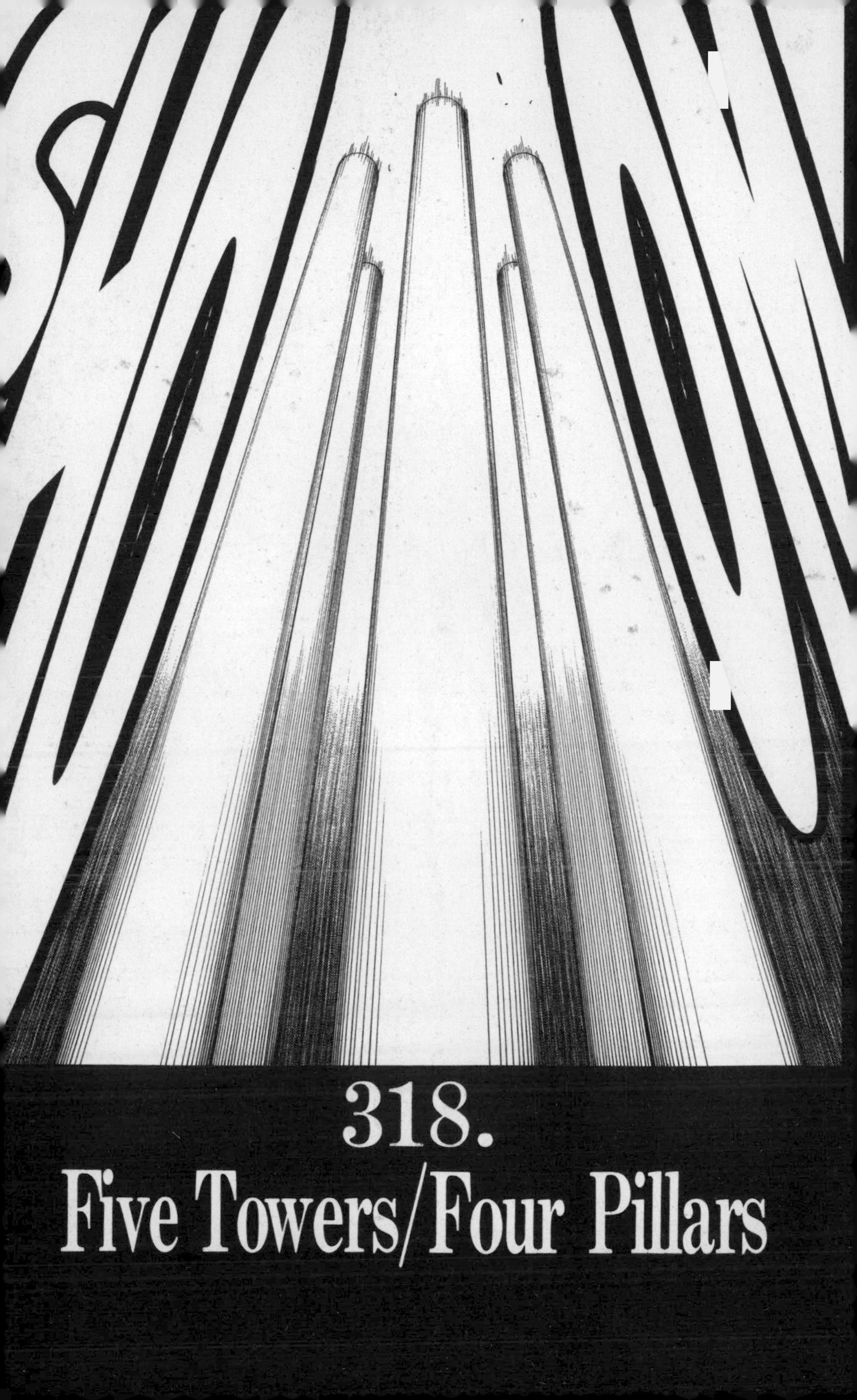

318.
Five Towers/Four Pillars

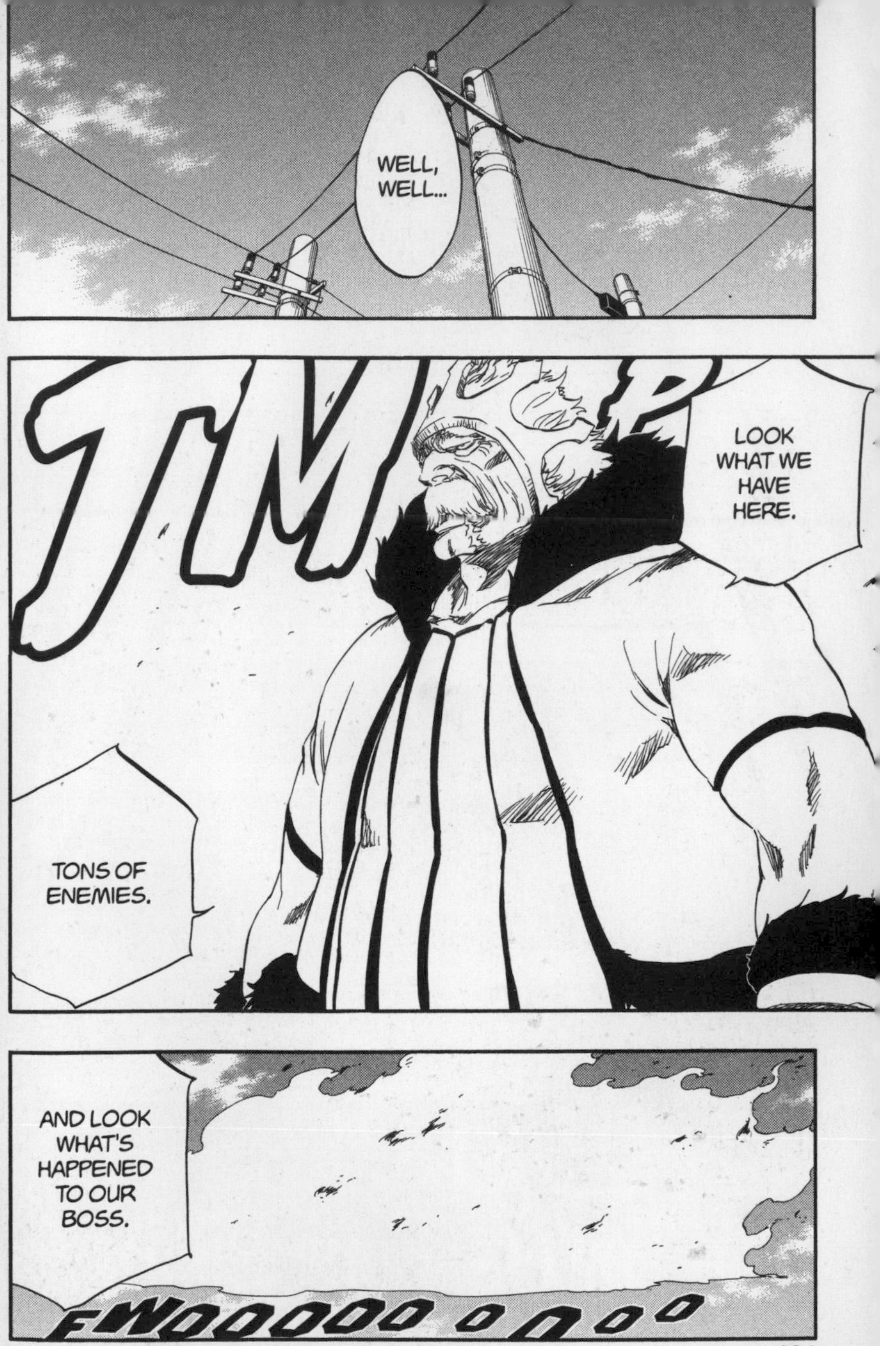
WELL, WELL...
TMP
LOOK WHAT WE HAVE HERE.
TONS OF ENEMIES.
AND LOOK WHAT'S HAPPENED TO OUR BOSS.
FWOOOOOOOOO

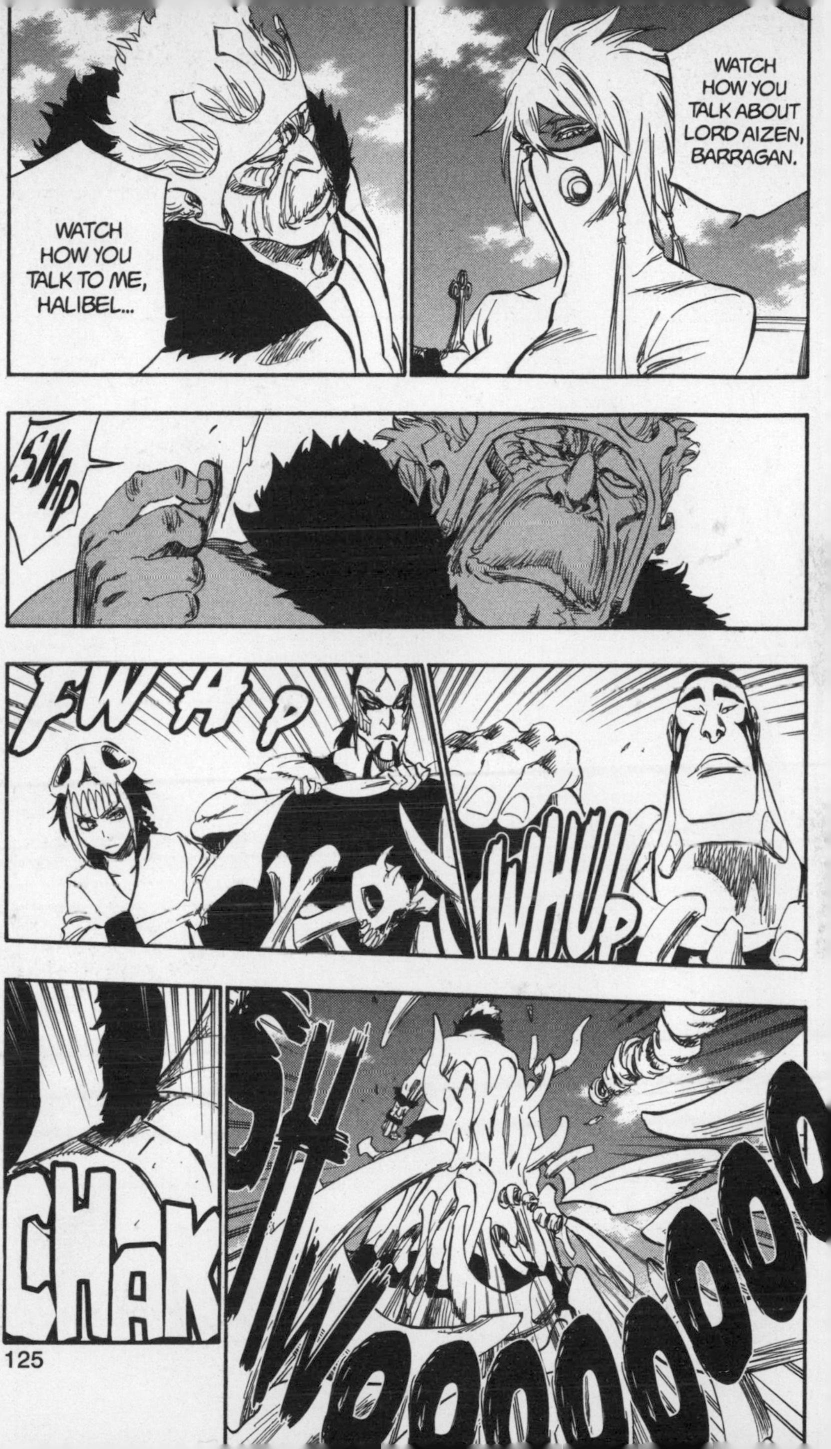
WATCH HOW YOU TALK ABOUT LORD AIZEN, BARRAGAN.
WATCH HOW YOU TALK TO ME, HALIBEL...
SNAP
WHUP
FWAP
WOOOOOOOOO
CHAK

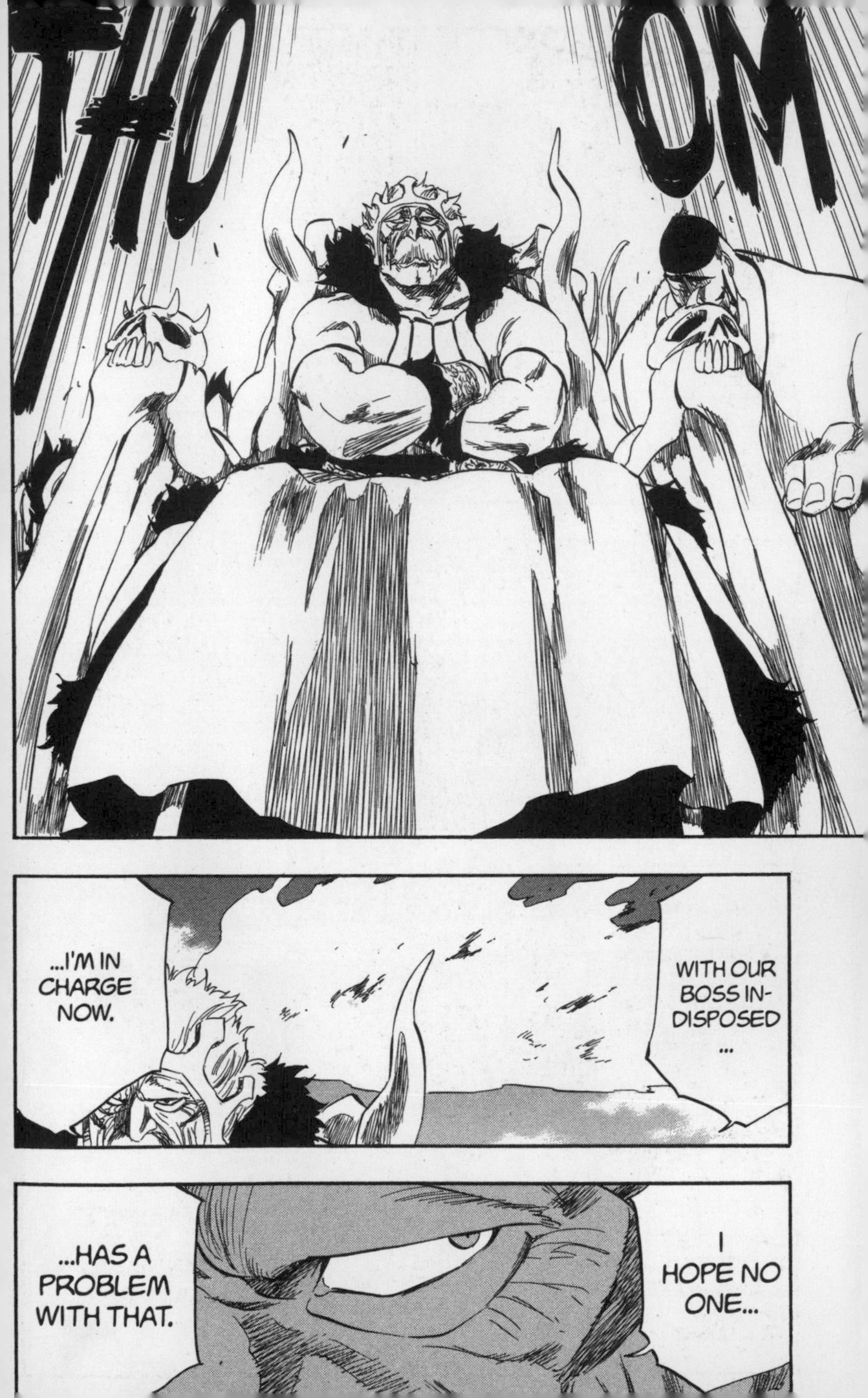
THOOM
WITH OUR BOSS IN-DISPOSED ...
...I'M IN CHARGE NOW.
I HOPE NO ONE...
...HAS A PROBLEM WITH THAT.

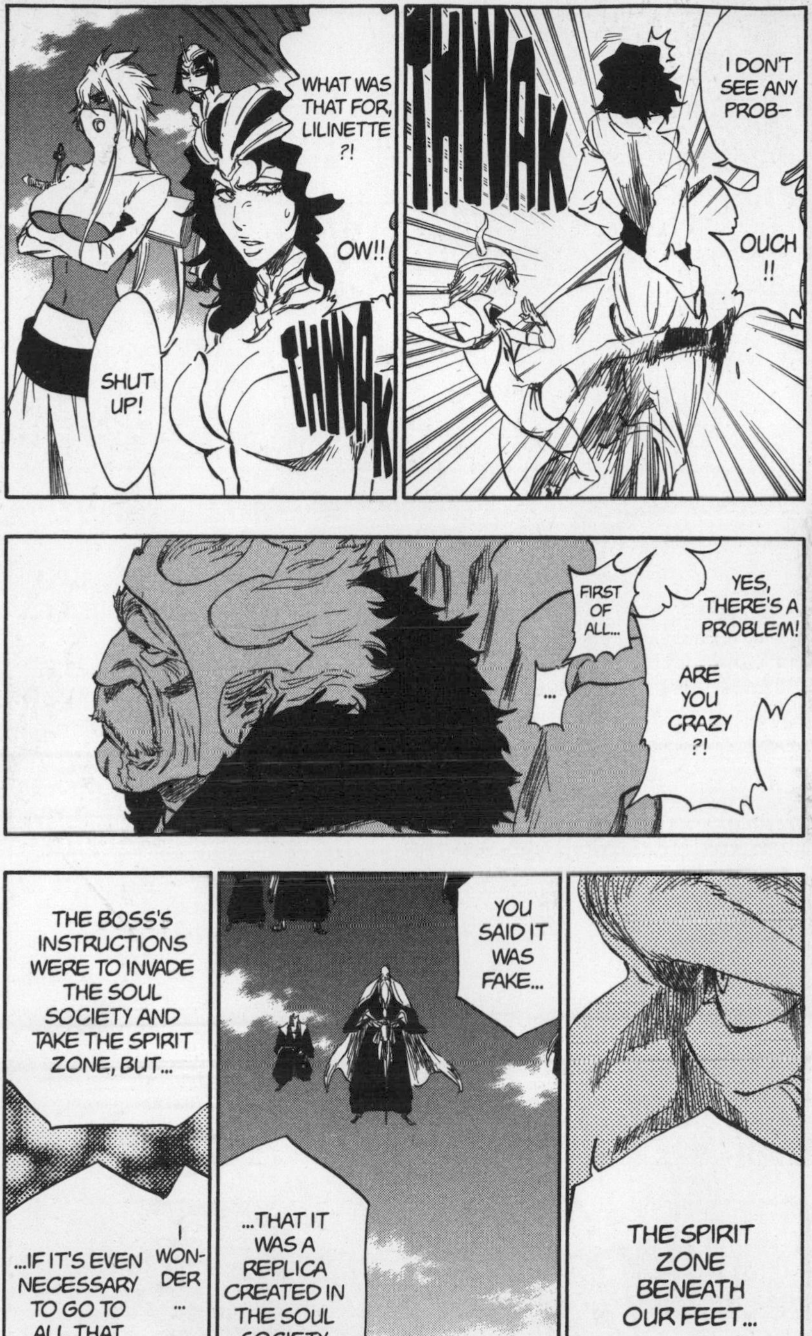
I DON'T SEE ANY PROB—
THWAK
OUCH!!
WHAT WAS THAT FOR, LILINETTE?!
OW!!
THWAK
SHUT UP!
YES, THERE'S A PROBLEM!
ARE YOU CRAZY?!
FIRST OF ALL...
...
THE SPIRIT ZONE BENEATH OUR FEET...
YOU SAID IT WAS FAKE...
...THAT IT WAS A REPLICA CREATED IN THE SOUL SOCIETY.
THE BOSS'S INSTRUCTIONS WERE TO INVADE THE SOUL SOCIETY AND TAKE THE SPIRIT ZONE, BUT...
I WONDER...
...IF IT'S EVEN NECESSARY TO GO TO ALL THAT TROUBLE?

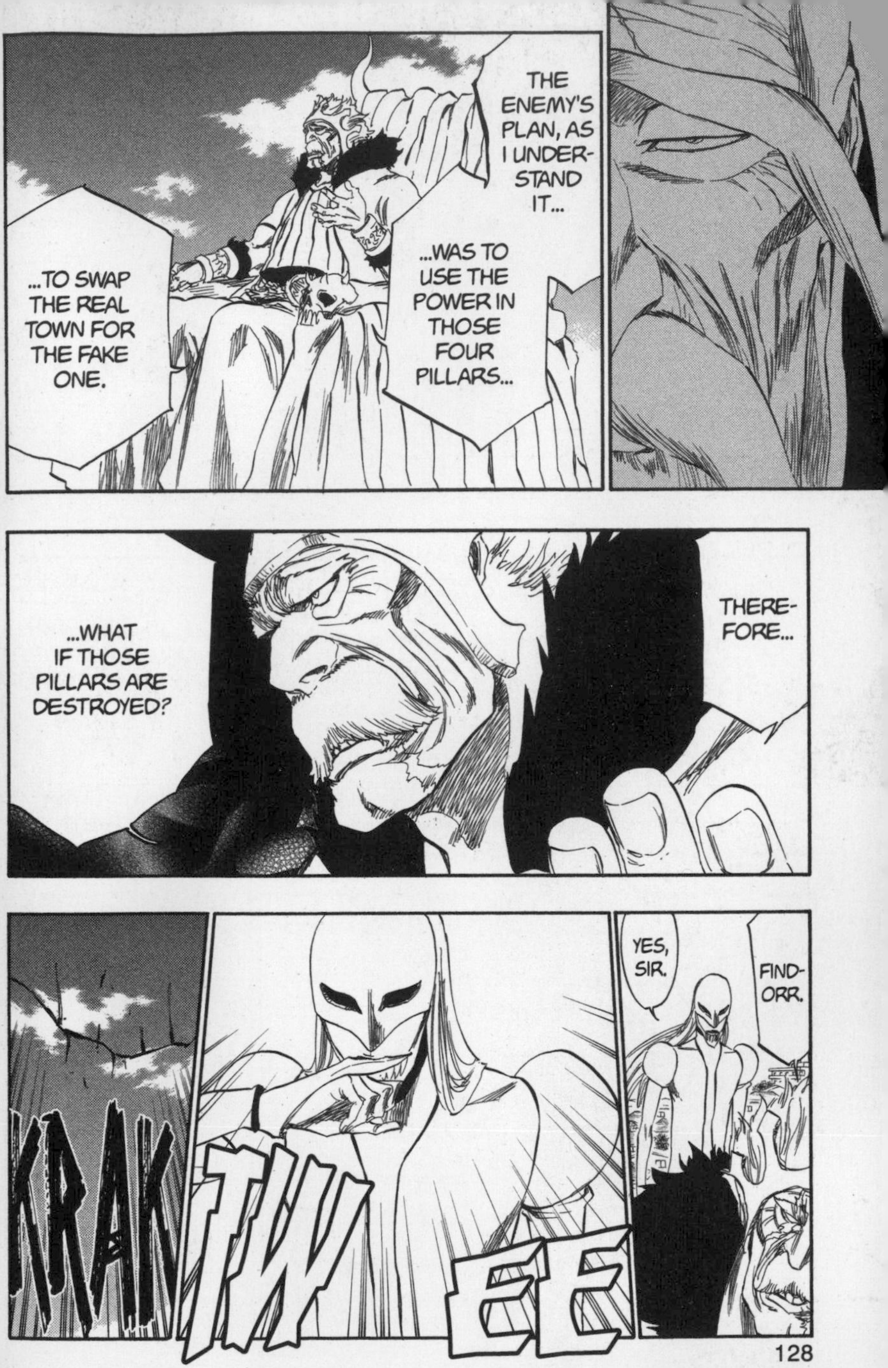
THE ENEMY'S PLAN, AS I UNDER-STAND IT...
...WAS TO USE THE POWER IN THOSE FOUR PILLARS...
...TO SWAP THE REAL TOWN FOR THE FAKE ONE.
THERE-FORE...
...WHAT IF THOSE PILLARS ARE DESTROYED?
FIND-ORR.
YES, SIR.
TWEE
KRAK

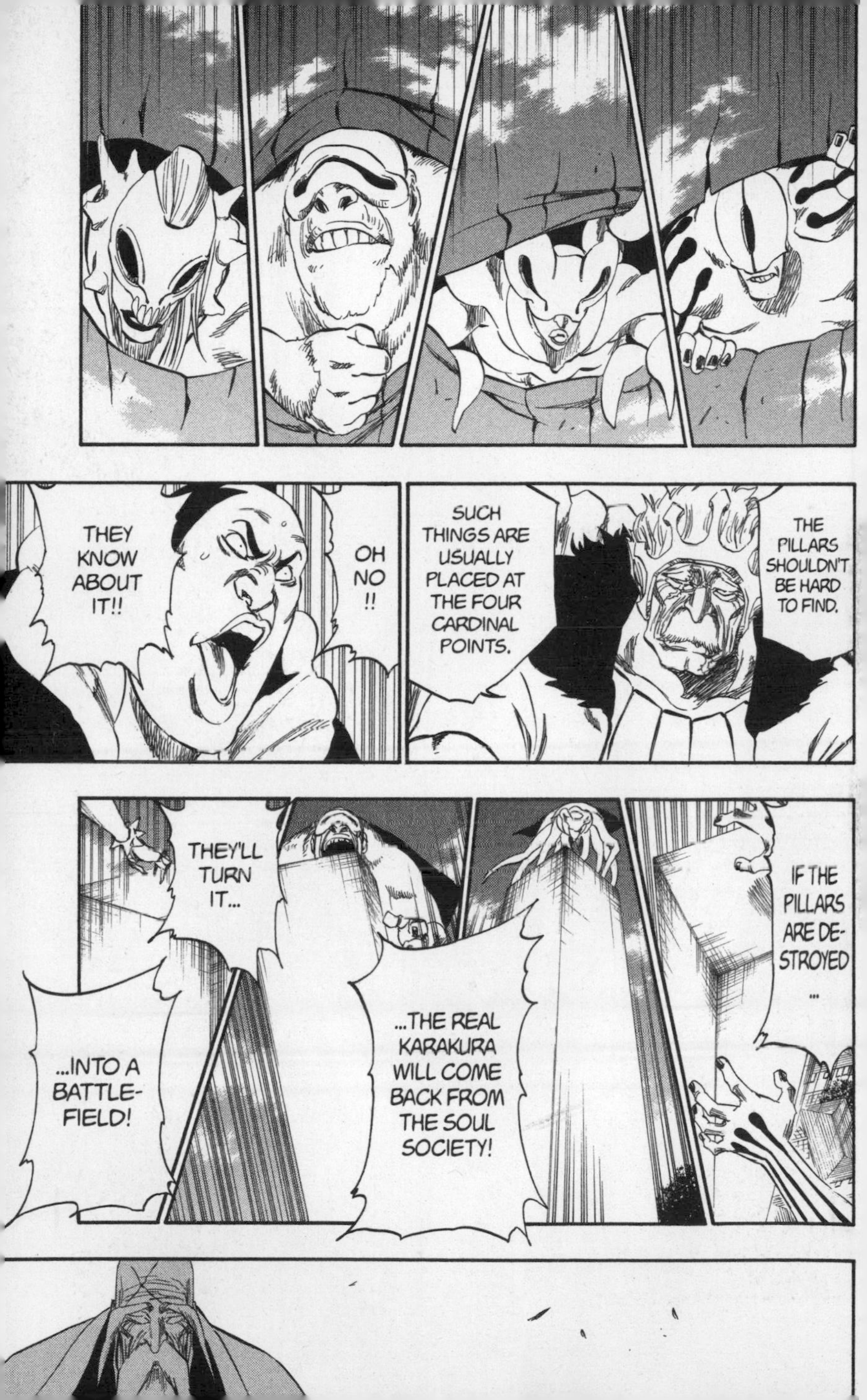
THE PILLARS SHOULDN'T BE HARD TO FIND.
SUCH THINGS ARE USUALLY PLACED AT THE FOUR CARDINAL POINTS.
OH NO!!
THEY KNOW ABOUT IT!!
IF THE PILLARS ARE DESTROYED...
...THE REAL KARAKURA WILL COME BACK FROM THE SOUL SOCIETY!
THEY'LL TURN IT...
...INTO A BATTLEFIELD!

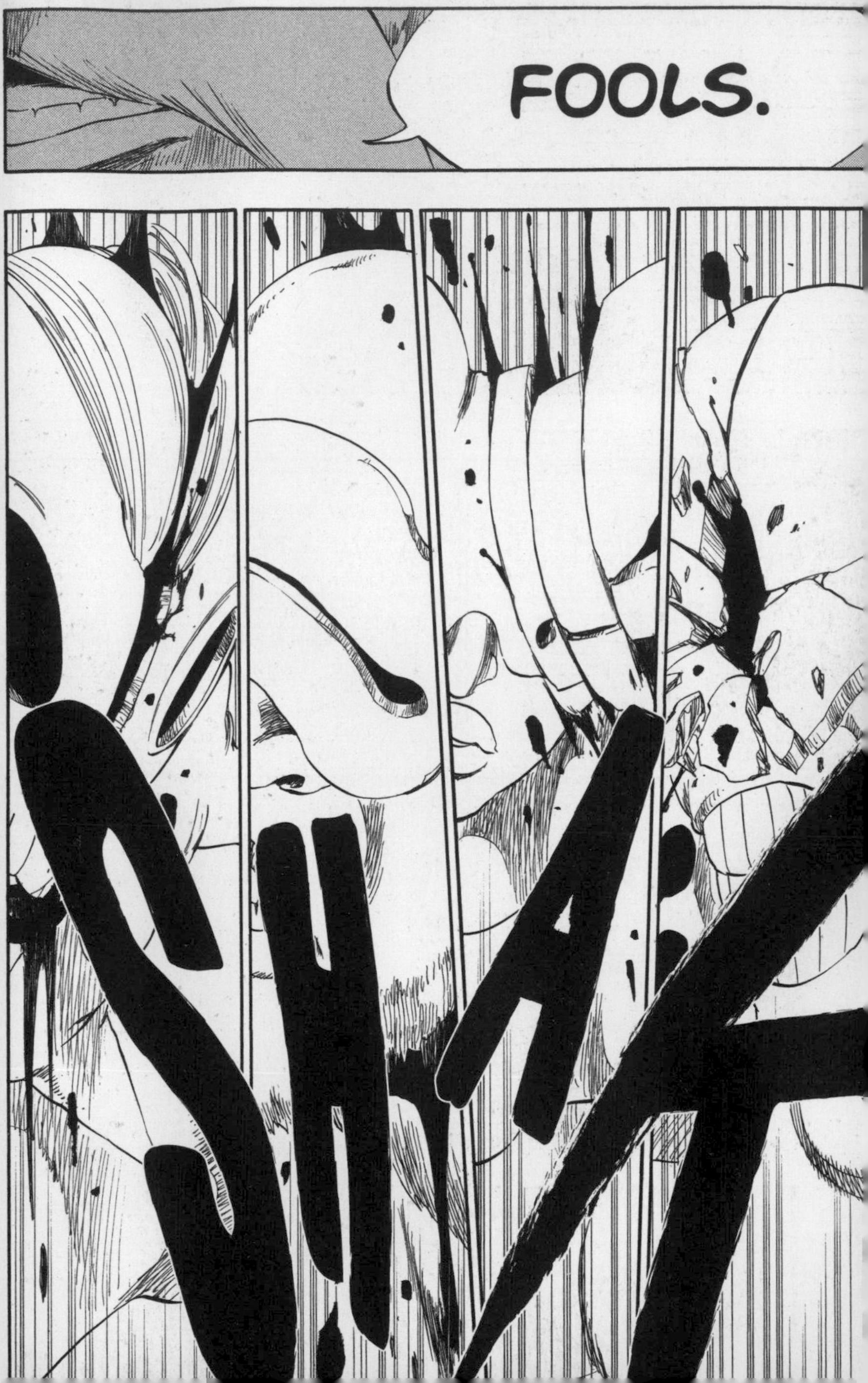
FOOLS.
SHAK

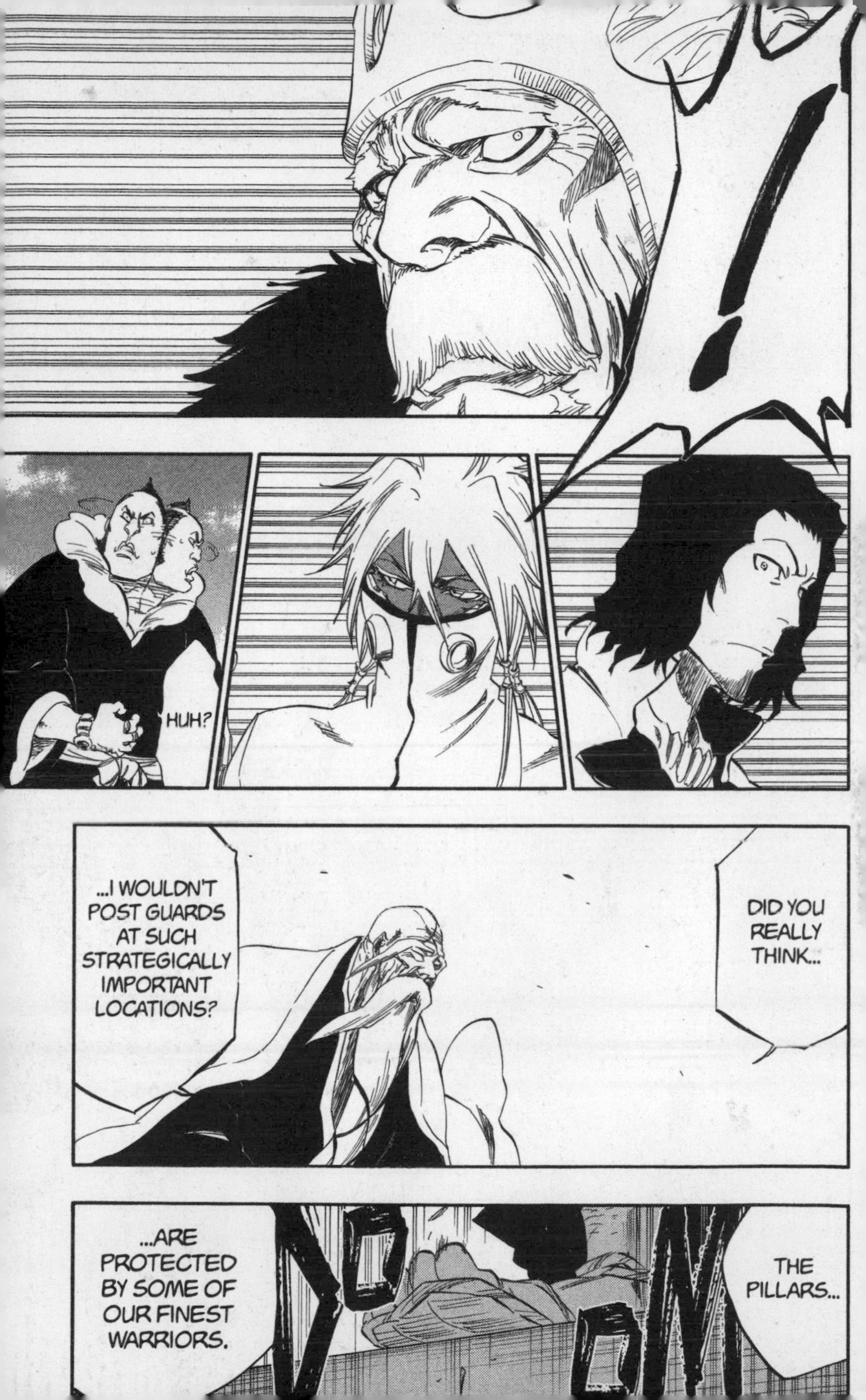
HUH?
DID YOU REALLY THINK...
...I WOULDN'T POST GUARDS AT SUCH STRATEGICALLY IMPORTANT LOCATIONS?
THE PILLARS...
...ARE PROTECTED BY SOME OF OUR FINEST WARRIORS.

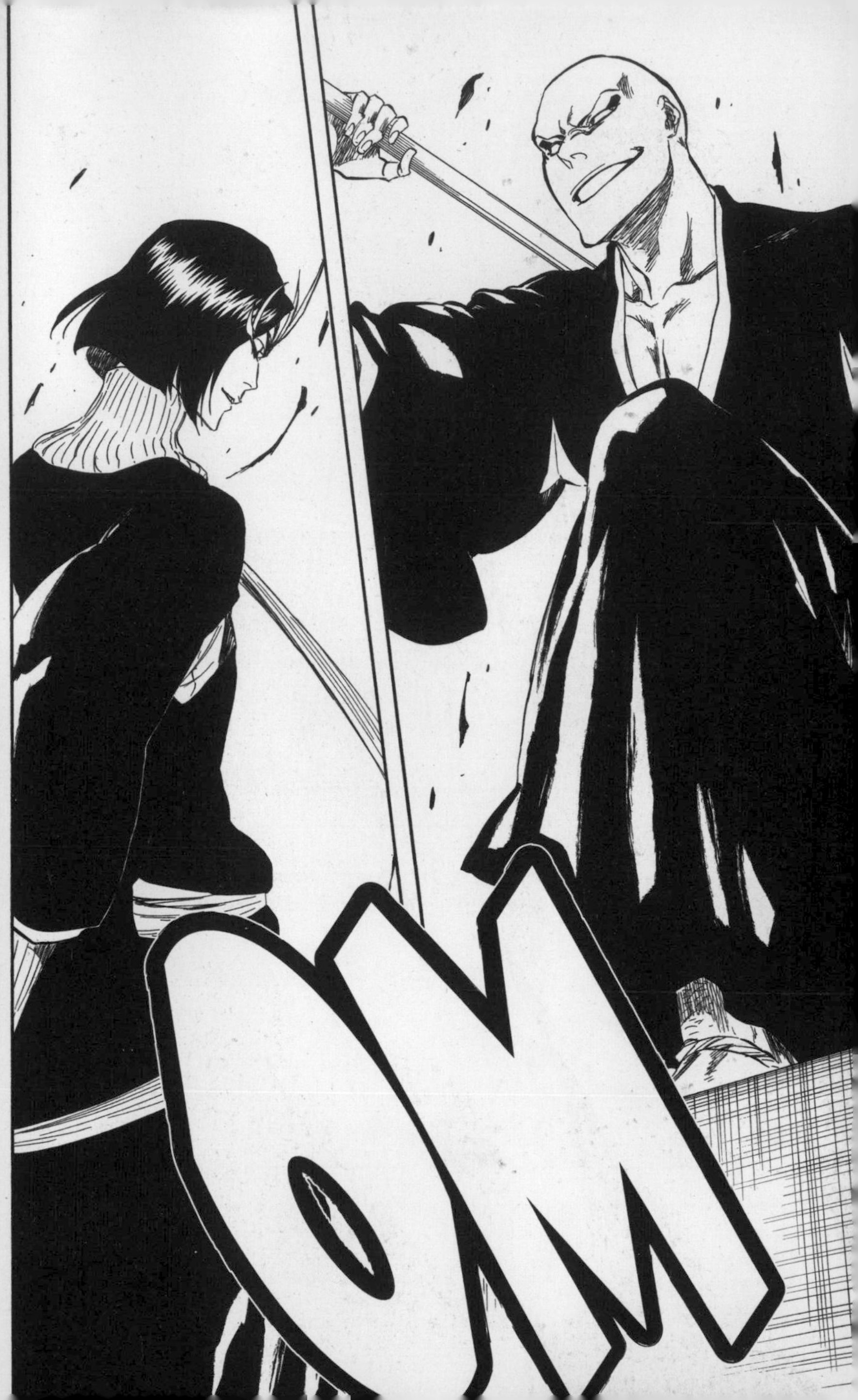
OMM

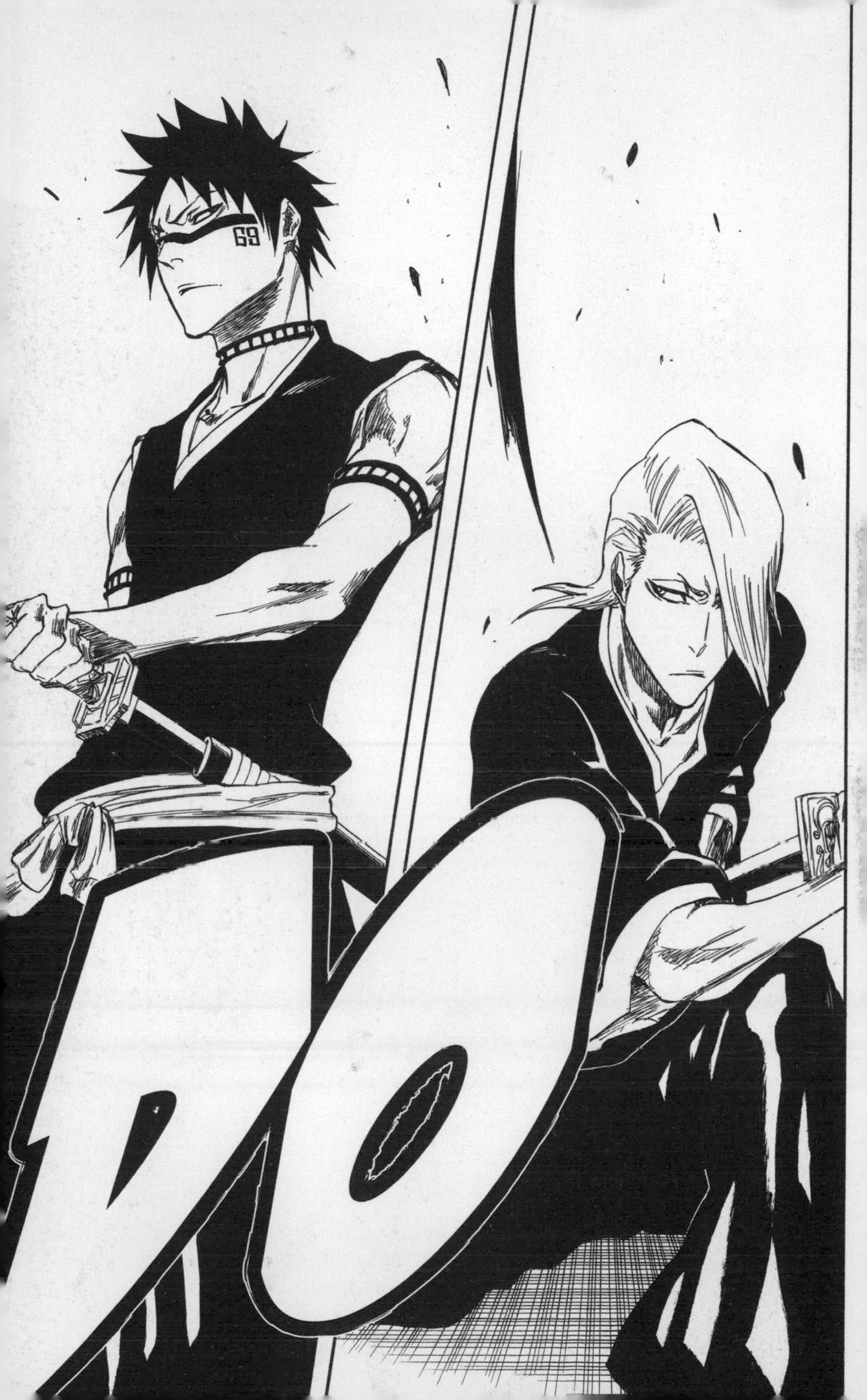
DO

MY FIRST APPEARANCE IN SO LONG...
I HOPE HISAGI HASN'T FORGOTTEN HOW TO DO THIS.

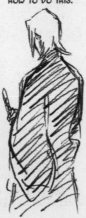

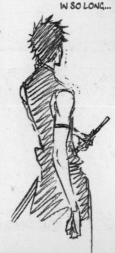

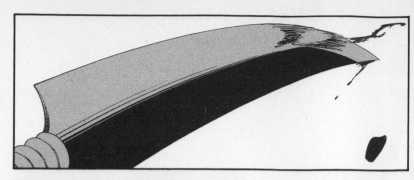

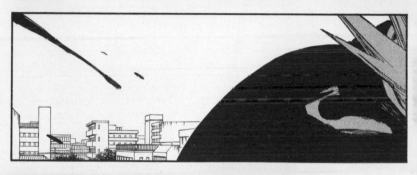

319. Ants and Dragons

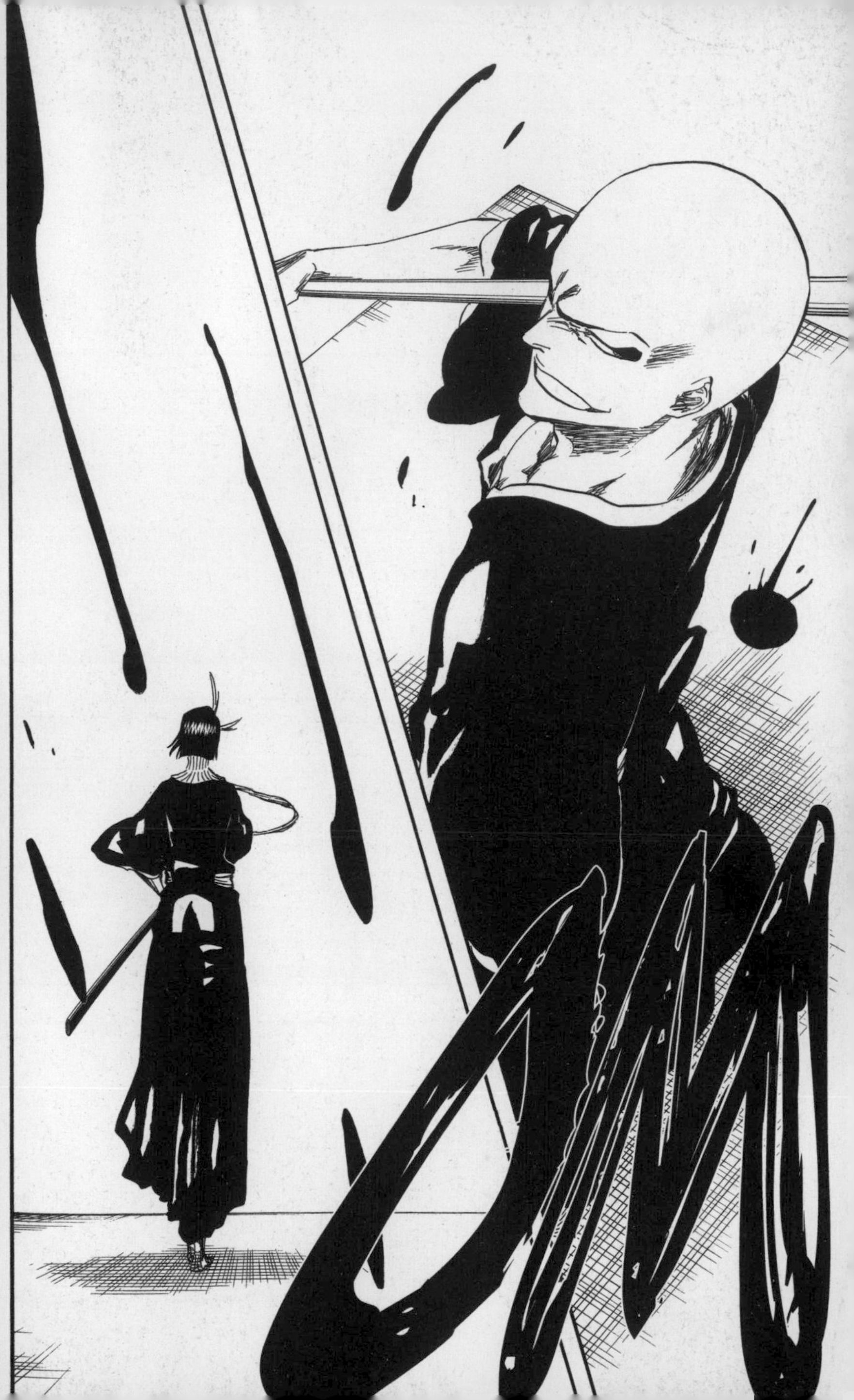

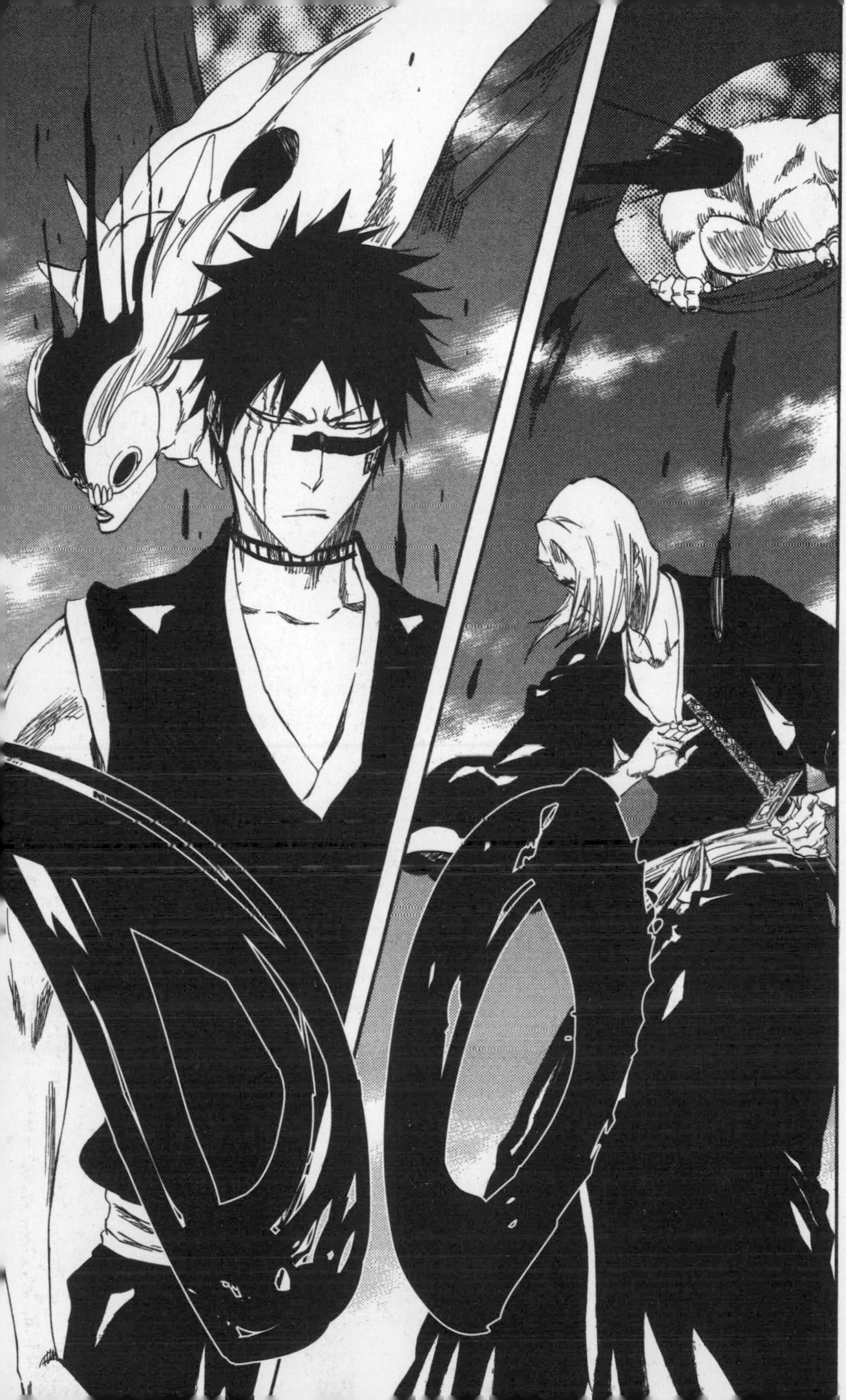

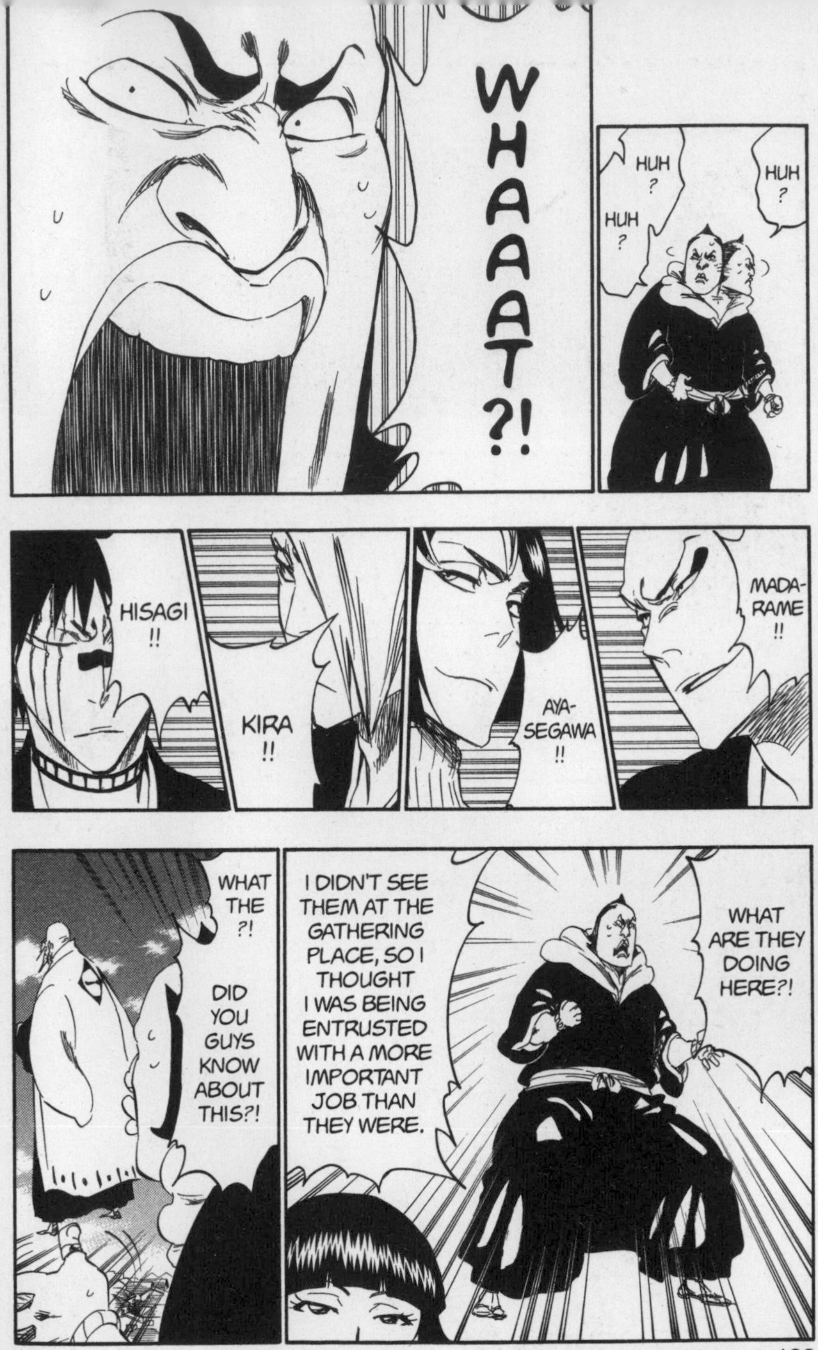
HUH?
HUH?
HUH?
WHAAAT?!
MADA-RAME!!
AYA-SEGAWA!!
KIRA!!
HISAGI!!
WHAT ARE THEY DOING HERE?!
I DIDN'T SEE THEM AT THE GATHERING PLACE, SO I THOUGHT I WAS BEING ENTRUSTED WITH A MORE IMPORTANT JOB THAN THEY WERE.
WHAT THE?!
DID YOU GUYS KNOW ABOUT THIS?!

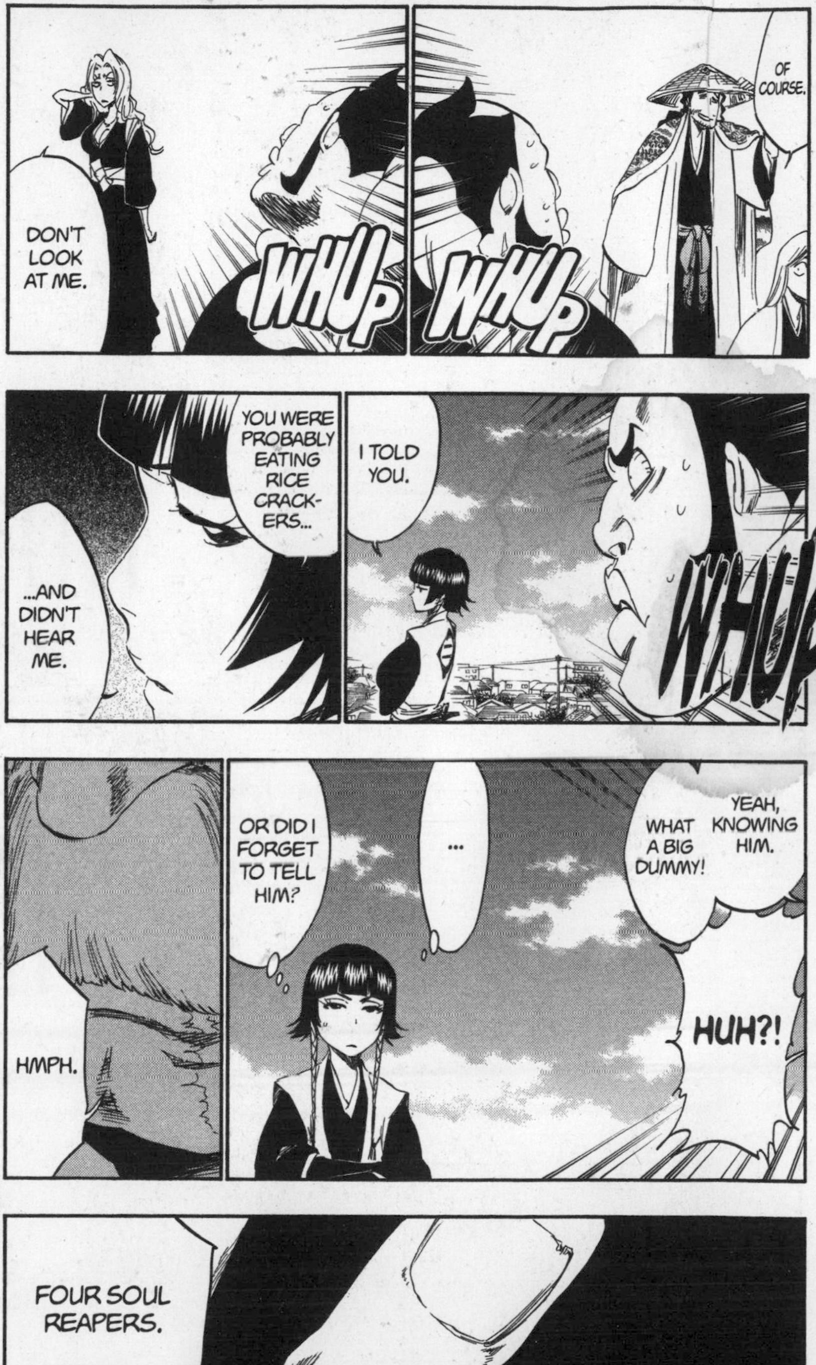
OF COURSE.
WHUP
WHUP
DON'T LOOK AT ME.
WHUP
I TOLD YOU.
YOU WERE PROBABLY EATING RICE CRACK-ERS...
...AND DIDN'T HEAR ME.
YEAH, KNOWING HIM.
WHAT A BIG DUMMY!
...
OR DID I FORGET TO TELL HIM?
HUH?!
HMPH.
FOUR SOUL REAPERS.

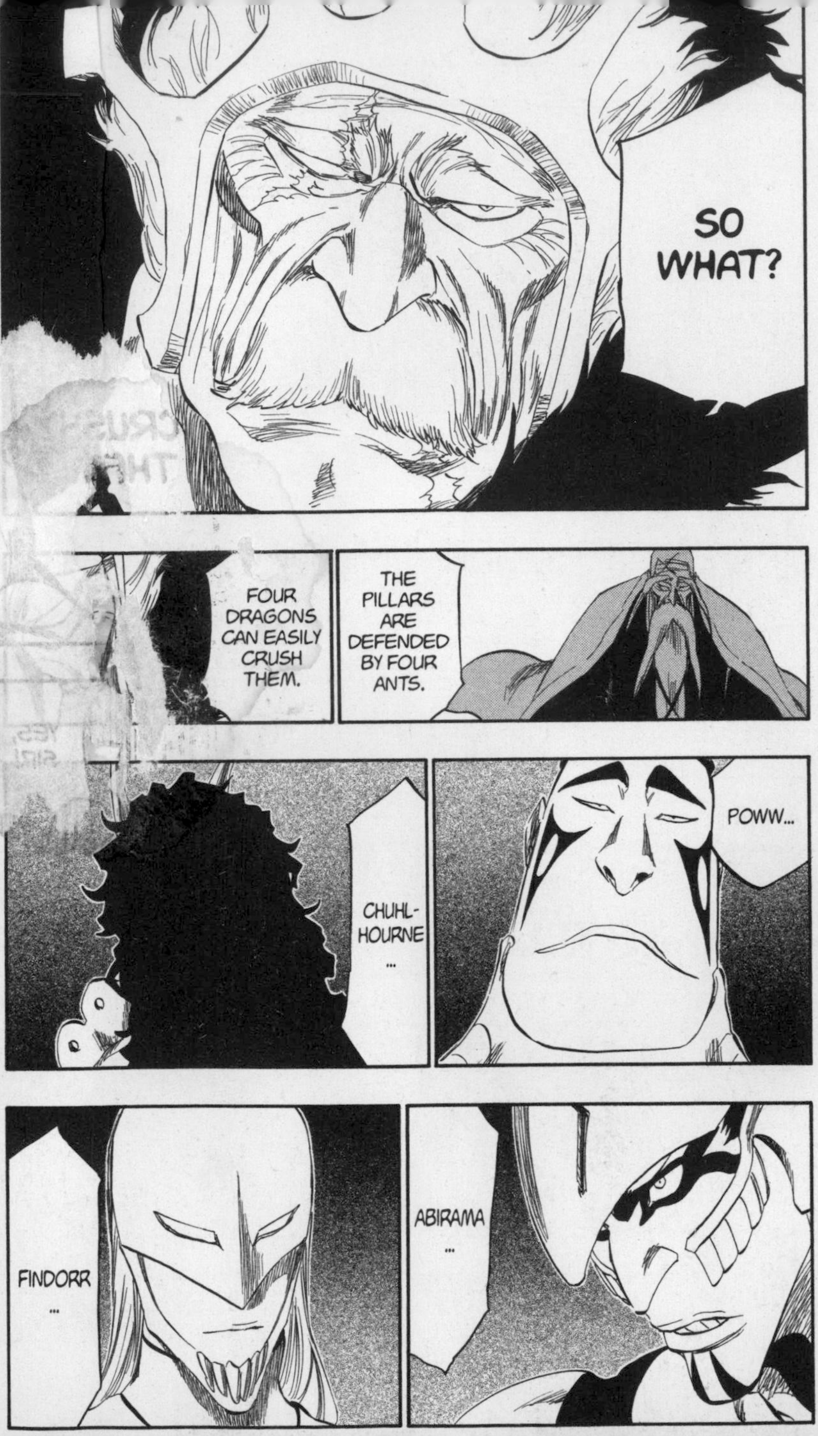
SO WHAT?
THE PILLARS ARE DEFENDED BY FOUR ANTS.
FOUR DRAGONS CAN EASILY CRUSH THEM.
POWW...
CHUHL-HOURNE...
ABIRAMA...
FINDORR...

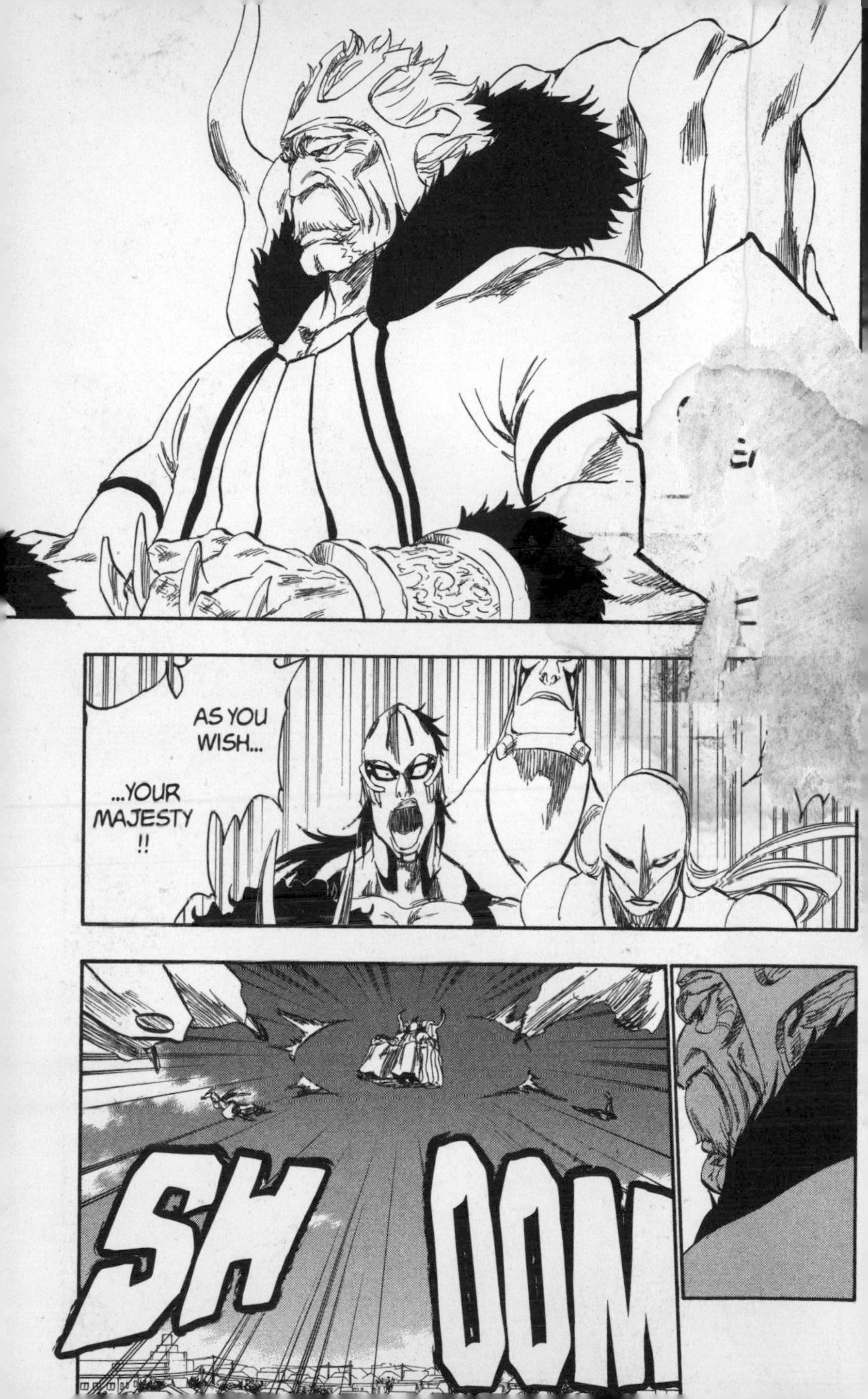
AS YOU WISH...
...YOUR MAJESTY !!
SH OOM

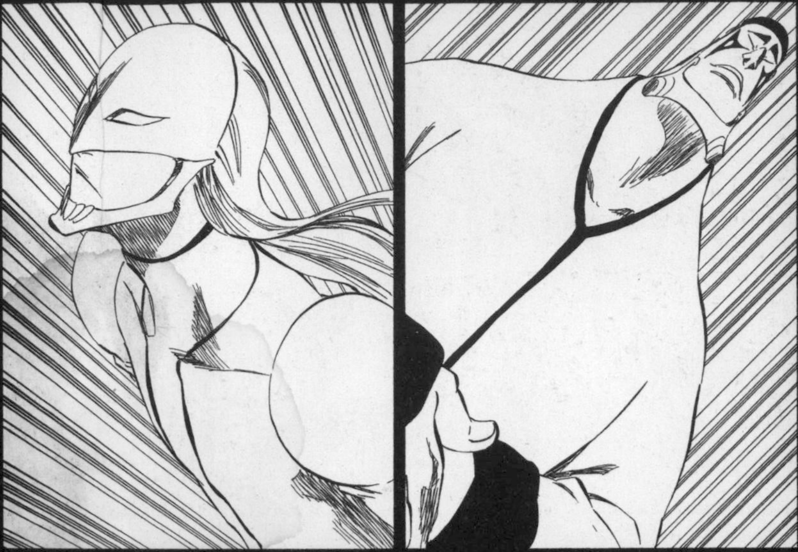

BLEACH

319. Ants and Dragons

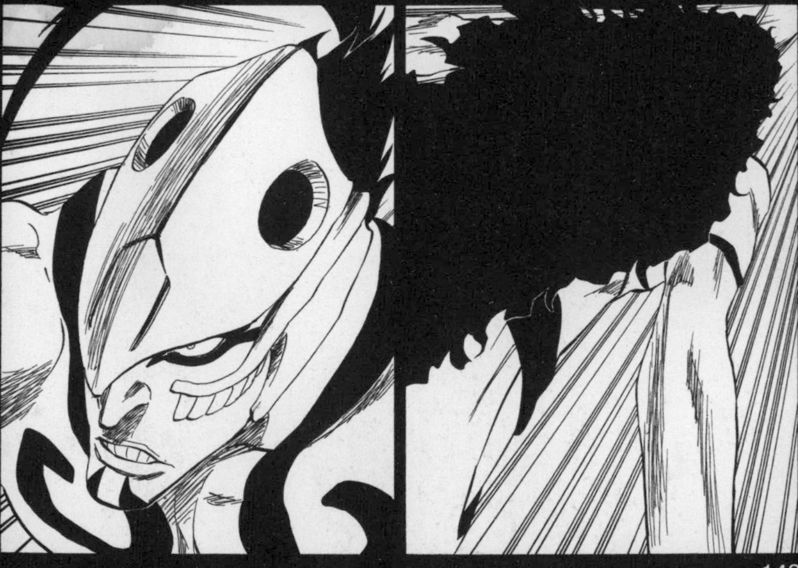

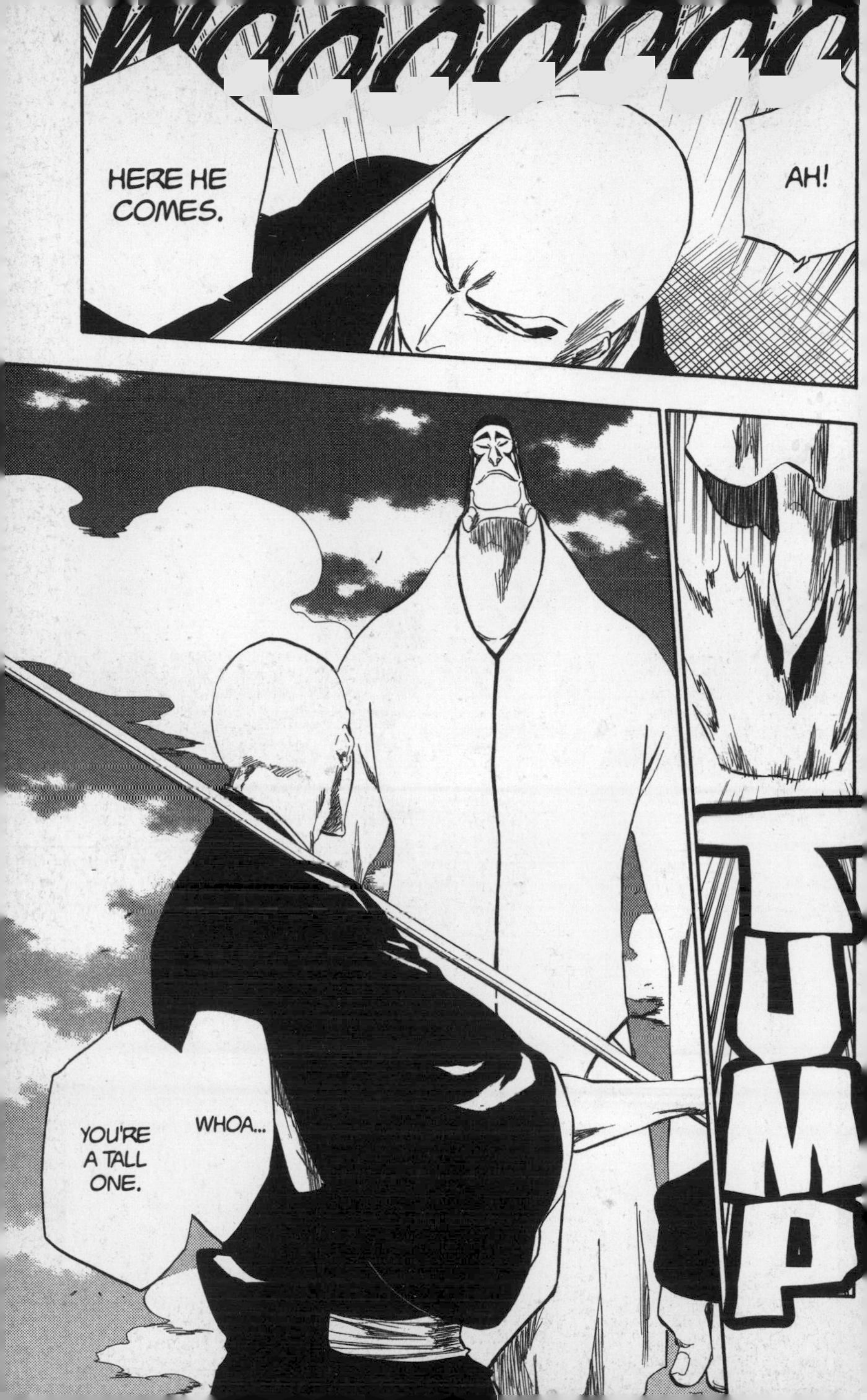
AH!
HERE HE COMES.
TUMP
WHOA...
YOU'RE A TALL ONE.

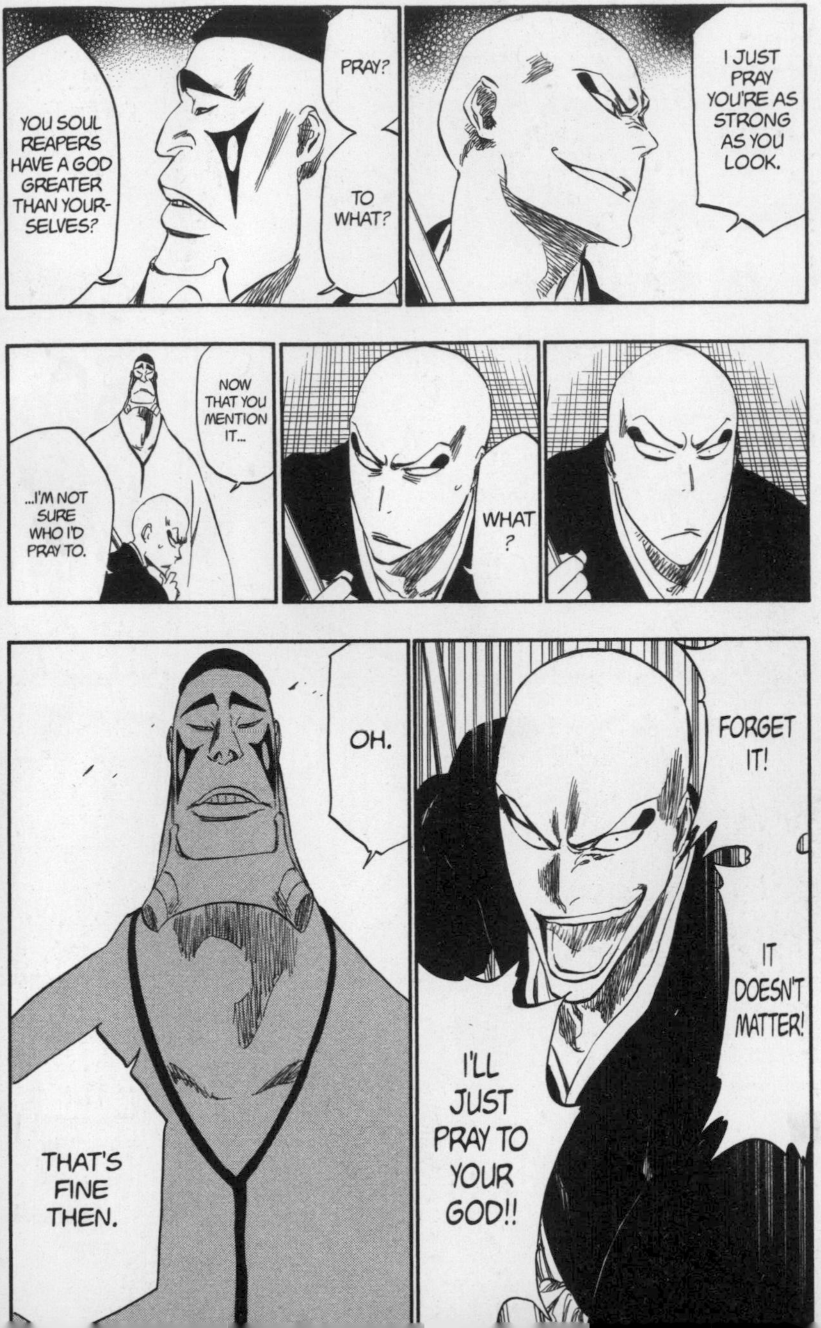
I JUST PRAY YOU'RE AS STRONG AS YOU LOOK.
PRAY?
TO WHAT?
YOU SOUL REAPERS HAVE A GOD GREATER THAN YOUR-SELVES?
WHAT?
NOW THAT YOU MENTION IT...
...I'M NOT SURE WHO I'D PRAY TO.
FORGET IT!
IT DOESN'T MATTER!
I'LL JUST PRAY TO YOUR GOD!!
OH.
THAT'S FINE THEN.

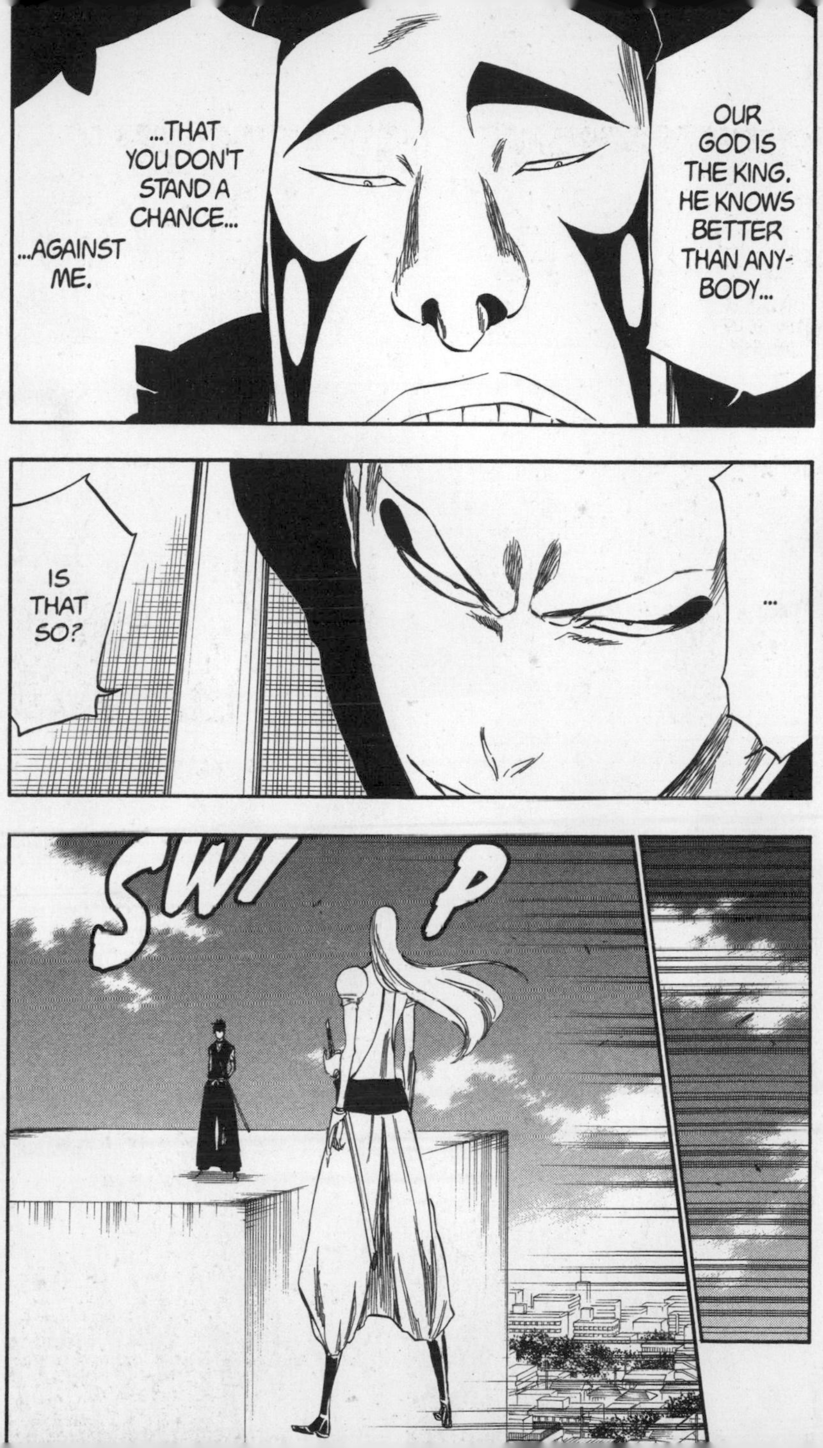
OUR GOD IS THE KING. HE KNOWS BETTER THAN ANY-BODY...
...THAT YOU DON'T STAND A CHANCE...
...AGAINST ME.
...
IS THAT SO?
SWIP

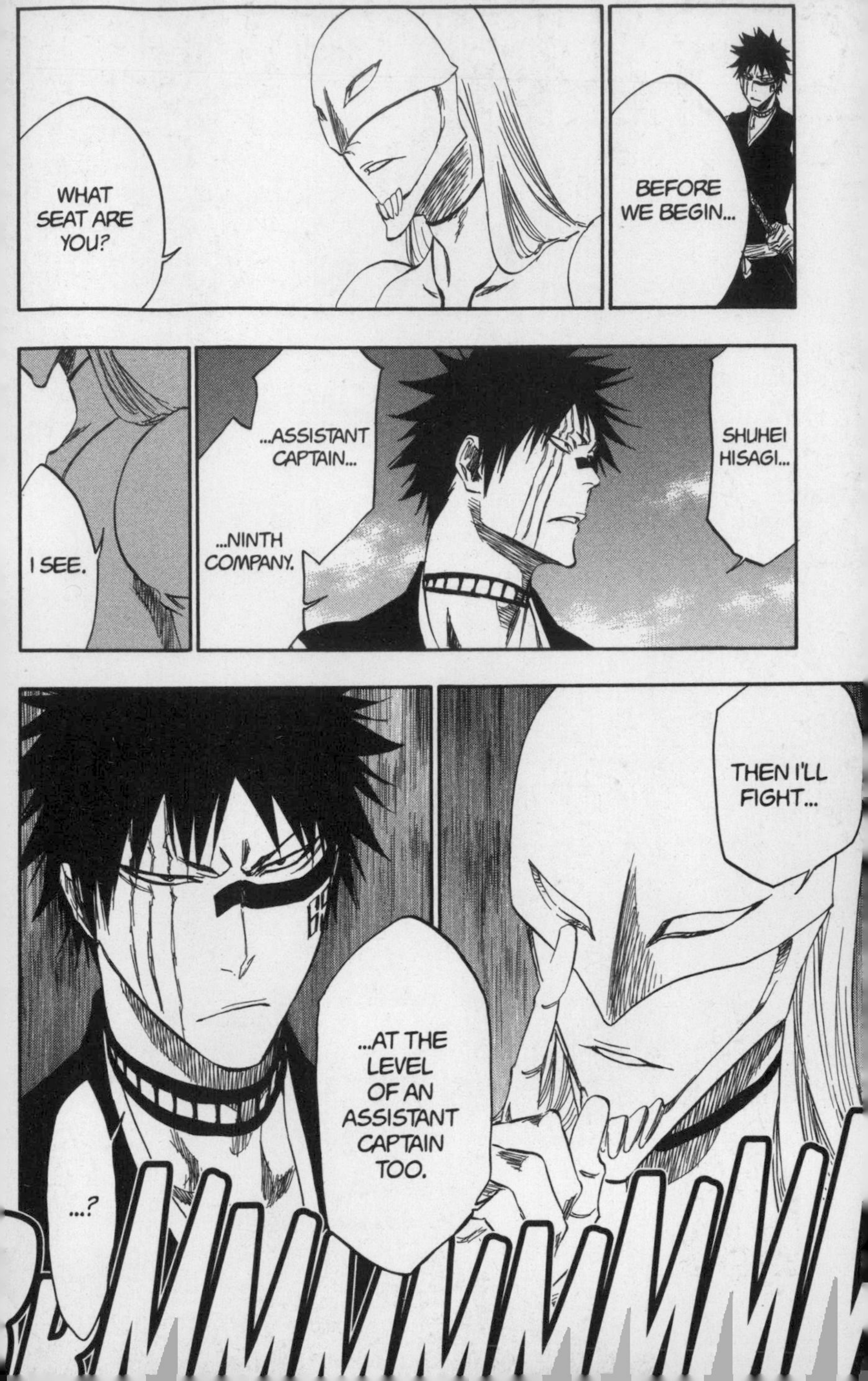
BEFORE WE BEGIN...
WHAT SEAT ARE YOU?
SHUHEI HISAGI...
...ASSISTANT CAPTAIN...
...NINTH COMPANY.
I SEE.
THEN I'LL FIGHT...
...AT THE LEVEL OF AN ASSISTANT CAPTAIN TOO.
...?

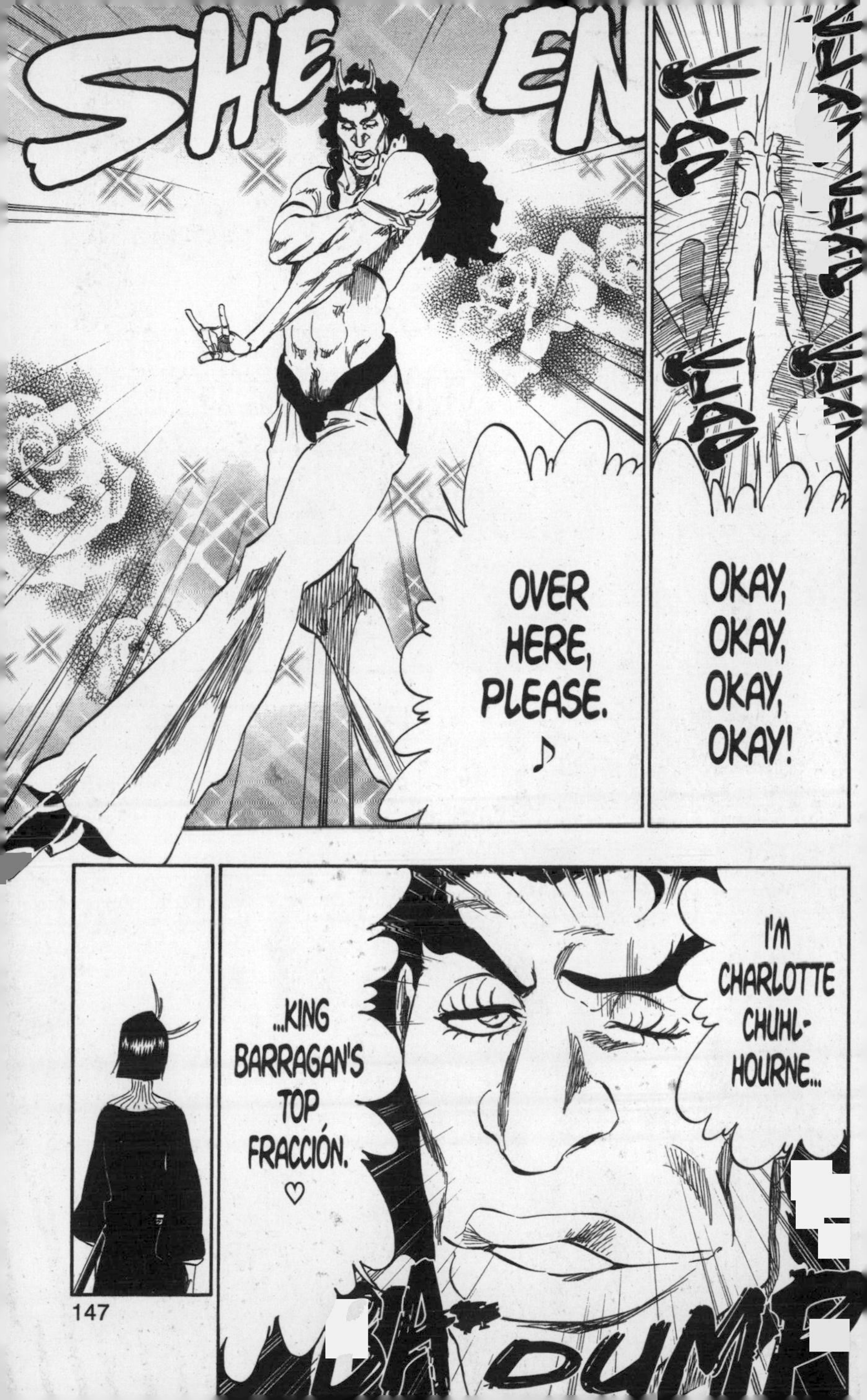
OKAY, OKAY, OKAY, OKAY!
OVER HERE, PLEASE. ♪
I'M CHARLOTTE CHUHL-HOURNE...
...KING BARRAGAN'S TOP FRACCIÓN. ♡

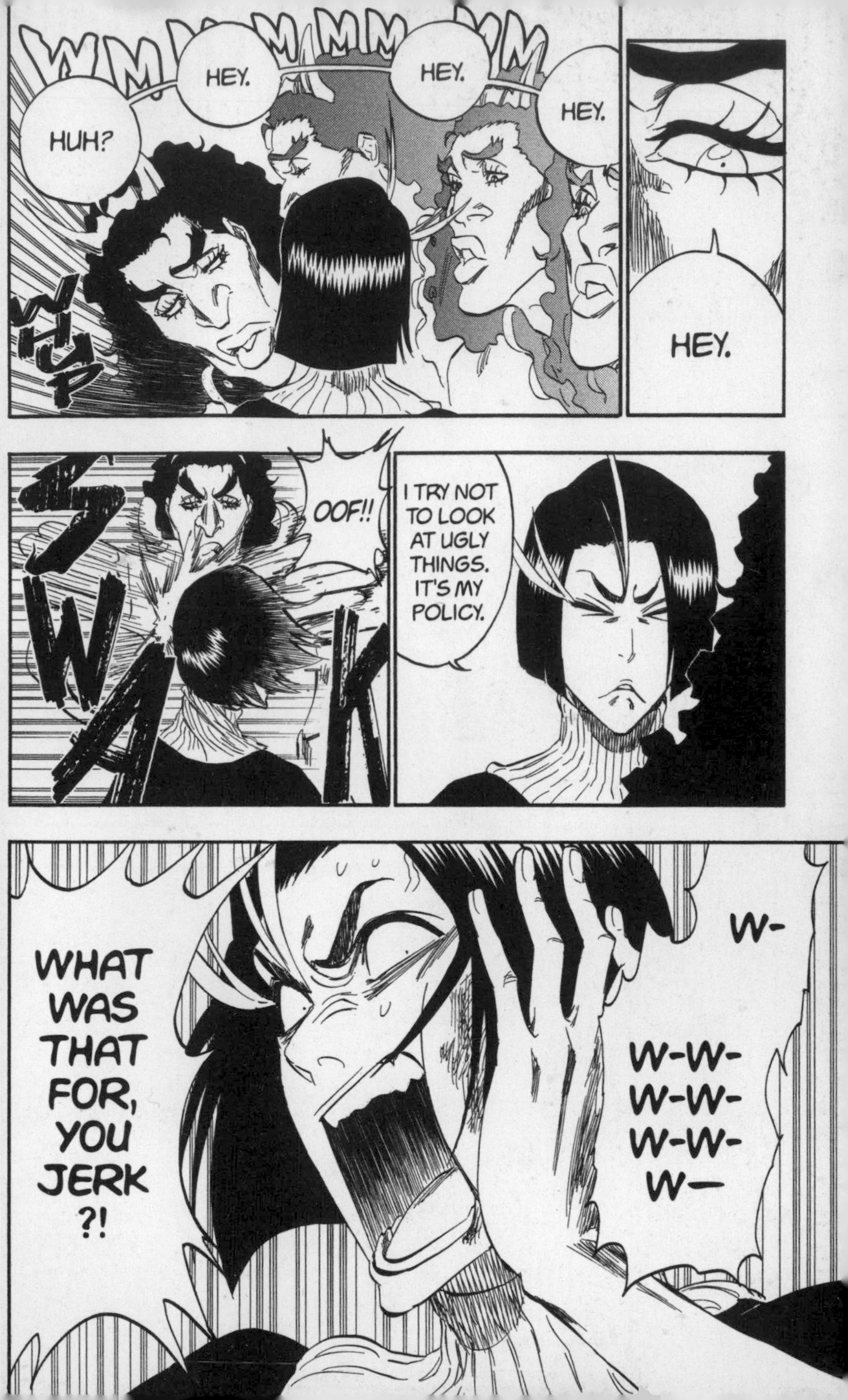
HEY.
HEY.
HEY.
HEY.
HUH?
WHUP
I TRY NOT TO LOOK AT UGLY THINGS. IT'S MY POLICY.
OOF!!
SWAK
W-
W-W-W-W-W-W-W—
WHAT WAS THAT FOR, YOU JERK?!

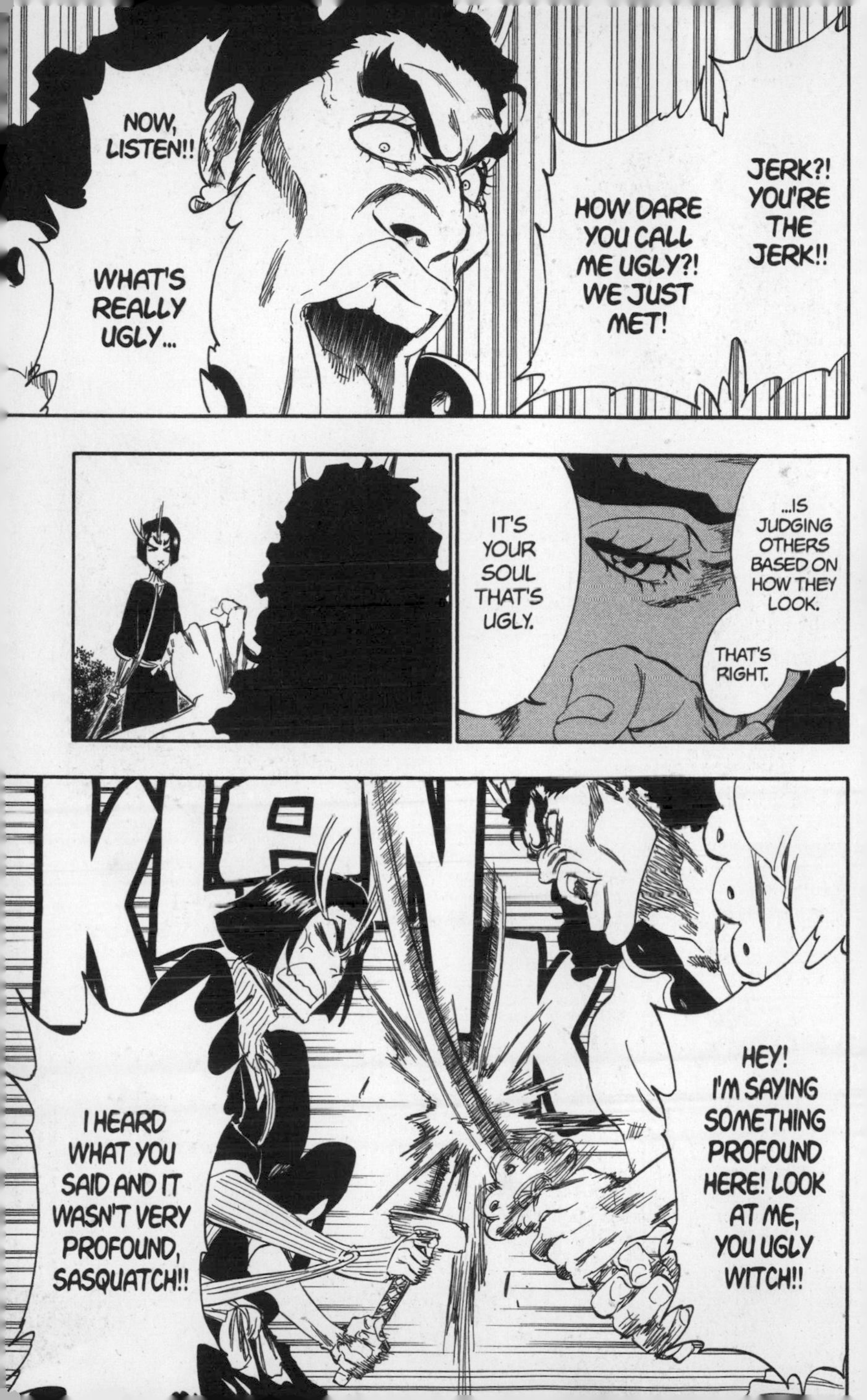

JERK?! YOU'RE THE JERK!!
HOW DARE YOU CALL ME UGLY?! WE JUST MET!
NOW, LISTEN!!
WHAT'S REALLY UGLY...
...IS JUDGING OTHERS BASED ON HOW THEY LOOK.
THAT'S RIGHT.
IT'S YOUR SOUL THAT'S UGLY.
HEY! I'M SAYING SOMETHING PROFOUND HERE! LOOK AT ME, YOU UGLY WITCH!!
I HEARD WHAT YOU SAID AND IT WASN'T VERY PROFOUND, SASQUATCH!!

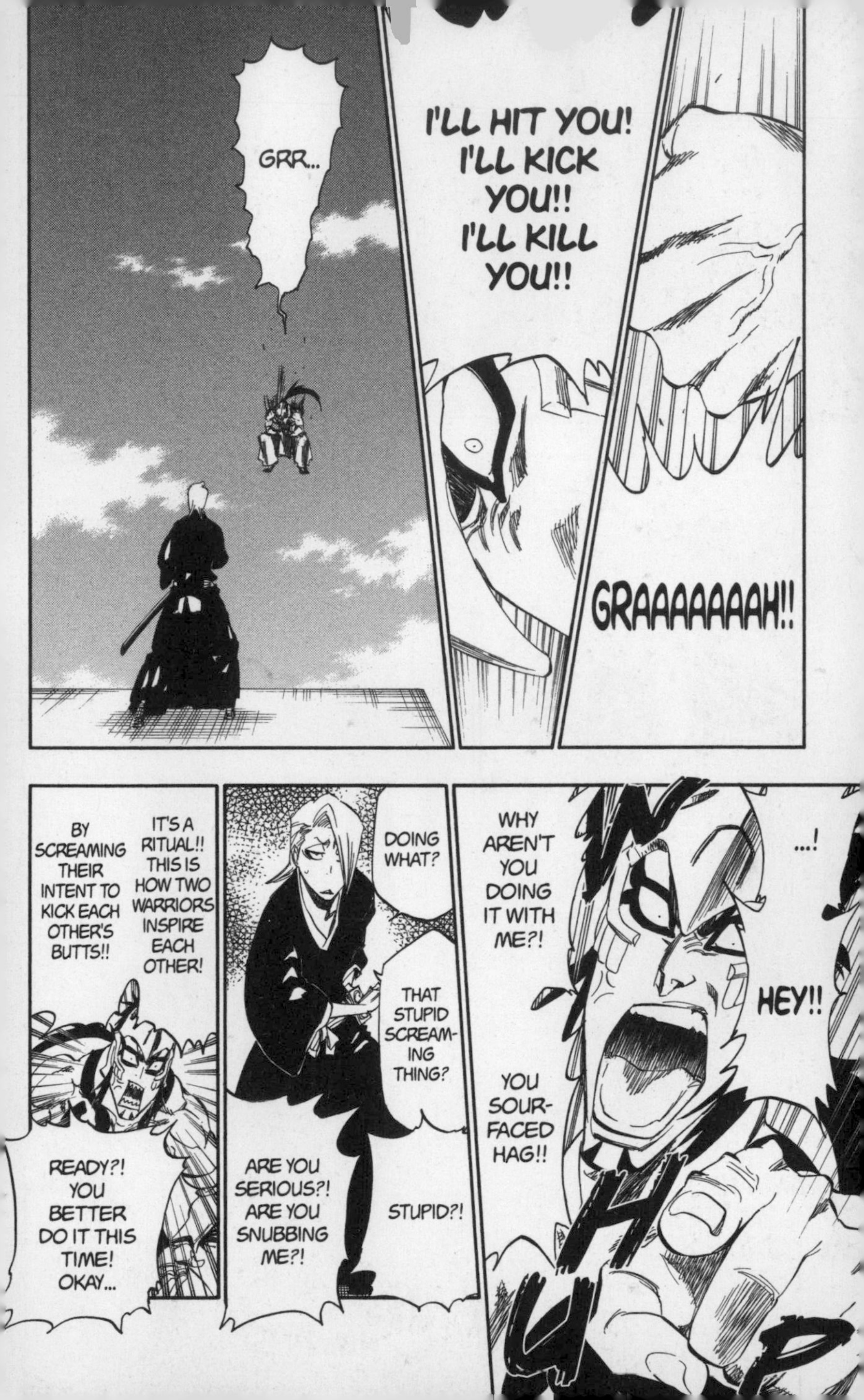
GRAAAAAAH!!
I'LL HIT YOU! I'LL KICK YOU!! I'LL KILL YOU!!
GRR...
...!
HEY!!
WHY AREN'T YOU DOING IT WITH ME?!
YOU SOUR-FACED HAG!!
DOING WHAT?
THAT STUPID SCREAM-ING THING?
STUPID?!
ARE YOU SERIOUS?! ARE YOU SNUBBING ME?!
IT'S A RITUAL!! THIS IS HOW TWO WARRIORS INSPIRE EACH OTHER!
BY SCREAMING THEIR INTENT TO KICK EACH OTHER'S BUTTS!!
READY?! YOU BETTER DO IT THIS TIME! OKAY...

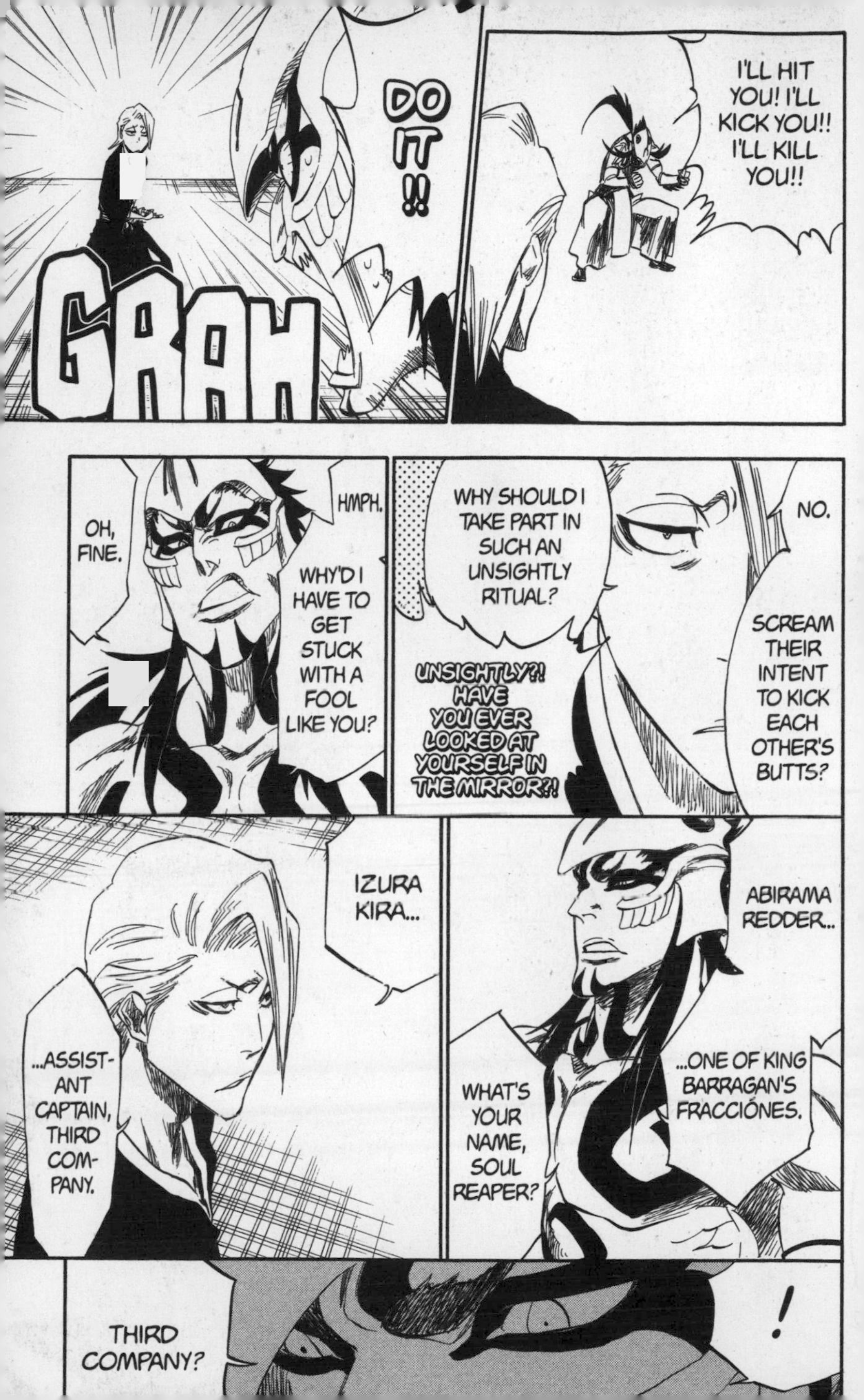
I'LL HIT YOU! I'LL KICK YOU!! I'LL KILL YOU!!
DO IT!!
GRAH
NO.
WHY SHOULD I TAKE PART IN SUCH AN UNSIGHTLY RITUAL?
SCREAM THEIR INTENT TO KICK EACH OTHER'S BUTTS?
UNSIGHTLY?! HAVE YOU EVER LOOKED AT YOURSELF IN THE MIRROR?!
HMPH.
WHY'D I HAVE TO GET STUCK WITH A FOOL LIKE YOU?
OH, FINE.
ABIRAMA REDDER...
...ONE OF KING BARRAGAN'S FRACCIÓNES.
WHAT'S YOUR NAME, SOUL REAPER?
IZURA KIRA...
...ASSIST-ANT CAPTAIN, THIRD COM-PANY.
!
THIRD COMPANY?

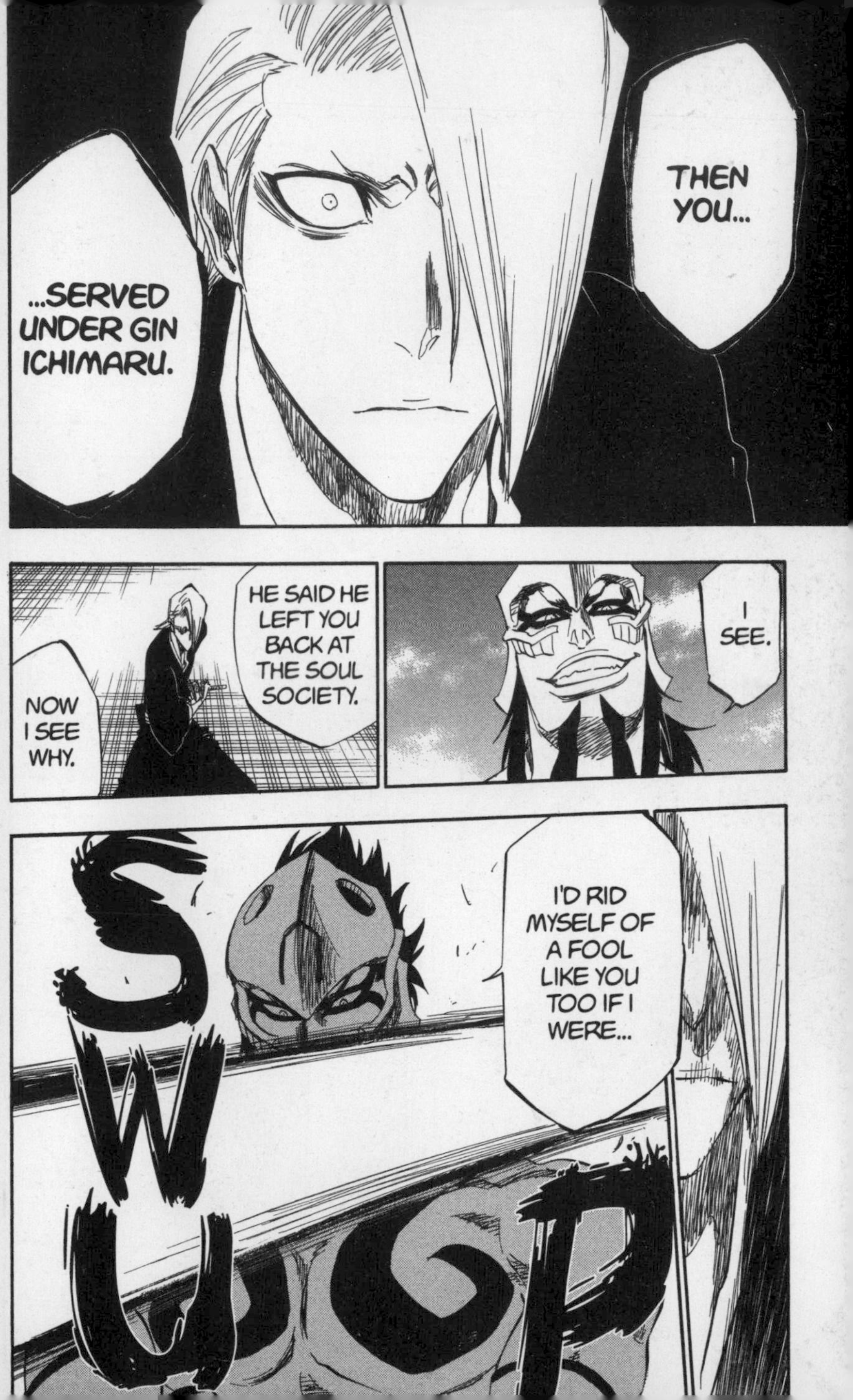
THEN YOU...
...SERVED UNDER GIN ICHIMARU.
I SEE.
HE SAID HE LEFT YOU BACK AT THE SOUL SOCIETY.
NOW I SEE WHY.
I'D RID MYSELF OF A FOOL LIKE YOU TOO IF I WERE...

READ THIS WAY

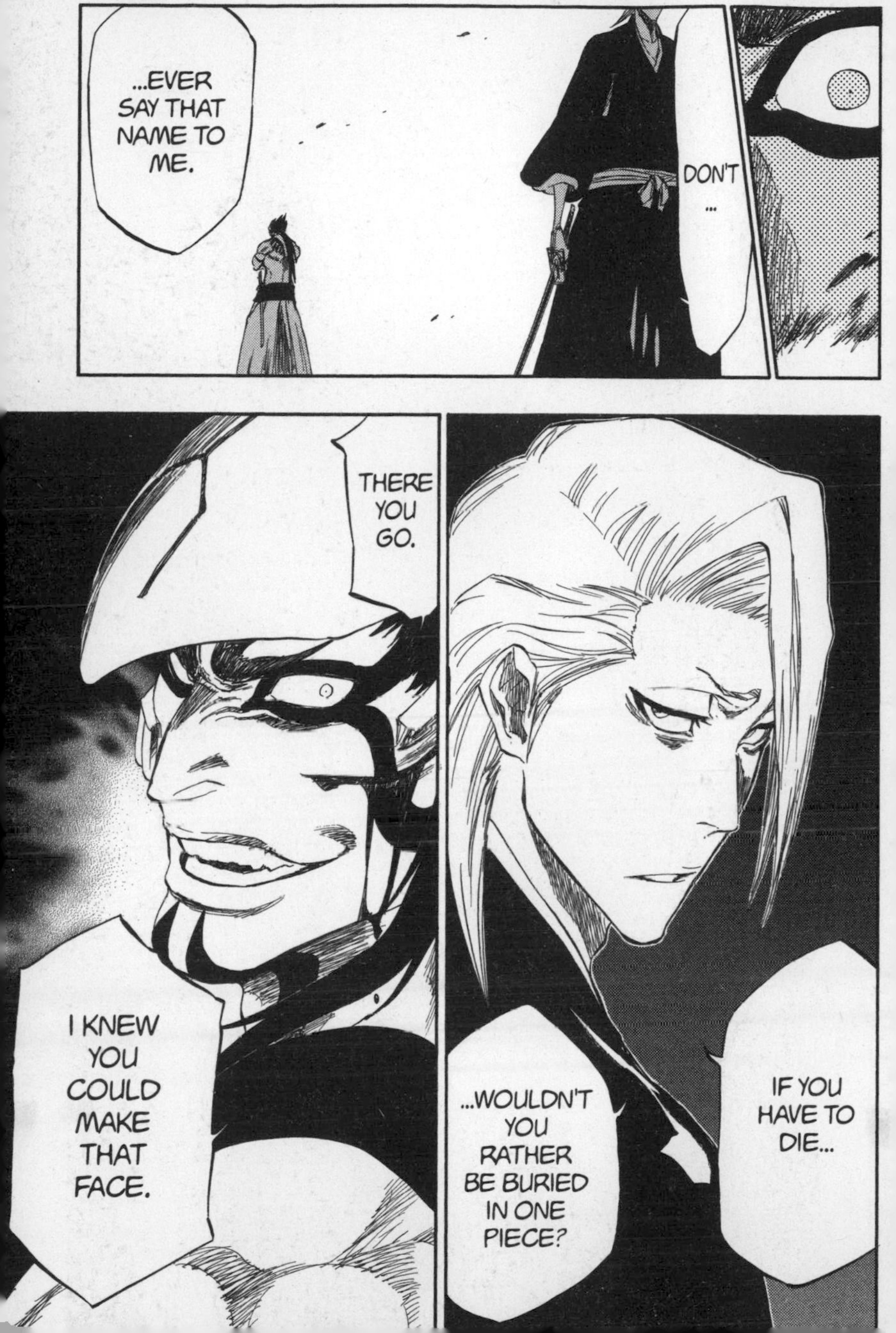
DON'T ...
...EVER SAY THAT NAME TO ME.
IF YOU HAVE TO DIE...
...WOULDN'T YOU RATHER BE BURIED IN ONE PIECE?
THERE YOU GO.
I KNEW YOU COULD MAKE THAT FACE.

WHAT'S WITH THIS AREA...?
I'D BETTER MAKE SURE NOT TO STRIKE THERE.

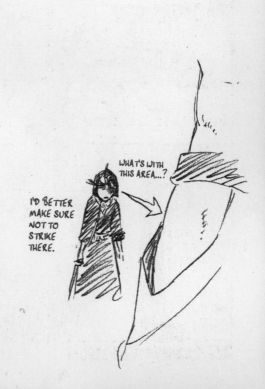

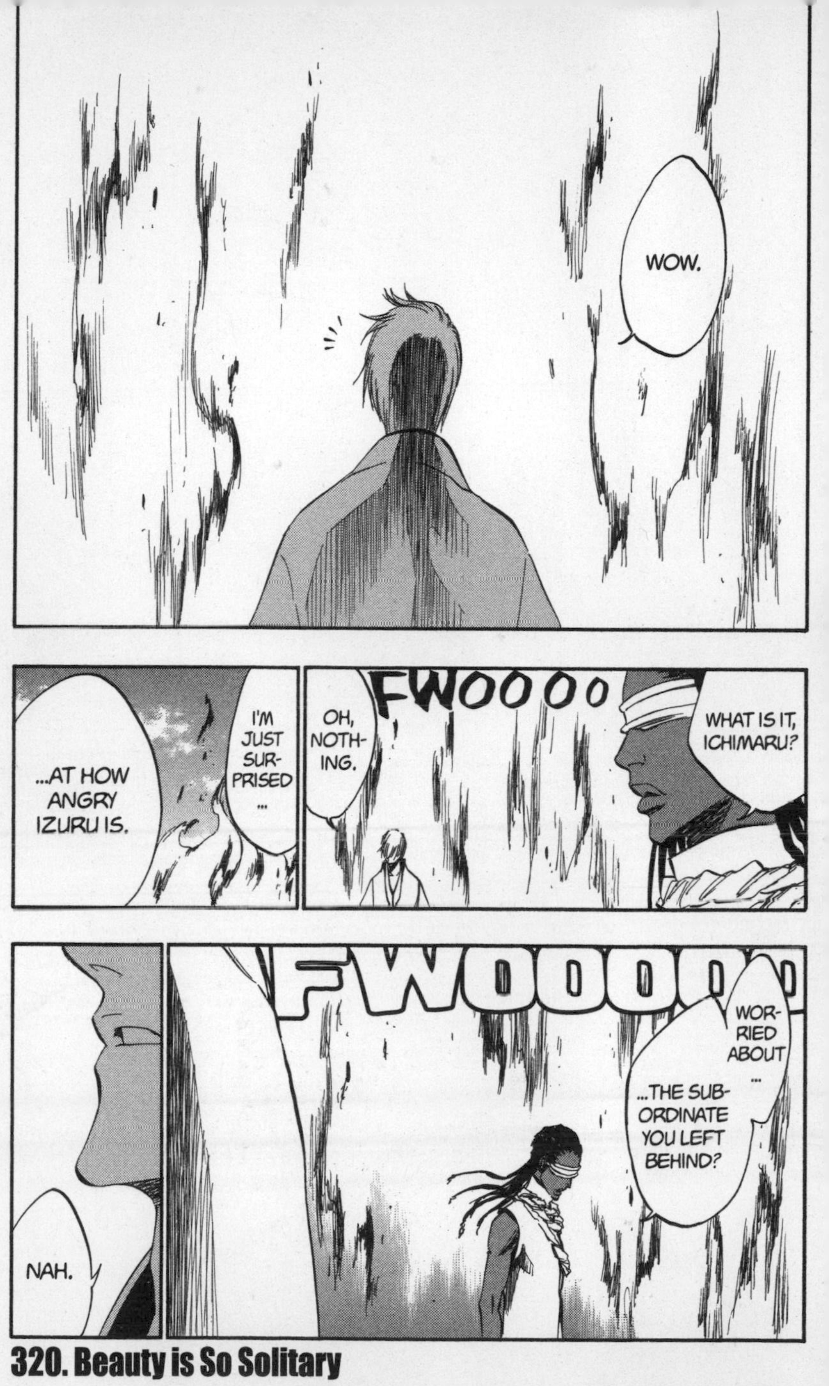
WOW.
FWOOOO
WHAT IS IT, ICHIMARU?
OH, NOTHING.
I'M JUST SURPRISED...
...AT HOW ANGRY IZURU IS.
FWOOOOO
WORRIED ABOUT...
...THE SUBORDINATE YOU LEFT BEHIND?
NAH.

320. Beauty is So Solitary

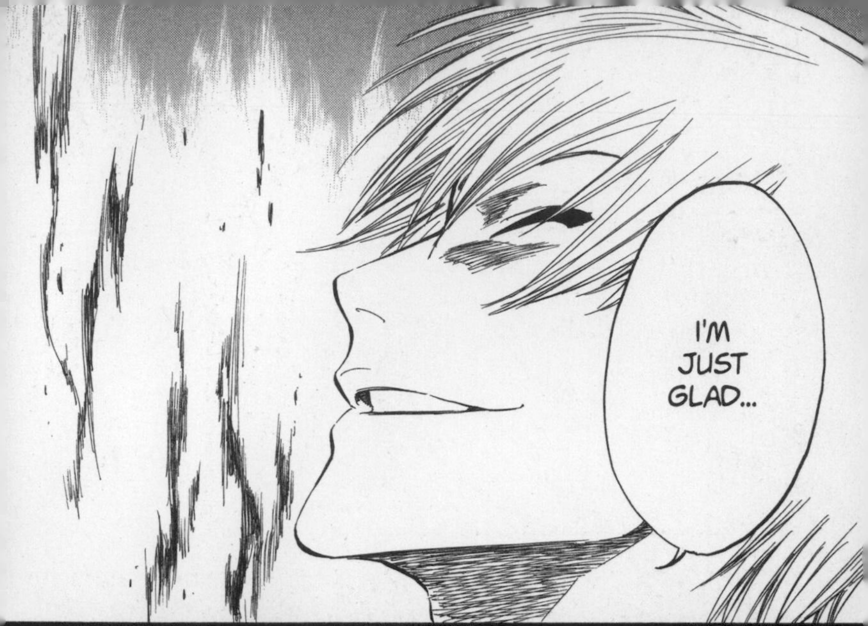
I'M JUST GLAD...

BLEACH320. Beauty is So Solitary

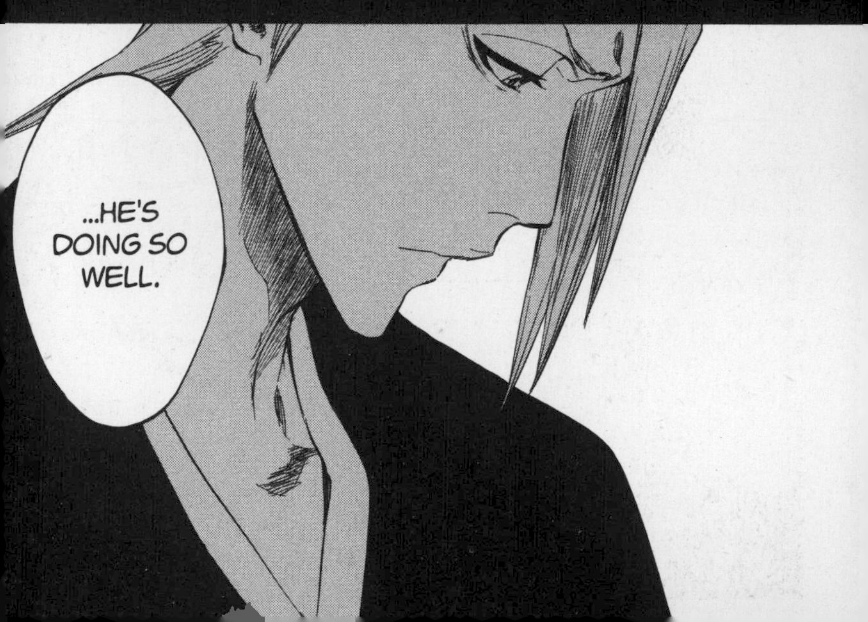
...HE'S DOING SO WELL.

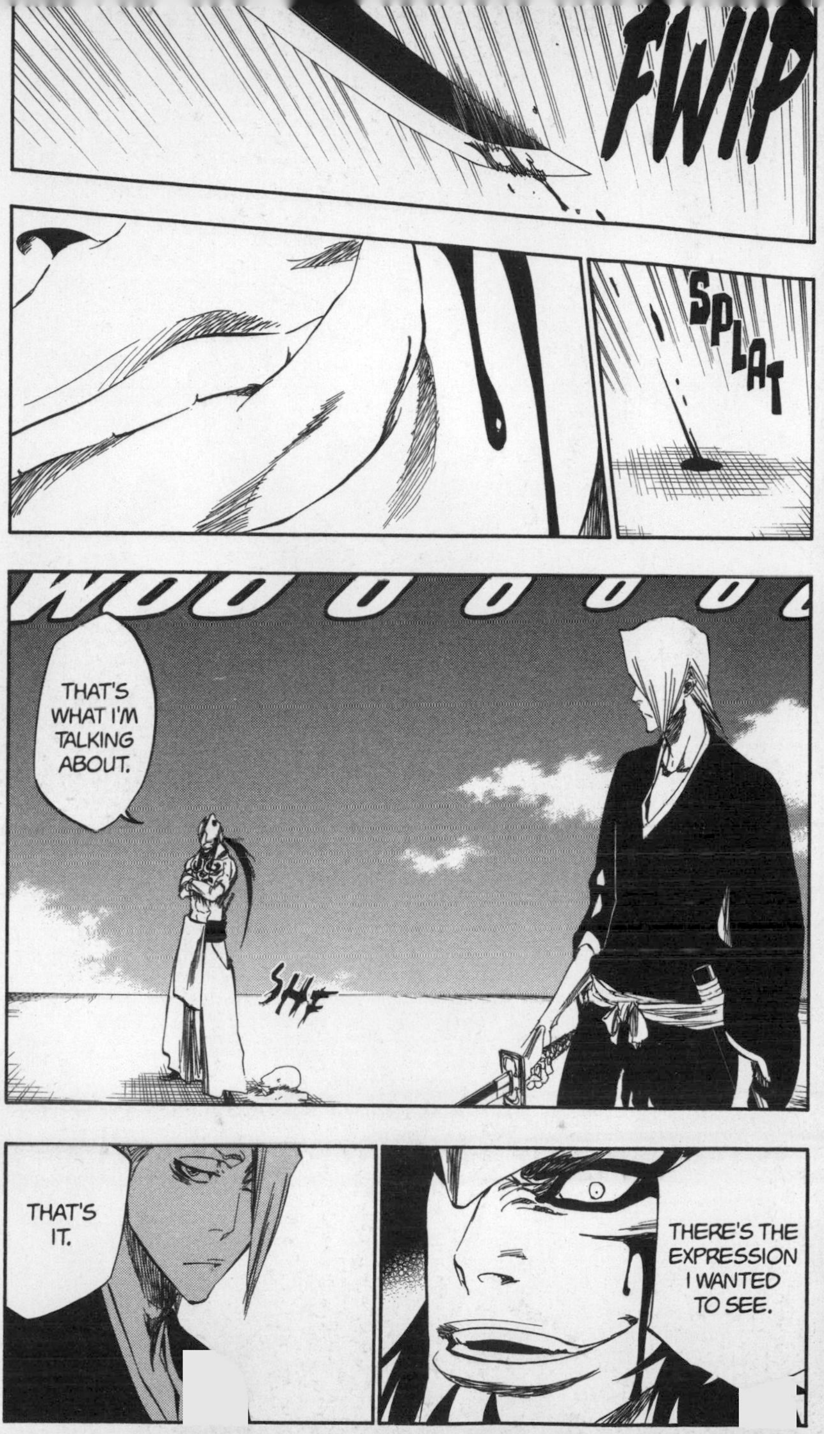
FWIP
SPLAT
WOOOOOOO
THAT'S WHAT I'M TALKING ABOUT.
SHF
THERE'S THE EXPRESSION I WANTED TO SEE.
THAT'S IT.

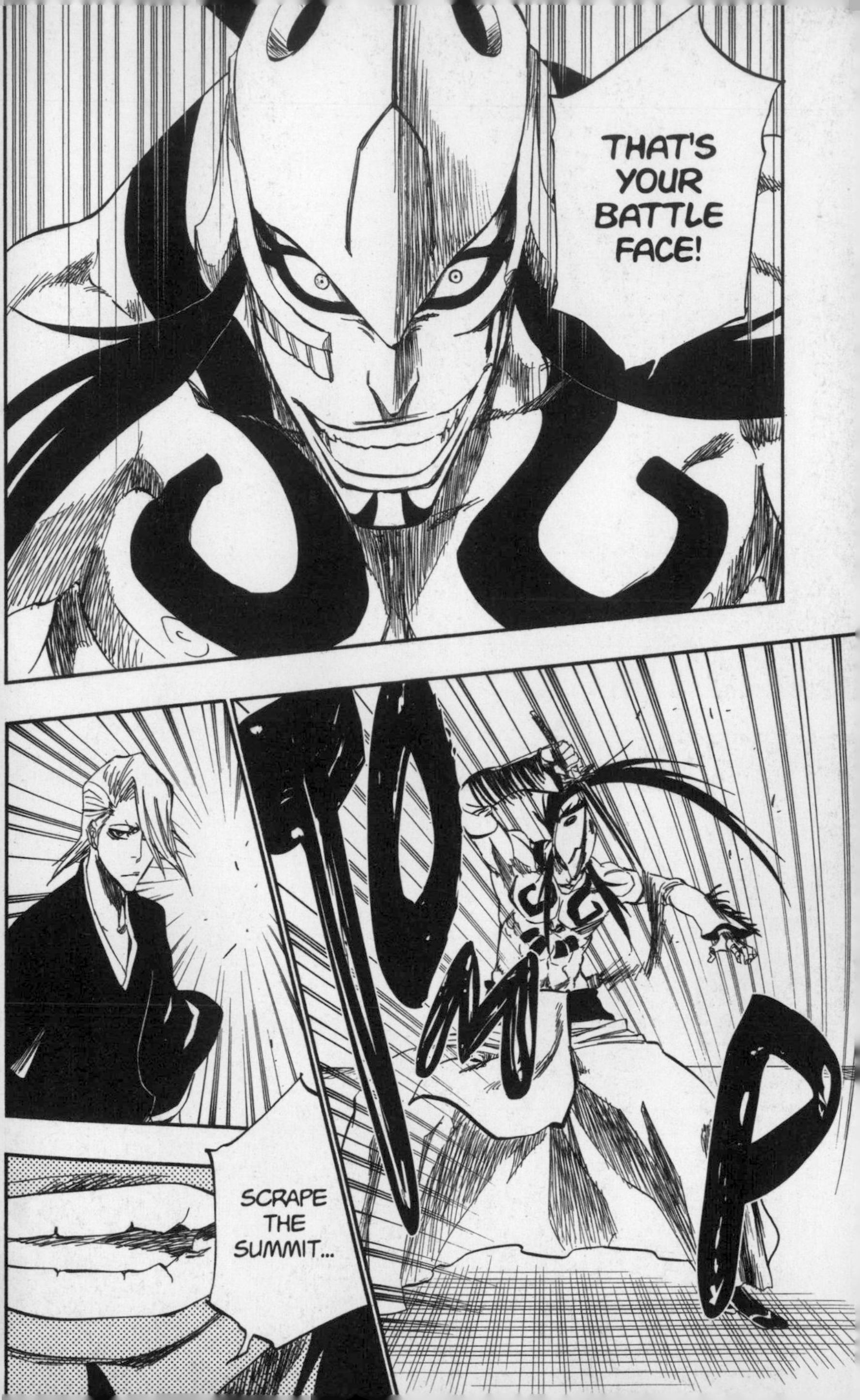

THAT'S YOUR BATTLE FACE!
SCRAPE THE SUMMIT...

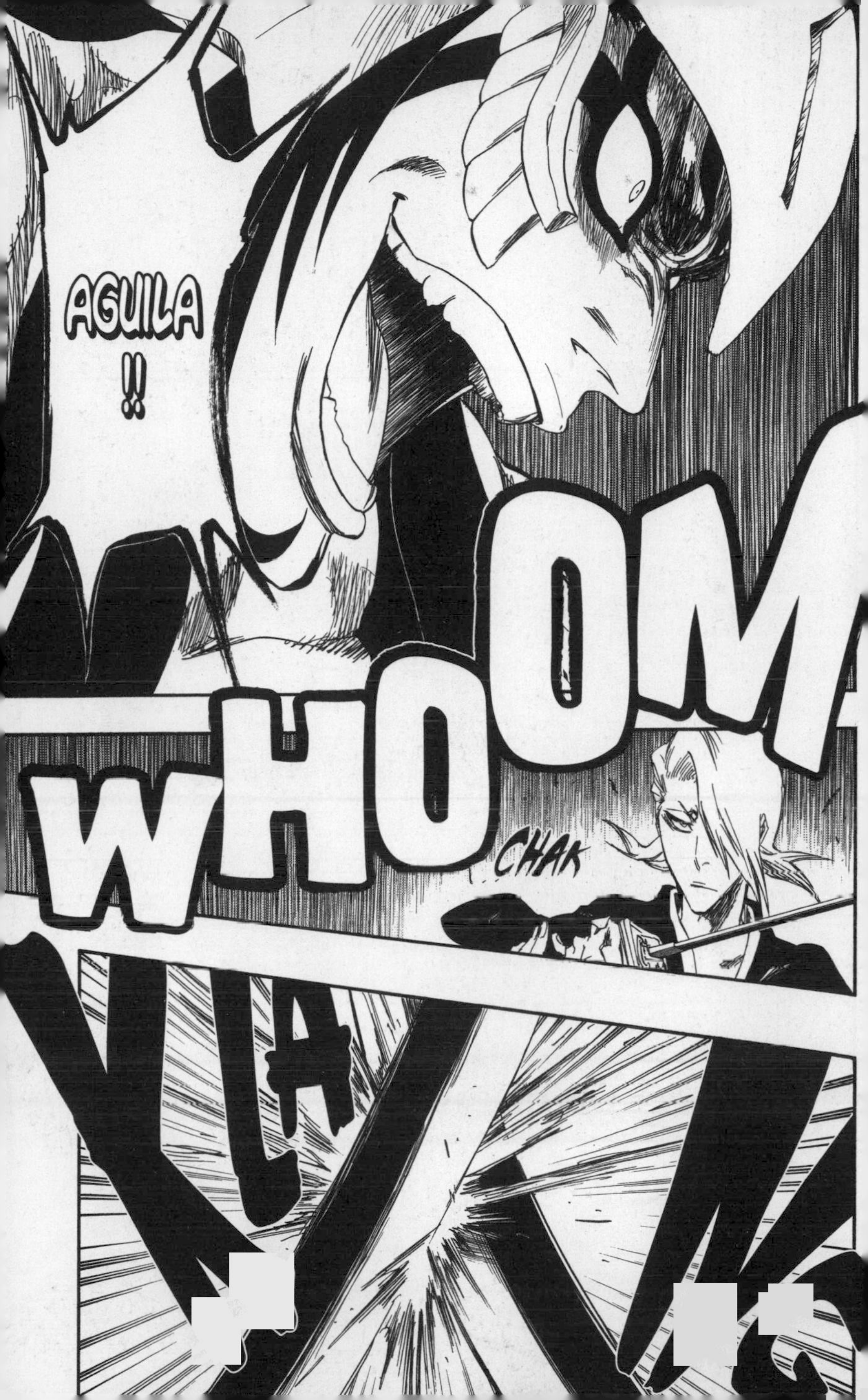
AGUILA !!
WHOOM
CHAK

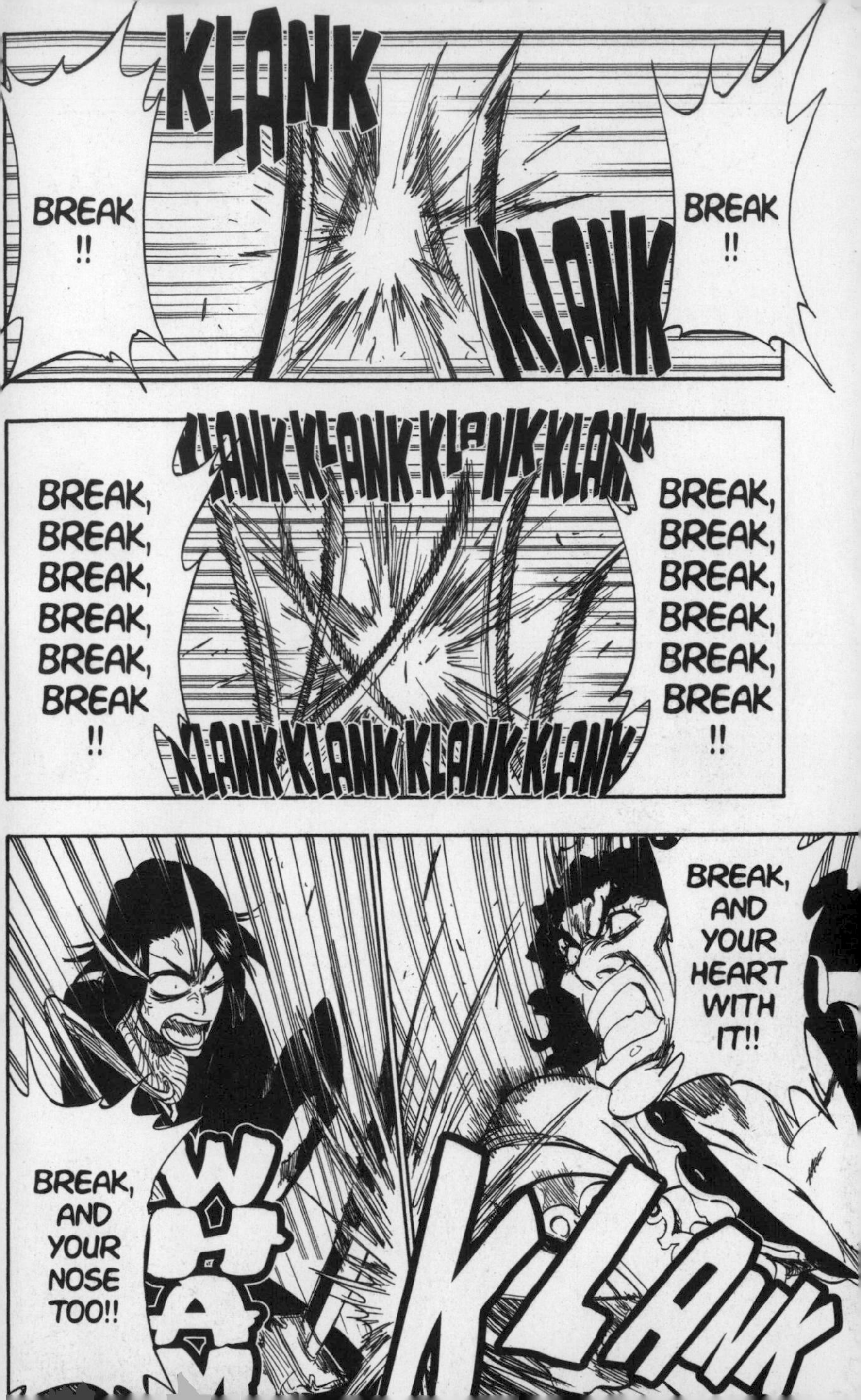
KLANK
BREAK !!
KLANK
BREAK !!
KLANK KLANK KLANK KLANK
BREAK, BREAK, BREAK, BREAK, BREAK, BREAK !!
BREAK, BREAK, BREAK, BREAK, BREAK, BREAK !!
KLANK KLANK KLANK KLANK
BREAK, AND YOUR HEART WITH IT!!
KLANK
BREAK, AND YOUR NOSE TOO!!
WHAM

READ THIS WAY

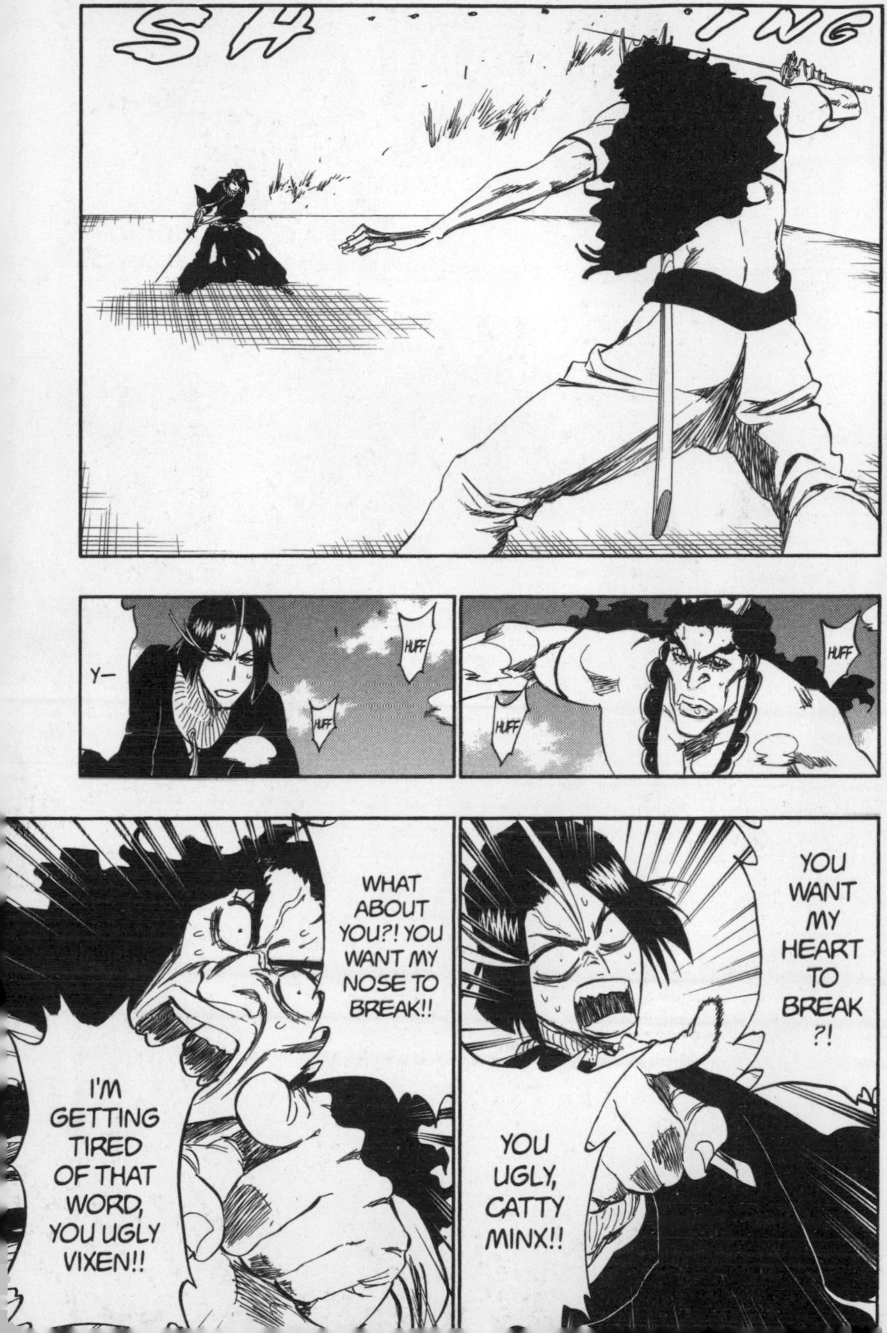
SH...ING
HUFF
HUFF
HUFF
HUFF
Y—
YOU WANT MY HEART TO BREAK?!
YOU UGLY, CATTY MINX!!
WHAT ABOUT YOU?! YOU WANT MY NOSE TO BREAK!!
I'M GETTING TIRED OF THAT WORD, YOU UGLY VIXEN!!

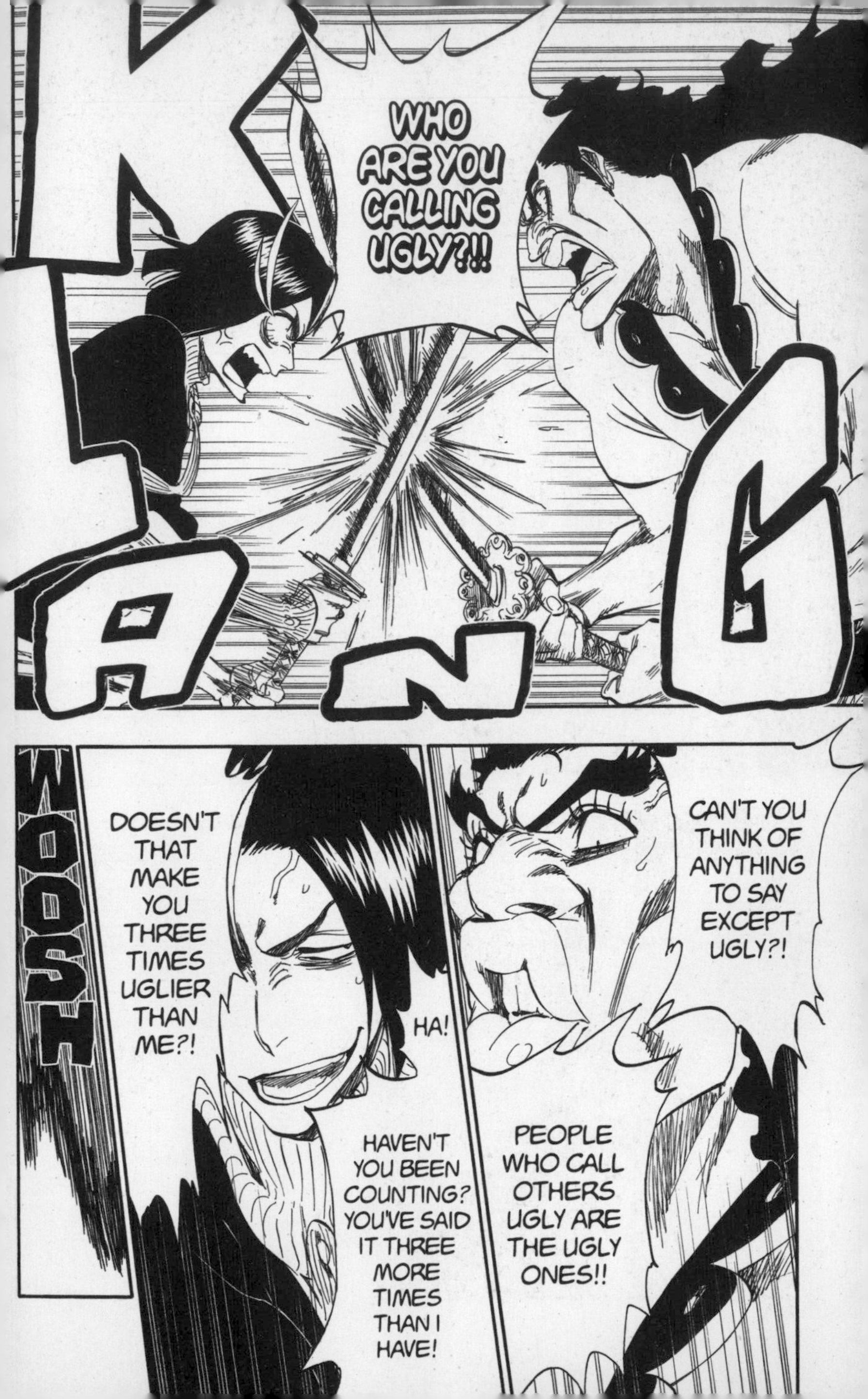
KANG
WHO ARE YOU CALLING UGLY?!!
CAN'T YOU THINK OF ANYTHING TO SAY EXCEPT UGLY?!
PEOPLE WHO CALL OTHERS UGLY ARE THE UGLY ONES!!
WOOSH
HA!
HAVEN'T YOU BEEN COUNTING? YOU'VE SAID IT THREE MORE TIMES THAN I HAVE!
DOESN'T THAT MAKE YOU THREE TIMES UGLIER THAN ME?!

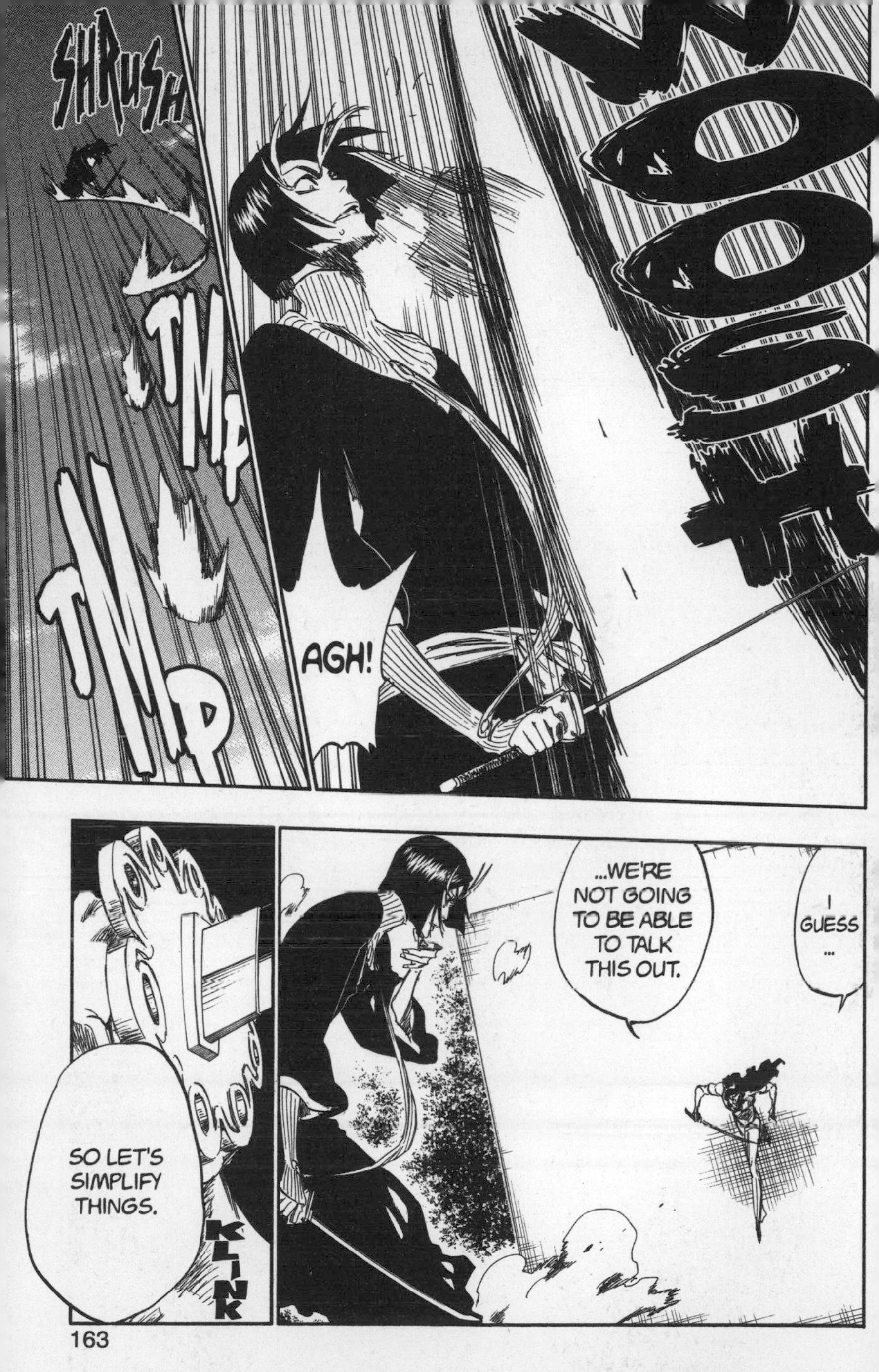
WOOSH
AGH!
SHRUSH
TMP
TMP
I GUESS...
...WE'RE NOT GOING TO BE ABLE TO TALK THIS OUT.
SO LET'S SIMPLIFY THINGS.
KLINK

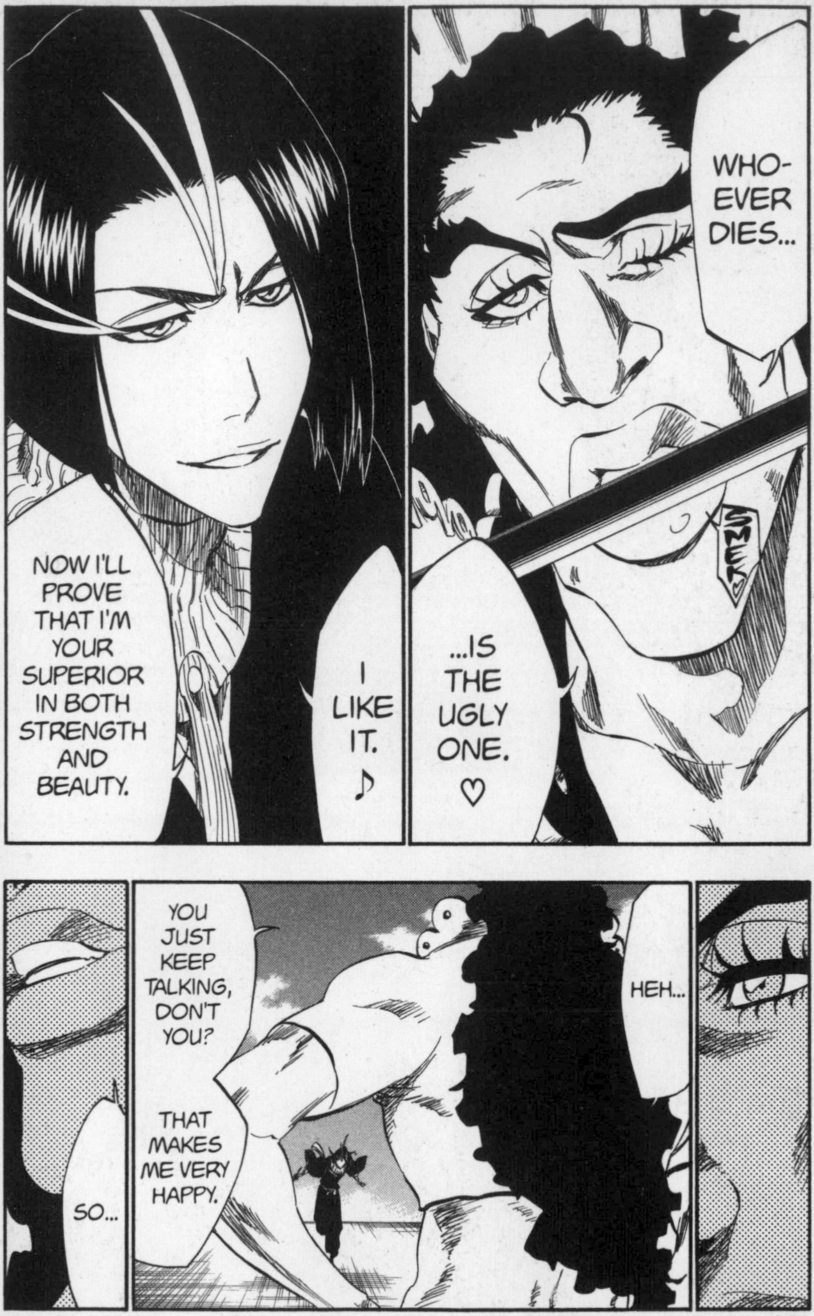
WHO-EVER DIES...
SMEK
...IS THE UGLY ONE. ♡
I LIKE IT. ♪
NOW I'LL PROVE THAT I'M YOUR SUPERIOR IN BOTH STRENGTH AND BEAUTY.
HEH...
YOU JUST KEEP TALKING, DON'T YOU?
THAT MAKES ME VERY HAPPY.
SO...

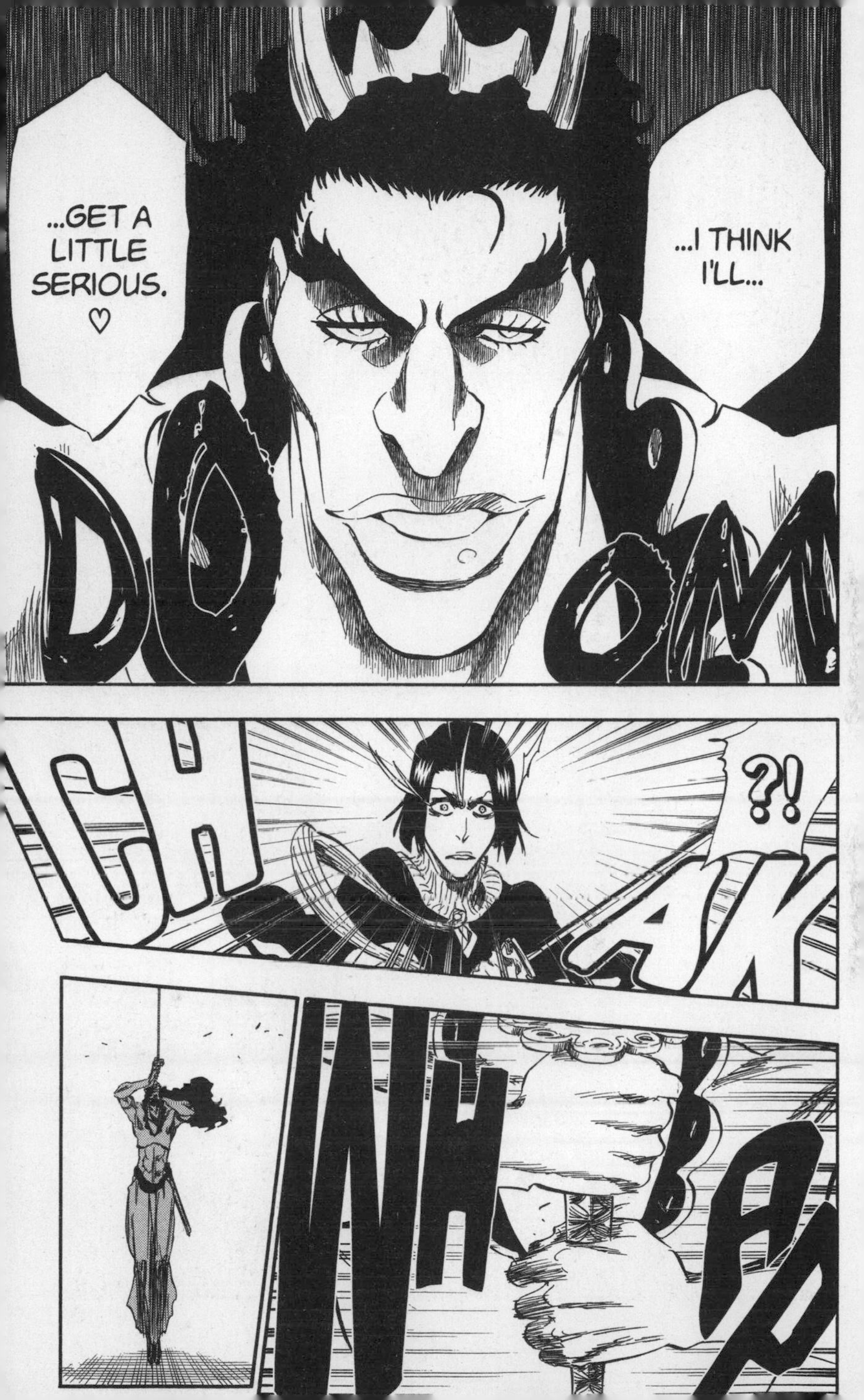
...I THINK I'LL...
...GET A LITTLE SERIOUS. ♡
DOOM
?!
CHAK
WHAP

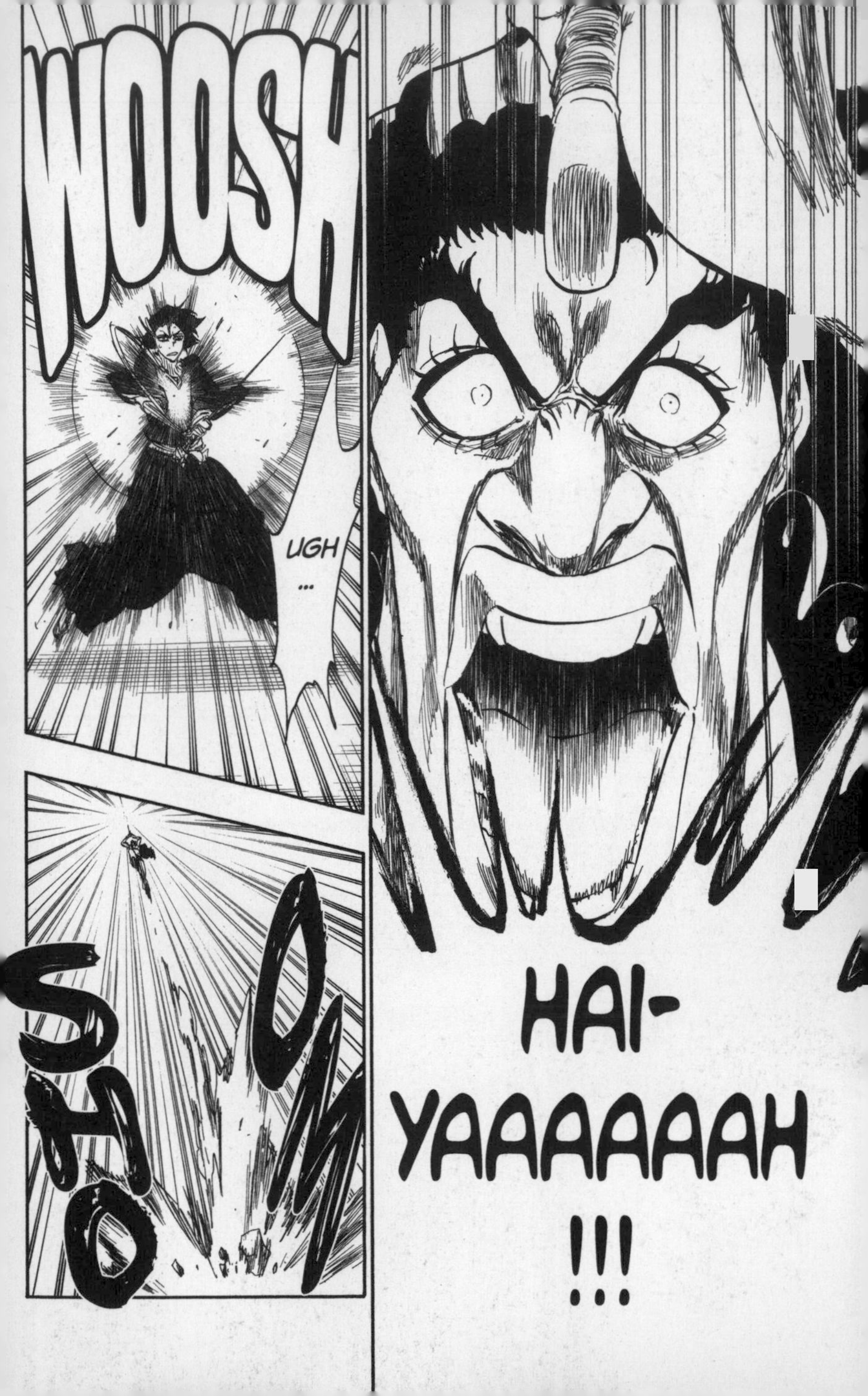
HAI-YAAAAAAAH!!!
WOOSH
UGH...
WOOSH

READ THIS WAY

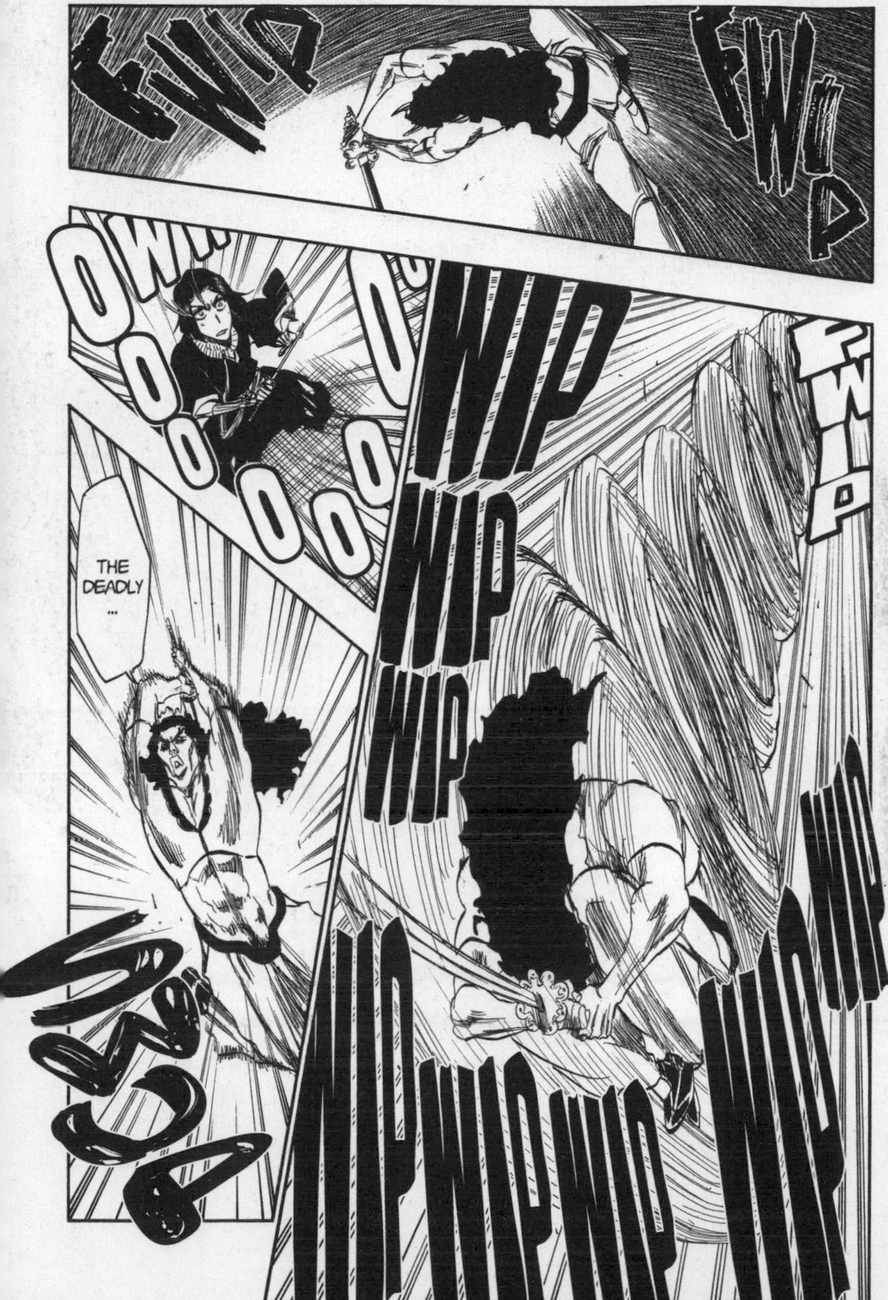
FWIP
FWIP
FWIP
WIP
WIP
WIP
THE DEADLY ...
WIP WIP WIP WIP

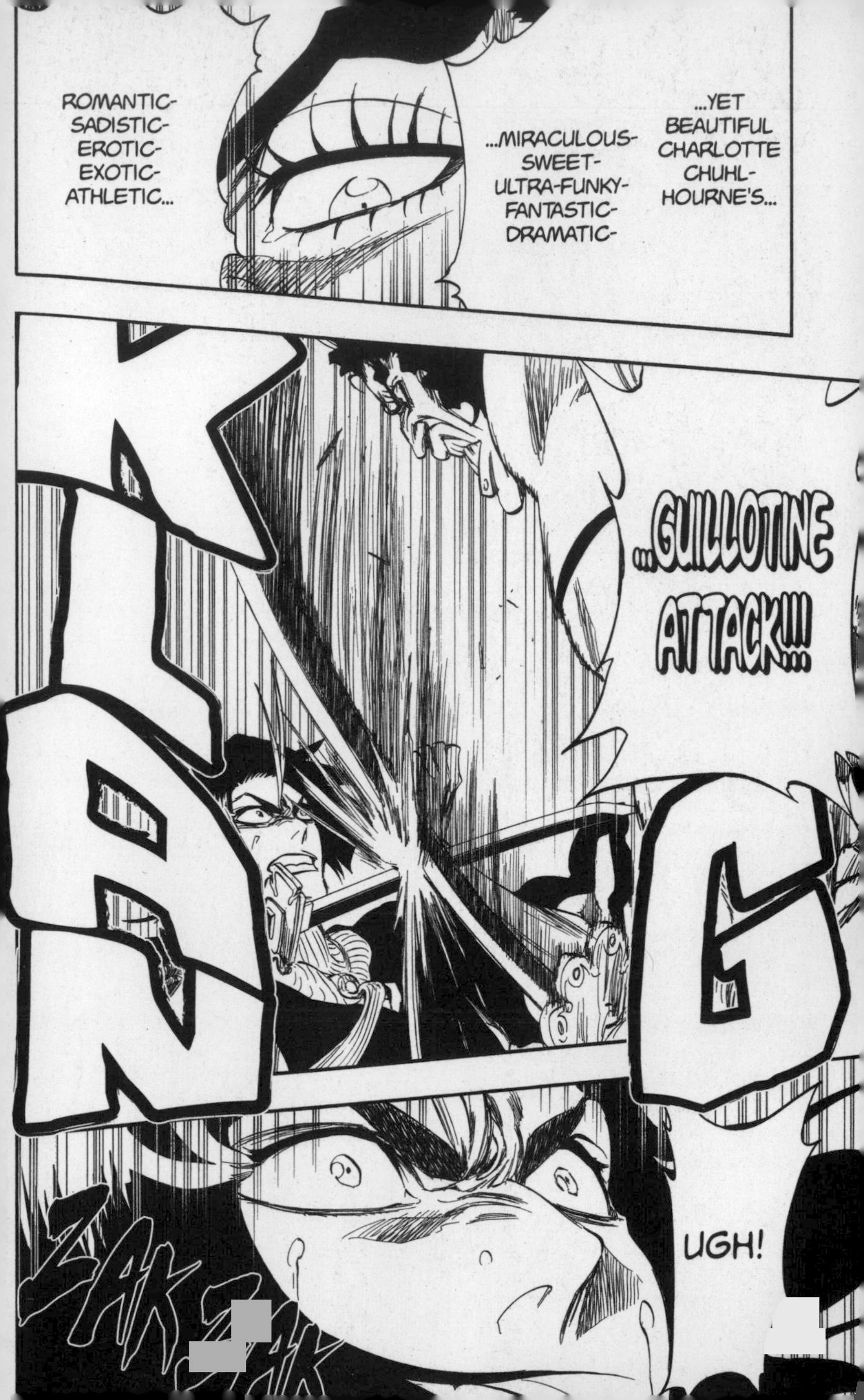
ROMANTIC-SADISTIC-EROTIC-EXOTIC-ATHLETIC...
...MIRACULOUS-SWEET-ULTRA-FUNKY-FANTASTIC-DRAMATIC-
...YET BEAUTIFUL CHARLOTTE CHUHL-HOURNE'S...
...GUILLOTINE ATTACK!!!
UGH!
ZAK ZAK

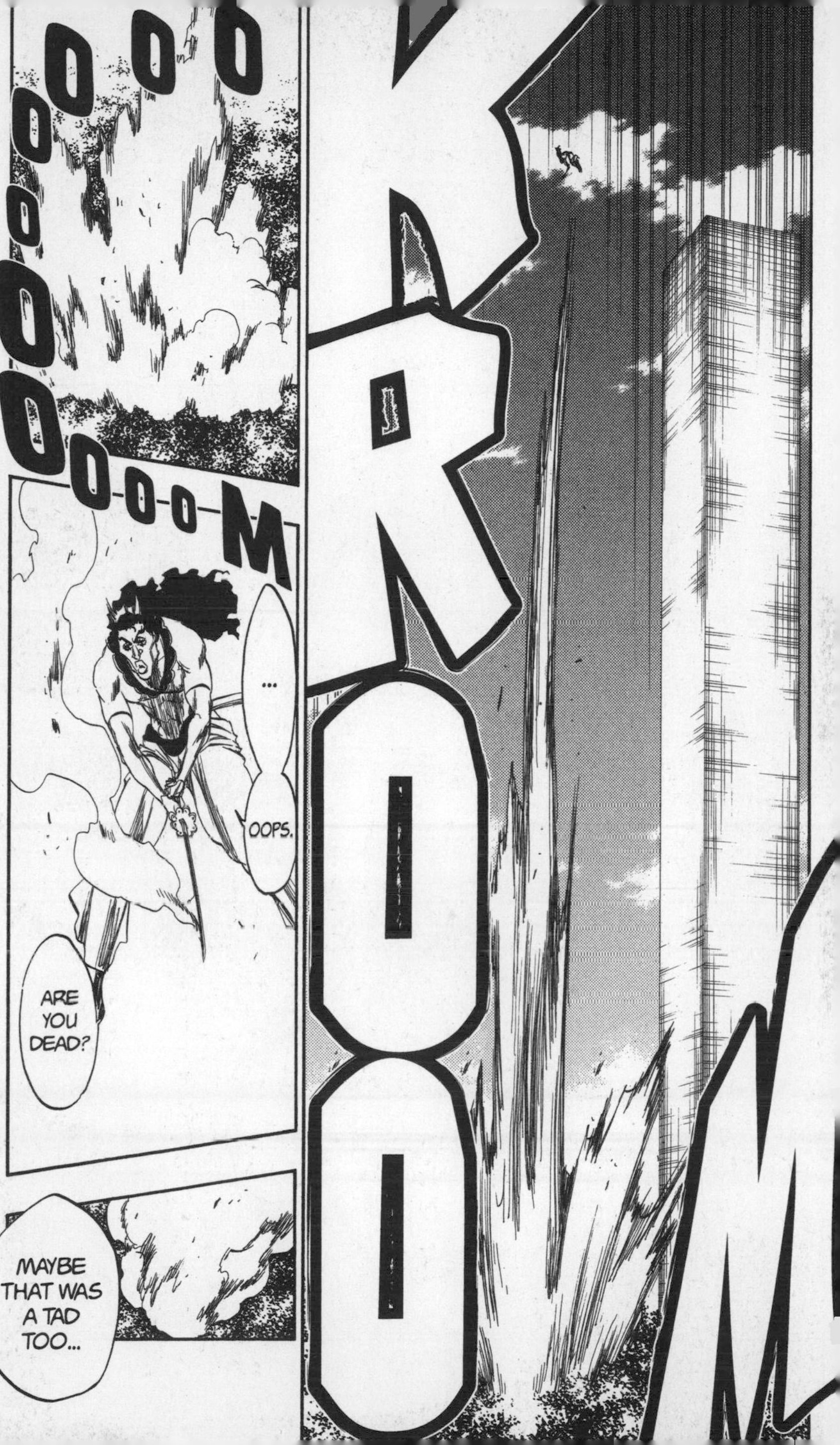
ROOM
OOOOOOOOOOOM
...
OOPS.
ARE YOU DEAD?
MAYBE THAT WAS A TAD TOO...

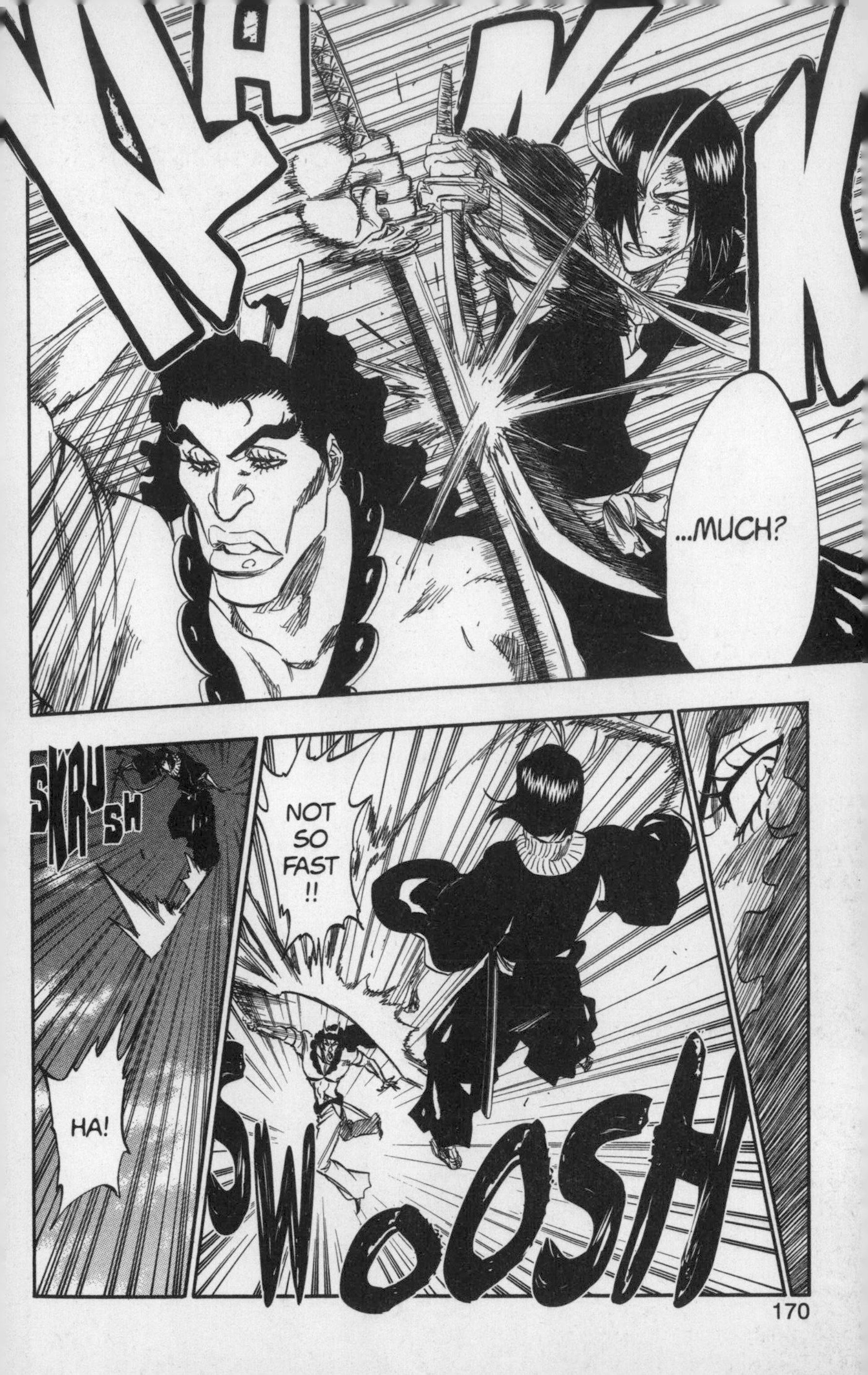
...MUCH?
NOT SO FAST!!
WOOSH
SKRUSH
HA!

READ THIS WAY

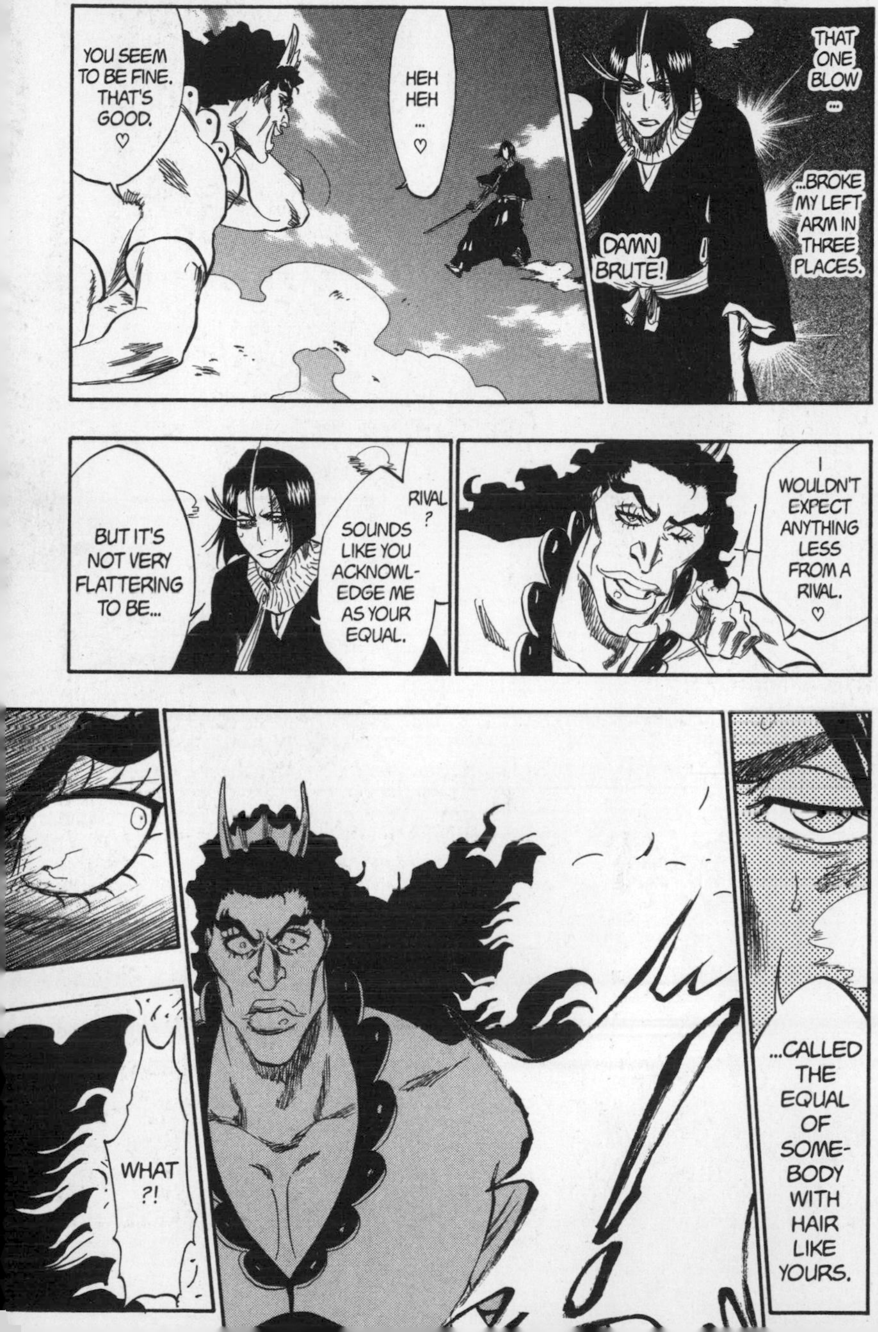
THAT ONE BLOW...
...BROKE MY LEFT ARM IN THREE PLACES.
DAMN BRUTE!
HEH HEH... ♡
YOU SEEM TO BE FINE. THAT'S GOOD. ♡
I WOULDN'T EXPECT ANYTHING LESS FROM A RIVAL. ♡
RIVAL?
SOUNDS LIKE YOU ACKNOWL-EDGE ME AS YOUR EQUAL.
BUT IT'S NOT VERY FLATTERING TO BE...
...CALLED THE EQUAL OF SOME-BODY WITH HAIR LIKE YOURS.
WHAT?!

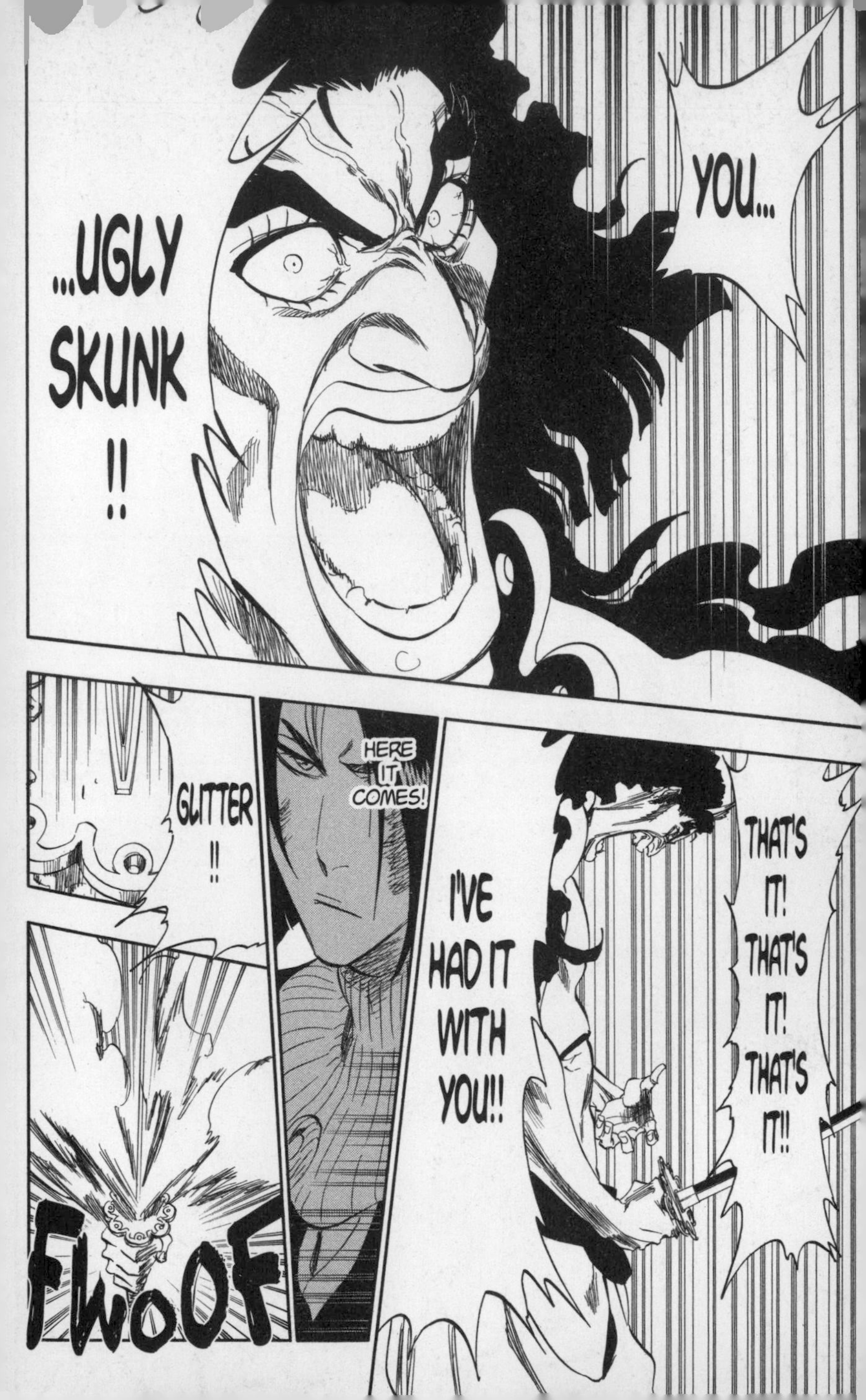
YOU...
...UGLY SKUNK !!
THAT'S IT! THAT'S IT! THAT'S IT!!
I'VE HAD IT WITH YOU!!
HERE IT COMES!
GLITTER !!
FWOOF

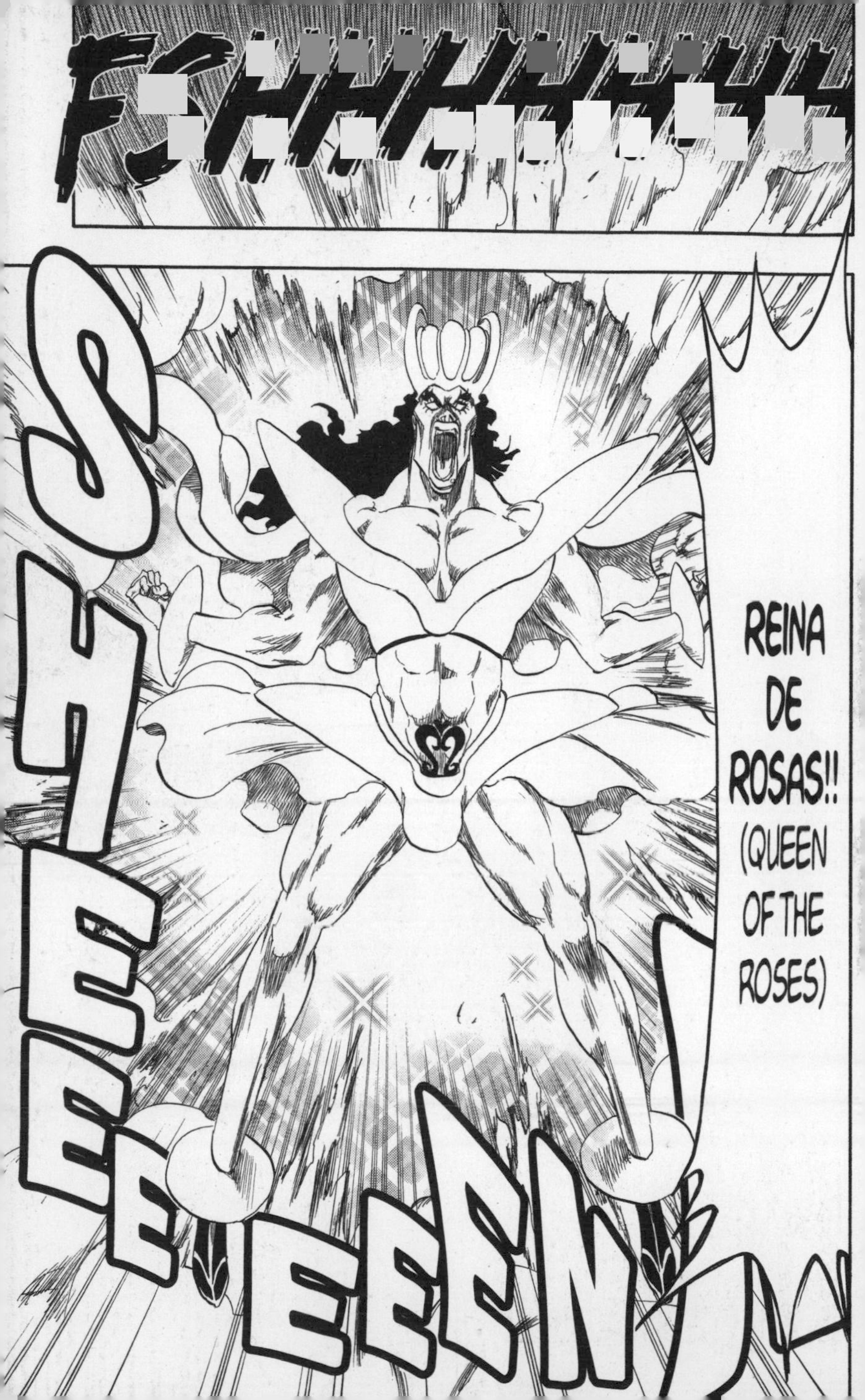
REINA DE ROSAS!! (QUEEN OF THE ROSES)

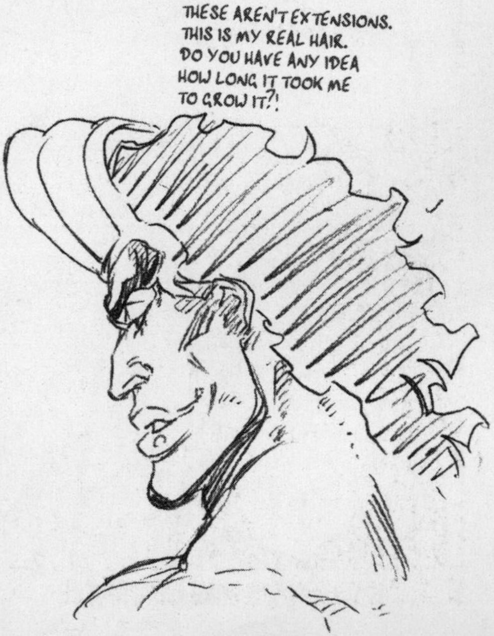
THESE AREN'T EXTENSIONS.
THIS IS MY REAL HAIR.
DO YOU HAVE ANY IDEA
HOW LONG IT TOOK ME
TO GROW IT?!

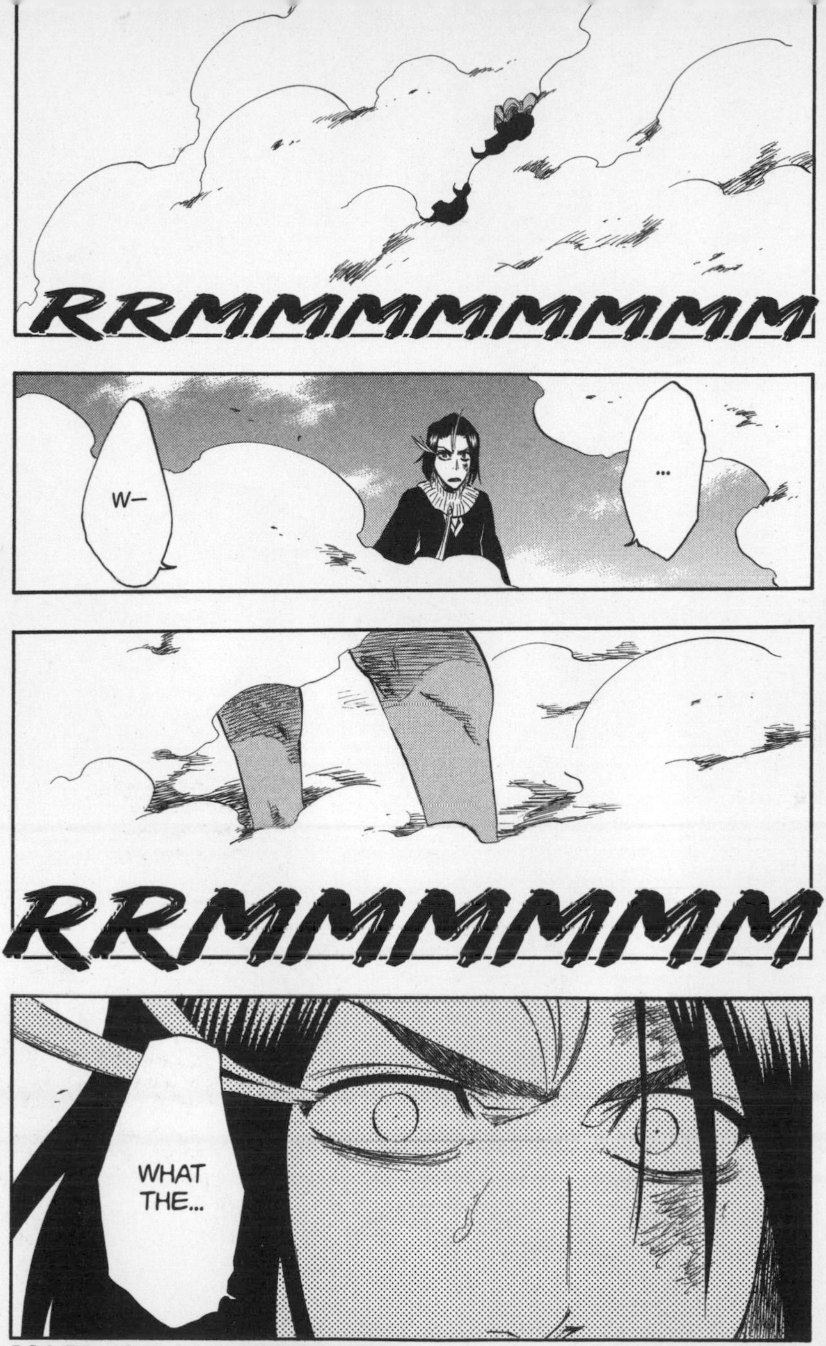
RRMMMMMMMMMM
...
W—
RRMMMMMMM
WHAT THE...

321. Black Briars and Brambles

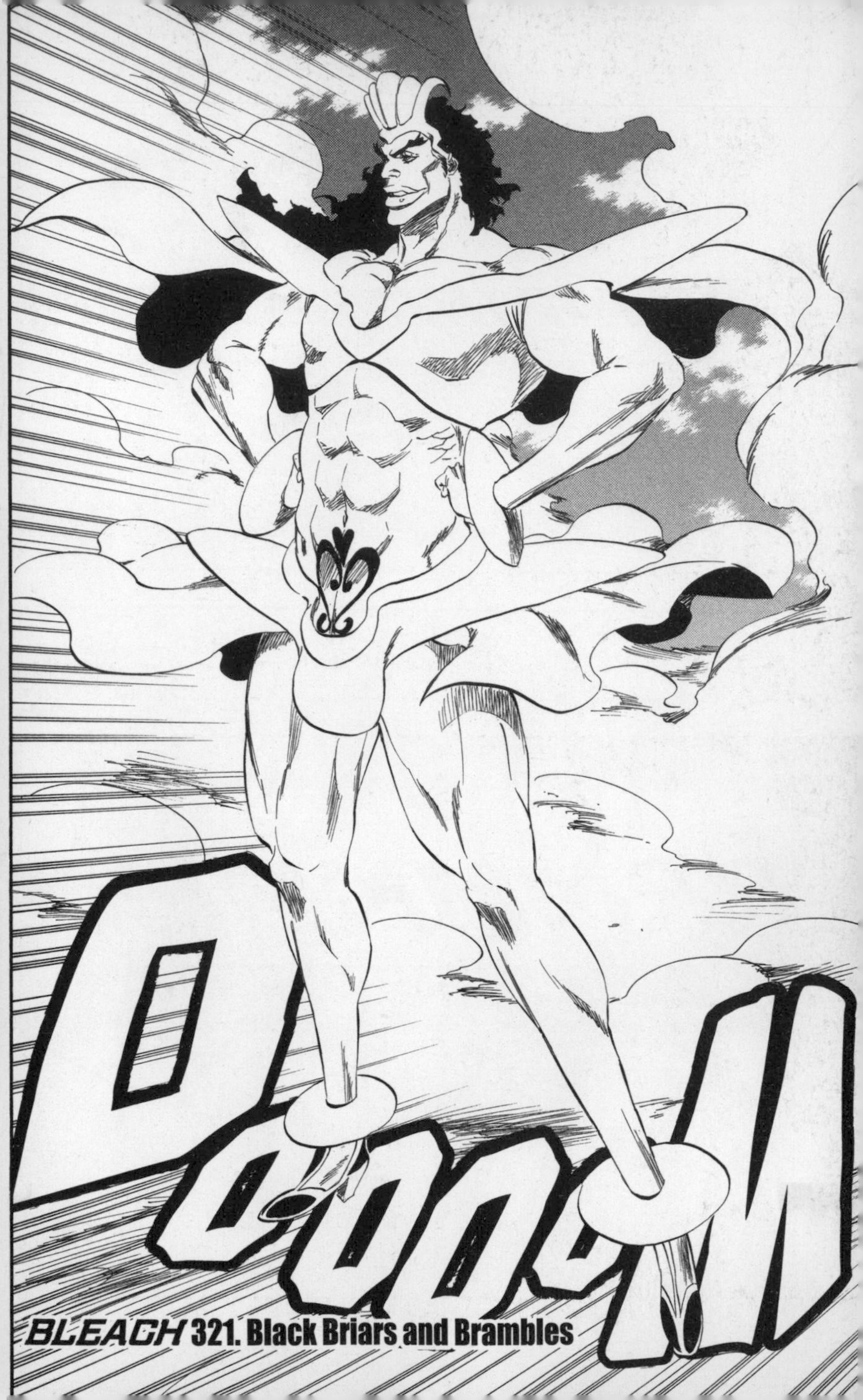

BLEACH 321. Black Briars and Brambles

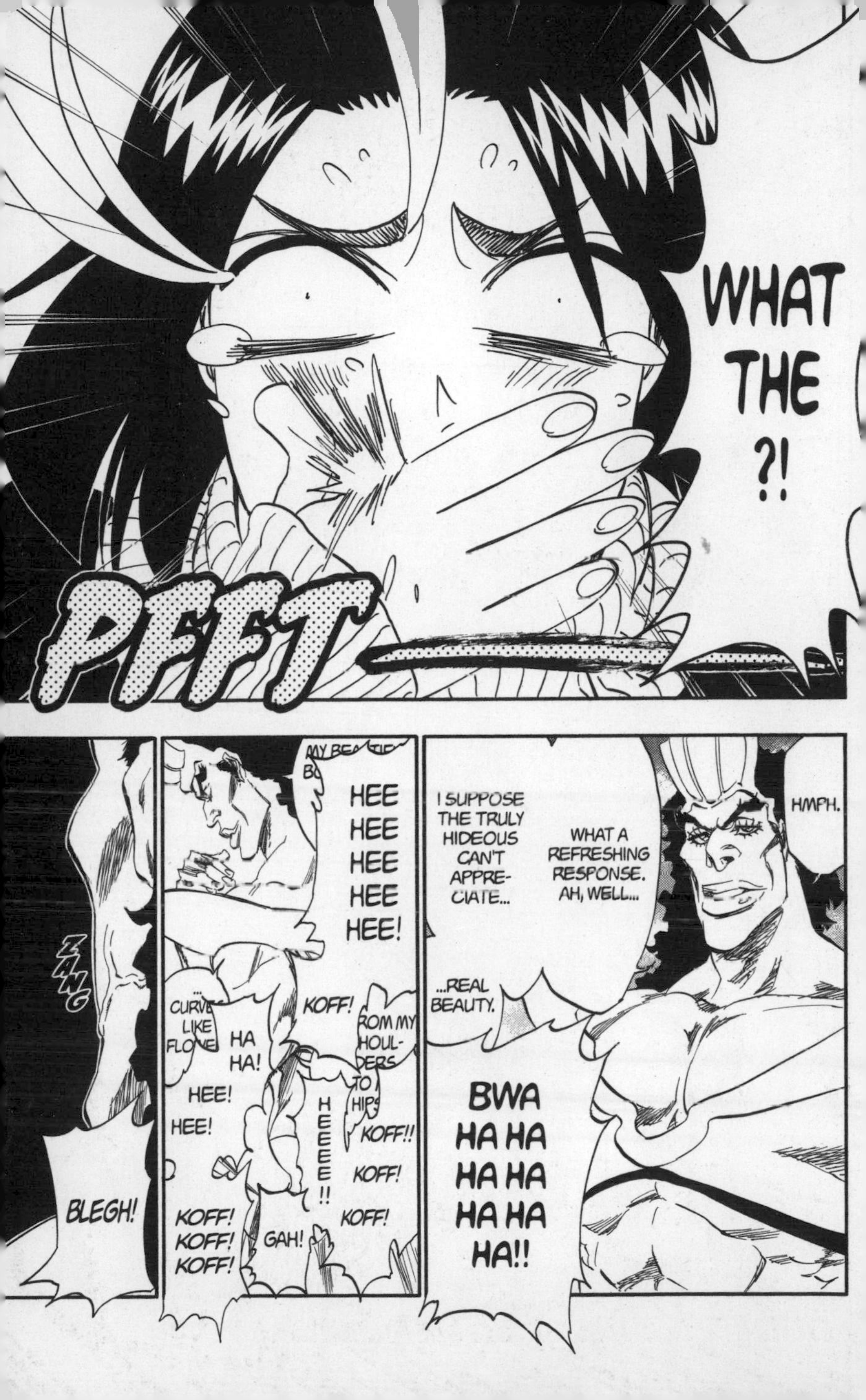
WHAT THE ?!
PFFT
HMPH.
WHAT A REFRESHING RESPONSE. AH, WELL...
I SUPPOSE THE TRULY HIDEOUS CAN'T APPRE-CIATE...
...REAL BEAUTY.
BWA HA HA HA HA HA HA HA!!
HEE HEE HEE HEE HEE!
KOFF!
HEEEEE!!
KOFF!!
KOFF!
KOFF!
HA HA!
HEE!
HEE!
GAH!
KOFF! KOFF! KOFF!
ZANG
BLEGH!

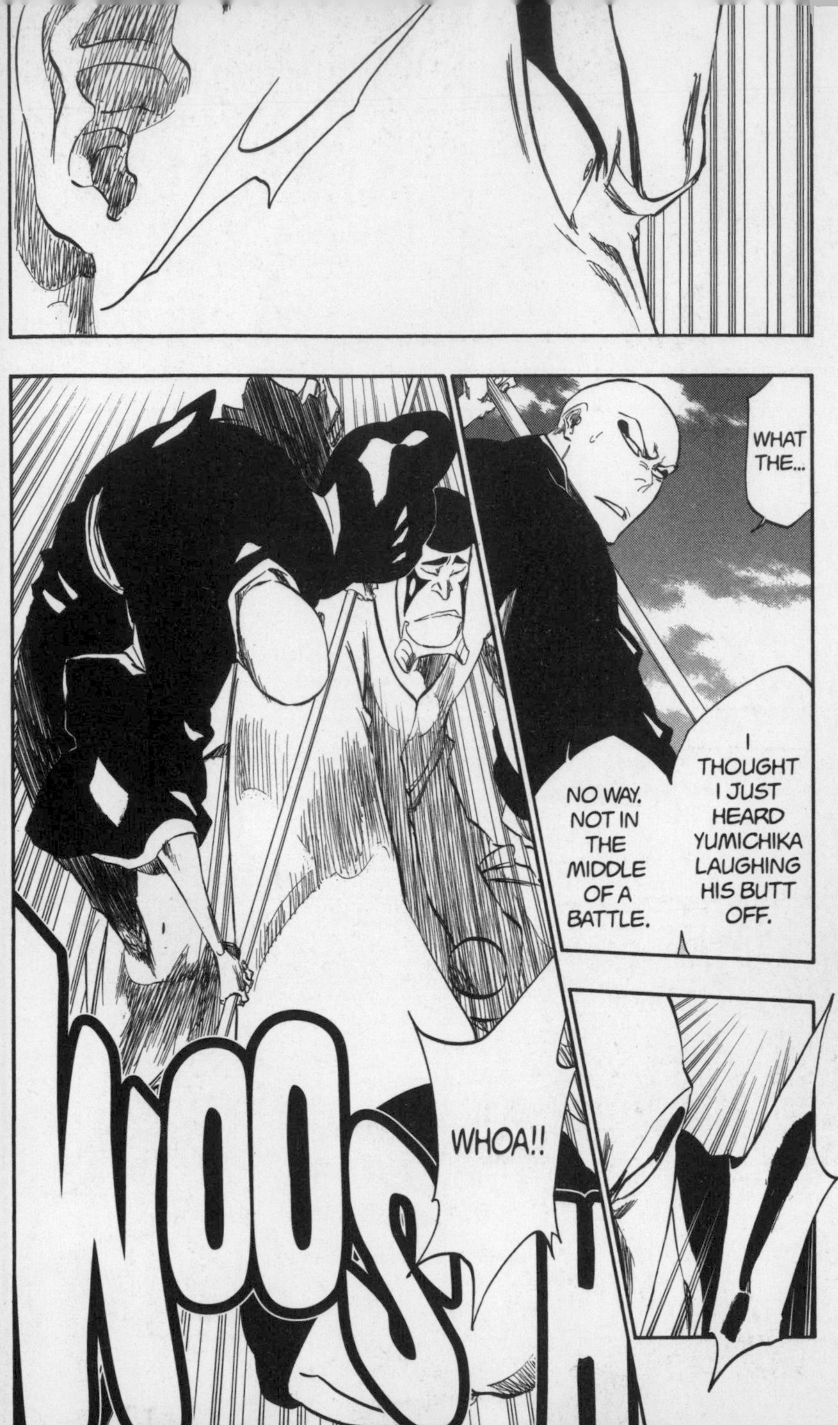
WHAT THE...
I THOUGHT I JUST HEARD YUMICHIKA LAUGHING HIS BUTT OFF.
NO WAY. NOT IN THE MIDDLE OF A BATTLE.
WHOA!!
WOOSH!!

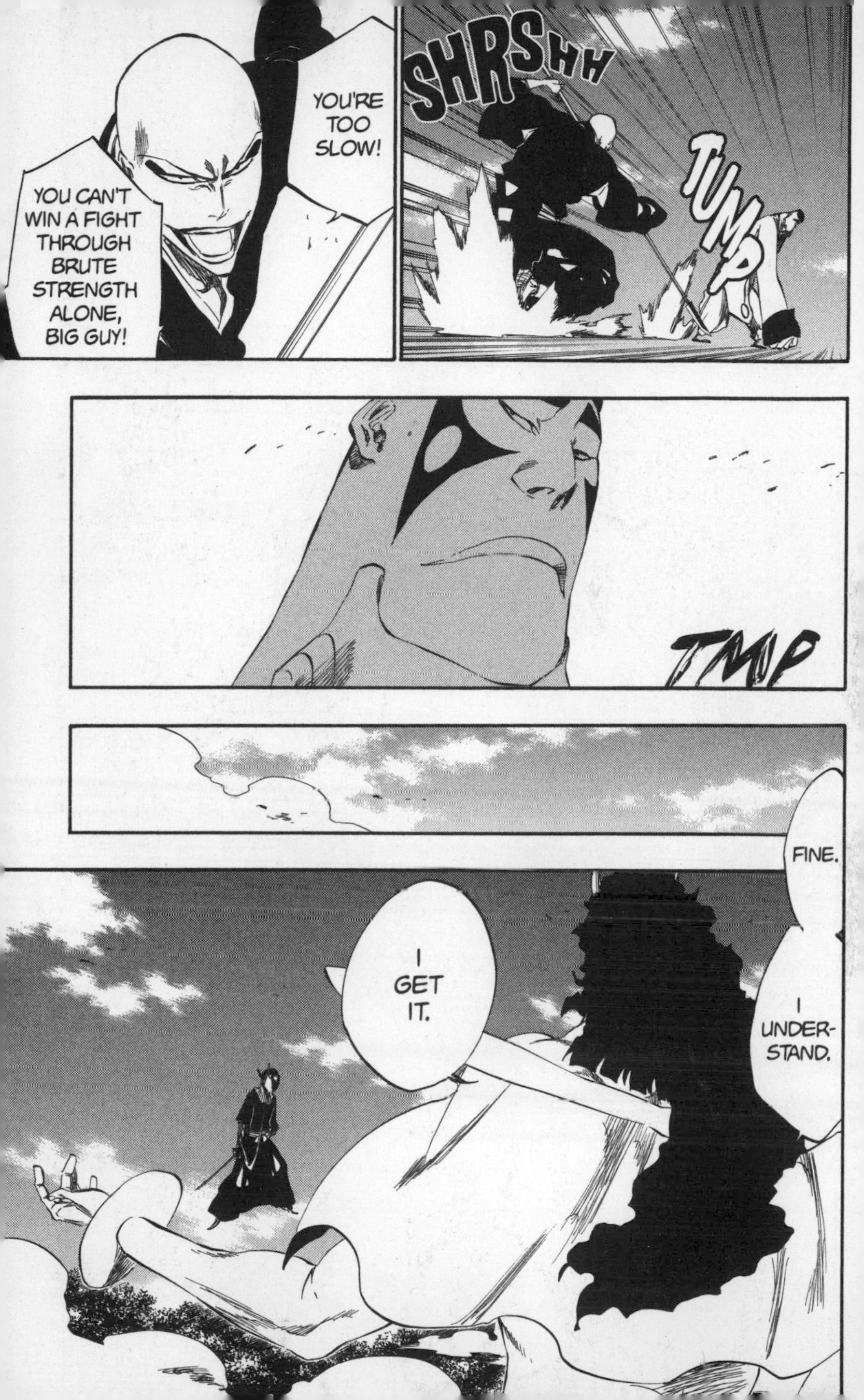
SHRSHH
TUMP
YOU'RE TOO SLOW!
YOU CAN'T WIN A FIGHT THROUGH BRUTE STRENGTH ALONE, BIG GUY!
TMP
FINE.
I UNDERSTAND.
I GET IT.

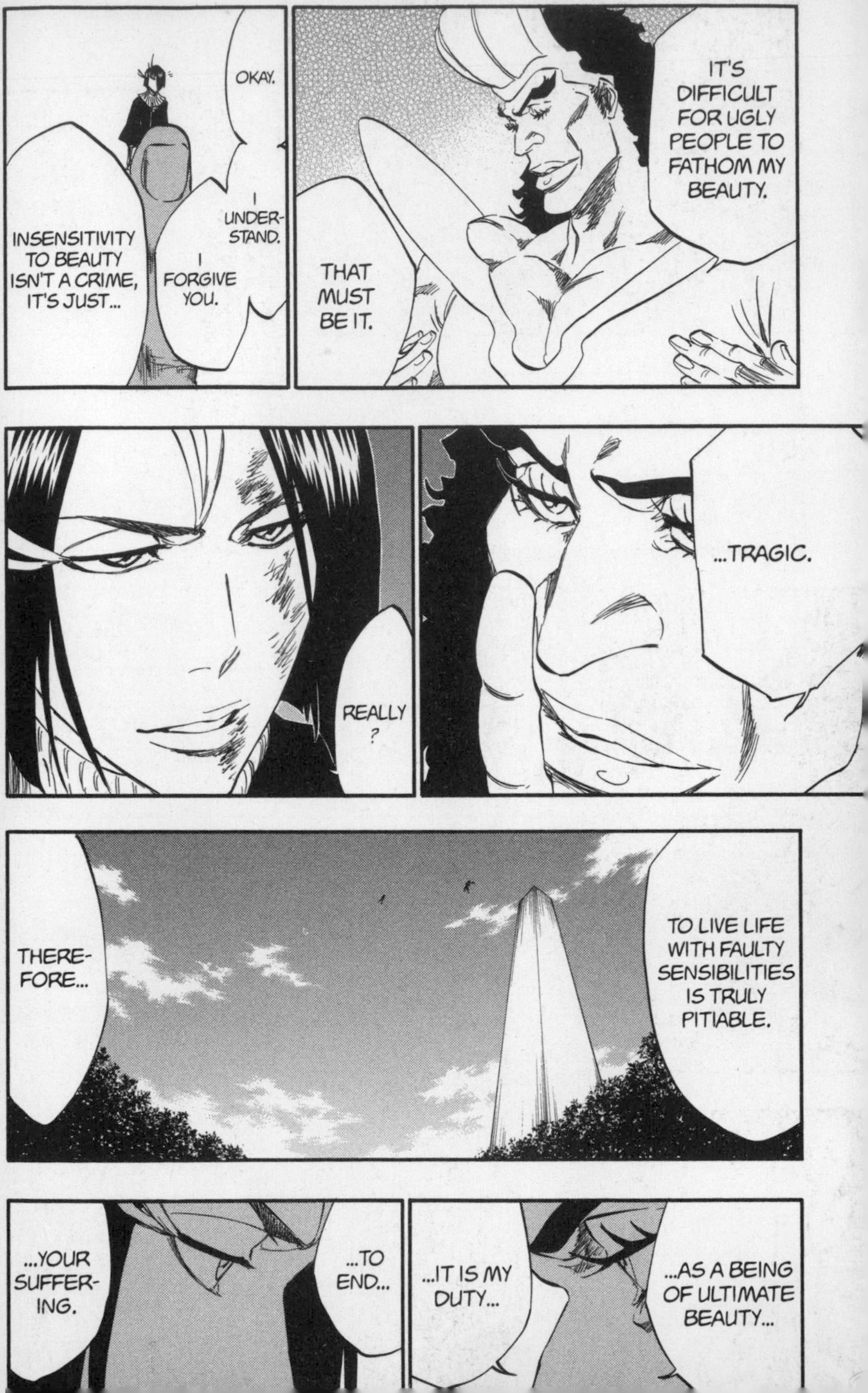
IT'S DIFFICULT FOR UGLY PEOPLE TO FATHOM MY BEAUTY.
THAT MUST BE IT.
OKAY.
I UNDERSTAND.
I FORGIVE YOU.
INSENSITIVITY TO BEAUTY ISN'T A CRIME, IT'S JUST...
...TRAGIC.
REALLY?
TO LIVE LIFE WITH FAULTY SENSIBILITIES IS TRULY PITIABLE.
THEREFORE...
...AS A BEING OF ULTIMATE BEAUTY...
...IT IS MY DUTY...
...TO END...
...YOUR SUFFERING.

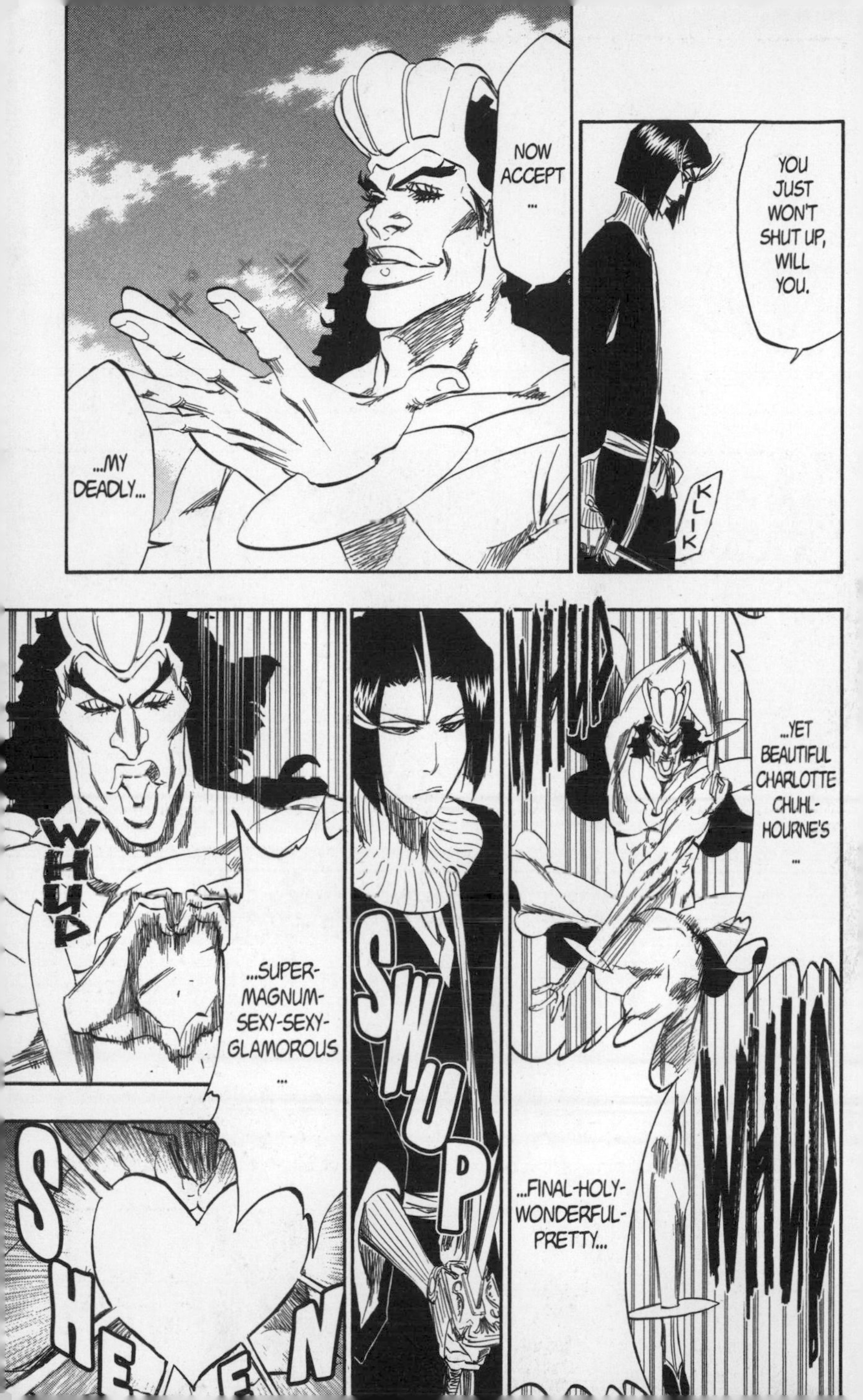
YOU JUST WON'T SHUT UP, WILL YOU.
KLIK
NOW ACCEPT...
...MY DEADLY...
WHUP
...YET BEAUTIFUL CHARLOTTE CHUHL-HOURNE'S...
WHUD
SWUP
...SUPER-MAGNUM-SEXY-SEXY-GLAMOROUS...
...FINAL-HOLY-WONDERFUL-PRETTY...
WHUP
SHEEN

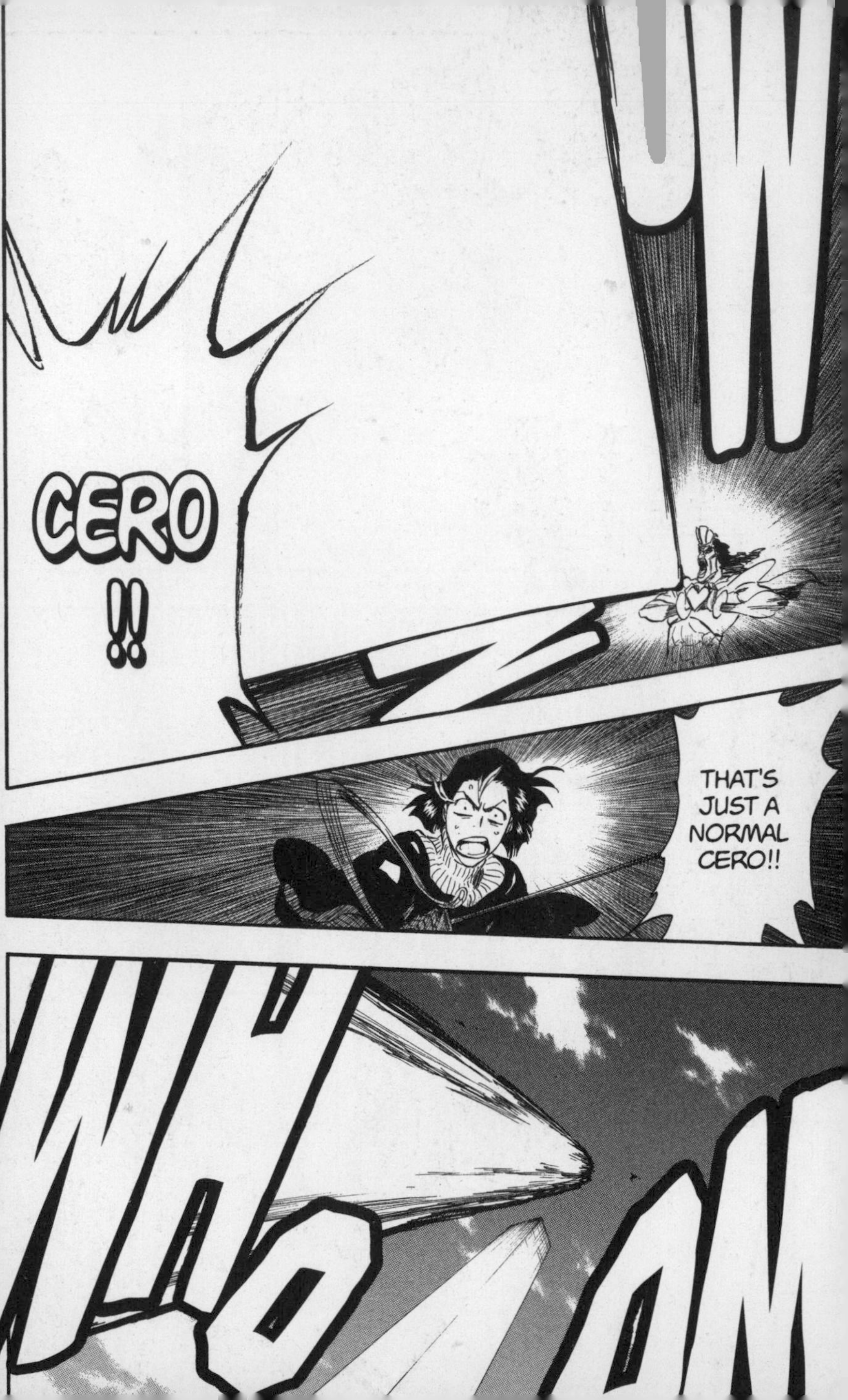
CERO!!
THAT'S JUST A NORMAL CERO!!

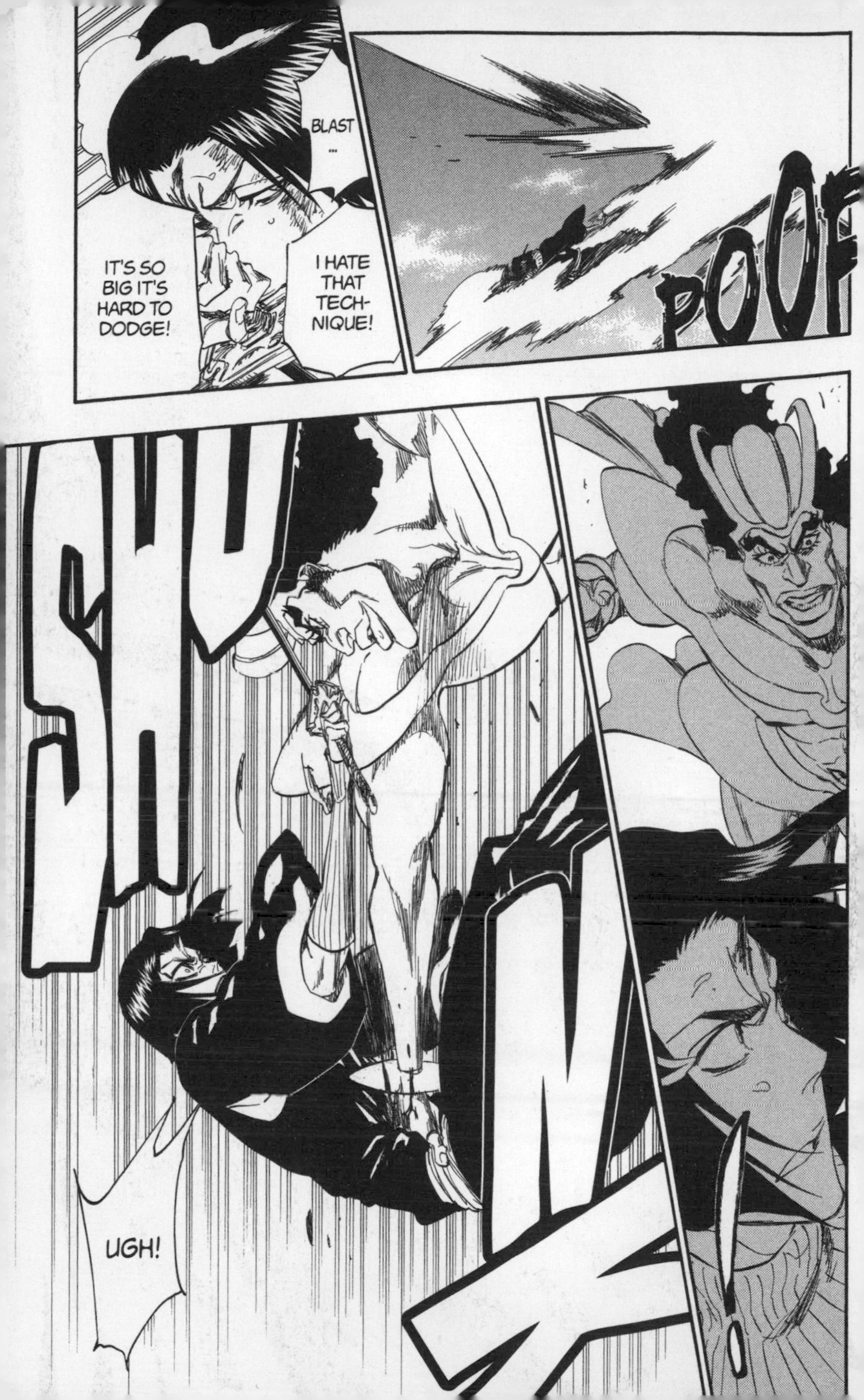
POOF
BLAST ...
I HATE THAT TECHNIQUE!
IT'S SO BIG IT'S HARD TO DODGE!
UGH!

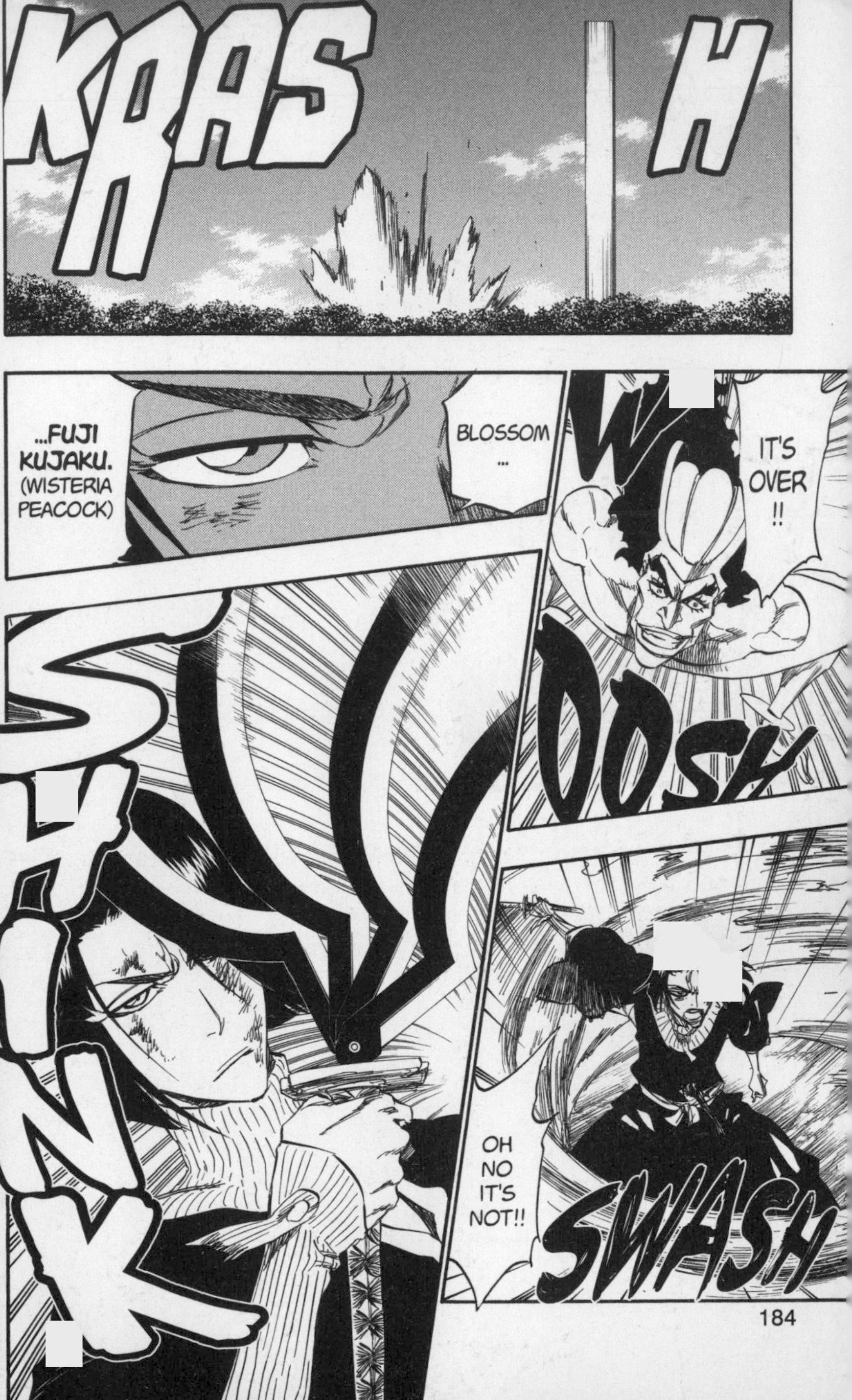
KRAASH
IT'S OVER!!
OOSH
BLOSSOM...
...FUJI KUJAKU. (WISTERIA PEACOCK)
SHINK
OH NO IT'S NOT!!
SWASH

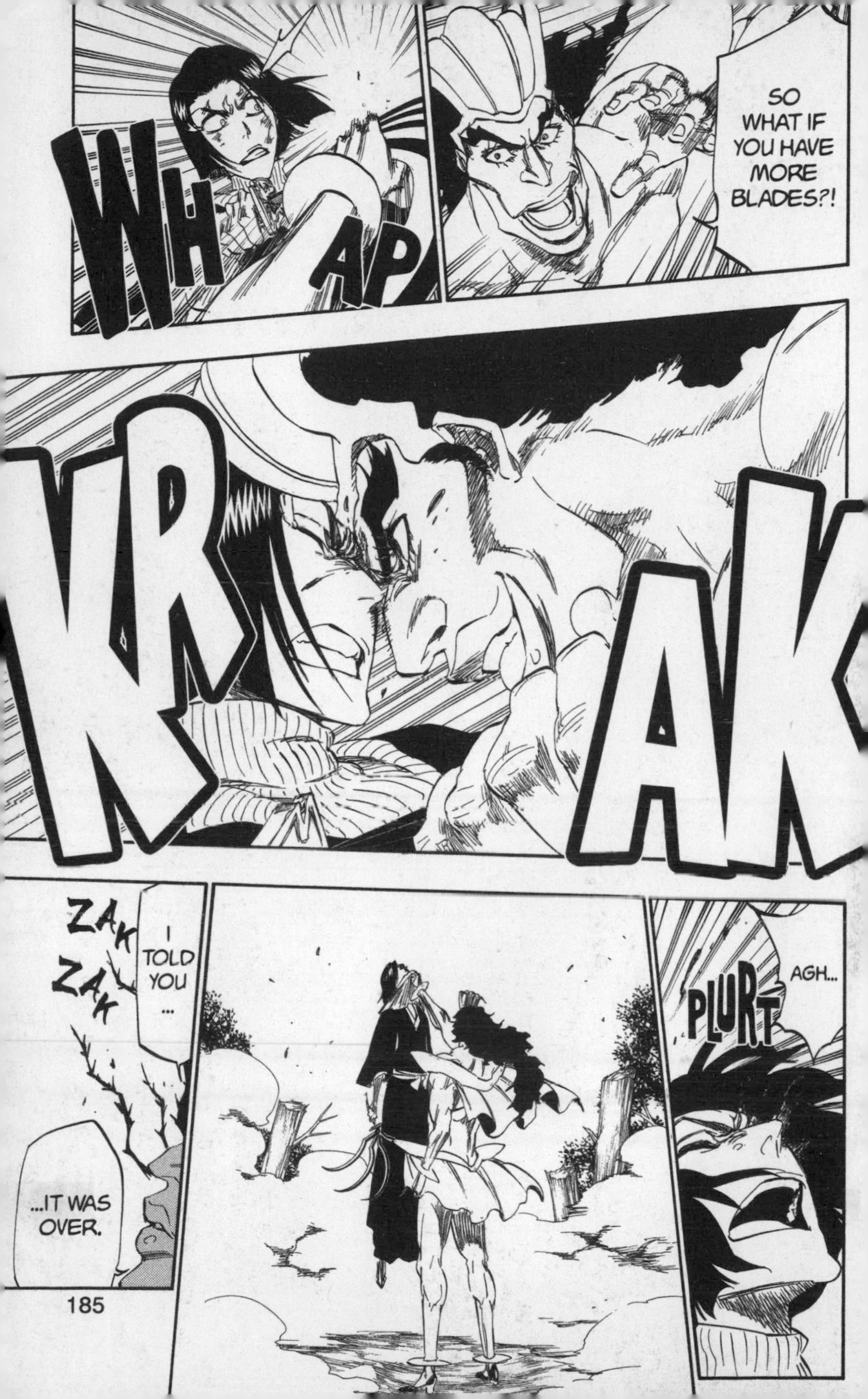
SO WHAT IF YOU HAVE MORE BLADES?!
WHAP
KRAK
AGH...
PLURT
ZAK ZAK
I TOLD YOU ...
...IT WAS OVER.

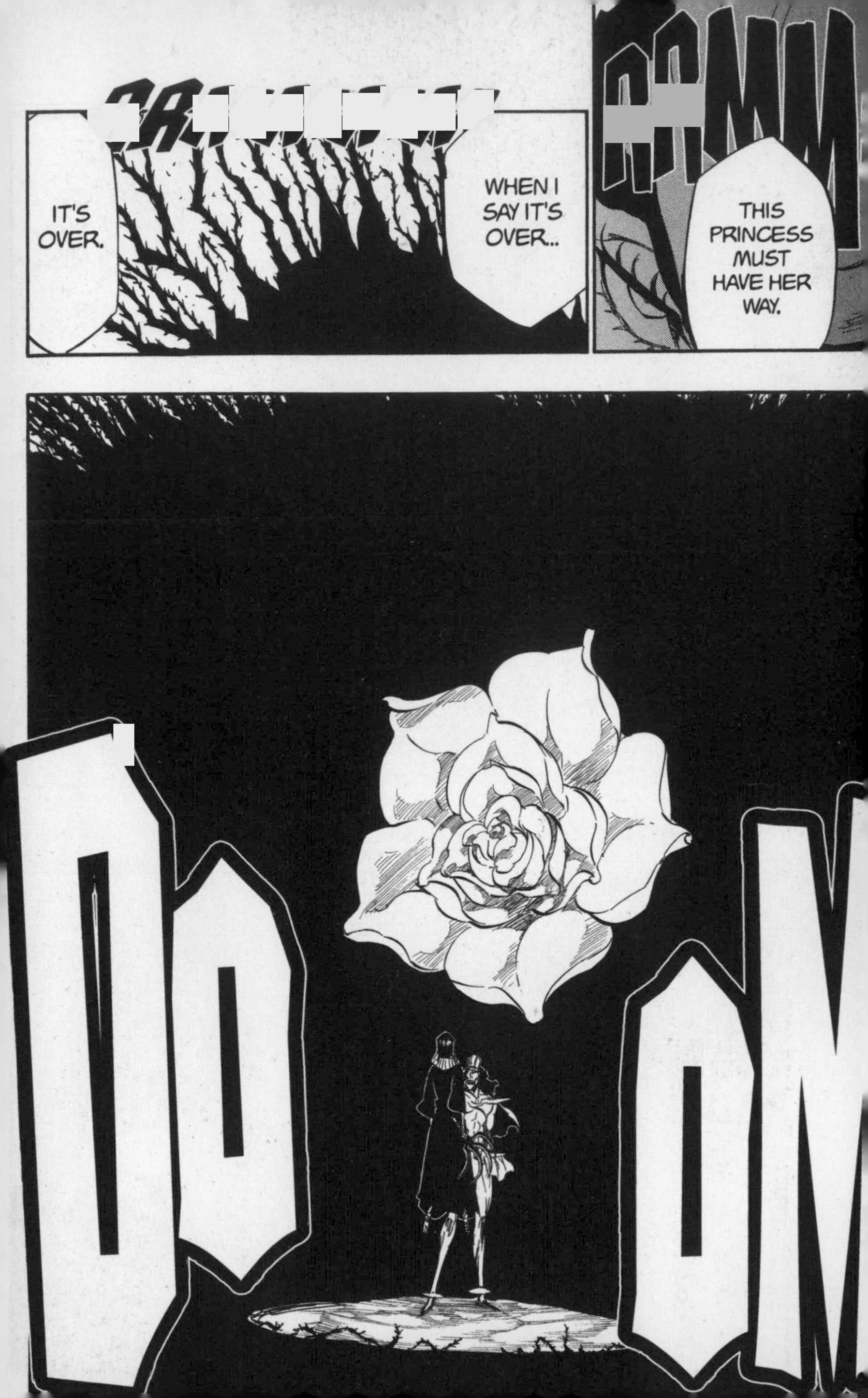
THIS PRINCESS MUST HAVE HER WAY.
WHEN I SAY IT'S OVER...
IT'S OVER.

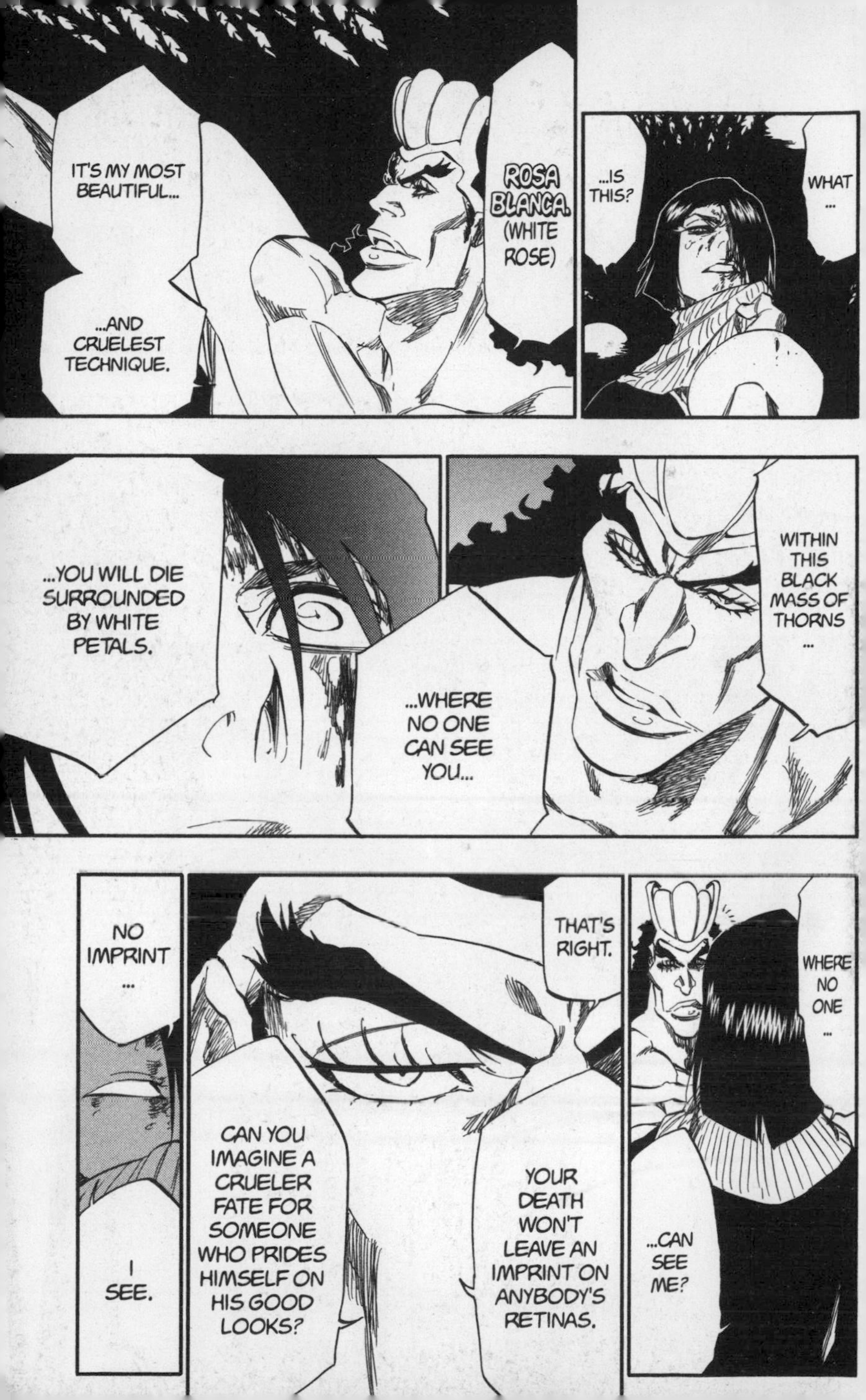
WHAT ...
...IS THIS?
ROSA BLANCA. (WHITE ROSE)
IT'S MY MOST BEAUTIFUL...
...AND CRUELEST TECHNIQUE.
WITHIN THIS BLACK MASS OF THORNS ...
...WHERE NO ONE CAN SEE YOU...
...YOU WILL DIE SURROUNDED BY WHITE PETALS.
WHERE NO ONE ...
...CAN SEE ME?
THAT'S RIGHT.
YOUR DEATH WON'T LEAVE AN IMPRINT ON ANYBODY'S RETINAS.
CAN YOU IMAGINE A CRUELER FATE FOR SOMEONE WHO PRIDES HIMSELF ON HIS GOOD LOOKS?
NO IMPRINT ...
I SEE.

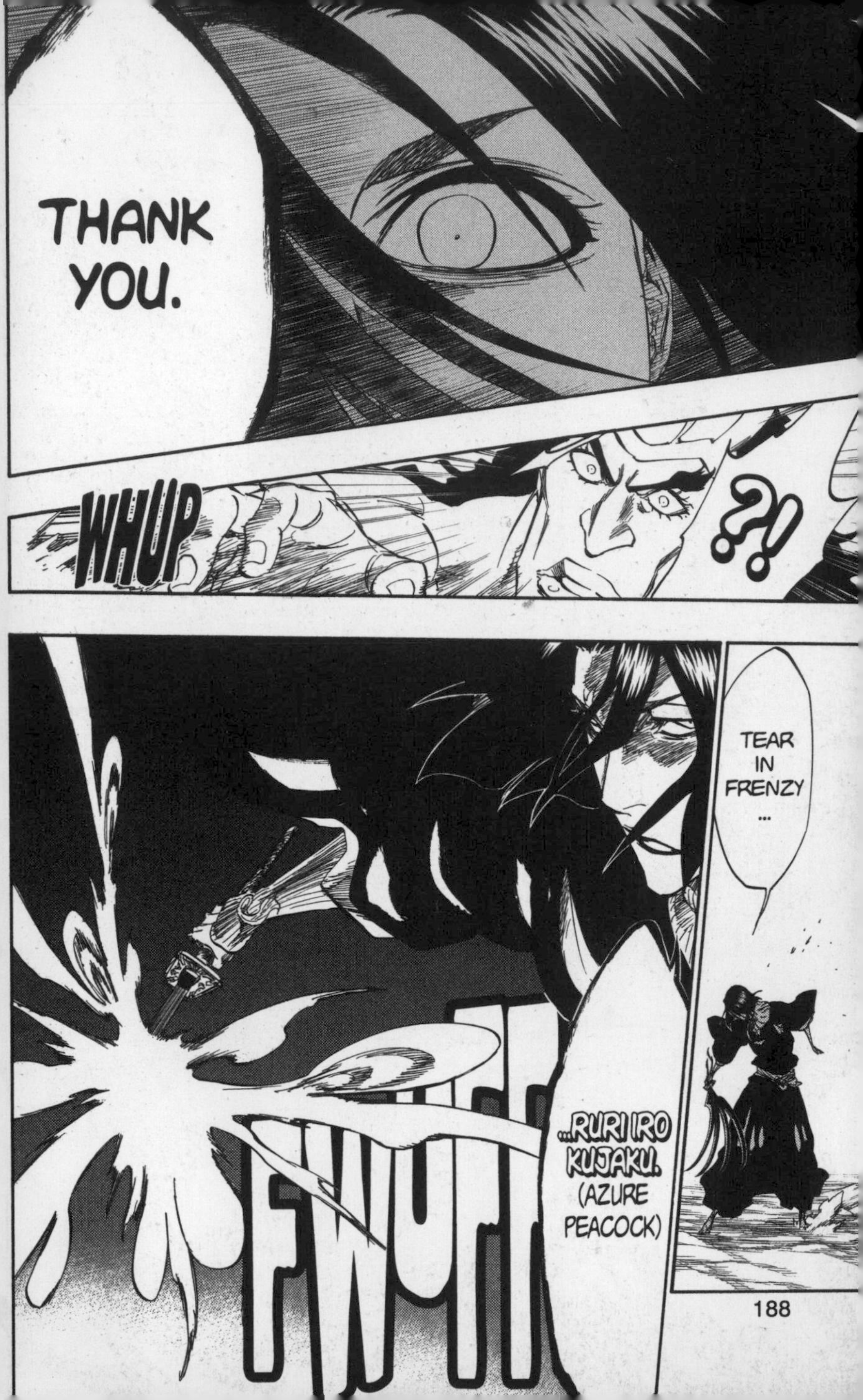
THANK YOU.
?!
WHUP
TEAR IN FRENZY ...
...RURI IRO KUJAKU.
(AZURE PEACOCK)

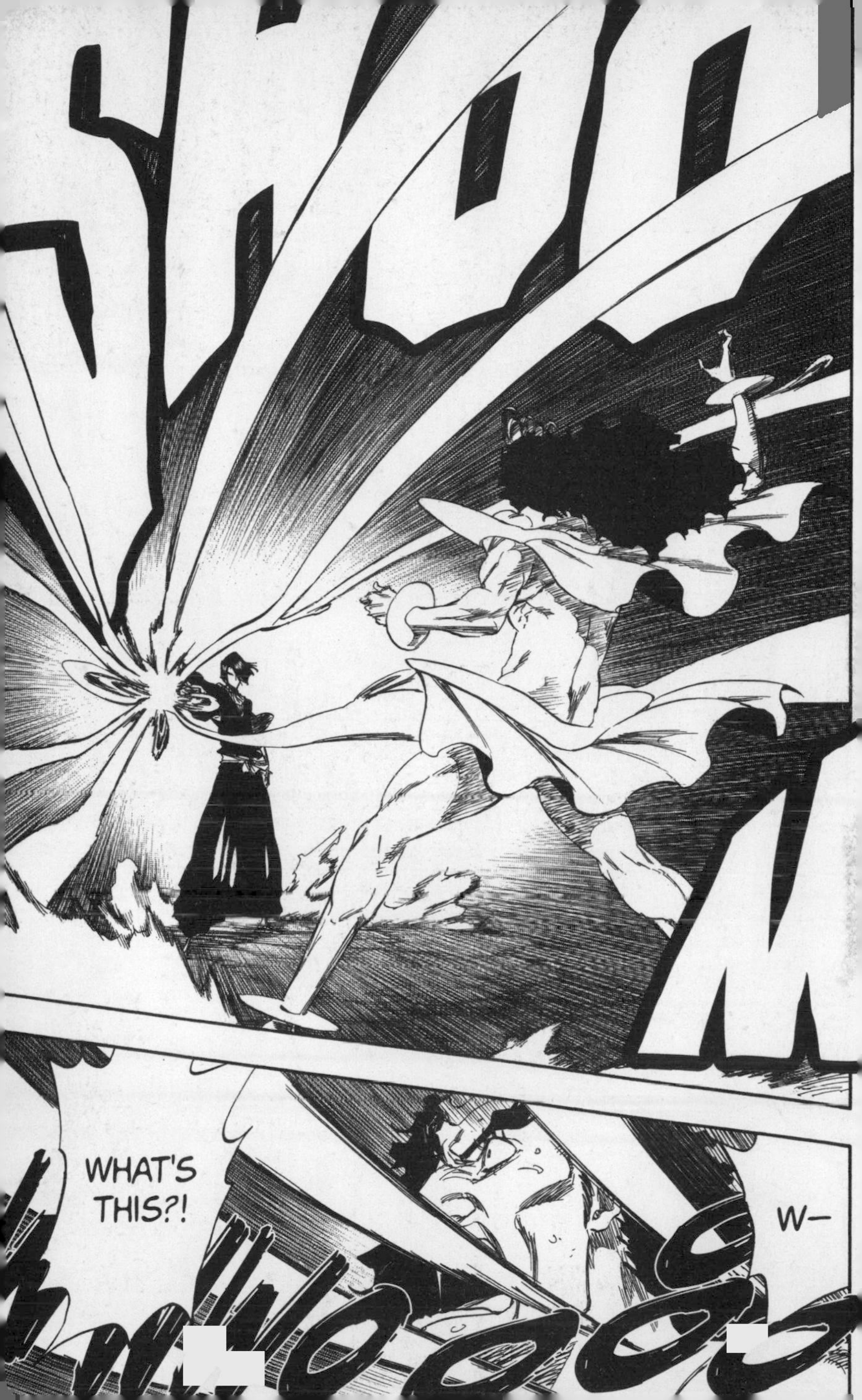
W–
WHAT'S THIS?!

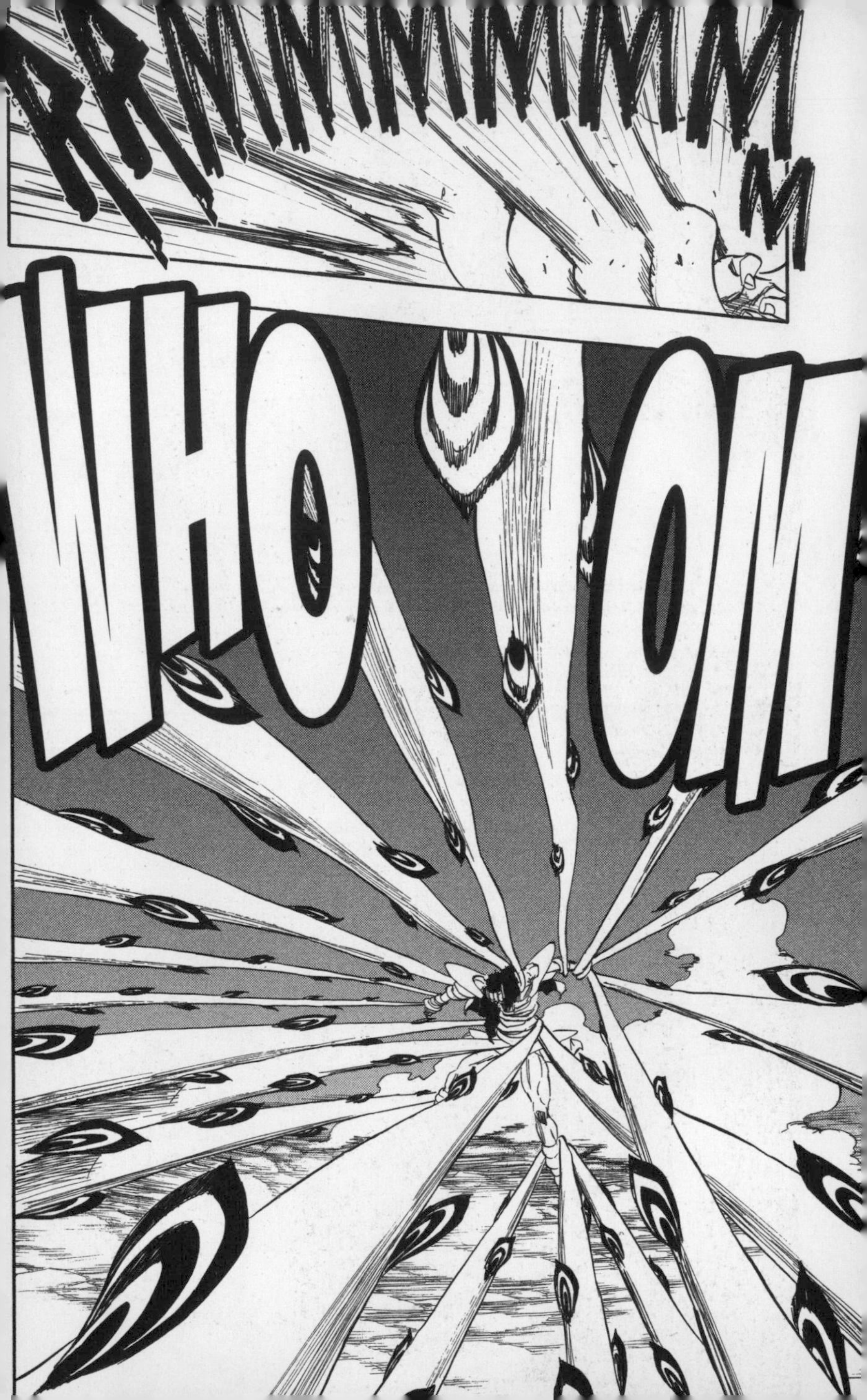
WHOOM

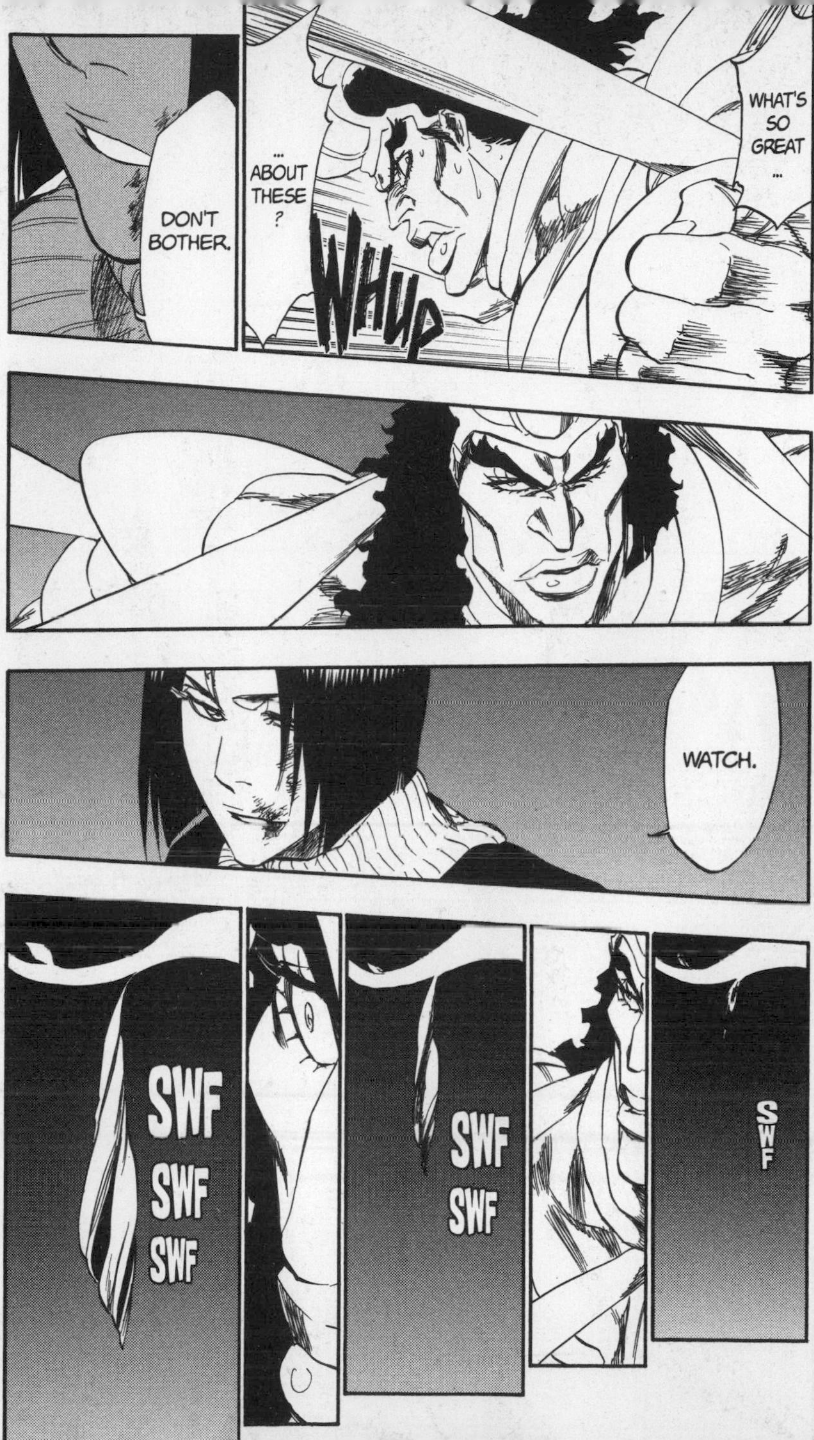
WHAT'S SO GREAT ...
... ABOUT THESE ?
WHUP
DON'T BOTHER.
WATCH.
SWF
SWF SWF
SWF SWF SWF

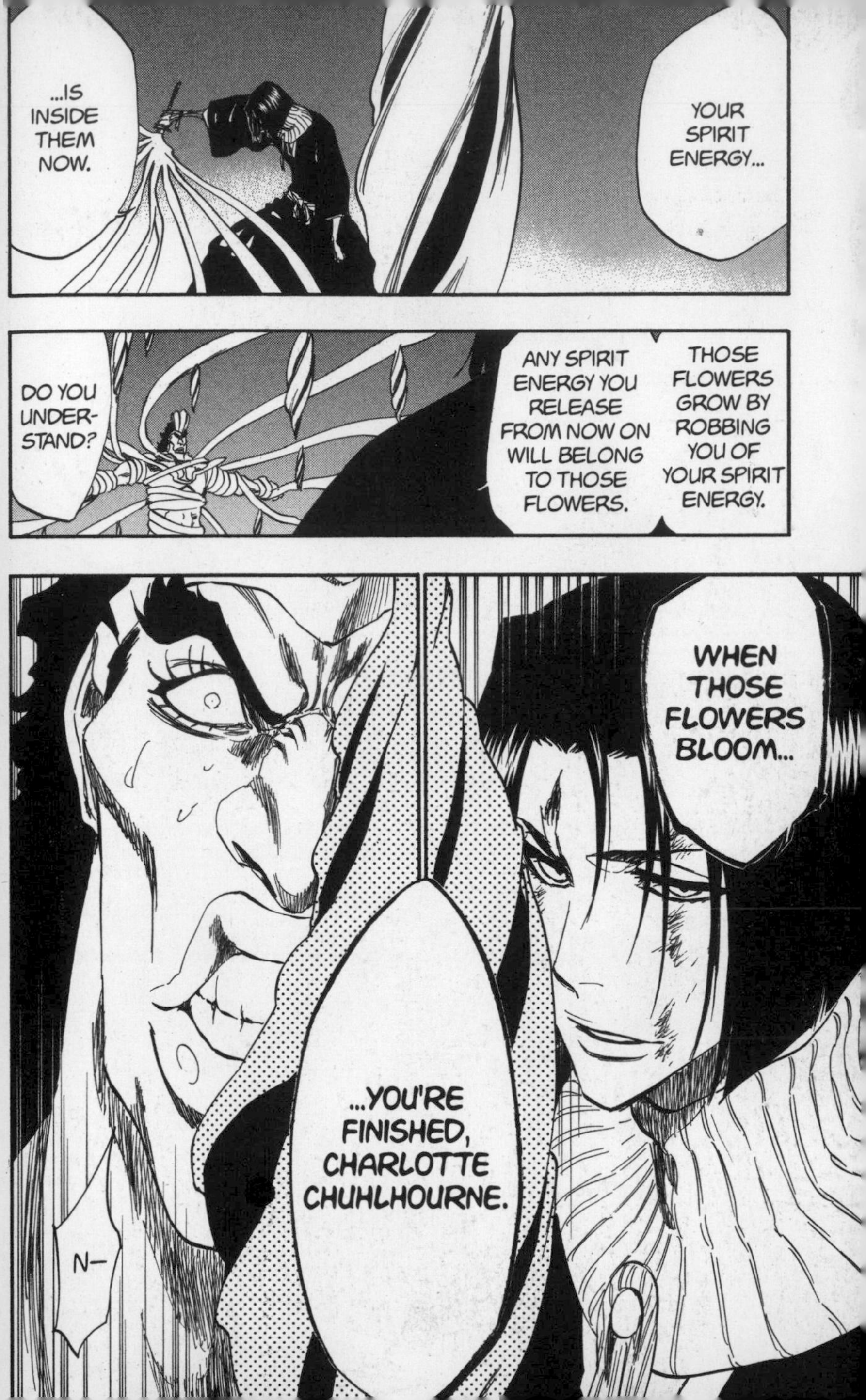
YOUR SPIRIT ENERGY...
...IS INSIDE THEM NOW.
THOSE FLOWERS GROW BY ROBBING YOU OF YOUR SPIRIT ENERGY.
ANY SPIRIT ENERGY YOU RELEASE FROM NOW ON WILL BELONG TO THOSE FLOWERS.
DO YOU UNDER-STAND?
WHEN THOSE FLOWERS BLOOM...
...YOU'RE FINISHED, CHARLOTTE CHUHLHOURNE.
N—

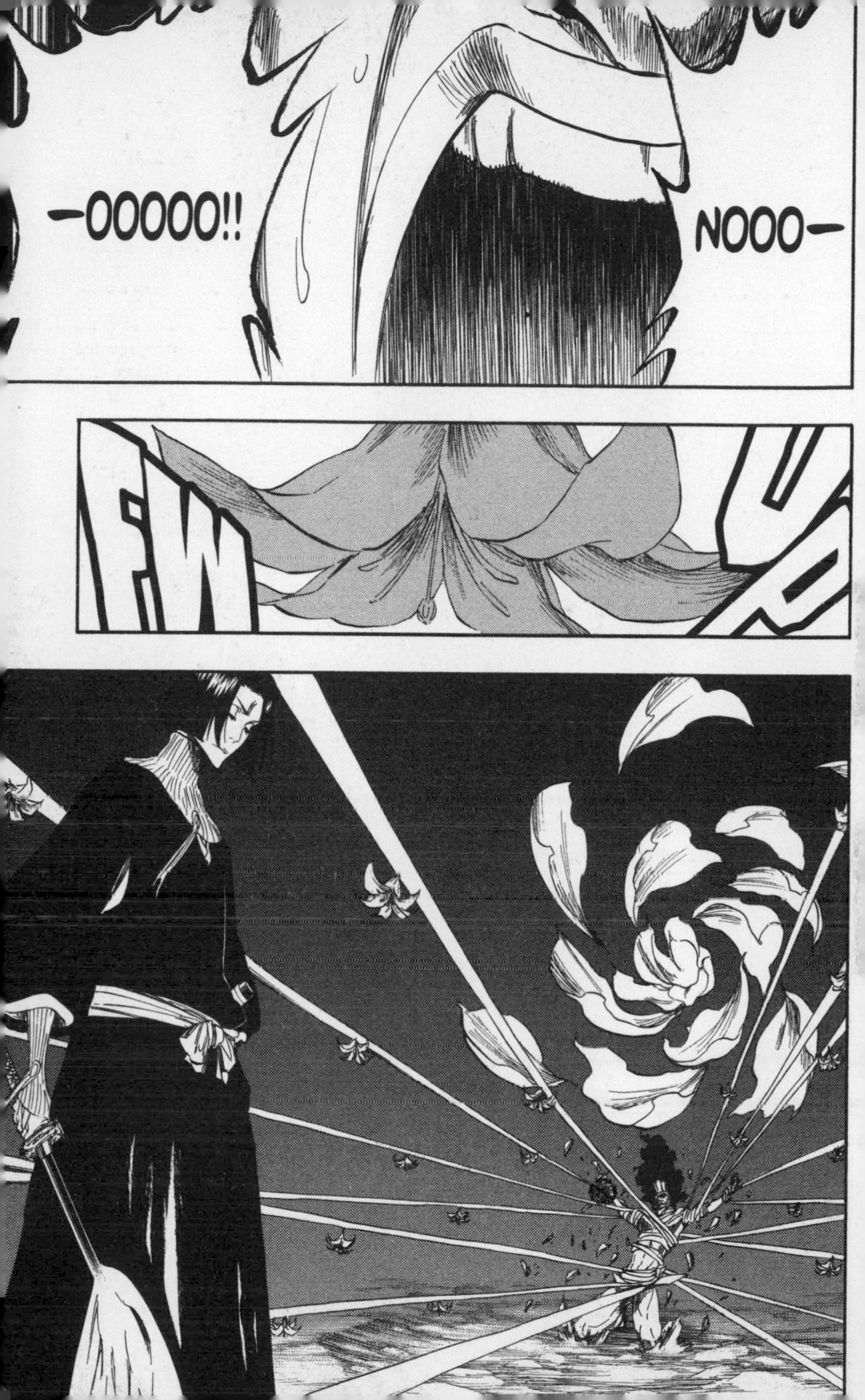
NOOO—
—OOOOO!!

322. Oath Under the Rose

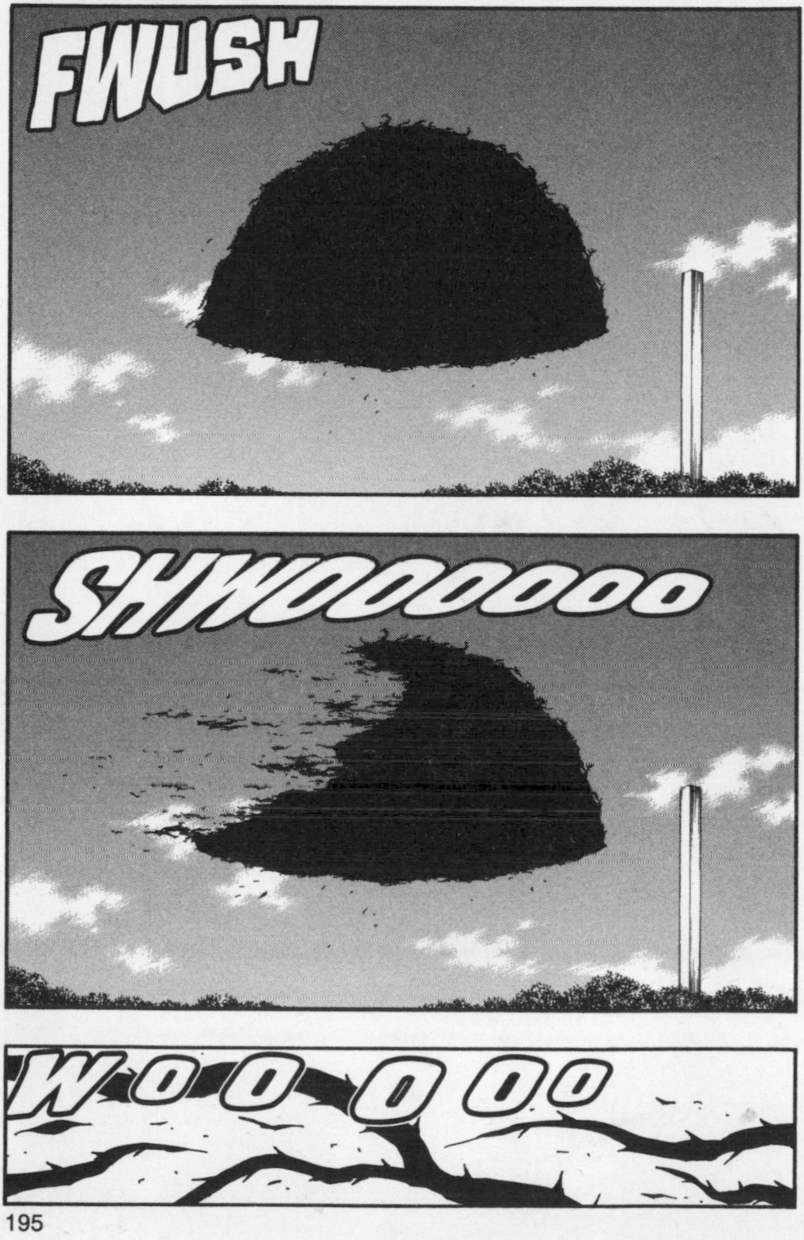
FWUSH
SHWOOOOOOO
WOOOOO

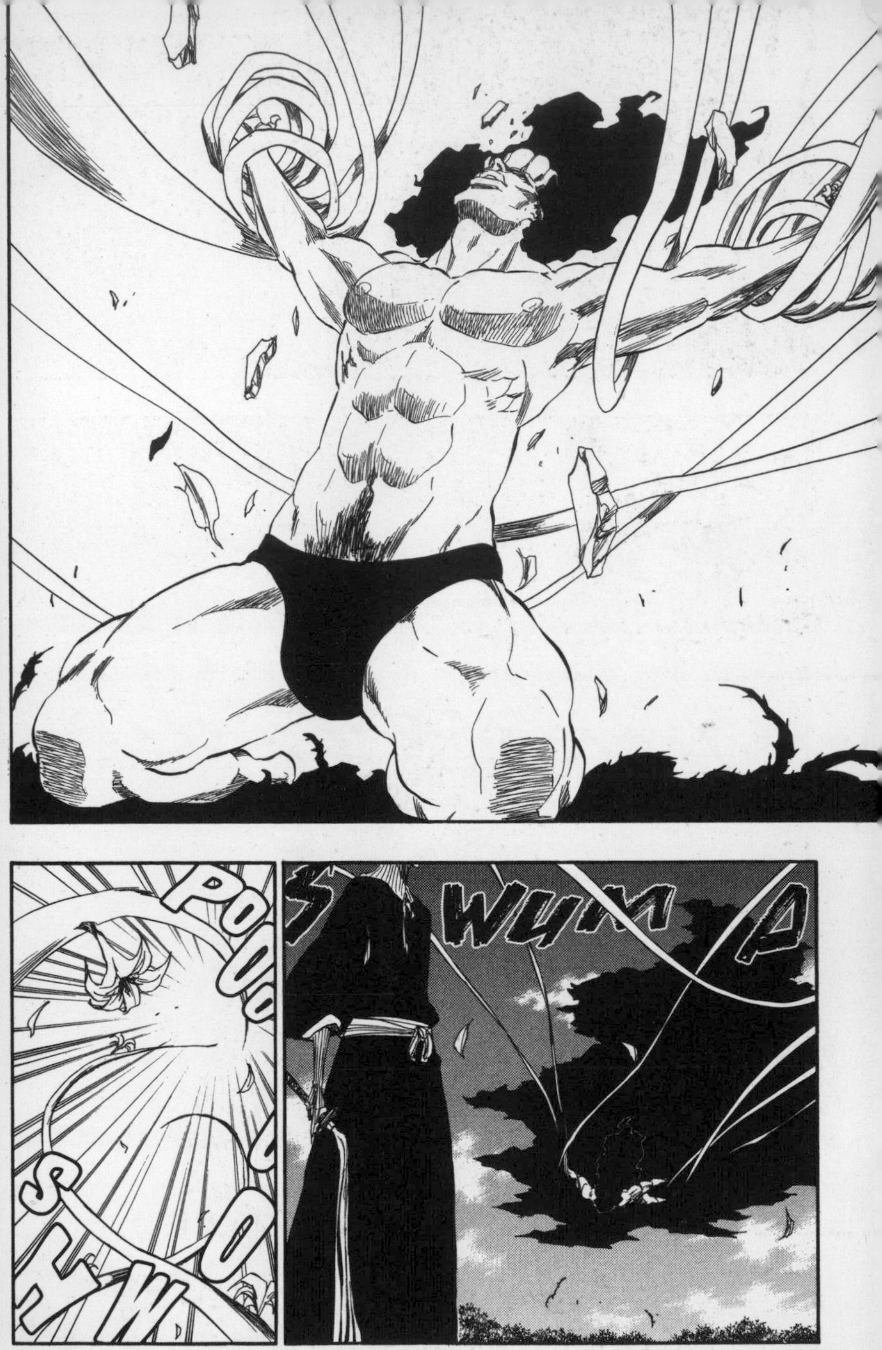
SWUMP

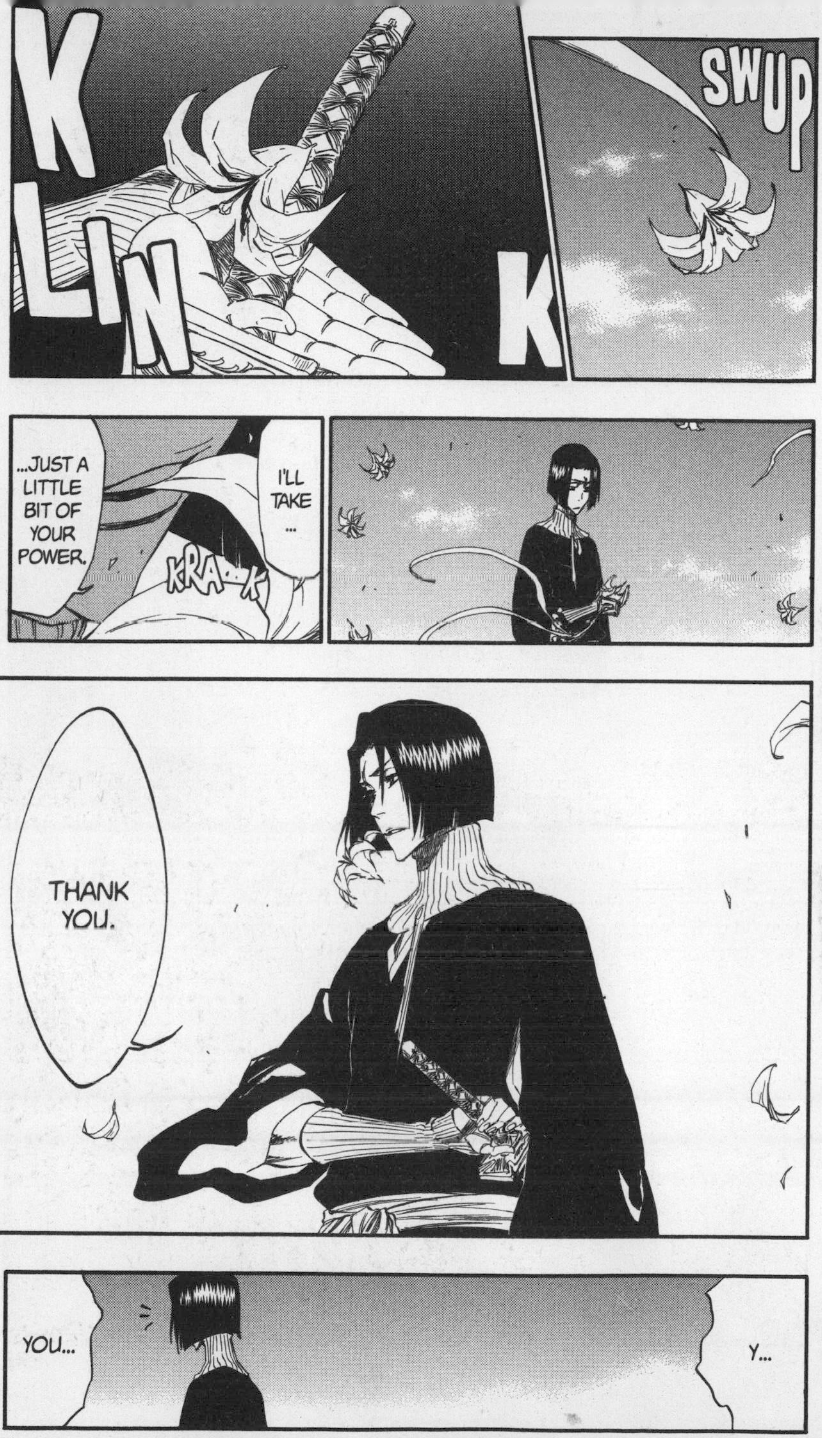
SWUP
KLINK
I'LL TAKE ...
...JUST A LITTLE BIT OF YOUR POWER.
KRA..K
THANK YOU.
Y...
YOU...

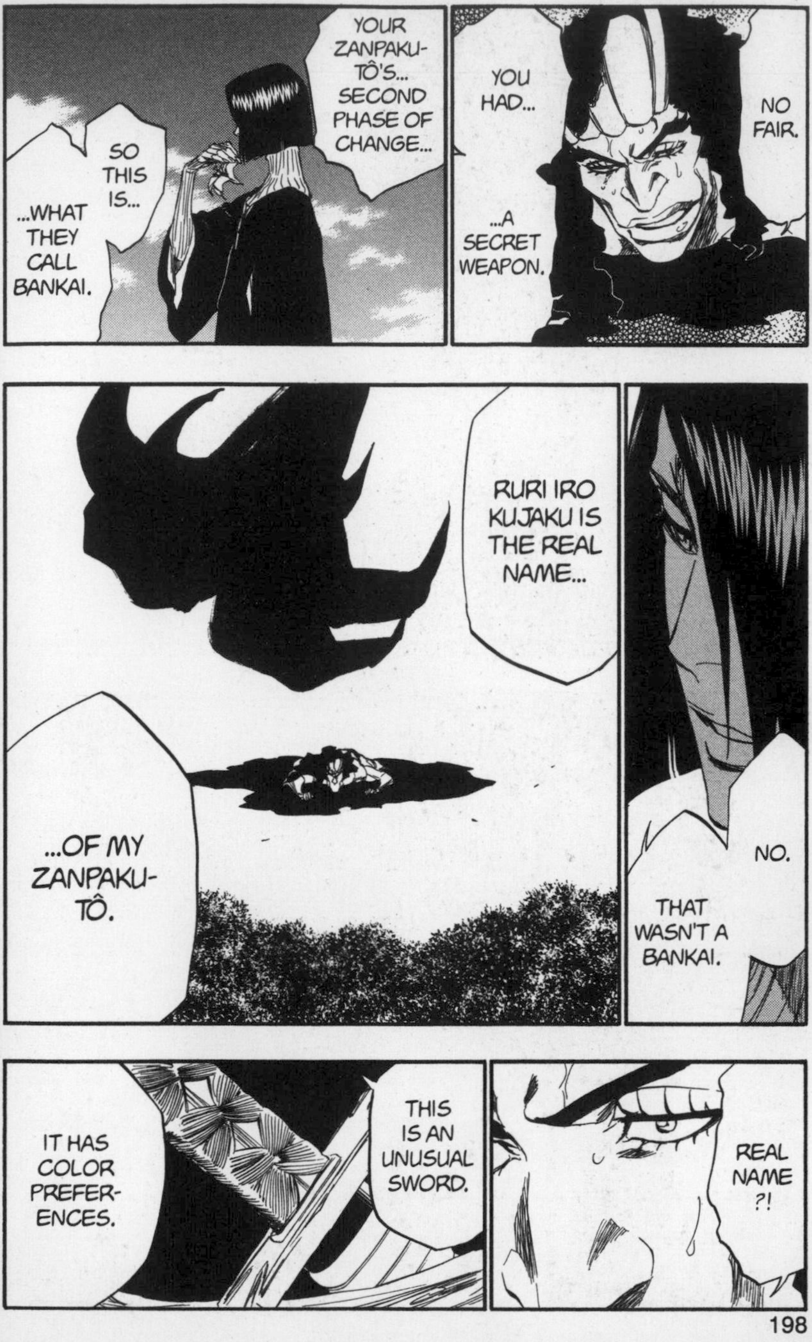
YOU HAD...
...A SECRET WEAPON.
NO FAIR.
YOUR ZANPAKU-TÔ'S... SECOND PHASE OF CHANGE...
SO THIS IS...
...WHAT THEY CALL BANKAI.
NO.
THAT WASN'T A BANKAI.
RURI IRO KUJAKU IS THE REAL NAME...
...OF MY ZANPAKU-TÔ.
REAL NAME ?!
THIS IS AN UNUSUAL SWORD.
IT HAS COLOR PREFERENCES.

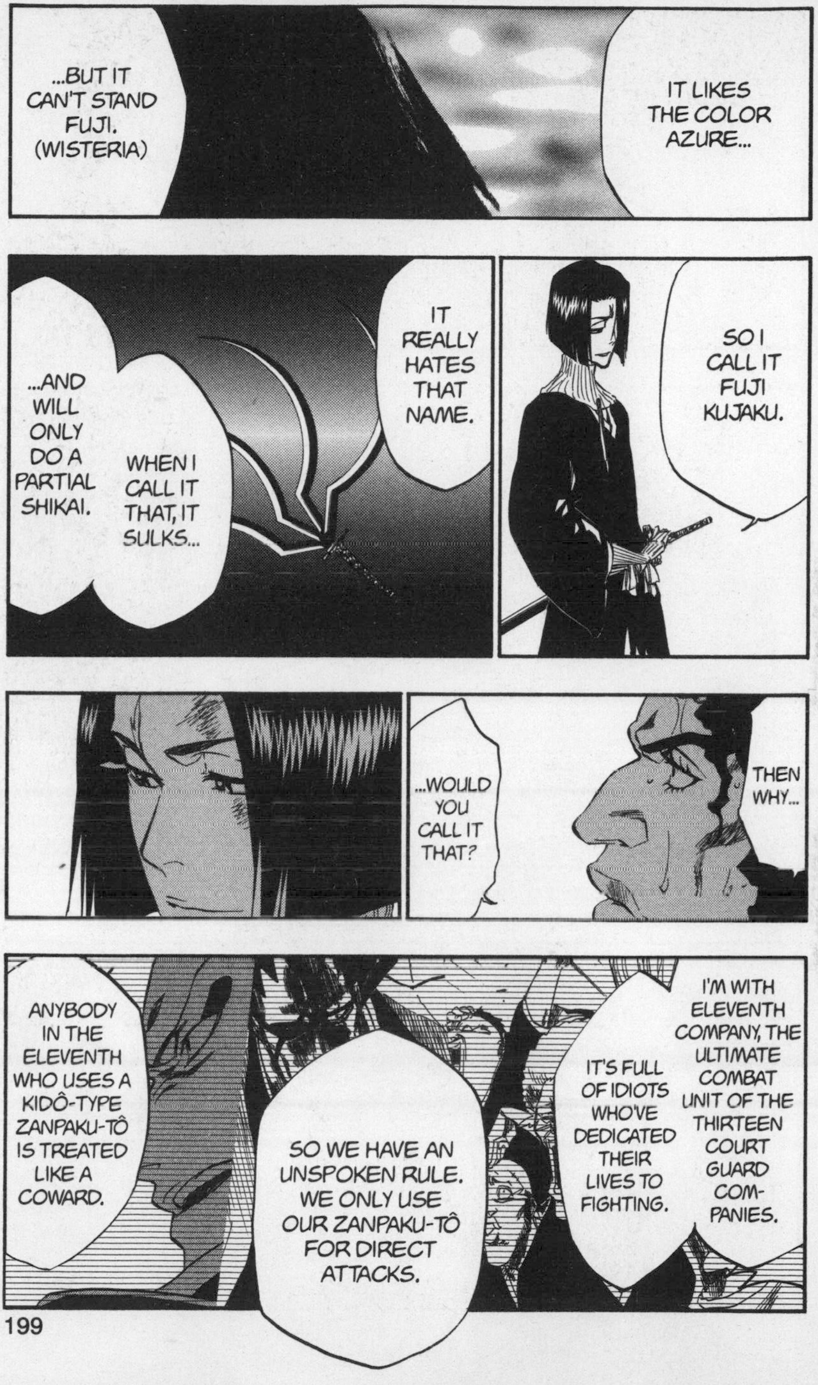
IT LIKES THE COLOR AZURE...
...BUT IT CAN'T STAND FUJI. (WISTERIA)
SO I CALL IT FUJI KUJAKU.
IT REALLY HATES THAT NAME.
WHEN I CALL IT THAT, IT SULKS...
...AND WILL ONLY DO A PARTIAL SHIKAI.
THEN WHY...
...WOULD YOU CALL IT THAT?
I'M WITH ELEVENTH COMPANY, THE ULTIMATE COMBAT UNIT OF THE THIRTEEN COURT GUARD COMPANIES.
IT'S FULL OF IDIOTS WHO'VE DEDICATED THEIR LIVES TO FIGHTING.
ANYBODY IN THE ELEVENTH WHO USES A KIDÔ-TYPE ZANPAKU-TÔ IS TREATED LIKE A COWARD.
SO WE HAVE AN UNSPOKEN RULE. WE ONLY USE OUR ZANPAKU-TÔ FOR DIRECT ATTACKS.

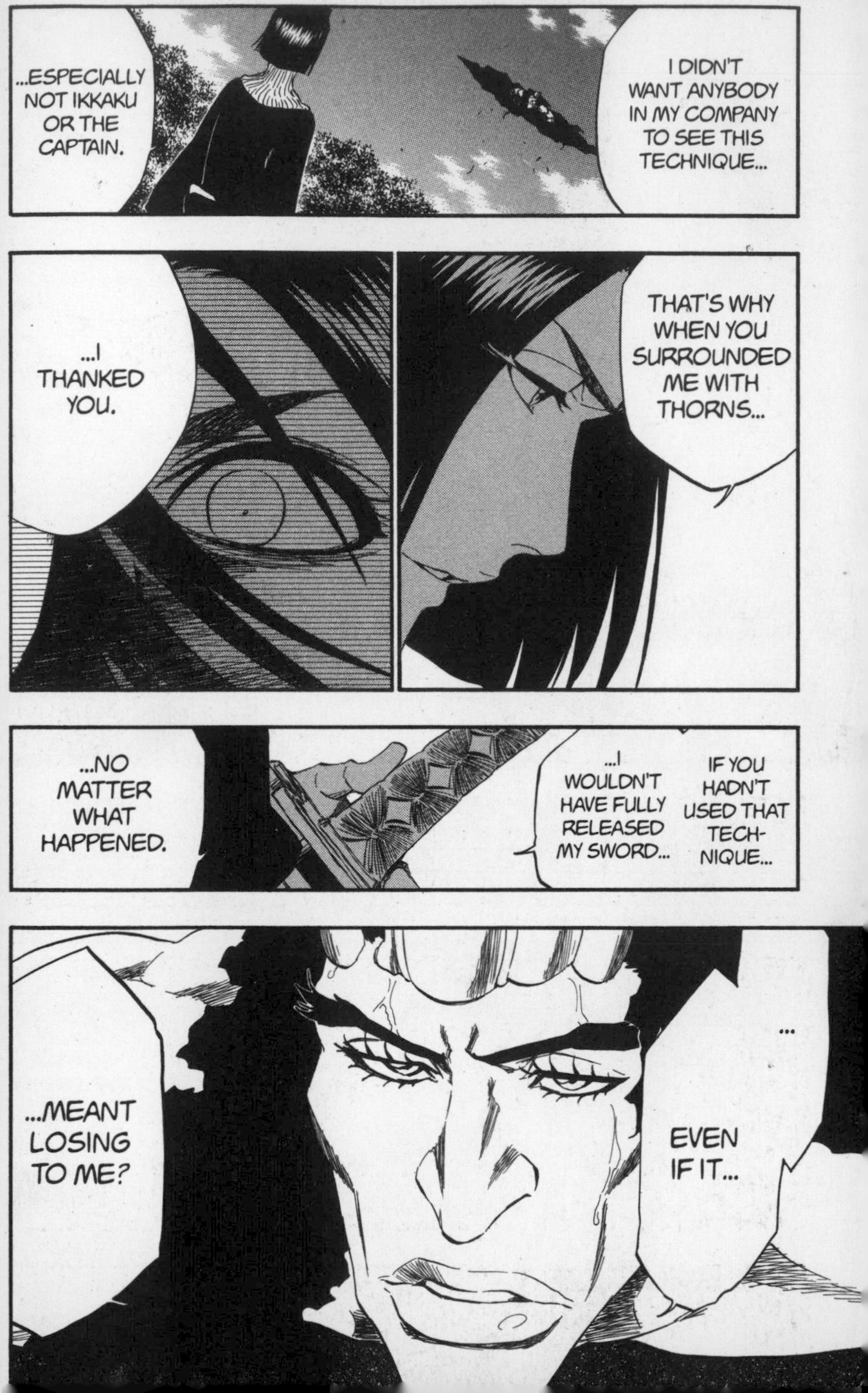
I DIDN'T WANT ANYBODY IN MY COMPANY TO SEE THIS TECHNIQUE...
...ESPECIALLY NOT IKKAKU OR THE CAPTAIN.
THAT'S WHY WHEN YOU SURROUNDED ME WITH THORNS...
...I THANKED YOU.
IF YOU HADN'T USED THAT TECH-NIQUE...
...I WOULDN'T HAVE FULLY RELEASED MY SWORD...
...NO MATTER WHAT HAPPENED.
...
EVEN IF IT...
...MEANT LOSING TO ME?

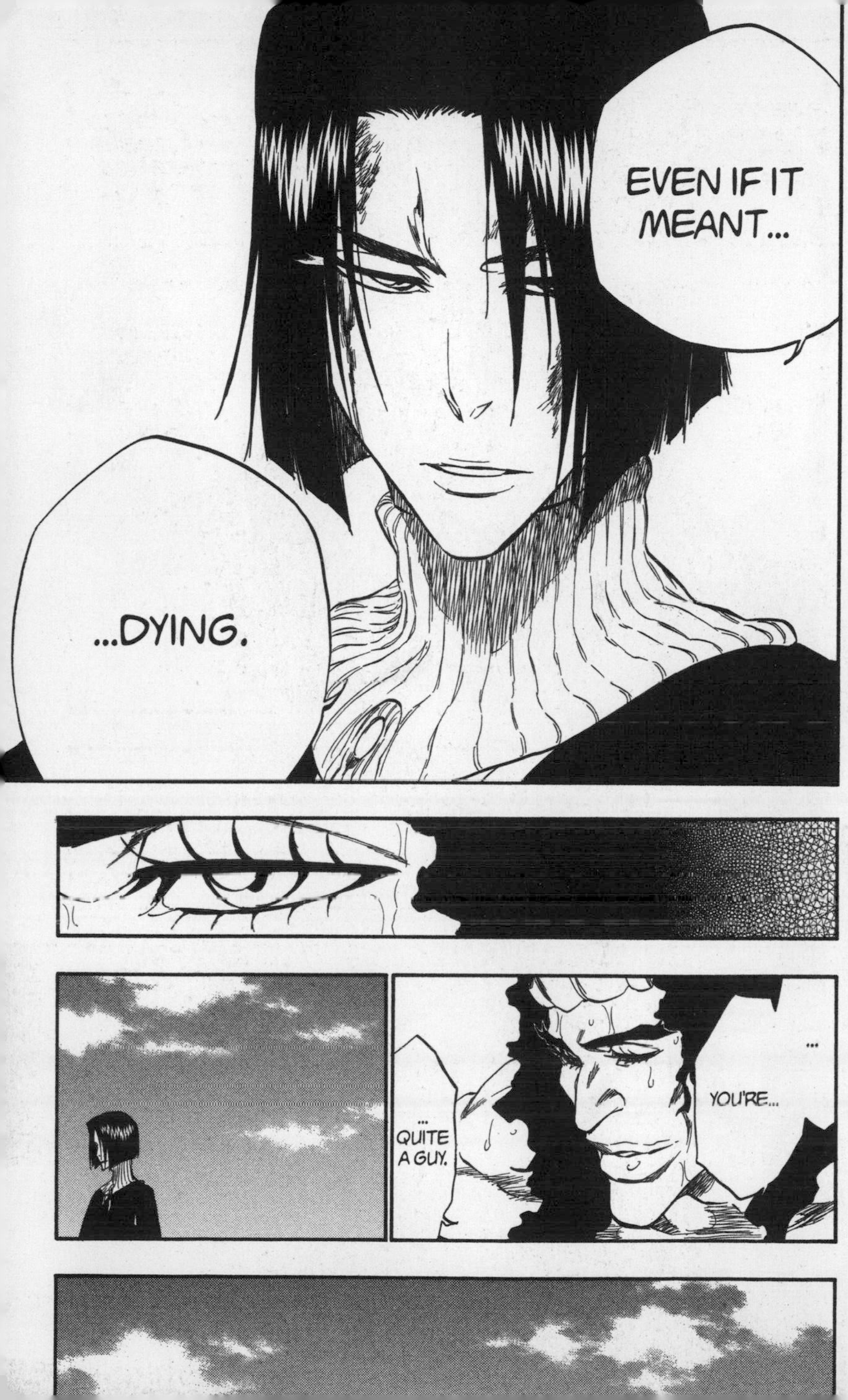
EVEN IF IT MEANT...
...DYING.
...
YOU'RE...
... QUITE A GUY.

BLEACH 322. Oath Under the Rose

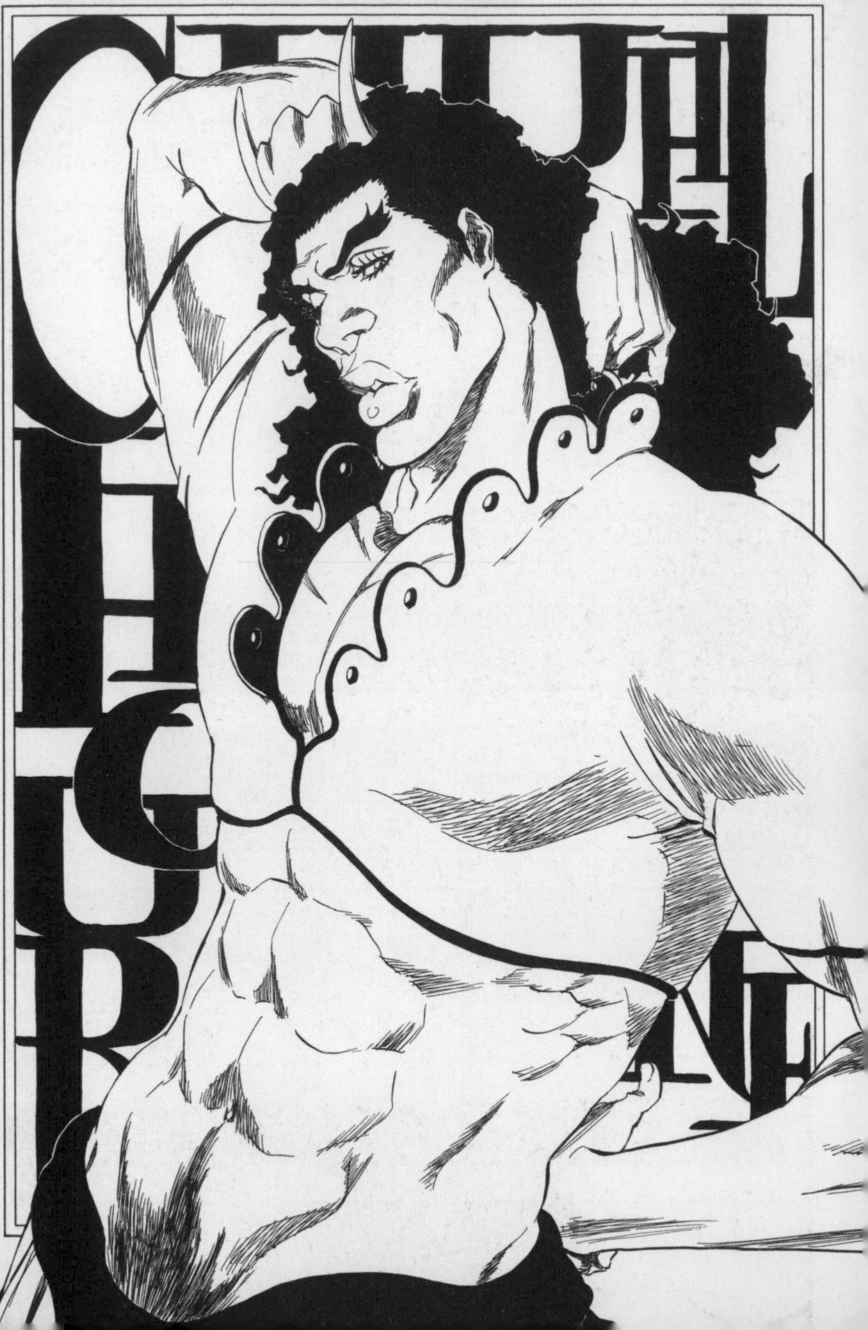

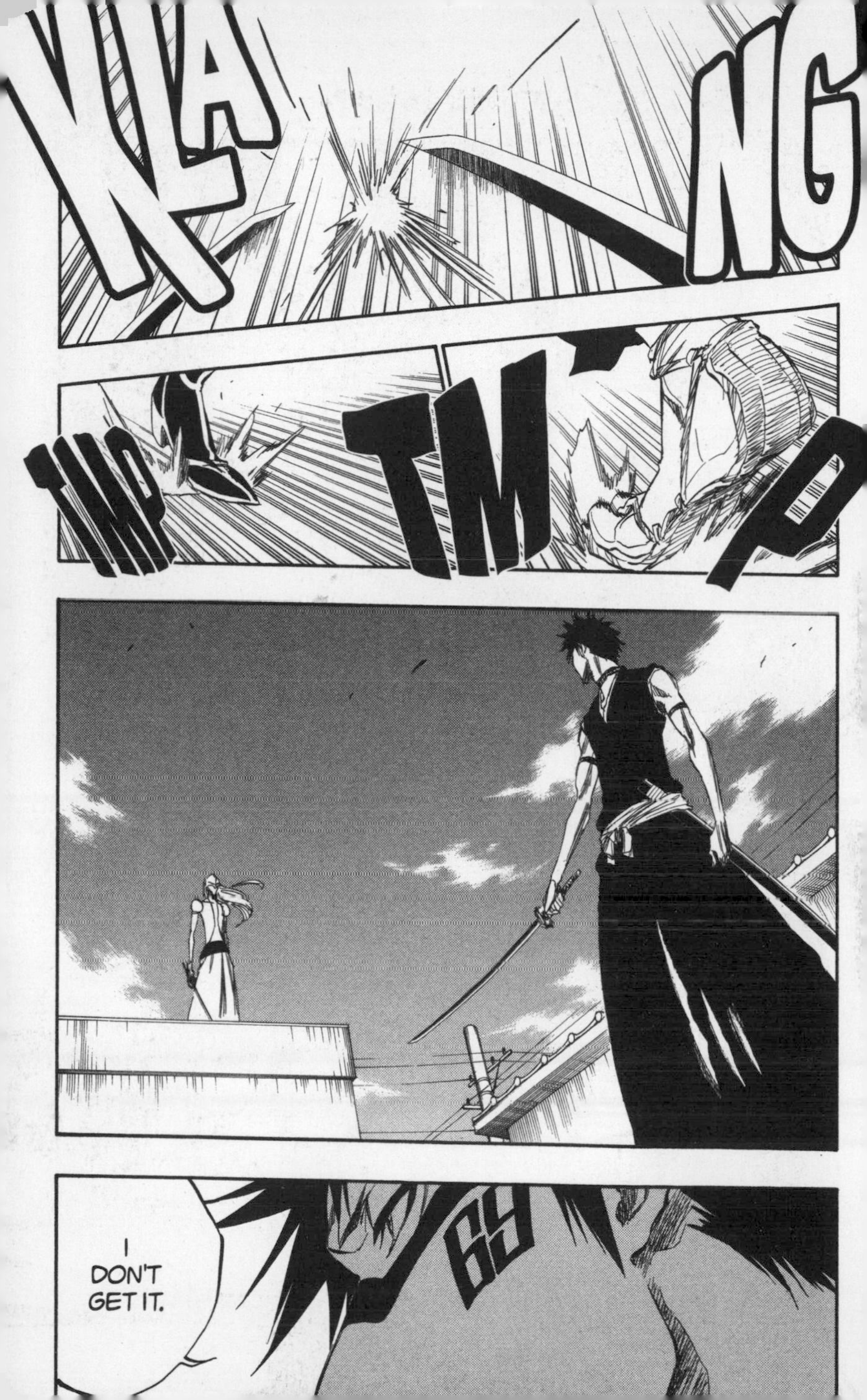
KLANG
TMP
TMP
I DON'T GET IT.

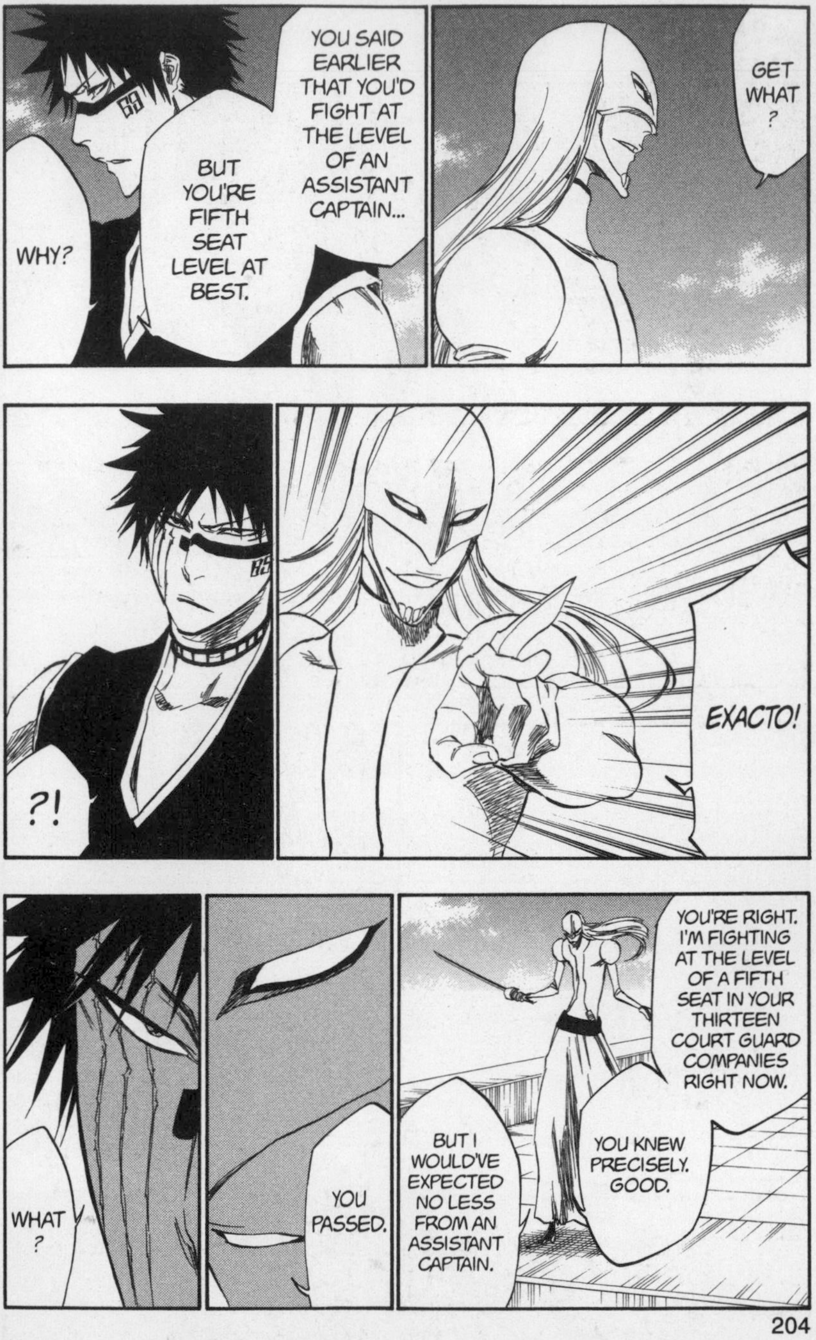
GET WHAT ?
YOU SAID EARLIER THAT YOU'D FIGHT AT THE LEVEL OF AN ASSISTANT CAPTAIN...
BUT YOU'RE FIFTH SEAT LEVEL AT BEST.
WHY?
EXACTO!
?!
YOU'RE RIGHT. I'M FIGHTING AT THE LEVEL OF A FIFTH SEAT IN YOUR THIRTEEN COURT GUARD COMPANIES RIGHT NOW.
YOU KNEW PRECISELY. GOOD.
BUT I WOULD'VE EXPECTED NO LESS FROM AN ASSISTANT CAPTAIN.
YOU PASSED.
WHAT ?

READ THIS WAY

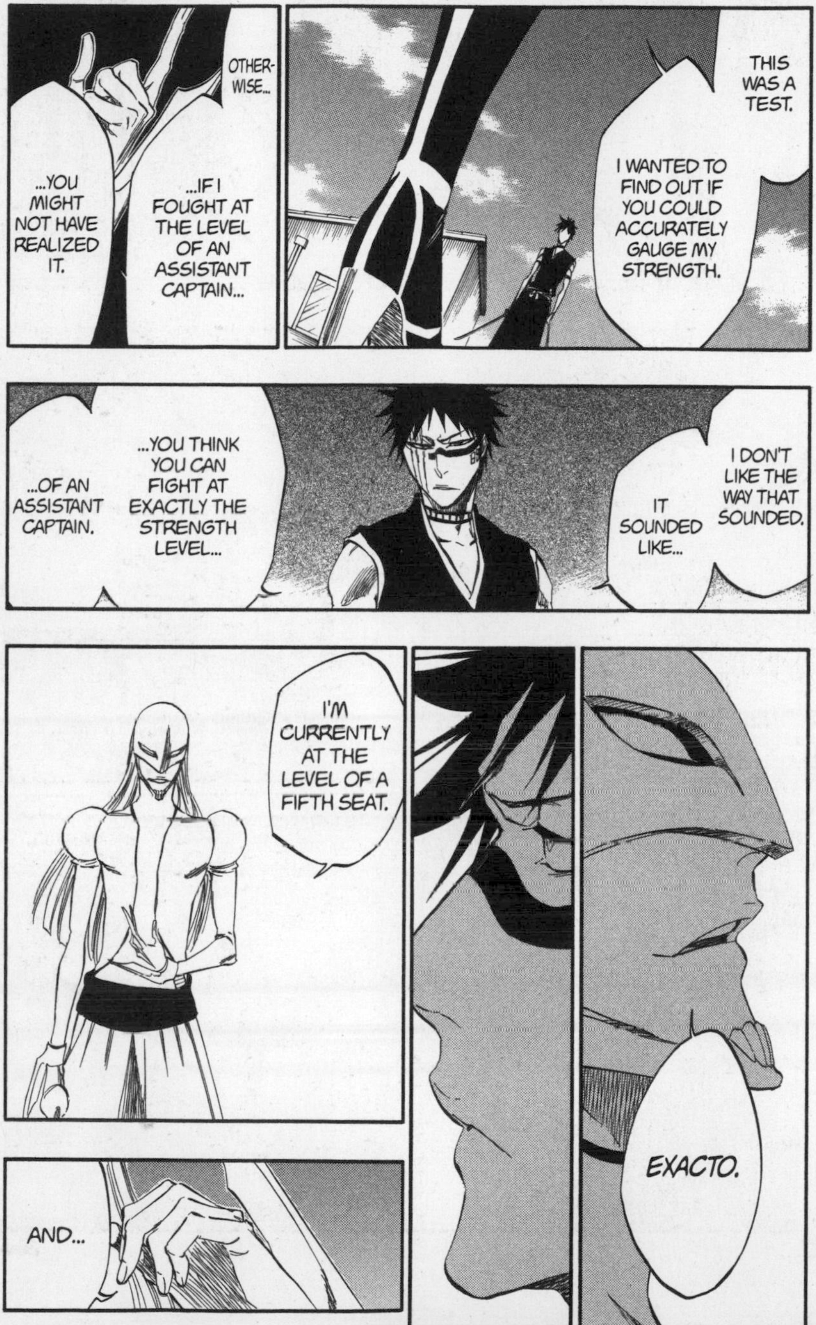
THIS WAS A TEST.
I WANTED TO FIND OUT IF YOU COULD ACCURATELY GAUGE MY STRENGTH.
OTHER-WISE...
...IF I FOUGHT AT THE LEVEL OF AN ASSISTANT CAPTAIN...
...YOU MIGHT NOT HAVE REALIZED IT.
I DON'T LIKE THE WAY THAT SOUNDED.
IT SOUNDED LIKE...
...YOU THINK YOU CAN FIGHT AT EXACTLY THE STRENGTH LEVEL...
...OF AN ASSISTANT CAPTAIN.
EXACTO.
I'M CURRENTLY AT THE LEVEL OF A FIFTH SEAT.
AND...

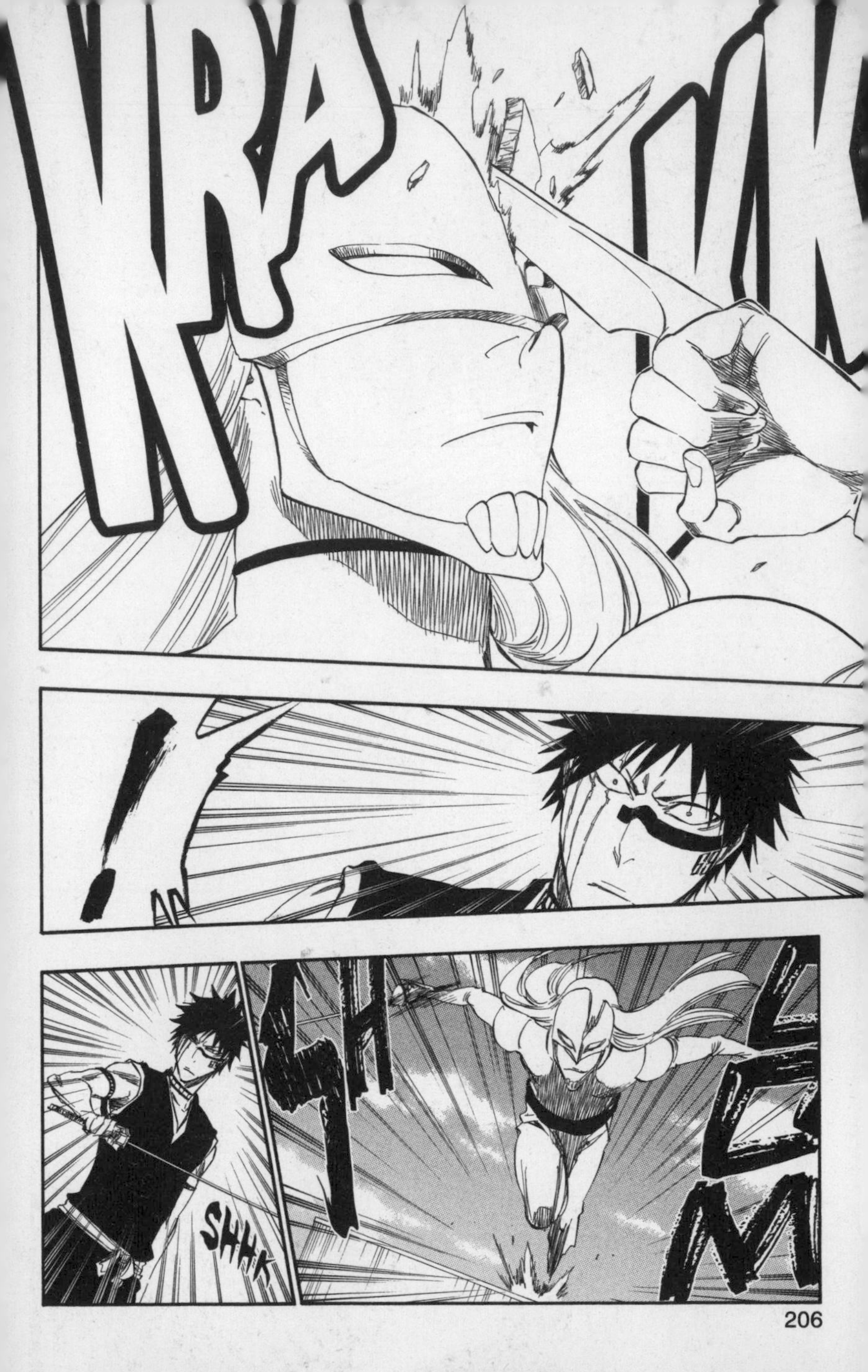
SHHK

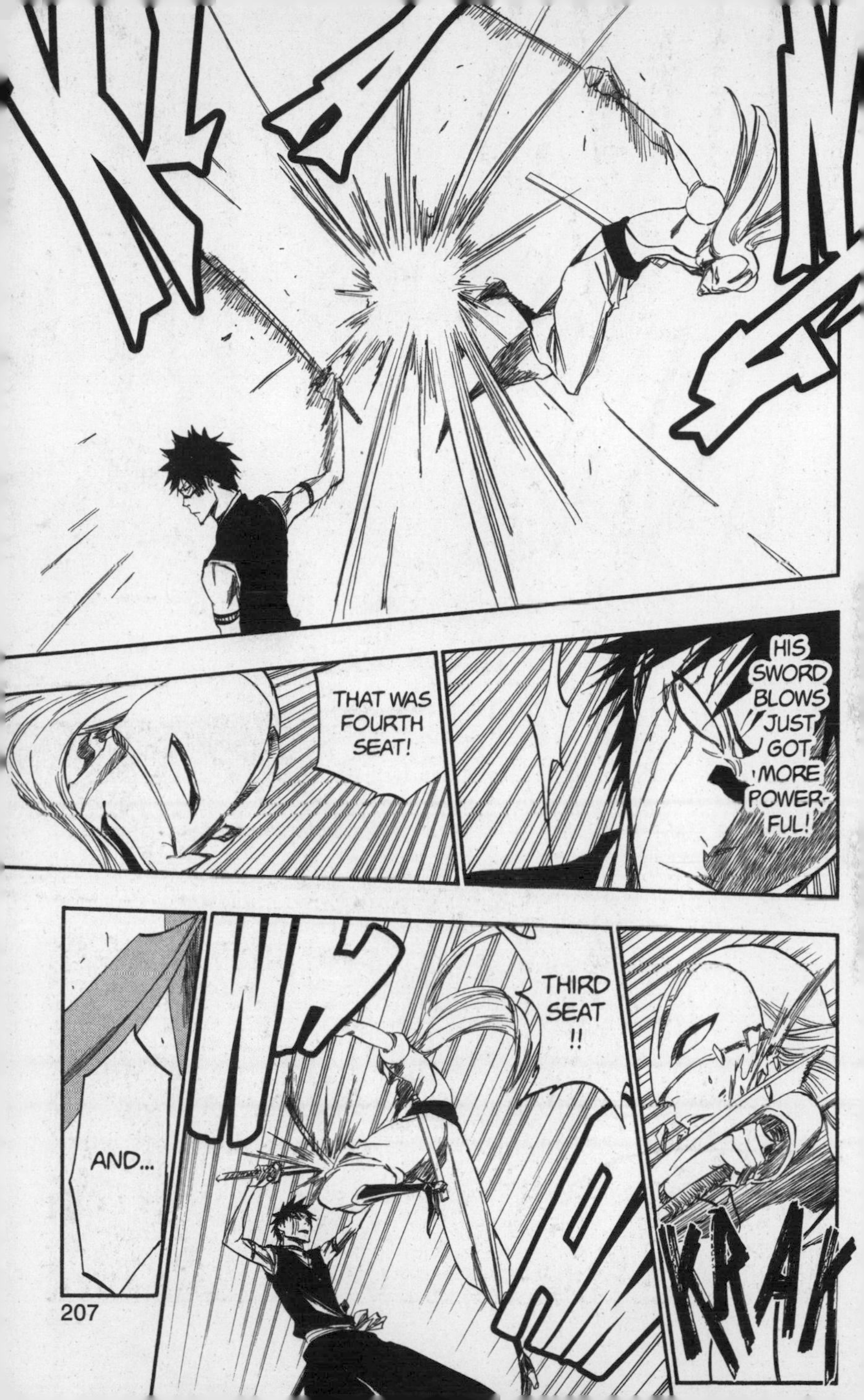
HIS SWORD BLOWS JUST GOT MORE POWERFUL!
THAT WAS FOURTH SEAT!
KRAK
THIRD SEAT !!
AND...

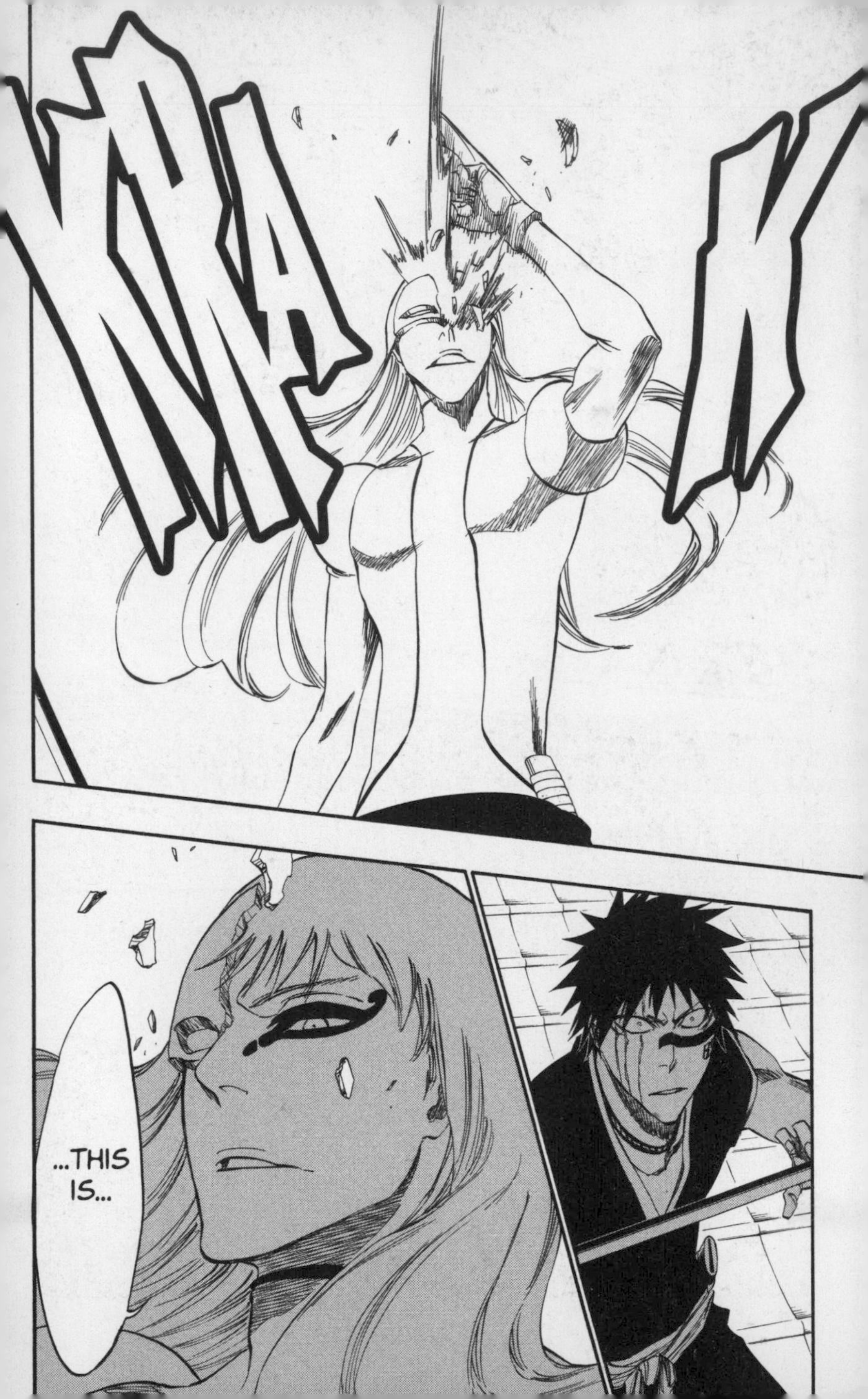
KRAK
...THIS IS...

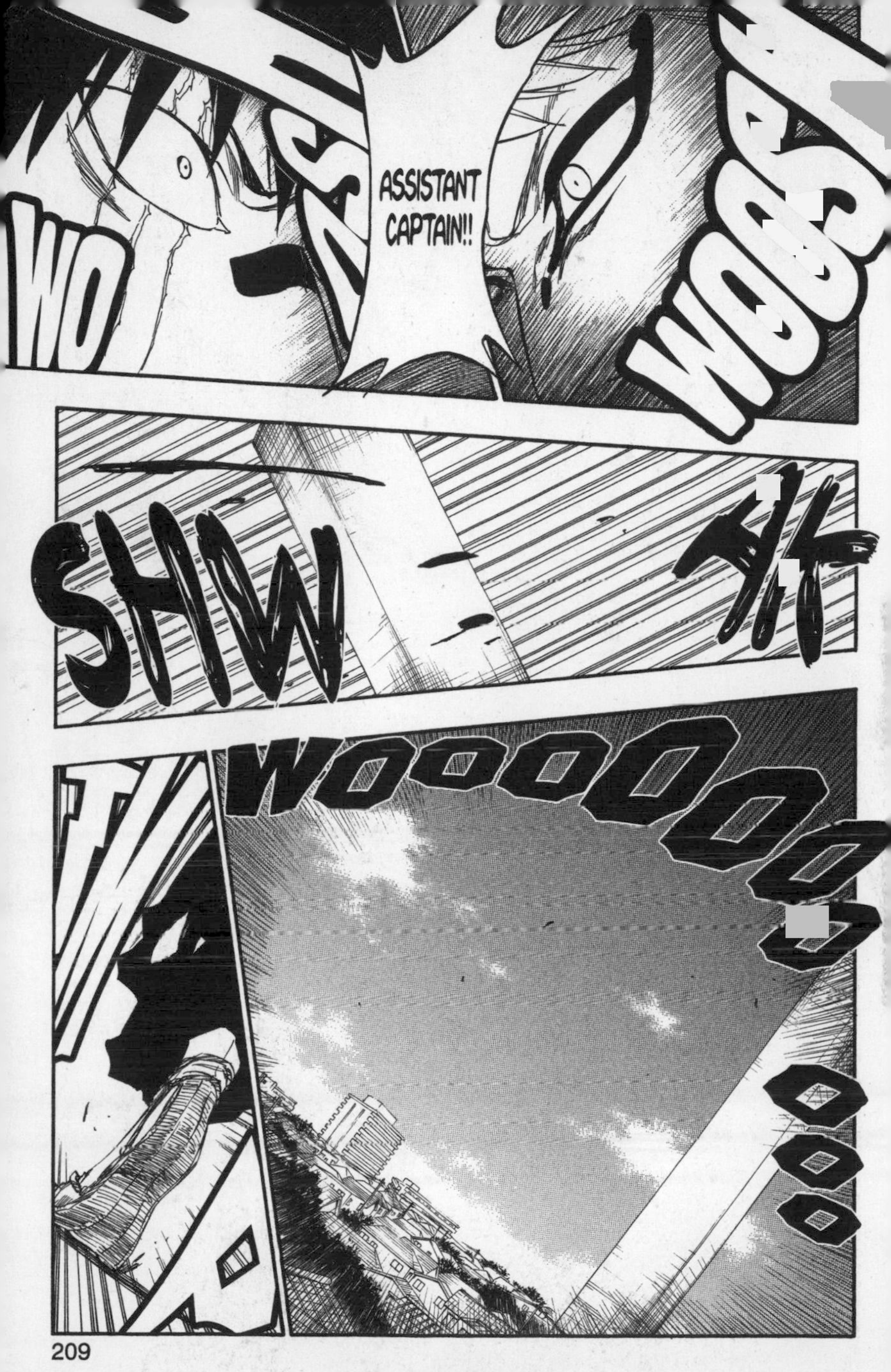
ASSISTANT CAPTAIN!!

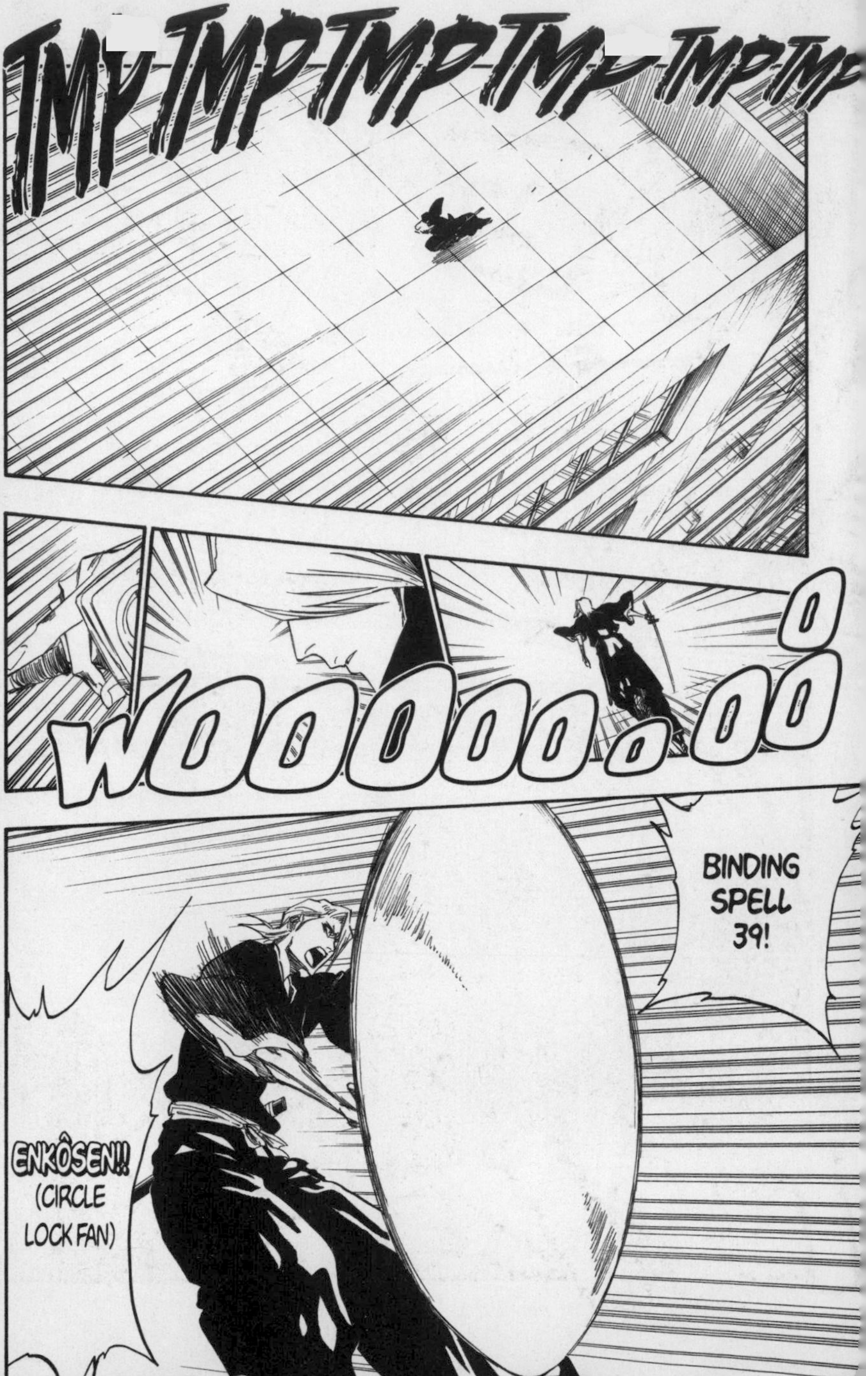
TMPTMPTMPTMP TMPTMP
WOOOOOO...OO
BINDING SPELL 39!
ENKÔSEN!!
(CIRCLE LOCK FAN)

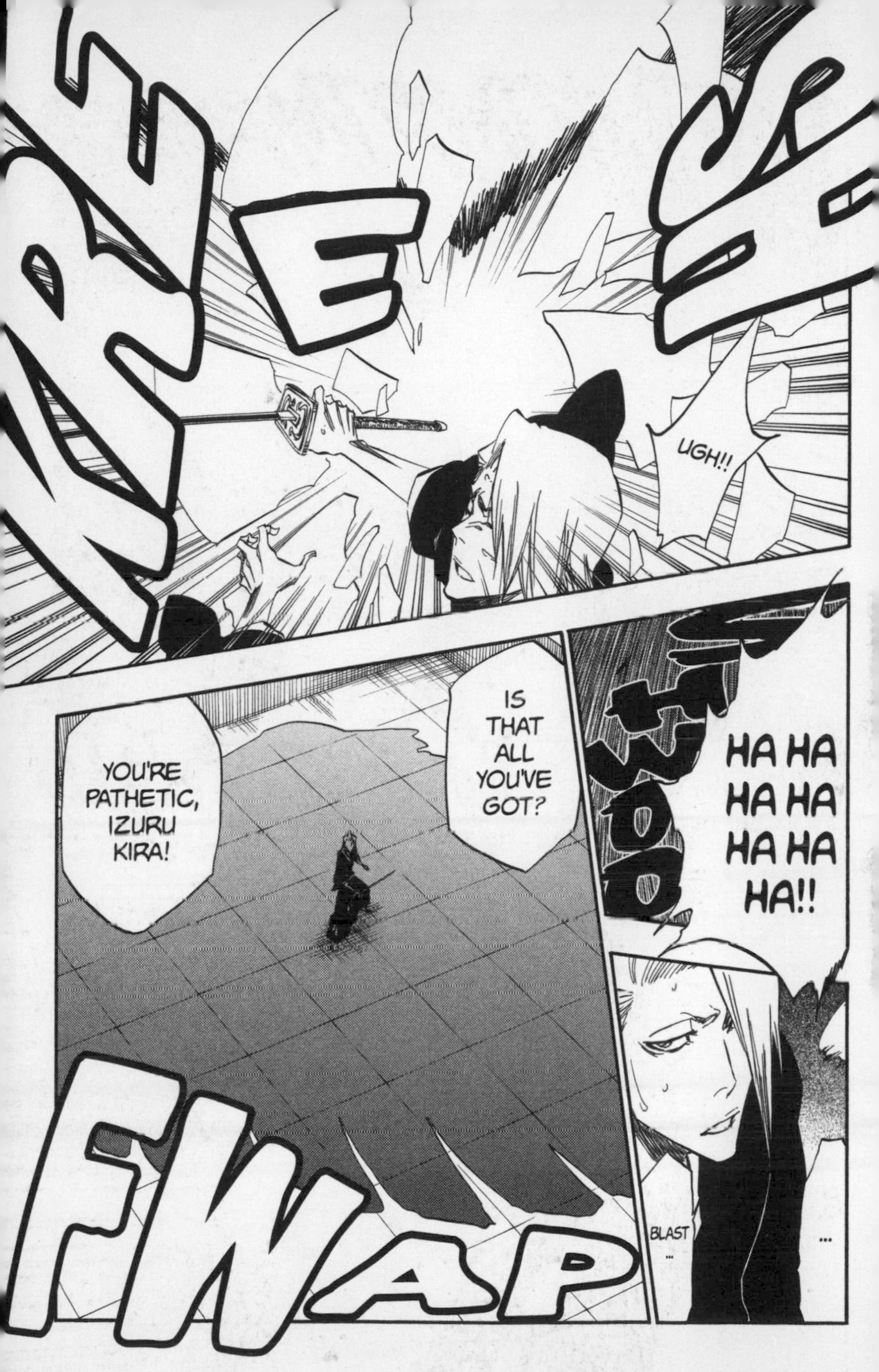
UGH!!
HA HA HA HA HA HA HA!!
...
BLAST ...
IS THAT ALL YOU'VE GOT?
YOU'RE PATHETIC, IZURU KIRA!
FWAP

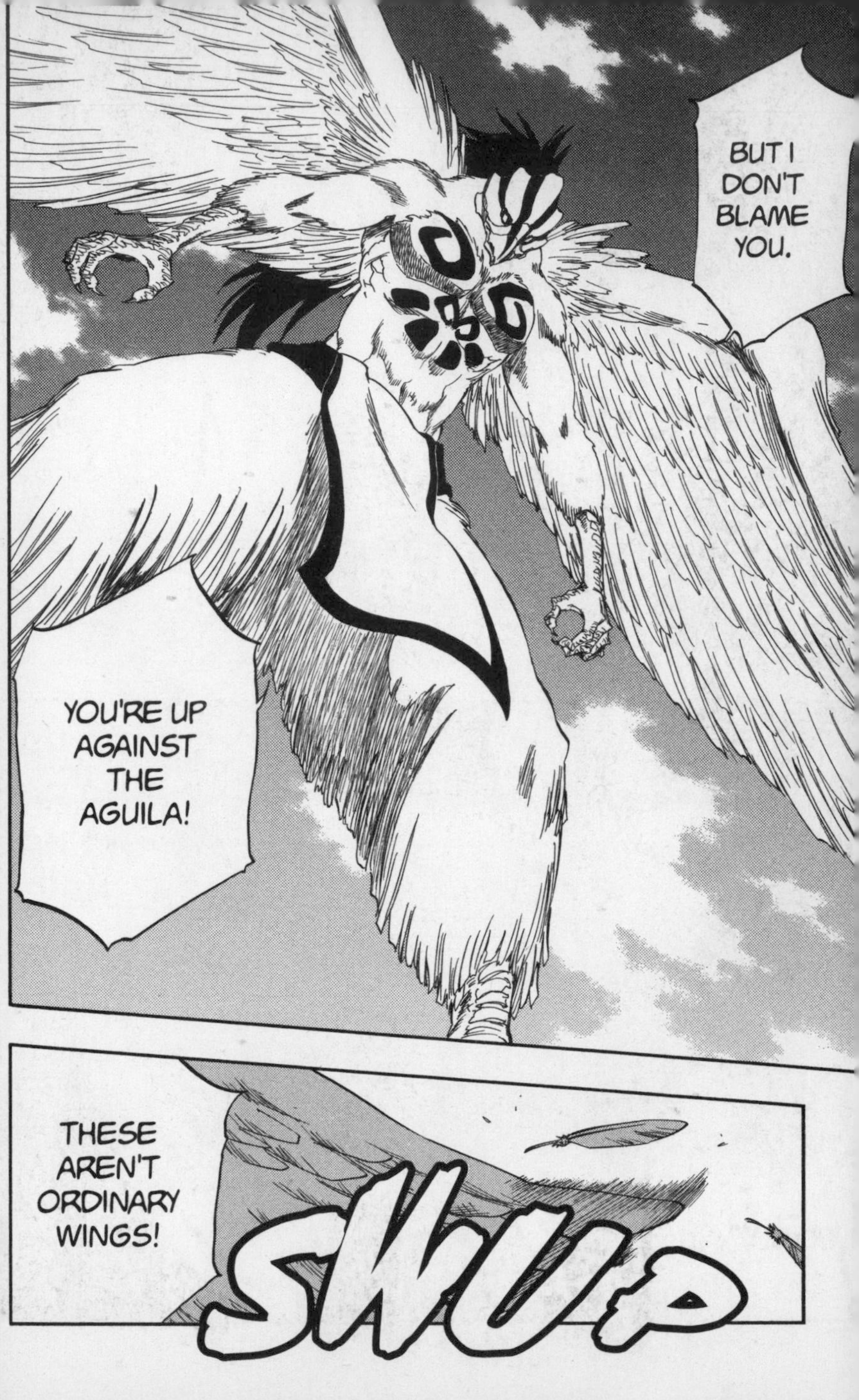
BUT I DON'T BLAME YOU.
YOU'RE UP AGAINST THE AGUILA!
THESE AREN'T ORDINARY WINGS!
SWUP

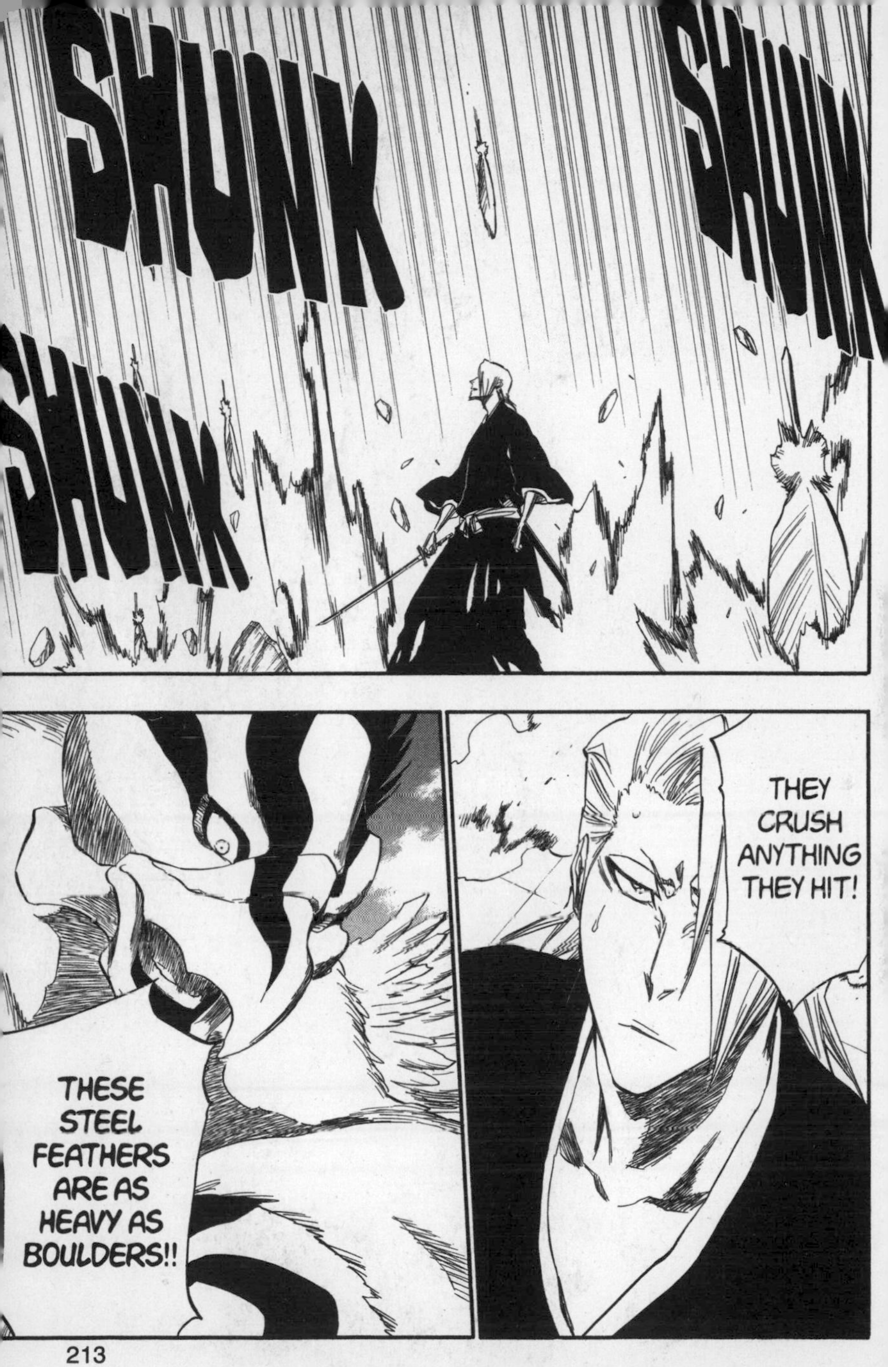
SHUNK
SHUNK
SHUNK
THEY CRUSH ANYTHING THEY HIT!
THESE STEEL FEATHERS ARE AS HEAVY AS BOULDERS!!

CONTI
NUED
IN
BLEACH
38